WHITE ON WHITE/ BLACK ON BLACK

WHITE ON WHITE/ BLACK ON BLACK

Edited by
George Yancy

ROWMAN & LITTLEFIELD PUBLISHERS, INC.
Lanham • Boulder • New York • Toronto • Oxford

ROWMAN & LITTLEFIELD PUBLISHERS, INC.

Published in the United States of America
by Rowman & Littlefield Publishers, Inc.
A wholly owned subsidiary of The Rowman & Littlefield Publishing Group, Inc.
4501 Forbes Boulevard, Suite 200, Lanham, Maryland 20706
www.rowmanlittlefield.com

PO Box 317
Oxford
OX2 9RU, UK

British Library Cataloguing in Publication Information Available

Library of Congress Cataloging-in-Publication Data

White on white/black on black / edited by George Yancy.
p. cm.
Includes bibliographical references and index.
ISBN 0-7425-1480-3 (alk. paper) — ISBN 0-7425-1481-1 (pbk. : alk. paper)
1. Race awareness. 2. Blacks—Race identity. 3. Whites—Race identity.
4. Race—Philosophy. I. Yancy, George.
HT1521.W45 2005
305.8—dc22

2004023613

Printed in the United States of America

∞™ The paper used in this publication meets the minimum requirements of American National Standard for Information Sciences—Permanence of Paper for Printed Library Materials, ANSI/NISO Z39.48-1992.

For Susan
"Joansie"

Contents

Foreword

I DO NOT RECALL WHEN I FIRST MET GEORGE YANCY but I do remember that our meeting left a grand impression on me. He was driven by a deep love of philosophy and a deep hatred of white supremacy. He was bewildered by the silence of most academic American philosophers on the most explosive issue and rawest nerve in American life: race.

George Yancy has made major contributions toward shattering the silence of academic philosophers in regard to race. His historic collection of seventeen conversations with African American philosophers, published in 1998, has made it difficult to ignore the challenge of race in contemporary philosophical discourse. The rich cacophony of voices in his collection revealed the diverse streams and strains of the black philosophical community. And his voice is a significant one among the others in his text. His timely critical reader in 2001 on my own work brought together for the first time in American history a set of reflections on a living black philosopher by his colleagues. This courageous work included essays by many of the most celebrated black philosophers of our time as well as the greatest academic philosopher in America—Hilary Putnam. My own contribution to this volume—"Philosophy and the Funk of Life"—remains the most sustained commentary of my philosophic work. And I am grateful to him for this tribute and opportunity.

His next work, published in 2002, focused on the existential dimension of academic philosophers: the tacit personal experiences that inform and influence thinkers who rarely write in the first-person present tense. This focus is consistent with Yancy's own interests in continental philosophy and in literary matters. It is the first text I know that highlights the messy background conditions that prefigure the smooth philosophic language of the dominant genre of the academy. This book was followed by another groundbreaking text in 2004 in which Yancy called African American philosophers to grapple seriously with the question of whiteness.

This recent volume—*White on White/Black on Black*—is another pioneering work. Never before have academic philosophers candidly engaged the subtle role of race in their writings, especially white and black philosophers within the same text; and specifically, the various ways in which constructions of whiteness operate among white philosophers and experiences of blackness (in response to constructions of whiteness) influence black philosophers. Yancy has laid bare how the nearly lily-white philosophic academy can be demystified and deconstructed by some of the leading philosophers in the country. He shows that despite all of the genuine calls for pluralism and diversity in American academic philosophy, most philosophers have yet to interrogate and examine seriously their "raciated" identities as practitioners in their profession and life. Ironically, his text is exemplary in its own pluralism and diversity of orientations, methods, and approaches. He has produced not only a "teachable" text but also a subversive work that boldly challenges some of the most unexamined assumptions of the American philosophic academy, for example, color blindness.

George Yancy is a unique voice in the American intellectual scene. His profound interest in a wholesale questioning of the monumental silence of most U.S. philosophers on fundamental issues like race or existential identities has made him an indispensable and unavoidable figure in American philosophy. We all must do philosophy differently owing, in large measure, to his invaluable work.

Cornel West
Class of 1943, University Professor of Religion
Princeton University

Acknowledgments

FIRST AND FOREMOST I WOULD LIKE to thank Eve DeVaro, philosophy editor at Rowman & Littlefield, for her inspirational collaborative effort with regard to the genesis of this book and its title. I would also like to thank Tessa Fallon, editorial assistant, for her cordiality and wonderful efficiency. Kimberly Ball Smith, assistant editor in production, is to be thanked for her hard work, professionalism, and dedication in seeing this book to its completion. Each contributor is to be thanked for showing tremendous endurance and for bringing honesty and critical reflection to bear upon their contributions. In this regard, I would especially like to thank philosophers Janine Jones and Chris Cuomo. Both wrote their chapters with incredible speed within a very tight time schedule. Thanks for your commitment and dedication. Philosophers Clarence Sholé Johnson, Eleanore Holveck, and Manomano M. M. Mukungurutse are to be thanked for providing helpful feedback on my chapter. I would especially like to thank Manomano for his camaraderie, shared intellectual hunger, and for such spirited dialogues in "the cave."

At New York University, where I received my second M.A. in Africana Studies, I would like to thank scholars Kamau Brathwaite, Manthia Diawara, Michael Dash, Leonard Wantchekon, and Robert Hinton. Hinton is to be thanked for allowing me the latitude to write about subjects that were relevant to my own projects, while guiding that writing in the larger service of the thematic framework of his courses. I would especially like to acknowledge Ramona Knepp, administrative assistant in the Africana Studies Department. She was always available, cordial, and personable, even while under difficult stress. Ramona, thanks for making my temporary transition from Duquesne University to New York University such a delightful experience.

At Columbia University, I would like to thank scholars Farah Griffin and Donna Daniels. In particular, I would like to thank Griffin for directing my M.A. thesis in Africana Studies, and Daniels whose course was most rewarding. Daniels is to be thanked for demonstrating just how complicated and fascinating issues of race and gender can be within the Black Diaspora.

I would also like to thank my uncle William L. Banks for his continued show of interest in my work, James G. Spady for his continued support, Ruth Yancy, Artrice and Carson McGill for their show of support and love. I would also like to thank Brother El who encouraged above all things that I should seek wisdom. Now the student has become the teacher and the mirror reflects back the advice in love: "Father, above all things seek wisdom, don't abandon her. Don't allow those words to echo back to you, empty, and without a show of your most dedicated effort and sincerest conviction." I would like to thank my in-laws Lillian and Geoff Hadley for giving of themselves to help out while I went off to fulfill one of my passions.

Adrian, Gabriel, and Elijah: "I don't call you sons because you *shine*; I call you sons because you're *mine*." Always strive to take delight in sunsets and the larger universe. Don't judge the value of your contributions to the world by comparing your work to that of others. Let them do their *own* thing and congratulate them when appropriate. Nurture *your own* projects with dedication and a clear conscience. It's not about competition, but honesty. And never forget to take tremendous delight in the sheer mystery of your own existence.

To Susan, my wife, thanks so very much for entering my life at just the right moment, not too soon and not too late. You're the woman from "down under" who hadn't planned to stay so long. Paths crossed, social borders breached, "sitting on the dock of the bay," hiding behind sunglasses, lunch, dinner, late nights, flowers and balloons, shared secrets and shared tears, mutual acceptance, two extraordinary boys, a once tabooed shared love. You have made this book, and several before, so incredibly less stressful. Thanks for your show of love in the things that you *do*. I dedicate this book to you.

Introduction

George Yancy

WHEN I FIRST HEARD about the dehumanizing events that took place at Abu Ghraib Prison, whether it was a prisoner with a leash around his neck like a dog, or Iraqi prisoners in the nude depicted in very suggestive sexual acts and forming pyramids, I immediately thought of *race*. From the many commentaries that I read or heard, the dynamics of race were absent. The content of much of the commentary that I read and heard focused around the issue of America's contradictory messages. Of course, many were quick to point out that the events that took place at the prison were isolated, limited to a few inexcusable cases only. Such discourse, however, aims to render the pervasiveness of racism invisible under the banner that most white Americans are "color blind." Acts of white racism are then deemed individual instances of *prejudice*, perhaps even categorized as hate crimes, claims that attempt to sidestep the systemic and structural nature of white racism. Indeed, President Bush announced, "This is not the America I know." But "Whose America?" and "Whose knowledge?" Perhaps it is here that Bush's "knowledge" about America might be framed within the context of the epistemology of ignorance, whereby he is blinded by a certain historically structured and structuring (white) opacity, "a particular pattern of localized and global cognitive dysfunctions (which are psychologically and socially functional), producing the ironic outcome that whites will in general be unable to understand the world they themselves have made."[1] Bush's comment only further confirmed my conviction that critics and pundits had failed to explore and interrogate the subtext of race that I theorized had been performed at Abu Ghraib. Such themes as sadistic brutality, sexual violence, xenophobic paranoia, the reduction of fellow human beings to brute beasts, played themselves out against a silent, though familiar, backdrop of a long history of America's racist drama: the racializing, stigmatizing, and brutalizing of the marked "Other." Why is it that the events at Abu Ghraib took the form of *sexual* humiliation? The photos had a spectacle and ceremonial feel to them, as if the larger semiotic message, the narrative of violence, sex, and "darkies," was intended to communicate what many white racist Americans have always thought: that the Iraqi prisoners were "sand Niggers," swarthy in complexion, morally "dark" in their deeds, bestial, and lacking in the "progressive" values of modernity.

As the events at Abu Ghraib unfolded, I found myself bombarded with thoughts of the racist historical processes of "Niggerization" and hypersexualization that Blacks in North America have undergone. Were these prisoners being "Niggerized" and hypersexualized? The events that took place at Abu Ghraib reminded me precisely of the America that I knew and know. Recall that it was only in 1997 that, in New York, Abner Louima, a Black man, had a wooden stick shoved into his rectum and mouth by white police officers while his hands were cuffed behind his back. What is the nature of the satisfaction that white men derive from shoving a phallic object into the rectum of a Black man and then shoving it into his mouth? This is the America that I know. Then again, what desire is satisfied by getting so-called sand Niggers to perform in the nude before white onlookers? What is the anatomy of this perverse desire? The ritual sounds so familiar. Themes of white sadism, illusions of (white) absolute power and freedom from responsibility, white male phallocentrism, and feelings of psychological impotence "overcome" through pernicious acts of brutalizing the Other pervaded the white ritualism at Abu Ghraib.

I found the recent beheadings in Iraq to be despicable acts.[2] And it is only right that the world protests such acts. But at the same time, let us not forget America's history. Again, in 1997, white men hung a Black man, Garnett Paul Johnson, on a cross, poured gasoline over his body and then *beheaded* him with what I understand to have been a dull ax. "A year later," as African American writer David Bradley notes, "near a town called Jasper, Texas, three white men kidnapped a black man named James Byrd, Jr., spray-painted him white, chained him to the bumper of a pickup, and dragged him until his body parts [*head included*] were distributed along two miles of country road."[3] As much as we should be horrified by what is happening to white Americans abroad, which is by no means acceptable, Blacks at home are also being beheaded and brutalized.

Abner Louima experienced firsthand white America's pernicious racism toward the dark Other. He understood how it is not enough to be physically brutalized. He understood what it meant to be sexually abused/humiliated, symbolically "fucked" by white male members of a power structure that saw themselves as giving him what he "desired." After all, or so the mythopoetic reasoning goes, those darkies are oversexed anyway. Louima knew what it was like to experience a "torture chamber" or a "torture room." If only American prison walls could name the horrors that occur there daily, the sadism, the horror of forced rape of both men and women, forced sodomy, forced humiliation. Abu Ghraib was no exception to the rule of America's racist brutality and sexually perverse practices. Such events at the Iraqi prison were profoundly disturbing, but not new, not surprising.

Consider Claude Neal, a twenty-three-year-old Black man who, on October 19, 1934, was arrested in Greenwood, Florida, for allegedly raping and killing a white woman. It is said that, while in the hands of white men, he "confessed" to the crime. With all the signs of whiteness gone mad (predictably so, when it comes to the need to punish "oversexed" Black male "beasts" who prey on the purity, sanctity, and innocence of white women), Neal was taken from his jail cell by white men and horribly brutalized. Neal was branded. They cut off his penis and made him eat it. They then cut off his testicles and made him eat them, forcing him to say that he liked them. His sides were sliced with knives. Whites would go on to decide to cut off a finger or toe. They burned him with hot coals. During this act of *white terrorism*, Neal had a rope tied around his neck. The white racist terrorists made sure that he did not lose consciousness. When there was no doubt that he was on the brink of losing consciousness, he was quickly resuscitated. He was then terrorized all over again, and again, and again. The experience of terrorism is not new to Black people living in racist white America. Neal's dead body was later run over by cars, stabbed with knives, beaten with sticks, and kicked by white men, women, and children. Many pictures were taken of his mutilated body only to be sold. Like Sam Hoes, who was lynched in Georgia, who had slices of his heart and liver sold, and whose Black knuckles were on display in a store, Neal's fingers and toes were exhibited as prize possessions for all to see.

W. E. B. Du Bois was cognizant of the ritualistic nature of the lynching of Black bodies. It was not so much about whether the Black victim was guilty or not; it was about the ceremonial rite/right of taking the life and spilling the blood of *any* Black, for if you were Black you were guilty. On this score, Blackness *is* the state of always already being guilty. White anger could not be propitiated until the ritual was complete, until the body had been castrated, dismembered, burned, and beaten. It was only then that the white mob could rest peacefully, knowing that it had preserved the white order of things. Du Bois said:

> We have seen, you and I, city after city drunk and furious with ungovernable lust of blood; mad with murder, destroying, killing, and cursing; torturing human

> victims because somebody accused of crime happened to be of the same color as the mob's innocent victims and because that color was not white! We have seen—Merciful God! in these wild days and in the name of Civilization, Justice, and Motherhood—what have we not seen, right here in America, of orgy, cruelty, barbarism, and murder done to men and women of Negro descent.[4]

W. E. B. Du Bois, Malcolm X, and Paul Robeson were well aware of the dialectic that existed/exists between white supremacy and Black degradation/brutalization. Malcolm X and Du Bois were so tired of white America's misanthropic ways that each felt the moral obligation to call upon the United Nations to hear the pernicious crimes that America had committed against its Black "citizens." Indeed, Paul Robeson was head of a New York delegation who took it upon themselves to petition the United Nations for action against the U.S. policy of genocide against Black Americans. The petition was entitled, "We Charge Genocide: The Crime of the United States Government against the Negro People."

My point here is that when we point to and construct "enemies" abroad, and become overwhelmed and seduced by a false, precarious, and short-lived sense of "national unity," as if America is not fundamentally divided by race, it is important that we remember the history of America, recall its racist past and present. Here is where historical memory can function as a weapon. To recall appropriate historical memories at the appropriate historical time has the power to silence those who would have us believe that America is the paragon of ethical leadership. The America that I know is an America that paints the world in white and black, good and evil, us and them, civilized and barbaric, peacekeepers and warmongering terrorists. In short, America has created its own Manichean divide(s). The divide that is most important to the task at hand, and within the body of this text, is that between white and Black. Of course, this divide is by no means uncomplicated, always fixed, and neatly delineated. Indeed, it has, at moments, proven to be extremely murky, coalescing at significant points of shared interest, political struggle, and so on. Even within each hemisphere of the divide, as it were, there are tensions, contradictions, fundamental differences, rivalries, schisms, and further complex divisions and splits. What I am saying here does not overlook other sites of tension, hatred, violence, and division such as exists along lines of class, gender, religion, politics, and sexual orientation. Moreover, Blackness and whiteness are systemically interlocked along axes of class, misogyny, heterosexism, political affiliation, and so on. However, this does not negate the reality that America, at its core, is structured in the form of a systemically racist Manichean (white-Black) divide. Of course, there have been whites who have come to America and have gained psychological, moral, and material power by being designated as "white" or as identifying themselves as white. In this case, the boundary is expanded, thus negatively impacting more of those who are excluded, rendered Other and politically nugatory. Perhaps the Kerner Commission's report, which was published in 1967, had profound prescience. We are divided along racial lines, two societies, one Black, one white. Assimilation theory appears to be dead in the water. Donald R. Kinder and Lynn M. Sanders note:

> Certainly economic and social inequalities continue to divide Americans along racial lines. Even with the postwar progress taken into account, large racial differences in employment, income, and wealth remain. Blacks are twice as likely to be unemployed; they earn less when they are employed; the average black household commands less than one-tenth the financial assets of the average household; black children are more likely than not to be born into poverty [almost three times]; and it goes on.[5]

The reality continues. Blacks are six times more likely than whites to be incarcerated. Blacks constitute 40 percent of those executed. Although Blacks are about one-eighth of the national population, some 1.2 million Blacks are under lock and key.[6] White males make up a little over 35 percent of the population, yet they constitute more than 80 percent of the Forbes 400 group, those who are worth well over $240 million. Of course, within the political sphere, white males dominate as state governors and in the Congress. White males are also dominant in numbers when it comes to such areas as tenured college faculty, daily-newspaper editors, television news directors, corporate management, you name it.[7] Noting differences, it is still incredibly amazing how opinion was divided along white-Black "racial" lines when it came to the O. J. Simpson trial,[8] the events that took place in Los Angeles after the first verdict was handed down for the police officers in the Rodney King beating, and the racial binarism of opinion regarding the case of the Central Park jogger. Concerning the last case, Joan Didion points to the extreme schism over the event. She notes:

> One vision, shared by those who had seized upon the attack of the jogger as an exact representation of what was wrong with the city, was of a city systematically ruined, violated, raped by its underclass [that is, people of color]. The opposing vision, as an exact representation of their own victimization, was of a city in which the powerless had been systematically ruined, violated, raped by the powerful [white folk].[9]

In the above example, it is as if Blacks and whites have gotten hold of two radically different world pictures or paradigms admitting of no common ground.[10] The "no common ground" reality, however, is made all the more clear when one looks at the material ways in which America is divided, as I suggest above.

Although his book is entitled *Beyond Black & White*, Manning Marable provides very insightful comments regarding what it means to be Black in America. What he points to are some of the everyday lived realities of many Black people. Such realities have profoundly psychological and material consequences. The reader will note the effective use of the resounding refrain, "To be black." Marable maintains:

> To be black means that when you go to the bank to borrow money, despite the fact that you have a credit profile identical to your white counterpart, you are nevertheless two or three times more likely to be denied the loan than the white. To be Black means that when you are taken to the hospital for emergency health-care treatment, the quality of care you receive will be inadequate and substandard. To be black means that your children will not have the same academic experiences and access to higher learning resources as children in the white suburbs and exclusive urban enclaves. To be black means that your mere physical presence and the reality of your being can trigger surveillance cameras at shops, supermarkets, malls and fine stores everywhere. To be black, male, and to live in central Harlem in the 1990s, for example, means that you will have a life expectancy of forty-nine years of age—less than in Bangladesh.[11]

Marable does not leave small quotidian white racist aggressions—though powerful in their impact upon Black and other subaltern people—unturned. He notes such manifestations as:

> The white merchant who drops change on the sales counter, rather than touch the hand of a black person; the white salesperson who follows you into the dressing room when you carry several items of clothing to try on, because he or she suspects that you are trying to steal; the white teacher who deliberately avoids the upraised hand of a Latino student in class, giving white pupils an unspoken yet understood advantage; the white woman who wraps the strap of her purse several times tightly around her arm, just before walking past a black man; the white taxicab drivers who speed rapidly past African-Americans or Latinos, picking up whites on the next block.[12]

I would like to make it clear that I realize that the self-Other divide is not exhausted by the white-Black divide. This will, I hope, preempt any critique that I am trapped by a white/Black binary that trumps other forms of complex social tensions. After all, Native Americans, Latin Americans, Mexicans, Asian Americans, and Arabs have been Othered by the axiological, political, and material power of whiteness, and have felt the negative impact of the color line. My wish is not to render invisible these groups. There is no aim to erase, even by implication, the significance of such groups—their political struggles, their pain and suffering, and their cultural richness—by focusing on the white-Black divide. We are a nation that is "visibly mixed race, multiethnic, and multiracial."[13] Indeed, I fully acknowledge the fact that poor whites and poor Blacks constitute another hemispheric divide vis-à-vis both wealthy whites and Blacks.

So, why the focus on the white-Black divide? First, within the context of this text, the focus speaks to my own "racialized" positionality. As a Black male, I am interested, indeed, existentially invested, in the dynamics that continue to create and reinforce the color line between whites and Blacks. After all, it was white people who created and segregated the social, political, and economic spaces that my Black great-grandparents, grandparents, and mother and father lived through. I, thereby, have intergenerational links to the history of their suffering, derailment, and degradation. Of course, I am also socio-ontologically and existentially linked to all of those subaltern voices and bodies (Native Americans, Latin Americans, Mexican Americans, and Asian Americans) in North America who have suffered and continue to suffer under white racist hegemony. Second, I am specifically interested in how white and Black philosophers conceptualize whiteness and Blackness, respectively. It is one thing for white and Black philosophers to theorize race as an epistemologically bankrupt category. It is quite another for them to engage the issue of whiteness and Blackness in terms of what these social categories have come to mean for them personally, and how, despite their critical philosophical analyses of race, they existentially live the sociopolitical dimensions of their whiteness or Blackness. Indeed, on a personal level, beyond the abstract conceptual domain of rejecting the concept of race, the integrity of my dark body continues—from a semiotic and physical perspective—to be under attack. And white bodies continue to reap the rewards and respect of the historical weight of presumptive innocence, intelligence, and worthiness.

Hence, the title of the book: *White on White/Black on Black*. The objective was not to buttress the already white-Black racial binary. The racial binary in America existed long before this text. Each philosopher within the text has inherited the discourse of race, its history, its link with power/powerlessness, its material relations, its structured social relations, and its valuational structures. The idea was to get white and Black philosophers to explore how they understand the implications of living within one or the other of the "racialized" hemispheres, again, keeping in mind that these hemispheres are by no means static and easily drawn. My aim was to get white and Black philosophers to name and theorize their own raciated identities within the same philosophical text. By combining both white and Black philosophical voices within the same text, these voices are designed to function to establish a form of dialogue, speaking within a common thematic framework. This approach was designed to create a space for discursive diversity, broad conceptual scope, and diverse philosophical approaches vis-à-vis race. Having the chapters appear within the same text, readers are given the opportunity to engage the text in terms of how white and Black philosophers are differentially invested in the language of racial identity, how they normatively understand such identities, how they more generally understand the epistemological and ontological status of whiteness and Blackness, and how such identities are inextricably linked to broader historical, cultural, politico-economic, ideological, and aesthetic sites. My aim was to create a teachable text, that is, to create a text whereby readers will be able to compare and engage critically the similarities and differences found within and between the critical cadre of both white philosophers and Black philosophers.

There are multiple questions that can be raised as points of critical entry into this text. For example, how do white and Black philosophers understand the concept of race? How do they read their identities in terms of the historical backdrop of race discourse? Do they manage to articulate notions of whiteness/Blackness that avoid essentialism? Is whiteness/Blackness socially constructed? If socially constructed, what does this say about the *lived* reality of race? How do white and Black philosophers *live* their raced identities differently? In what ways do white/Black philosophers seek to reconstruct whiteness/Blackness? How does one reject whiteness and yet still benefit from whiteness? Intrapsychologically, what does Blackness/whiteness normatively register for Black and white philosophers? In what ways are Blackness and whiteness ways of *becoming* and not simply static descriptor terms? To what extent do Blackness and whiteness constitute important sites of philosophical embarkation? What impact does living one's identity as Black or white have on how one does philosophy or lives one's philosophical projects, particularly in recognition of the deeply political implications of such identities? How is the phenomenon of *naming* differentially used (or deployed) in the process of critiquing or embracing whiteness/Blackness? In what way does ethical and aesthetic discourse intersect with race within the text? How is this intersection critiqued, embraced, theorized?

As a reader, professional philosopher or not, how important is *your* "racialized" identity in terms of your philosophical standpoint? More specifically, as a professional philosopher or a student of philosophy, *should* "race" matter in terms of your philosophical project? Or do you think that because you specialize (or intend to specialize) in the pre-Socratics, Plato, Aristotle, medieval metaphysics, epistemology, value theory, the philosophy of mind, or the like, that your "racialized" identity has no bearing on how *you* philosophically conceptualize the world? *White on White/Black on Black* dared to ask philosophers to explore the messiness of racialized consciousness. The contributors within this text enthusiastically accepted my request to engage what it means to be white/Black. What follows is a summary of the fascinating results.

White on White

Robert Bernasconi, noting his existentialist approach to race from the outset, insightfully engages the philosophical autobiographical terrain, providing readers with a rich description of what it was like to *become* white once he moved to Memphis. He explores the importance of critiquing and disrupting whiteness but argues that whiteness, as a site of privilege, is also not simply a matter of choice. He goes on to explore the ramifications of the whiteness of philosophy and what ought to be done to address it.

Chris Cuomo, writing in a style that is refreshingly free of philosophical formality, opens her chapter with a powerful plea for help to fight against her own whiteness. She critiques naming processes that are tied to racial hierarchy and raises very powerful imagery regarding the need to have one's (white) sense of self shaken at its core. Engaging in a process of re-naming her multiple positions, Cuomo ends with advice for those whites who desire to remain shaken in their identities, to preserve the cracks.

Crispin Sartwell provides an engaging exploration of what it means to be a "wigger," which is a white person who acts like a Black person. Locating his own identity within the wigger tradition, Sartwell provides the cultural space within which his wigger identity emerged. He takes the reader on a journey through the prehistory of the wigger, shows how music is an important site of wigger formation, and moves on to the self-critical dimensions of wiggerism in terms of how it can function as an expression of the rejection of whiteness, and how this form of wiggerism is best exemplified by William Upski Wimsatt and rapper Eminem.

Greg Moses makes it clear that as a white philosopher he has long "been interested in the form that philosophy takes along the color line." He challenges whites to engage in an ethic of whiteness that is motivated to *name* and *unmask* the complex ways in which whiteness resists being named, which is actually a function of its power. He goes on to challenge the assumption that there are no modes of whiteness that are desirable. Moses draws from the work of Lucius Outlaw, revealing how an "Africology of whiteness" is capable of deconstructing the transcendental pretensions of whiteness.

Anna Stubblefield, drawing critically upon her experiences as a white woman philosopher who teaches Africana philosophy, argues that race is a social construction, but that it is very real in terms of its material manifestations. She advances a postsupremacist philosophy, one that is nurtured in the spirit of interdisciplinarity and challenges white hegemony, gender hierarchy, and so on. She boldly recommends that white philosophers should choose to be "bad" philosophers, that is, philosophers who do not fail to take the white normative dimensions of philosophy for granted, but wage powerful critiques against not only whiteness in philosophy, but philosophy's supremacist and elitist tendencies as these negatively impact Native American, Asian, and Middle-Eastern students, disabled students, and others who desire to engage the field of philosophy as a career.

Monique Roelofs moves the reader into a complex space of "racialized aestheticization" and "aesthetic racialization." Roelofs provides an insightful tracing of problematic racist links between Enlightenment philosophers and the notion of the aesthetic in terms of an engaging analysis of taste as an expression of whiteness and other cultural vectors. Recognizing the dialectic that exists between whiteness and Blackness, she also explores ways that "racialized aestheticization" and "aesthetic racialization" get reproduced or challenged in the work of Jamaica Kincaid, Franz Fanon, Angela Davis, and others. She ends with a critique of the white self-confessional mode in much of critical whiteness studies.

Bettina G. Bergo raises the very significant phenomenological question of what it means to "see." Speaking in my own voice as editor, I believe that this is a crucial place to begin with respect to issues of race and the dynamic of "seeing" others (or one's own identity) as raced. She interrogates perception (as intentionality) as understood within a phenomenological frame of reference, emphasizing the importance of the *cultural* and *symbolic* sphere that generates values vis-à-vis the process of "seeing" white, Black, Other. Bergo goes on to explore her own whiteness, emphasizing that "seeing whiteness" is not a solitary act.

Black on Black

Clarence Sholé Johnson provides a historical exploration of the Enlightenment conception of Blackness. He delineates three procedural elements involved in the social construction of Blackness, a construction grounded in the utility value of Black bodies, and the hegemonic aims of whites. He also explores the meaning of "becoming" Black, rejecting an essentialist characterization of Blackness and stressing the importance of transcending the negative valuation of Blackness, and not the natural pigmentation of skin color. Dialectically locating his own position, Johnson critically addresses various points raised by such race theorists as David B. Wilkins, Naomi Zack, and Lucius Outlaw. He ends his chapter with an insightful description of how he personally enacts his Blackness—that is, Blackness as *resistance*—through philosophy.

Molefi Kete Asante explores the meaning of Blackness as an ethical trope. On this score, Blackness is not reduced to skin color or, for example, the ability to speak Ebonics. Blackness, for Asante, signifies an ethic of resistance and human liberation. As for Johnson, "Blackness" for Asante functions as a descriptor that can be applied to whites who enact forms of resistance against injustice and oppression. Blackness, for Asante, points to a post-Western mode of sociopolitical existence; for Blackness, in terms of its anti-imperialist history, emphasizes the centrality of a social universe governed by mutual respect and an ethical fervor against national and international injustice.

Janine Jones's use of language is provocative, calling seriously into question the normative discourse found in much of philosophical writing. She moves the reader through philosophical insights, personal memories, and a powerful form of performative discourse. She says, "I was born black." This assertion undermines the kind of voluntarism implied in a form of social constructionism that holds that simply by changing the name of a thing one can generate something entirely different. She interrogates so-called "white curiosity" and "white innocence," revealing how these performative sites of whiteness have negatively impacted Black people. Jones's chapter moves the reader through a personal recollection of a complex performance by Helmutt and Brenda Gottschild on the tragic African female figure known as Hottentot Venus. It is through the recollection and strategic appropriation of this performance that Jones explodes the often hidden realities of whiteness, its perverse imaginary, and its unconscionable acts of ocular and physical vivisection vis-à-vis the Black body.

In my own chapter, I explore the meaning of Blackness through the medium of whiteness. This is by no means to suggest that "Blackness" is limited to the white imaginary. Rather, I locate Blackness within the historical space of whiteness so as to emphasize how the emergence of Blackness is itself dialectically linked to whiteness. Like Jones, I integrate a performative discourse, one that appears as breaks within the body of the chapter. The breaks are designed to engage Blackness as historical memory, ancestral heritage, along magical realist lines, in terms of deep interreferential cultural signs and symbols. Like Jones, I also engage the narrative life of the so-called Hottentot Venus. My larger aim is to explore the structure of the white gaze, to reveal, like Bergo, its historical, cultural, and semiotic embedded nature.

Robert Birt explores the possibility of Blackness as a form of authenticity. He answers in the affirmative. Arguing that whiteness "*is* self-delusion and abandonment of responsibility," Birt argues that authenticity is grounded in the recognition that both facticity and transcendence is part of human reality.

Black authenticity is achieved through the process of reclaiming Blackness as a site for liberation and the rejection of "thingification." Of course, this also involves the acceptance of one's facticity, one's Blackness, and not maintaining that one is simply human; for this would involve another form of flight and hence movement toward inauthenticity. According to Birt, Black people cannot affirm human transcendence or existence without affirming their existence in Black. He then links the notion of self-affirmation with that of Black communal affirmation.

John H. McClendon III opens with a self-narrative regarding his experience of Blackness as something that was coded as negative when he and a group of other young Black students were told (ironically, by a Black teacher) not to act their color. McClendon draws links between the negativity associated with his dark skin—coming from the outside world—with his own eventual identity as a Black philosopher. This sets in motion a deep affirmation of his Blackness, a choice that would have implications for his life project as a Black philosopher, scholar, and activist. He then discusses the emergence of Black philosophy, linking it to larger sociopolitical movements initiated by Black people, and the importance of the work of Black philosopher William R. Jones in terms of the latter's affirmation (unlike Black philosopher William Banner) of the very legitimacy of Black philosophy. Drawing from his own political standpoint, McClendon provides an analysis of Blackness in terms of what he calls a minimalist definition of Blackness (MDB).

Kal Alston explores Blackness in terms of its epistemology, ontology, and axiology. Alston draws from her own personal experiences as a Black philosophy graduate student and as a Black woman philosopher. She is aware of how the history of philosophy is indeed a history of the conceptual and social consolidation of race. She emphasizes the importance of "knowing Blackness" in terms of how it "is always bound up with critical, dialectical thinking." Out of this epistemic awareness of engaging philosophy in Black grows the importance of becoming and valuing Blackness. Alston very insightfully explores how she "became" Black more than once. The second time she describes as coming to terms with the significance of her Blackness "beyond my phenomenal experience." The implications here in terms of identity formation as a dynamic process and the claim that Blackness is an *essential thing* (once and for all) are very intriguing. After all, Black consciousness changes relative to historical specificity and sociopolitical stasis/disruption. Black knowing, becoming, and valuing can be significantly aided through the liberatory actions of others. In Alston's case, her parents were very influential in this regard. Alton also explores how valuing Blackness must lead to positive actions. She then insightfully suggests ways that philosophy itself might engage in the process of valuing Blackness.

Edited books are collaborative efforts. Even if the project is conceived while sitting in the park alone, the coming into being of an edited book occurs through the combined efforts of contributors, a publishing industry, copy-editors, indexers, readers, bookstores, capital, and so on. In other words, this book (and any book for that matter) came to be within a shared space. In fact, *White on White/Black on Black* came into existence as the result of a single conversation. That conversation took place with Eve DeVaro, philosophy editor at Rowman & Littlefield. I suggested the idea to Eve of editing a work similar in structure to another project of mine that was under contract with another publisher, and has since been published as *What White Looks Like: African-American Philosophers on the Whiteness Question.* My idea was to edit a book that would complement this text but that would exclusively deal with white philosophers examining whiteness. It was at this juncture that Eve suggested two possible projects: (a) either a book where Black philosophers wrote on whiteness and white Philosophers wrote on Blackness or (b) a book where white philosophers wrote on whiteness and Black philosophers wrote on Blackness. I was much more excited about the second idea than I was about the first. The rest, as they say, is history. As Eve says, "And so the project *White on White/Black on Black* was born."

Notes

1. Charles Mills, 1997, *The Racial Contract*, Ithaca, NY: Cornell University Press, 18.
2. At the time of this writing this included Americans Daniel Pearl, Nicholas Berg, and Paul Johnson, and South Korean Kim Sun-il.
3. David Bradley, 2002, "To Make Them Stand in Fear" in Bernestine Singley (ed.) *When Race Becomes Real: Black and White Writers Confront Their Personal Histories*, Chicago, IL: Lawrence Hill Books, 117.
4. W. E. B. Du Bois, 1995, "The Souls of White Folk," in David Levering Lewis (ed.) *W. E. B. Du Bois: A Reader*, New York: Henry Holt and Company, 455.
5. Donald R. Kinder and Lynn M. Sanders, 1996, *Divided by Color: Racial Politics and Democratic Ideals*, Chicago, IL: University of Chicago Press, 285.
6. Glenn C. Loury, 2002, *The Anatomy of Racial Inequality*, Cambridge, MA: Harvard University Press, 137.
7. See *The Philadelphia Tribune Magazine*, April 1999, 9.
8. Although making it clear that she had not been polled and that polls are always inflected by such variables as gender, class, education, religion, location, etc., Ann DuCille, 1996, notes: "Although percentages fluctuated throughout the trial, the reported polarity remained constant: a majority of white Americans—anywhere from 60 to 80 percent—believed Simpson guilty, and a majority of black Americans judged him innocent." See her book, *Skin Trade*, Cambridge, MA: Harvard University Press, 147.

9. As quoted in Kinder and Sanders, 1996, *Divided by Color*, 288.

10. Kinder and Sanders, 1996, *Divided by Color*, 288.

11. Manning Marable, 1996, *Beyond Black and White: Transforming African American Politics*, New York: Verso, 6.

12. Marable, *Beyond Black and White*, 7.

13. Johnnella E. Butler, 2000, "Reflections on Borderlands and the Color Line," in Shirley Geok-Lin Lim and Maria Herrera-Sobek (eds.) *Power, Race, and Gender in Academe: Strangers in the Tower?* New York: The Modern Language Association of America, 8.

I

WHITE ON WHITE

1

Waking Up White and in Memphis

Robert Bernasconi
University of Memphis

HOW DO I EXPLAIN WHAT WHITENESS HAS come to mean to me? Particularly because I favor an existential approach to race, there seems little alternative, if I am to address the questions that George Yancy has put to me and the other contributors, but to offer some autobiographical observations, albeit it is a form of address with which I have never felt comfortable. And never less so than when talking about race. Like many white people, I am never more nervous than when the topic turns to race, though this has not stopped me from writing about it on a number of occasions. With race everything is always overdetermined, and context is decisive. What is racist in one context will be emancipatory in another, and vice versa. And yet one cannot control the context in which the written word will be read. However, my discomfort at talking about race, although no doubt fed in part by the common and not always honorable fear of causing offense, would not account for my obsession with the topic. That has more to do with the shock of waking up white in Memphis, as I try to explain here. Because my remarks are largely autobiographical and refer to my fifteen years living in Memphis, the focus falls on Black-white relations. Read in San Francisco or Miami, or read from the perspective of Memphis's own changing demographics, what I have to say about my life in Memphis may probably seem as alien as my life in England, but I am not trying to produce a universal theory; rather, I am trying to be true to my limited experience.

The context in which I have been led to think about race is Memphis. To say that coming to Memphis woke me from my dogmatic slumbers would be to claim too much, but when, in 1988, I moved to Memphis from England, I was largely ignorant of the history of the United States and particularly of its race relations to a degree that I now find frightening. I was surprised, for example, to find that in Memphis I was perceived as white. Scholars of the negritude movement who have read how Paulette Nardal, Aimé Césaire, and Frantz Fanon were each surprised to find on their arrival in France that they were perceived as Black will at least be familiar with the phenomenon, even if they remain astonished at my naïveté. I did not think of myself as white, but as English. It took me a while to understand how little I understood my new environment.

The first time I was confronted by a form asking me to check the box that corresponded to my racial self-indentification I sought help. I knew enough to know that I wanted to opt out of the system from the outset. I wanted to know how long I could get by with the waiver: I am not white but English. Certainly in England at that time whiteness was not an important category. This is not to say that Britain did not and does not have racial problems or racial consciousness, to go along with all the issues of class and region that permeate life there. However, the English are so focused on the Scottish, the Irish, and the Welsh, not to mention the French, that whiteness was not the salient category. Today, whiteness as a label has more currency in Britain than it had fifteen years ago, but it is a discourse that has largely been imported from North American mass culture and, to the extent that it has been adopted, it does not conform entirely to the specific experiences—and prejudices—operative there. Whiteness is not an exclusively North American phenomenon, or a North American invention, but it is in the United States that it has received one of its most vicious modern forms: a society of unprecedented wealth whose benefits are unevenly distributed largely along racial lines. However, I have to admit that it was by coming to the United States that I understood British racism, British classism, and British sexism, much better.

In any event, if I ever seriously contemplated resistance to being categorized, I was soon disabused: I was seen as white, whether I liked it or not. It is a story that, with reference to a somewhat different environment, Albert Memmi tells brilliantly in *The Colonizer and the Colonized*, a book about Tunisia under French occupation that explains complicity in a system: an outsider coming from Europe into a colonial environment cannot stay for long without becoming a colonizer, because one immediately is a beneficiary of the privileges of the colonizer, whether one wants them or not. Privilege is guaranteed by the institutions, the customs, and the people. Pressure is put on the newcomer to adopt the mannerisms and prejudices of the colonizers, but whether one does or does not, the privileges remain.[1] Initially my most decisive encounters were with native white Memphians who clearly regarded me as suspect, simply by virtue of my being a new arrival from England. I was frequently put to the test, or that is at least how I experienced it at the time, as if they correctly surmised that I did not share what to me were their unconscionable sensibilities on the race issue. A mildly racist remark would be inserted into the conversation to see how I would react. If I let it pass, or if my protest seemed halfhearted, then another more provocative comment would follow. My love of soul music, which is widespread among British people of my generation, with the result that I was drawn to the Black clubs of Memphis, made me particularly suspect.

Whiteness is an alliance, but it is not an alliance in which all partners are equal. There was some suspicion of me among white Southerners because I was from elsewhere, a suspicion that seemed to arise from a recognition that their practices were questionable. However, the fact that I was English more than made up for it. For the first and only time in my life I was exotic. To white Memphians my Englishness was a kind of hyperwhiteness, which, of course, is also how it tended to be conceived in North America in the eighteenth century. I was invited to address a meeting of a society that euphemistically described itself as English-speaking. I knew what they meant, so when I made it clear I would love to come with a Black friend I introduced them to, I was not surprised that I heard no more from them. They did not know and would not have understood that my Englishness also made me more acceptable to the African American community, according to a logic that I perhaps should have protested more vehemently than I did: "This is Robert. He's all right. He's from England. Don't mess with him." Furthermore, my Italian surname seemed to gain me entry into a small group of influential Italian Americans, who were even less Italian than I was, and who greeted me with open arms until I made it clear that I could not give a lecture in honor of Columbus for the five hundredth anniversary of his arrival in America. Whiteness, in North America, but not in Africa, for example, assumes racial purity, but it is a shifting identity and always some are more white than others. This is because whiteness has expanded its boundaries so that the core group—the Anglo Saxons—can retain their privileges and power.

Tired of constantly having to negotiate the anti-Black racism of white Memphians, it became clear that if I was to have a social life away from the closed world of the university, it would be among African Americans, but this happened more by accident than design. African Americans welcomed me with open arms into their homes and their churches. I have a particularly fond memory of Reverend Melvyn Rodgers, the pastor of New Bethel Missionary Church, Ball Road, announcing during service, "I know some of y'all hate white people, but let's sing 'Happy Birthday' to Robert anyway." It is also true

I overheard on occasion one or other of my new friends being warned not to trust "whitey." But given what I learned from listening to their casual conversation about the conditions under which they lived, I could not complain. Nor could I help myself from trying to calculate the ages of "Pops" or "Big Mama" when I was introduced to them: why were they so welcoming after all they had suffered at the hands of whites?

I also learned that most African Americans in Memphis wanted to be seen as such. In Walter Mosley's *Devil in a Blue Dress*, Easy Rawlins finds that his conversation with Todd Carter, a rich white man, proceeds "like we were best friends—even closer." "I could tell that he didn't have the fear or contempt that most white people showed when they dealt with me." But he then suspects that Carter was "so rich that he didn't even consider me in human terms." Rawlins complains, "it was the worst kind of racism. The fact that he didn't even recognize our difference showed that he didn't care one damn about me." This last sentence shows how deceptive, more precisely, how self-deceptive, the stance of the white liberal in contemporary America can be. The white liberal fails to recognize how whiteness functions within society and how Easy Rawlins wants to be respected, not as a man, but as a Black man.[2]

One long hot summer in Memphis, with my application for a Green Card pending, so that if I left the United States I would not be able to return, I anticipated a productive summer writing on Heidegger, Levinas, and Derrida. Instead, I experienced a debilitating writing block. I was incapable of making sense of my new situation, and paralyzed by my inability to find a place in it. In addition to listening to the people around me, I sought understanding by reading books on the history of race thinking and of the United States. It took a while for me to realize it, but this was a rebirth of my philosophical life. Insofar as I conceive philosophy as a quest for illumination set off by the experience of something bewildering, addressing my comprehension of my new surroundings gave me a partial resolution of the problem of how to live as a white philosopher in the United States. It was only a partial resolution because I could see for myself that racism was not primarily about individual comments or intentions. That is only an epiphenomenon of the underlying racism, which we try to gesture at with the phrase *institutional racism.* Furthermore, insofar as racism is a system that reproduces itself—through the cycle of poverty, for example—then only a major reorganization of society will address it, not simply a revision of personal attitudes where everything else remains the same. Personal attitudes are not the main source of the problem and they cannot provide the solution.

I experienced my whiteness as a label attached to me on the basis of my appearance in order to assimilate me to one group and assign me the appropriate privileges. That is to say, I experienced this process of labeling not simply as a lesson in language usage, but as an indication of the advantages that accrued to me in a polarized society. Memphis, like most urban communities in the United States, is characterized by de facto segregation—separate and unequal: for Blacks, poorer housing, poorer education, poorer health care, lower life expectancy, not to mention fewer job opportunities, higher unemployment, and lower income. The statistical data also play a role in forming the expectations that govern personal encounters. I could see that I was the beneficiary of white privilege, even if I had not yet heard the phrase, because in a group I was often treated differently from the way the African Americans in that same group were treated. That is why poor whites prefer to identify themselves in racial terms. Coming from a country obsessed with class and regional differences, I was struck by the fact that when people in the United States talk about class and about regions it is usually to talk about race without talking about race explicitly.

If the choice is between thinking of race as a biological essence or a social construction, then it is the latter. However, I do not believe that either notion was particularly helpful, either for coming to terms with the racial history we each inherit or for negotiating the problems that individually and collectively we have to face now. To say that something is a social construction is a first step toward clarifying its ontological status, but it does not clarify its existential status. It can foster false beliefs about the extent to which it is under a society's control, and one can see that in the current enthusiasm among certain politicians and philosophers for refusing to acknowledge race in what is undeniably a racialized society. This is more likely to contribute to perpetuating racism than it is to eradicating it. This is because racism today has less to do with individual prejudices than it has to do with an institutionalized system of oppression. Societies may have constructed a hierarchy of races, but that does not mean that any society knows how to dismantle the insidious effects of that hierarchization. However, I am not saying that things won't change. The only question will be whether they change for better or worse. We must be prepared to impact that change, if it happens in our lifetime.

When I landed in Memphis I cannot say that I experienced race as a social construction, so much as, to use a term from continental philosophy, a facticity, which means I cannot tell how much it is my or society's imposition and how much it is in things but is nevertheless my responsibility. I can celebrate my race or feel guilty about it, I can even renounce it, but I have no choice as to which race I get to renounce. I experienced race as a fact of life that I had no alternative but to address because to my eyes, coming from elsewhere, the absurdity of the taboos it imposed were as conspicuous as race itself seemed to be to the local population. Descartes tells us that travel is good for revealing one's own prejudices to oneself. Of course, it is even better at making apparent the prejudices of other people.

Not all whites share equally in white privilege, but the fact of white privilege makes the renunciation of one's whiteness a tempting prospect. One could abolish whiteness, leaving other identities in place, so as not to insult the collective memory of all those who have been persecuted because of race and the cultures that were formed in part to nourish that memory. This position was developed by the *Race Traitor* manifesto of Noel Ignatiev and John Garvey. The truth underlying the *Race Traitor* movement of the early 1990s was that privilege, the summit from which all other races are to be judged, is so much part of the inherited meaning of whiteness that whiteness cannot take its place alongside other racial categories without being submitted to radical critique. They concluded that whiteness should be abolished. However, I see this as a way of evading our responsibilities as whites rather than of meeting them. On an individual basis, divesting oneself of one's whiteness, or at least transforming it by disruptive strategies so that it ceases to be a site of privilege, seems attractive, but it ignores the fact that my identity is not simply up to me. It is not a matter of choice. We are responsible for who we are irrespective of how little choice one has in the matter. It is not for whites to decide if, when, and how whiteness is to be abolished, particularly as it may simply conceal the structures of white privilege already in place. Whites must turn to other racial groups and listen to them to find out who we are and what the meaning of our histories is. It is not obvious to me that whites know more about what it means to be white than other racial minorities do, although I do believe that Blacks, for example, know a great deal more about being Black than any other groups. This is because of the nature of racial identities in a racist society. Hence there is a responsibility on whites to listen. Whites associate whiteness with civilization, while overlooking its barbarity; they associate it with generosity, while overlooking its cruelty; and they associate it with justice, while overlooking its injustice. But for those races that have experienced slavery, genocide, or colonialism at the hands of whites, this is not possible.

We are all familiar with the way that the citizens of the United States, as a group, seem unwilling and unable to see themselves as others see them and that this hurts the country's pursuit of its foreign policy interests. After 9/11 it seemed that a concerted effort was made to correct this, but what other countries say about the United States ran so counter to its image of itself that the disconnect was intolerable and the attempt could not be sustained. Something similar happens with whites as a group in spite of the fact that here too there is a mass of material to go to in order to correct the deficiency. Instead, many whites today seek out other races because they want acceptance and acknowledgment. This clearly puts an intolerable burden upon those who are thus victimized by what amounts to a new form of exploitation. It is difficult to guard against because white desire for acceptance does not necessarily operate wholly at the conscious level.

Among whites, avowed racists seem more ready to admit it than the liberals who are worried about causing offense, but it has long been known there is an allure to racial difference, the allure of the exotic. In academia this can play out as multiculturalism, or in ordinary life as travel to exotic places or, as Frantz Fanon reminds me, in one's musical tastes.[3] Whites reach out to the racial Other in the expectation of receiving what is foreign to us. It is easier to document how dangerous this gesture has been, than the good it has done.

The fact that I had chosen to move to Memphis meant that, even though I had not at the time recognized all the implications, I had a clearer sense of the advantages of my position there and the responsibilities that came with it than I had had in England. What strikes this alien resident is the extraordinary inability of whites in the United States to acknowledge the racial crimes that constitute its history. Nor do these crimes belong only to what, to the American mind, is the distant past. The effects of enforced segregation and the denial of civil rights continue to this day. The failure of whites to acknowledge this history seems to be all of a piece with a tendency to run away from current racial problems, where possible, by emigrating to suburbia or, better yet, postsuburbia. No wonder that few people have the imagination to see that the magic of the consumer society is sustained less by hard work and low taxes, than it is by the low wages of Third World workers whose lives are consumed by our greed.

It seems to me that the dishonesty that whites in the United States show in respect of their failure to address the past crimes of which they are beneficiaries is also characteristic of philosophy as a discipline. Philosophers are largely in denial not only about the role of some of the most exalted philosophers in the history of racism and in preparing for other crimes against humanity, but also about philosophy's current problems: the fact that philosophers in the United States are overwhelmingly white; the fact that Black philosophers, like women philosophers, often seem to have to leave philosophy for other disciplines in order to get a senior position; the fact that non-Western philosophy, although it is much sought after by undergraduates, is rarely taught and that graduate schools do not prepare new Ph.D.s to teach it; and the fact that the philosophical canon alone in the humanities has not been revised to accommodate multiculturalism. Furthermore, I believe, although this is not the place to run the argument, that the philosophical establishment in the United States with its championing of individualism and of analytic thought operates to conceal the impact of racism, much as the reigning ideology of the United States has always done.

There is no discourse of white responsibility in the United States to match that produced by the German philosophers after the Second World War; there is not even a debate about the need for it, outside the discourse of reparations, which has largely been confined to African American philosophers. White philosophers need to take up this issue but also need to clarify that "reparations" is not a means of purification, of paying off a debt, of making amends. That presents a false expectation. How could the Germans ever pay off the Jews or white Americans make amends to American Indians? However, because as whites we have a disproportionate share of the resources and because it is as whites that we will be judged, whites have a historical responsibility to address these crimes. Where once there was a triumphalist history in which past crimes—for example, the Atlantic slave trade, the genocide of American Indians—were justified because they led to the civilization of the present, we are moving into a world where whites will be judged by history's victims. For the same reason, within the context of globalization, future generations will hold us in the West responsible for the tragedies that are taking place in Africa: the millions of war deaths in the Congo, the AIDS epidemic, and above all the deaths from starvation. How does the West present international debt as a problem that the Third World has in relation to the richest countries in the world? Should not the question be the debt that the West owes to those it has robbed and exploited? The same is true for whites in the United States in respect to racism. Wherever we find ourselves in a setting that is overwhelmingly, if not exclusively white, whether it be a class in the university or a fancy restaurant or a suburb, we know that that is a consequence of a violent shameful history and we know that it is sustained only by a society for its self-protection that refuses to address societal solutions to societal problems, preferring to pretend that we are all only individuals like atoms or nomads.

Individually and collectively philosophers must take responsibility for what is taught, who does the teaching, and who is taught. The whiteness of philosophy must be addressed with the same energy as the maleness of philosophy is beginning to be. The right wing press would have one believe that academics are dominated by political correctness. But one does not hear how women candidates for academic positions are often subjected to more scrutiny than their male counterparts and that the same happens with nonwhites. To be sure, my evidence for that is anecdotal and not scientific, but we do have very strong reason to believe that having Black, American Indian, or Hispanic philosophy professors in the classroom can have a very real impact on the overall education of all students and that this is largely underestimated by appointment committees. We each need to commit ourselves to doing more to change the face of philosophy in the United States. We must keep the issue of racism, especially institutional racism, constantly at the forefront of attention in every context in which we operate: whether it be college admissions, recruiting majors, or curriculum development.

Notes

1. Albert Memmi, *Portrait du colonisé précédé du portrait du colonisateur*, Paris: Gallimard, 1985, 45, trans. Moward Greenfield, *The Colonizer and the Colonized*, Boston: Beacon Press, 1967, 17.
2. Walter Mosley, *Devil in a Blue Dress*, New York: Pocket Books, 1990, 119.
3. Frantz Fanon, *Les damnés de la terre*, Paris: Gallimard, 1991, 291, trans. Constance Farrington, *The Wretched of the Earth*, New York: Grove Weidenfeld, 1991, 242–43.

2

White and Cracking Up

Chris Cuomo
University of Cincinnati

I'm asking for mercy. Could somebody please help me with whiteness—that elusive form, that pillar of America, that line meant to mark some fundamental difference between them and us (perhaps you on one side, me on the other). I am so sick of whiteness, and the world that the drive for white supremacy fosters and the legacies it has created, sometimes I don't know where to turn. I know I shouldn't complain to you, but some day I'm just going to crack up. Whiteness is so fucking unfair, so boring, so overdetermined and fake, so tight, so ridiculous. I am sick of going to work where the professors are white and the custodians are black, where ten percent of the students are black, most of the black students are criminal justice majors, and everyone thinks that's a big victory for diversity. Gee, why do so many of my black students know they can have great careers in prison administration?

I hate this racist world.

Where hierarchical racial distinctions operate, racial names such as *black, indigenous, latino/latina, asian, white,* and *mixed* (the American race names currently in vogue) are explicitly or implicitly given to everyone at birth, or even before. Unlike sex or intelligence or physical ability, in America the racial categorization of any child-to-be is knowable before it is even conceived, because the logic of racial categorization is strictly genealogical.

Racial naming need not be so hierarchical or judgmental. Indigenous peoples the world over have referred to imposing Europeans as whites, for example, but that color-coded name generally did not imply the belief that white folks were inherently less valuable or less fully human. As a case in point, a Crow woman named Pretty Shield described a first encounter in the 1860s as follows:

> When I was six snows old . . . these white men, trappers, with many packhorses, came to our village. At first my people did not call the white man Masta-cheeda (yellow eyes) as they do now. Our first name for the white man was Beta-awk-a-wah-cha (Sits on the Water) because my people first saw the white man in a canoe on Big river. The canoe was far off. The white man in it looked as though he sat on the water; and so my people named him, and his tribe.[1]

Around the same time, Walt Whitman published *Leaves of Grass*, calling to his white American brethren as fellow pioneers:

> Come my tan-faced children,
> Follow well in order, get your weapons ready,
> Have you your pistols? Have you your sharp-edged axes?
> Pioneers! O pioneers![2]

Even when sun-kissed, white Americans were often violent conquerors and exploiters of indigenous communities and the land. Because of the ways white folks act in even the best circumstances—pistols and axes in hand—for many nonwhites the name "white" came to be associated with yellow-eyed dishonesty, moral inferiority, and spiritual weakness, and among many people of color that association continues to this day.

The white supremacist racial system that is still so influential in the United States was popularized and solidified through the hierarchies of eighteenth-century science and philosophy, with "natives" and "blacks" (nature) presumably occupying the low end in relation to which "whites" or "caucasians" (knowers) hold themselves high. Theories described existing social hierarchies as natural and inevitable, as though the human species actually consisted of physically and morally distinct subspecies, some inherently superior to others. As though profound inequalities resulted from the expression of natural difference, rather than the expression of oppressive power.

In racist societies, racial names are not equal, or morally equivalent. Given the history of their influence and meaning, it is not surprising that racial names themselves enact power. For example, the American rule of hypodescent attempts to keep whiteness distinct (or "pure") by assigning the children of racially diverse backgrounds the name of the less privileged group. That is why any bit of known African ancestry is sufficient to give someone the name "black." Legacies of slavery, including the extremely racializing logic deployed to maintain the institution in America, and the fact that the darkest human skin has come to symbolize the epitome of racial difference, has rendered the names "white" and "black" particularly potent here. Continuing violence, segregation, radical inequalities, exploitation, racist ideologies, and more spurious science have maintained white supremacist hierarchies and the power of the racial names we are born into. Nonwhites and antiracist whites continue to question the hierarchies, and the meanings of the names.

Names are unusually powerful words—the words "by which a person, thing, or class of things is known, called, or spoken to or of," such as signifying titles, or "words expressing some quality considered characteristic or descriptive of a person or thing," such as epithets.[3] We enter the world with many given names—first names, family names, names of race, names of gender, names of nationality. Some names refer to us as individuals, some are categorical. Although nicknames are always an interesting option, the name that is easiest to change is your family name, *if* you are a woman and *if* you legally marry a man and take on his family name. But if you want to change your name, you need another name to replace it. Some names cannot be changed at all, and it is not possible to have no racial name, no national name, no gendered name. To lack such a name makes you virtually a nonperson, or at least a freak, because those names are thought to refer to something necessary about one's body and genealogy—something "society" may be better able to determine than you are.

As part of the legacy of the mistaken American doctrine that racial names refer to deep and necessary differences, and that they are therefore very important, it is not currently possible to change your official racial name—the racial category listed on your birth certificate, college transcript, or job file.[4] Like a religious fiction, the idea that race denotes essential physical difference and that whiteness is inherently morally supreme, particularly admirable, or highly evolved, is remarkably difficult to supplant (at least in the minds of white people), probably because it is maintained by so much economic and epistemological power. When white folks are the knowledge makers, knowledge tends to serve white supremacy. At the same time, white people who despise racial hierarchies are no more able to relinquish their racial names than folks of color are able to abandon their racial categorizations.

Kurt said that all whites have cracks, like the fault lines endlessly emerging through the plaster walls of an old house. All whiteness has cracks because all whiteness is based on lies. Notice the thin veneer of lies about what it means to be white. Morally upstanding! Then why are white people so violent? Intelligent! Then why do white people create so many avoidable crises? Clean! Then why is such an army of servants necessary to help white people maintain themselves?

Naturally inclined to mix with others just like them! Then why such strong taboos against racial mixing and mingling?

If you've always assumed that you are the embodiment of normalcy, serious attention to the mythology that defines you as paradigmatically human (amid an incredibly diverse species), and to the ways your privilege depends on others' pain, may encourage you to crumble, may shake your firm sense of self. Have you ever felt your sense of self shaken? Perhaps you consider yourself an unusually intelligent person, but in the past you've been made to feel uncomfortable around someone much smarter, or someone who doesn't recognize your special intelligence. Or maybe you're a terrific athlete who suffered an injury that made it impossible to do the things you enjoy, and at the time you simply didn't feel like yourself. Or you've traveled to an unfamiliar place, and at some point on your journey you experience a deep uncertainty, even a terrific letting go of some idea about yourself that you'd always taken for granted before. Perhaps you know what it's like to lose someone you love, and to no longer know who or where you are.

When the foundation is cracking it's best to avoid denial. Don't hang on too tightly, and keep your feet on the ground. Admit your limitations and wait for new possibilities to emerge. Isn't that what white folks need to allow? Must we not crack up in order to be something new? But then where do we go, what do we become? I'm asking for mercy, for light!

No one can simply shed racial names or eliminate white supremacist systems and ideologies through force of will, but we can encourage the cracks in our privileged identities, whatever they may be. Paying attention to white privilege is one way for white folks to become more aware of the illusions masking the cracks in whiteness.[5] For example, a recent study showed that in many American cities, black drivers are three times more likely than white drivers to get pulled over by cops and cited for nonmoving violations.[6] Black drivers get cited more often because they are pulled over more often, because they are more likely to appear suspicious to cops who are taught that black folks are more likely than white folks to be drug dealers. The paradigmatic black drug dealer—upon whose shoulders rests the blame for violence in America—is the original profile that begins the chain of differential treatment, the necessary counterpoint to the paradigmatic upright white. That profile results in more black drivers bearing the stigma of arrest, incurring fines, and spending time in jail, all of which further contribute to the criminalization of African Americans; which allows cops to feel justified in detaining, beating up, and killing black and brown bodies.

I'm not afraid of *al Qaeda*—I'm afraid of *al Cracker*!

—Chris Rock

If the tables were suddenly turned, and white drivers were pulled over, questioned, and searched three times more often than black drivers, how many arrests would result? How many white drivers would be found driving without a license, registration, or insurance documentation? How many would find that the cops finally caught up with them regarding some old parking or speeding tickets they never paid? How many would be caught driving drunk or high, or without a seatbelt on? If you're a white person, would you suddenly feel a little bit hounded if you knew the cops in your city were going to start pulling white drivers over three times more often than black drivers? It might be difficult to maintain the myth that black folks are criminals and white folks are law-abiding citizens if the heat started to really come down on us in such a systematic fashion.

Noticing and encouraging cracks in whiteness is not just about interrogating privileges and imperfections. It is a matter of investigating the history behind the racial name and choosing the disintegration of its racist meanings. Attention to the ways white privilege reproduces itself through preferential treatment, segregation, miscegenation taboos, inheritance, and racist devaluations of people of color is the right place to begin. In addition to admitting and rejecting the injustices that maintain whiteness, if the goal is to shift the meaning of whiteness itself, whiteness must become something impure, dynamic, and healthy for people of all races. Whiteness would then become what it is not supposed to be. Instead of striving for self-maintenance, that project requires getting comfortable with the demise of white supremacy.

I see my own sins, my parents' silences, my grandparents' complicity, my government's violence, my priests' lies, my teachers' mistakes, and end up feeling guilty, ashamed, or overly righteous. Can noticing and encouraging the cracks in my whiteness transform it—transform me—into something else, something that is not just defensive or broken? Neither of those states help me move toward other people. Race can only be transformed collectively, in the company of difference and friendship.

Life is relationship, connection and negotiation, warm coming-together, tenuous questioning, and difficult work; it is searching for happiness, seeking security, and trying to make contributions. We are born into complex legacies and varying possibilities, unto places on complicated maps. We are only relational beings. It is therefore through our relationships and our work among others that we inhabit those maps, and compose new ones.

The political and emotional desire to live anti-racist whiteness inspires movement toward "white" identities that are consciously complex and hybrid, rather than pretending to be pure. Maria Lugones describes journeys toward hybridity as "the crossings that would initiate deep coalitions" against multiple oppressions:

> Fear is called for by crossing, because there is an impending sense of loss: loss of competence and loss of a clear sense of oneself and one's relation to others. A playful attitude is a good companion to fear; it keeps one focused on the crossing, on the process of metamorphosis.[7]

Sometimes we are a beautifully mixed-up group working or partying. Sometimes, even in the midst of play, we are working seriously together toward something we believe in, toward a different reality. The feeling of actually creating something worthwhile among others helps us feel like the world is a good place, that life is a good thing, so the work and the play can bring a sense of comfort that is complex, fleeting, and not reducible to ease. In that sort of place I'm still white, but I'm also so much more.

What names do our real relationships impart? The chosen names, the bestowed names of this adult being mitigate the silly pale name I cannot shed: Race traitor. Nature lover. Cool shoes. Pow-wow dancer. Lesbian. Admirer of Malcolm X. Music junkie. Student of Spanish. Naked giggler. Warrior for Justice. Good friend. Radical mother. Revolutionary. Niggerlover. Curryhead. The one who won't stop arguing for affirmative action. Cop magnet. Anti-racist teacher. Superfreak. Dove.

Add white and stir if you want, but our living relationships refuse the simplicity of race.

Sometimes mercy comes in the form of good advice, from the voices of experience. So, white folks who despise racial hierarchies:

1. Whatever your job is, do not stop working against racism, racist violence, and colonial legacies.
2. Be brave enough to find and face your cracks. Don't repair them. Instead, welcome the crumble of white supremacist lies.
3. Find or create communities of resistance and support. Spread anti-racist awareness, and remember that a playful attitude will help you to make friends along the way.
4. Allow your own multiplicity, your own complex names, to rise to the surface. Cultivate the places where you are known by those names.

Notes

1. Pretty Shield in *Native American Testimony: A Chronicle of Indian-White Relations from Prophesy to the Present, 1492–1992*, ed. Peter Nabokov (New York: Penguin Books, 1992), 29.

2. Walt Whitman, "Pioneers! O Pioneers!" in *Leaves of Grass* (New York: Bantam Books, 1983), 185.

3. Webster's *New World Dictionary*, Third College Edition.

4. People who've sued to change their racial designation, or name, have not argued that they have changed race, they've argued that the designation they were given at birth was incorrect.

5. For more on white privilege see Peggy McIntosh, "White Privilege: Unpacking the Invisible Knapsack," www.utoronto.ca/acc/events/peggy1.htm, and "Despising an Identity They Taught Me to Claim: Exploring a Dilemma of White Privilege Awareness," in *Whiteness: Feminist Philosophical Reflections*, ed. Chris Cuomo and Kim Q. Hall (Lanham, Md.: Rowman & Littlefield, 1999).

6. NBC Dateline, April 9, 2004.

7. Maria Lugones, *Pilgrimages/Peregrinajes: Theorizing Coalition Against Multiple Oppressions* (Lanham, Md.: Rowman & Littlefield, 2004).

3

"Wigger"

Crispin Sartwell
Dickerson College

THE WIGGER—THE WHITE PERSON WHO acts like a black person—is a stock figure of contemporary American comedy. A recent commercial, for example, depicts three white guys speaking in black argot and dressed in parody Hip Hop wear—sweat suits, head scarves, and sideways baseball caps—meeting three black guys dressed in conservative "prep" fashion à la Abercrombie and Fitch. The crossdressing seems symmetrical, but the black guys laugh at the white guys and not vice versa. The wigger is well-nigh ubiquitous: the Seth Green character in the film *Can't Hardly Wait*, or the pale rapper of *Malibu's Most Wanted*, and so on (if one lacks acquaintance with the term *wigger* or the accompanying concept, I'd suggest one of these films). The comic effect is achieved partly by the slight flavor of transgression that still attends the figure; the wigger plays with and in a variety of stereotypes. He (and it's indeed almost always he) indicates, first of all, that there is some sense in the idea of "acting black," that is, that there's still some current cultural distinction between the races. This, one would think, is hardly a controversial assertion, and yet it is anathema to a certain sort of liberal take on race, which holds that essentially any such distinction is a mere prejudice or stereotype without continuing purchase in reality. And indeed, the way that wiggers act black often has to do with a mere feeding off the media: an imitation of Hip Hop videos, for example. But of course the videos themselves make use of a variety of cultural norms and real vernaculars. The repertoire of race in contemporary American culture is incredibly rich and detailed, probably as much so as it has ever been, from gesture to costume to speech, from a way of walking to a way of being, and more or less everybody is capable of reading its semiotics.

Wiggerism is hence a cultural performance that draws whatever small frisson it may retain from the idea that race still has currency. As a standard comic persona, it resembles the Irishmen Pat and Mike of old, although oddly the wigger himself intends to privilege rather than ridicule the members of the group he imitates. But it is also a recognizable figure on the street, at a party, in a club, in a classroom: there really are wiggers, though we may think of the ones in the street as also being performers of a certain kind. The wigger outside the media often intends to convey the idea that he is more than a performer, and in some cases he may well be. That is, many wiggers will insist, with varying degrees of sincerity and varying degrees of truth, that his soul is not white. (One must bear in mind the possibility that a white person may actually grow up among black people, as the rapper Vanilla Ice falsely claimed about himself.) Incorporating the performative and comic aspects with the possibility of sincerity and seriousness, we might think of wiggerism (and hence of one form of blackness as perceived by the wigger) as an aesthetic: it centers around music, but it includes an entire, basically conscious art of self-presentation in body language, visual expression (such as graffiti), clothing, and so on. Wiggerism (and hence blackness as conceived by the wigger) is an aesthetic repertoire that pits itself against the aesthetic canons associated with whiteness. One of its important effects is that it makes both these aesthetic repertoires explicit. This is particularly interesting not for what it shows and what it distorts in black aesthetics, but for what it makes visible about white aesthetics, usually taken as unmarked and normative.

Just to lay down a few cards quickly: I emerge from the wigger tradition. I grew up in a mostly black city and attended mostly black schools. I associated coolness with blackness and clumsy stiltedness of manner with whiteness. I listened to black music, talked in black slang. Eventually, I immersed myself in the history of black music and learned to play the blues harmonica. Later I was a white rock critic writing about early Hip Hop music, which I must say I didn't understand very well. (But what publication had a black writer they could put on it?) Reading *The Autobiography of Malcolm X* in a junior high school black history class had been a formative experience. Eventually, I also immersed myself in African American literature, particularly autobiography. And you'll still hear black slang circa 1971 coming out my mouth, as well as Hip Hop coming out my speakers. Much of what I appreciated in black culture was, first, what I felt was missing in white culture, and, second, a construction of blackness by white culture for its spontaneity, expressiveness—even, dare I say, its rhythm.

The wigger is a problematic and complex figure. Does he signal a merging of the races, a transgression of whiteness that demonstrates that race is a social construction that can be destroyed by cultural crossings? Or does he demonstrate on the contrary—by his failure to offload his whiteness—that race is persistent and essential? Is he a liberatory figure or a mere reiteration of racist stereotypes? Does he contribute to a celebration of black arts, or does he take up a place in the vicious history of appropriation and exploitation of these arts and their practitioners by white people? Does he undercut and threaten white culture by the migration of its own children to blackness, or does he dilute black culture by his presence within it or at its periphery? Is he performing in blackface, or critiquing whiteness? And in our amusement at the figure in popular culture are we ridiculing white people for pretense, or are we ridiculing black people for their ridiculous mannerisms? The answer, as I guess you might imagine, is in every case "yes."

1. Prehistory of the Wigger

Let me begin with a brief set of excuses. In order to discuss this topic at all, it is necessary to resort to generalities. I have been and will be talking about "black culture" and "white culture," "black arts" and "white arts," or indeed "black people" and "white people." I will be purveying stereotypes even as I examine them. Many people—especially many academics—would stop me right there and accuse me of a false essentialism with regard to race. I should hasten to say that my own view of race is that it is entirely a social construction, and, furthermore, with regard to any given general characterization of black people or white people, that there are obviously numerous exceptions. But we need to be able to examine the content of these social constructions themselves, and we need to be able to acknowledge their continuing centrality to our experience: their status for us as realities. The fact is, when you see a wigger, you know what you're seeing, and you wouldn't if these categories were not current in our imagination. Indeed, you autonomically know what you're seeing; you deploy a set of categories you sucked in with your mother's milk. The fact that the categories are socially constructed does not entail that they are unreal for us now; quite the reverse. They are still *our* social constructions, and even as we criticize them we recognize and employ them. A benevolent egalitarianism determined not to use the language of race is little more than a semi-sweet self-delusion, and it is one that often itself carries racist overtones. On no subject is public discourse more dishonest than about race; on no subject are our thoughts so utterly distinct from our public pronouncements. So if you're worried about me throwing around terms like *we white folks*, or whatever, stop reading now or prepare to be irritated.

The history of white romanticization of black culture is exactly as long as the modern history of the contacts between the peoples, and exactly as long as the white destruction and exploitation of black peoples. It precisely tracks, we might say, philosophical and aesthetic modernism. It is rooted in the dualism of mind and body and its writ-large version, the distinction between culture and nature. And the romanticization is rooted also precisely in the oppression that is interpreted by these dualisms and which they drive. If high Western culture and its current American suburban manifestation identifies whiteness with mind, then we seek to exclude the body and its desires—in particular, sexuality, intoxication, and violence—from ourselves. And if we identify ourselves with culture, we seek to exclude from ourselves the primitive and savage festival: we imagine what we exclude as the blood rite or orgy, the precivilized evil of unleashed desire. This is not only the interpretation of, for example, Africa by eighteenth-century Europeans; it is the interpretation of the inner city black community by the contemporary suburban housewife. This structure underlies almost every racial stereotype and justifies almost every form of racial oppression. But it is fundamentally not about black people. It's about us and what we fantasize ourselves to be. We are souls or minds flitting hither and thither, barely spatially located. We are enlightened, educated; our civilization and knowledge are universal and represent progress or evolution from the savage state in which we find others. The basic function of the stereotype—besides the decided economic advantages that accrue to assigning other people the physical labor—is self-congratulation, the propping up of an always-tenuous self-image.

It goes without saying that the image is tenuous because, among other things, mind/body dualism is ridiculous. Even as we slap one another on the back for our purity and intellect and etiquette, we remain bodies grubbing around on the surface of a planet, mammals with the full range of mammalian desires. Indeed, in the familiar Freudian manner, the desires are intensified and twisted by their repression and by the privacy with which they are held and discharged. The primitive and black functions in the European and European American imaginative economy as the sign of desire per se; the essence of everything evil, desirable, and interesting. And so when it is time to discharge these desires, we seek what is black: we go slumming in Harlem, or we listen to the devil's music, or we turn the cap sideways. And since some white culture seems to have excluded almost everything interesting—indeed, almost everything real—from itself, we actually seek to migrate, to become black, for an evening or (in the case of the serious wigger) for a lifetime. It is also worth mentioning that the mirror image of this deflected desire is a black desire for assimilation. For one thing, the material and social rewards of whiteness seem all too obvious. And so while white people are slumming, black people are passing, and either of these activities can be engaged in to a variety of degrees.

From the beginning, then, there has been both an underground and an explicit privileging of "savagery" in the white mind: an association of blackness not only with the primitive, but with its neighbors honesty and simplicity and truth. This idea was present above all in romanticism: one of course sees it full-blown in Rousseau, but also in such figures as Thoreau and even Kierkegaard. Any conceptual system in which emotion is praised and the efficacy of reason doubted gets read as a praise of the primitive and an affirmation of the body. Such views are expressions of crossracial desire: a desire for desire itself, ejected by the tradition to which romanticism responds onto the bodies of black people.

This history of crossracial desire has been, on the whole, anything but liberating. It partly accounts, for example, for rape of black women by white slave masters and for a variety of other sexual practices that reproduce both racism and sexism, but which also largely account for America's signal racial impurity: the fact that most of us are mixed in one way or another. This in turn drives a certain kind of integration. But the fact that southern racists from Thomas Jefferson to Strom Thurmond seem to have had children with black women should surprise no one. And likewise, the basic structure of racism and crossracial desire drives the brutality displayed toward black men, who are invested in white imagination with a super- and sub-human masculinity and potential for violence that leads to their fetishization and to their brutalization. Indeed, the imagination of sexuality and violence attributed to black people by white people is what drives the actual sexuality and violence of white people directed at black people, a perfect hypocrisy in which we become what we imagine you to be: sexual predators, thugs, avatars of violence and twisted desire.

Such expressions took on a somewhat more nuanced form as the twentieth century proceeded from lynching to Jim Crow to the Civil Rights movement, though it always rests on a foundation of stereotype for its possibility. The tradition of rape proceeds into prostitution and various forms of concubinage. Lynch-law proceeds into the racially charged application of the death penalty. Malcolm X describes in detail the activities of white people in Harlem during the 1940s, when he was "steering" white men to black prostitutes, or simply enabling drunken or drug-addled nights on the town where white people could view some of the greatest musicians of the twentieth century, such as Billie Holiday or Duke Ellington. Such activities are, perhaps, more or less what one would expect out of human beings in general, and certainly the argument for going out to see Billie Holiday is one that ought to be universally valid. But what struck Malcolm about the white folks he was dealing with was that they regarded themselves as engaged in liberation, and not mere self-indulgence. They used their trips to Harlem as a way to congratulate themselves on their lack of prejudice. The most interesting thing about this claim, though Malcolm merely ridicules it, is that it is not wholly false. Many white people of the period would not associate with black people at all except as menials, much less go out clubbing with them. No doubt real conversations and real friendships eventuated; no doubt both cultures found out quite a bit about the other and occasionally entered into more understanding and sympathy than they showed previously. The recognition of the sophistication and power of black arts and politics as expressed in Harlem at that time no doubt had a real impact on the Civil Rights movement, as the presence of Adam Clayton Powell or of Malcolm himself would attest.[1]

But of course the structure of desire enacted in slumming fundamentally reproduces the American racial imagination. What makes Harlem attractive is the vacation it offers from whiteness: from tidy houses and tidy offices to the desires symbolized by the jitterbug or by the dark underside of the sex industry; from "good taste"—staid clothing and classical music—to the zoot suit and the rhythms of jazz: loudness. And what is perhaps most dangerous to say is that this experience is not completely false, and not, or not only, manufactured for commercial purposes by black people. Blackness really was a relief from whiteness, and whiteness really did have its privileges: the social constructions were in part made actual. That black taste of the period was by and large louder than white taste is not an assertion that you should really quibble with, nor the assertion that black dance was bolder and more athletic and more suggestive, nor the assertion that black music was . . . better.

2. Music

Music is absolutely central to the wigger persona, and it has been a central site of crossracial desire and crosscultural fertility since, at latest, the beginning of the twentieth century. Indeed, the history of world popular musics since that time is to an astonishing degree the history of white appropriation of black musical and performance styles. The swing music of Benny Goodman and Glenn Miller is a good example: it is a popularization of black jazz styles, cleaned up and made more palatable for white audiences. Its origin is the synthesis of European and African musical forms originating in Louisiana and elsewhere in the American south. The country blues of such distinctively American geniuses as Jimmie Rogers and Hank Williams emerges directly from the interchange of styles among largely dispossessed white and black people, and the mythology that attends such figures invariably includes scenes of the future performer crossing the tracks and listening at the window of a black juke joint, or learning their first few chords from a black bluesman. The origin of rock 'n roll music is similar, and certainly such figures as Elvis Presley or Jerry Lee Lewis owed not only their music but to some extent their personae to black musical traditions. Of course the music was widely received as transgressive by white society, and of course this had to do as much as anything with its association with blackness and the sexuality and criminality that were held to attend it. The British invasion launched by bands such as the Rolling Stones and the Beatles lionized American blues, and the idea of Mick Jagger was a knowing wink at blackness, down to the lips and the faux-American-black accent. Performers such as Eric Clapton and the Allman Brothers were archivists of the blues tradition as well as innovators within it. Disco emerged from black dance to the white mainstream, and Madonna, No Doubt, and countless others have made a living from black dance music. And finally, Hip Hop, which emerged from a synthesis of black American and Jamaican party styles in New York, is the dominant popular music of the day, as available and natural to white performers such as uber-wigger Eminem as to black ones such as Jay-Z or DMX.

This history is immensely complicated and immensely problematic. But it would certainly be wrong to think of it merely as exploitative or as merely having had a negative effect on black artists. Indeed, the history of black music has to a large extent been preserved by white performers and scholars, and many artists have gotten recognition and recording contracts and tours because they were the heroes and sources of famous white rockers. White appropriations of black music have not only at times compromised its artistic power, they have at times taken a cultural possession and disseminated it well-nigh universally, which is both an expansion and a dilution of its source. This has itself in part driven the history of black styles, which often seem to push quickly on once white folks get hold of them. The innovations are then eventually appropriated, and so on.

Hip Hop music enacts this entire history with peculiar intensity and peculiar self-consciousness. First of all, the various personae taken up by Hip Hop performers bear a remarkable set of relations to white stereotypes of black people. The gangsta or thug, embodied by 50 Cent or Tupac Shakur (who actually had "Thug Life" tattooed on his stomach,[2] and who died in a hail of bullets) feeds a white fantasy of black violence and hypermasculinity. Then there is the "ho" persona purveyed by L'il Kim or Eve, again a mirror of white conceptions of black female sexuality. This is not to say that the image these performers convey is insincere, or that it does not capture something real in their own experience, or that it is univocal. For example, for a black "thug" to appear in public space in full dress is not something permitted by white folks historically; there is no deference or self-effacement in these people. Quite the reverse: their art is a continual enactment of self-expression as defiance. And one might point out that the humor with which black rappers such as Ice T approach their material—which displays an immense capacity to play with stereotype and draw out its ironies—is often lost on white audiences. In addition, the personae themselves can be remarkably complex. Tupac is a good example: far from "celebrating" violence, for the most part he describes and mourns it, and obviously he knew what it meant as both victim and enraged man. And there is also a gentle, "sensitive" side to Tupac, found in his lyrics about love or about his mother, and perhaps in the vulnerability that came through in his face along with the aggression. Indeed, Tupac the family man or the religious man, Tupac the poet and dreamer, is not opposed to Tupac the gangsta: they are presented as aspects of a single coherent reality.[3] It's an extraordinary exercise of self-integration, one which attracts both black and white kids as a model for themselves.

One way to read the gangsta rapper is the stereotype manufacturing its own reality, which now returns to menace the people who invented it. And indeed, white culture has been duly menaced, in the form of Tipper Gore and a hundred other anti-Hip-Hop activists. It is as if our own exclusions constitute our destruction, which of course they do and must. The statement one gets about black experience in popular gangsta rap is limited, but important: it emerges from a real atmosphere of drugs, sex, and violence, and translates it into art, as the blues did with the hard labor and booze and chronic poverty of the early twentieth century. This is potentially a factor in its amelioration as well as its intensification. For one thing, Hip Hop is a form of music and art culture; it is designed for the party as a release from one's daily cares. But also, it puts into wide circulation a set of racial signifiers that now have to be grappled with by both black folks and white folks in public space: it makes the racial imaginary explicit, forces us all to confront it. This was true also of the blues, but Hip Hop is more explicit and more confrontational, and at this point more popular all over the world.

It is a familiar point that most people who buy Hip Hop records are white, though this should not be taken to mean (as it occasionally is) that it does not have a large black audience. And obviously as well, this affects its content to some extent, and any pop artist who is self-reflective will admit that what she does is not some sort of pure or unsullied self-expression but is also made in collaboration with an audience. By definition, pop artists want, or at least are willing, to sell a lot of records to a lot of people. Given the history that we've just traversed, it should surprise no one that white people not only buy Hip Hop records, but romanticize Hip Hop culture and seek to emigrate into it. So coding black is a way to rebel against one's own culture and one's own family, not just in some general sense in which each generation rebels against the previous one, but specifically against the content of whiteness as polite good taste, deference, and self-effacement. The culture we have made is immensely dull and safe, and we've made it specifically by excluding from ourselves anything interesting and dangerous. To say one might expect the occasional blackist backlash is an understatement: it's odd, in fact, that there are any really white kids left.

The wigger must be understood specifically in relation to Hip Hop music and culture. All the signifiers by which he codes black are essentially made within Hip Hop: the clothing, the slang, the music, the graffiti and other art. Hip Hop is the wigger's instruction manual, and since Hip Hop is available everywhere, wiggerism is available even in North Dakota or for that matter Paris, where, no doubt, it is even more interesting. Hip Hop is a visual as well as aural art: indeed, in the age of music video and pop soundtracks, music itself is a visual art. And Hip Hop is an art culture with well-nigh universal dissemination. There really is no reason any longer for anyone to act white, if they don't want to.

But passing also has its limits. We still believe that, for the most part, we can tell a white person from a black person by looking. We believe also that we can recognize the typical or identifying behavioral repertoire of black people and white people. And so we can *see* white people acting black, and for that matter black people acting white. And we still assert of this activity that it is a falsehood, or a betrayal of who one "really is"—that it is mere histrionics—and we ridicule people for it, however much they may protest their own authenticity. That is the essence of the wigger as comedy: he's pretending. Now this of course shows that we have all the racial understandings well-implanted in our heads: that we understand what it is to act black or to act white, and to be black or to be white. The ridicule to which the wigger is subjected is a policing of racial boundaries, but it's also an acknowledgment of realities: more or less, most of the time, the wigger *is* consciously acting out a role, though he may become very accustomed to it indeed. The ridicule is both an acknowledgment of the continuing reality of race and an enforcement of it.

At the center of the wigger's role is a critique of white culture. It is not a generalized critique (such as the one I've just issued) but a critique that gets down to the level of gestures: it is a completely specific attack on everything it means at a given moment to be white. In part this has to be seen as a self-critique: part of what most wiggers are attacking is themselves; part of what they are violating is the inscription of white culture on their own bodies and expressions. More explicitly in their own minds, perhaps, they are criticizing in ruthless detail their own parents and communities. They are expressing hatred for their lily-white suburbs, their excellent lawns, their good manners, their careers, their lockstep obedience to social conventions. They are trying to remake themselves into aliens in that atmosphere, and hence showing its power to alienate.

3. Two Cases: William Upski Wimsatt and Eminem

The comic effect of the wigger depends fundamentally on his lack of self-consciousness. The wigger of comedy is completely serious. So the wigger gets a kind of Quixote flavor, trying with the utmost seriousness to do something that is a priori impossible and inappropriate, like Quixote's mutation into a questing, chivalric knight. And yet from the start various wiggers have displayed the possibility of self-consciousness; this is true even of semi-ironic early wigger anthems such as "Play that Funky Music White Boy" or "Dirty White Boy." In this sphere, the first successful white Hip Hop artists—the Beastie Boys—provide a particularly clear example: in the midst of a set of Hip Hop recordings they were insistently, pointedly white: they actually made their whiteness, rather than their imitation of blackness, the key to their comedy, even as they made some excellent records. They were white kids *pretending to be white.*

Eminem is easily the most famous wigger who has ever lived. He certainly takes up a place in the history of white appropriations of black music styles, which we examined briefly above. And like Elvis, for example, he is more successful than any black artist working in the same style, though the style emerges from black communities. But what distinguishes Eminem in this history is his self-consciousness, which could hardly be more intense. Indeed, Eminem's overall approach is continuously confessional: he parades his neuroses and insecurities as explicitly as humanly possible: his raps are turned obsessively inward. In that context, his work on race is perhaps less surprising than it might be, but still:

> See the problem is I speak to suburban kids who otherwise would of never knew these words exist
> whose moms probably woulda never gave two squirts of piss,
> till I created so much motherfucking turbulence
> straight out the tube, right into your livingroom I came, and kids flipped. . . .
> That's all it took, and they were instantly right in, and they connected with me too because I looked like them.

This from the anthemic "White America," whose title more or less says it all: I doubt that white America has ever been so explicitly addressed in the white media by a white person, or criticized in such detail in that context. He calls unpolluted white children "Eric" and "Erica"—a characterization of their blandness—and attributes his own ability to pollute them to his own whiteness, as seen from his position as a race traitor or crossdresser. It is precisely Eminem's marginal status that allows him to deliver this message, that gives him leverage on his own people, that allows him to understand whiteness from a distance that one would usually associate with a black critique of white power. First of all, as he never tires of telling us, he grew up in a trailer park, as Detroit white trash. And second, he has worked with black people in a black style all his professional life. These factors allow him to understand white culture simultaneously from inside and outside, and he uses that understanding continuously. Eminem is not usually thought of as a political artist, but in fact politics marks all of his work, up to and including anti-war messages delivered in his own twisted way.

Eminem also manages to pay homage to Hip Hop history and to mentor black rappers such as 50 Cent. And his artistry is essentially collaborative, especially with regard to the great L.A. Hip Hop producer Dr. Dre. Indeed, in one song, Em credits Dre with bringing him a black audience, even as he credits himself with bringing Dre a white one. Such activities are not necessarily different in kind than those of white blues stars such as the Stones and Clapton, who also collaborated with black artists and provided career help. Nor is the irony essentially different; there are many extremely popular black Hip Hop acts (and no white ones other than Eminem in the top echelon), but nevertheless the single bestselling and artistically dominant Hip Hop performer is white. What is different is, again, the explicitness in the music itself of Eminem's racial positioning:

> No I'm not the first king of controversy
> I am the worst thing since Elvis Presley
> to do black music so selfishly
> and used it to get myself wealthy
> Hey! There's a concept that works
> Twenty million other white rappers emerge
> But no matter how many fish in the sea
> It'd be so empty, without me.

Em's excellent autobiographical movie *8 Mile* is largely an exploration of the trials and tribulations of being white in black neighborhoods, black styles, a black world. Here the wigger is portrayed seriously; one of the few such portrayals in the history of the persona. Eminem's character, "Rabbit," is played without irony, and though he deploys a set of black mannerisms, he does so with complete ownership of them, without any strain or exaggeration, simulation or comedy. It's about complexities and dangers, but also pleasures and the possibility of a small transcendence into the universal.

And maybe, despite the kinks in the wigger's consciousness and experience, that's what he's aiming for: a transcendence of the dualisms that constrain all of us to some degree. Eminem finds himself in the position to see and attack the dualisms from both sides at once, and that, we might say, is the hope embodied in the wigger, even though his very existence depends upon the dualisms in the first place. The wigger as presented by Eminem is a transitional phase in the breakdown of race; he's no less aware of race itself than a southern segregationist, or one might add, than the rest of us, black or white. But he has a different point of view on the whole matter, one that reveals aspects of it (as, among other things, performative, optional) that most Americans can't quite see. And what's unique about Eminem is that he then expresses these insights on the largest possible stage, to an audience of millions, which takes guts and creativity as well as understanding. Perhaps if this is pursued with enough self-reflection, a transcendence is possible, though it be small, halting, and itself of questionable value.

No self-proclaimed wigger other than Eminem has been more reflective and self-critical than William Upski Wimsatt, whose books *Bomb the Suburbs* and *No More Prisons* are minor classics not only as wigger manifestos but as anarchist-tinged political statements. Wimsatt, the son of a professor in Chicago (the quite famous philosopher who shares his name, sans the Upski), eventually became a serious graffiti artist and writer on Hip Hop for a variety of publications. He describes the dawning of his wiggerism like this:

> Midway through grammar school, I made a discovery. Michael Jackson, Prince, and most of the other rock stars I stood admiring one day in the record store display window, were black. From this massive insight followed others. Practically all of the wittiest, the coolest, the strongest, the most agile, and the most precocious kids I knew were black (in part this was because most of the whites I knew were unusually dull and spoiled). In the locker room, the black boys really did seem to have bigger dicks. Although it has been proven untrue scientifically, you couldn't have told me that at the time. Next to them, my voice was flat, my personality dull, my lifestyle bland, my complexion pallid.[4]

(I must note that this is strikingly similar to my own conversion, though that took place in the seventies rather than the eighties, in D.C. rather than Chicago, and involved James Brown and Isaac Hayes rather than Prince and Jackson.) Note that the romanticization of the black is coupled with an explicit attack on the white. And note also its sexual element: the big dicks of black men are, we might say, a synecdoche of all white attitudes toward black men, as is the sexual precociousness of black women, on the other side of the gender split (Mick Jagger: "Black girls just want to get fucked all night; I don't have that much jam"). So far, I think, so good: almost any wigger might tell a similar tale.

But Wimsatt goes on to examine both the racism and the liberatory potential in his own attitudes with a withering and absorbing self-reflection:

> [My whiteness] is the reason I am getting paid to write about Hip Hop while the people who taught me about Hip Hop are in jail, dead, or strugglin, scramblin 'n' gamblin. This is neither something to fight, nor to gloat about, nor to sit back and be thankful over. It is merely a moral debt. . . . "I'm confused about what your point of view is," an editor of mine once said. "I can't tell from reading this whether you are a hip-hopper or a racist, an insider in black society, or some kind of outside sociologist. Do you like black people or do you hate them?" My answer is that I'm human, meaning that I'm complex enough to be all these things at once.[5]

Wimsatt knows perfectly well that he didn't manage to offload his whiteness and his privilege even as he was trying with all his might to be "down." And he knew that his position was half participatory and half anthropological, studying an alien culture, a position that as much as anything crystallizes the relation of white to black culture in the minds of white people. An interesting analogy might be the work of W. E. B. Du Bois, who likewise continually faced the negotiation of a set of dualities: light-skinned black person from Massachusetts in the South, trained sociologist excluded in many ways from wide recognition because of his race, as well as race leader. He famously formulated the dilemma as "double consciousness." Wimsatt agrees, actually, but consciousness turned against itself is only one element; the doubleness is one of social positioning and its accompanying actions (for Wimsatt, graffiti and authorship), affiliations, educations, physical locations. Du Bois faced a double response from the black community too, to his "culture," his accent, his light skin, his "airs," all of which were on display during his conflicts with Booker T. Washington and Marcus Garvey, both of whom he despised. Wimsatt could expect the same were he to reach Du Bois's pitch of eminence.

The social scientist has a neutral view and no doubt good intentions; the target culture is basically described through its deviations from the culture of the social scientist. Wimsatt takes seriously his continual point of view as both-at-once, and both the racist and liberatory potential of each possible juxtaposition of affiliations. That the wigger himself is a location of racism is something he can almost never admit to himself. Like the slumming white folks of Malcolm's Harlem he believes that his romanticization of black culture and his emulation of it and seeking after membership in it is a demonstration of his transcendence of racism. But obviously the romance itself depends on a set of categories that in turn depends on the basic racist structure of mind/body dualism, and so forth. If this remains uninterrogated, the wigger is really not a liberatory figure, but if it becomes fully self-critical, it yields the kind of overall leverage on race that Eminem and Wimsatt display so conspicuously.

In the context of such self-criticism, wiggerism indeed becomes an agent of change, and race migration, with all its limitations, holds out the possibility of knowledge of black folks and knowledge of self. "The most promising thing about spilled milk," writes Wimsatt, "is that it has ventured from its container."[6] So, we might conclude, don't cry over the wigger.

Notes

1. Malcolm X as told to Alex Haley, *The Autobiography of Malcolm X* (New York: African-American Images, 1987 [1965]), chapters 5–7.
2. Tupac said that *Thug Life* was an acronym for "The Hate U Gave Little Infants Fucked Everybody" which is a pretty interesting political reading of gangsta life.
3. I owe this point to George Yancy.
4. William Upski Wimsatt, *Bomb the Suburbs* (New York: Soft Skull/Subway and Elevated, 2000 [1994]), 32.
5. Wimsatt, *Bomb the Suburbs*, 40–41.
6. *Bomb the Suburbs*, 32.

4

Unmasking through Naming: Toward an Ethic and Africology of Whiteness

Greg Moses
Independent Scholar

GIVEN THE LOUD AND PERNICIOUS HISTORY of white supremacy, obvious conclusions would encourage us to abolish all vestiges of racialized naming. Classic battles in civil rights have been fought to remove signs and labels. Appeals to whiteness and white identity have ugly legacies. Yet, power rarely works in simple ways. Consider the following proposition, made by Frederick Douglass to a meeting of Republicans in 1870: "I say, whenever the black man and the white man, equally eligible, equally available, equally qualified for office, present themselves for that office, the black man, at this juncture of our affairs, should be preferred." Or consider the practical method of Operation Breadbasket, pursued by Martin Luther King, Jr., and the Southern Christian Leadership Conference during the 1960s, in which black ministers would conduct demographic research into the customer base of a business in order to negotiate a larger share of black employment within that business. In these two examples, proffered by paradigmatic figures in the struggle for civil rights in the United States, the language of black and white is spoken as an explicit means of furthering racialized justice. In place of a plain history of injustice, Douglass and King propose a simple formula of fairness. Yet the Republican Party hardly followed the counsel of Douglass in 1870, and even today if one attempts the kind of practical method outlined by Dr. King's Operation Breadbasket, one is very likely to be called a reverse racist.

Nevertheless, following the plain formulas of Douglass and King, I think that justice still demands terms of racialized naming. If the terms *white* and *black* still name situations of collective injustice, then moral language requires their use. Whereas slogans, signs, and labels have long been obvious tools of power employed by white supremacy, so too are silences, erasures, and camouflage. One may mark the difference between old racism and new by generally shifting the weight of supremacy from codes of enunciation to codes of evasion. At about the same time that the new racism emerged, the so-called postmodern turn in philosophy began to call attention to the power of silence, erasure, elision, and all the things that don't get talked about every time we choose what to say. When we focus on racism as a legacy of unjust naming only, we neglect the newer half of the problem, because the power of white supremacy is also to be found in what is not named, what cannot be named, and why. For instance, why didn't the Republican Party simply adopt Douglass's fairness formula in 1870? Why wouldn't it be fair to pursue the kind of proportional representation that is called for under the procedures of Operation Breadbasket?

As a white philosopher, I have for more than a decade been interested in the form that philosophy takes along the color line. My long-time focus has been upon lessons taught by black philosophers. One of those lessons, exemplified by Cornel West's *American Evasion of Philosophy*, teaches us that white philosophy neither recognizes philosophy practiced by people of color nor recognizes itself as white philosophy. White audiences approaching black philosophy have a tendency to mark the field in advance as a project by and for other people, even when black philosophy addresses "Racism and the White Backlash," as did Martin Luther King, Jr. After several years considering what black philosophers have been saying about whites, white supremacy, and whiteness, I am beginning to explore what white philosophers should be saying. This chapter represents exploratory work for me, but it is not a new problem. In this chapter I want to raise the possibility of pursuing something called an ethic of whiteness. What I mean by this scandalous term is not complex to say. I mean that white folks should practice the art of naming themselves white precisely to establish the moral consequences that fall upon them for ending the injustices of white power.

If it is possible for white people to practice an ethic of whiteness, an important problem will concern the question of naming. When may it be morally helpful to name what is white, especially in reference to one's self, one's group, or one's history? If the symbolic power of whiteness is strengthened through practices of masking or denial, how may white supremacy be disempowered through strategies of unmasking or disclosure? In this chapter, I develop an ethic of reflective naming that may be deployed by self-identified white folks as we seek to become white allies in struggles against white supremacy. In particular, I attempt to demonstrate that strategic approaches to racialized naming may be useful in support of institutional integration and critical approaches to white studies.

The moral problem of racialized naming is exacerbated by a more-or-less progressive tenor of public discourse in the United States that continues to treat racism and white power as regrettable features of a past that has been largely disconnected from contemporary life. The less racism there is said to be, the less justification one has for racialized naming.

On the other hand, we may want to approach with suspicion the ongoing claims that racism and white power have been nearly vanquished from the social, political, or cultural scenes. If we define racism as the use of racialized categories to secure and perpetuate racialized hegemony, and if we understand the life of racialized categories in terms of widely shared institutions and subjectivities, then I think it is difficult to proclaim that the tide has turned.

In the introductory part of this chapter I briefly review claims that would remind us how whiteness still hides in ways that are strategically beneficial to the perpetuation of white supremacy. In the first part that follows the introduction, I defend a way of naming what is white to serve the purpose of inquiry and activity that would ameliorate supremacist tendencies. In the second part, I argue that strategic naming practices may provide one rationale for conscientious approaches to institutional integration. In the third part, I suggest an approach to critical white studies that would accentuate the project of disclosing whiteness for the purpose of understanding and resisting racialized hegemony.

To introduce the problem of naming, the work of Pamela Dykes will help begin a brief survey of arguments that would support the naming of white arenas for the purpose of critical disclosure. As Dykes argues in her provocative dissertation, a problem arises within progressive discourses when whiteness is not named as a focus of study. For Dykes, the contemporary predicament of race relations in the United States may be exemplified by the response that corporate managers have deployed to address demographic trends announced by the 1987 Hudson Institute Report, *Workforce 2000* (Dykes, 1). Facing evidence that the numerical ratio of white workers will steadily decline, corporations in the United States have been working for more than a decade to "manage diversity" through the use of consultants and sensitivity training.

For purveyors and consumers of corporate-diversity discourse, things have gotten better already, and they will continue to get better, because the wisdom of inclusiveness is now wedded to logics of profit and self-interest. In short, it is just plain stupid to exhibit prejudicial behaviors in today's competitive environment—so they say.

As Dykes points out, the move toward corporate diversity does many things, but one thing it does not do is investigate the meaning of whiteness itself. As Dykes argues, "the white male 'center' continues to remain concealed and undisclosed" even as the very practice of corporate-diversity management assumes that the problem to be confronted is the problem of white displacement. Management of white displacement that does not interrogate its own white-centered assumptions tacitly confirms scholarly suggestions that reigning standards have been created by white men (Dykes, 2). Argues Dykes:

> it is important to study this unarticulated space, the invisible center, or what is now called "whiteness." Whiteness refers to the everyday, invisible, subtle, cultural and social practices, ideas and codes that discursively secure the power and privilege of white people in the United States. Whiteness is a cultural phenomenon that reflects ways of being, knowing, and constructing meaning, and that ultimately affects the development and structuring of relationships within the workplace. (Dykes, 3)

For Dykes, the practical meaning of whiteness becomes especially apparent in the experience of nonwhite corporate workers who are "often required to change more than their speech and behavior—indeed, they are often required to change who they are" (Dykes, 4). Dykes thus argues for the articulation of whiteness as a strategy to disclose implicit pressures upon corporate workers who are required to exemplify an appropriate mode of being for the corporate workplace. While it is not the intention of this chapter to further develop the results of Dykes's research, the important point is taken, that there are situations where it is morally important to name and study whiteness.

If we follow the analysis that Dykes offers, then we can see how the optimistic tenor of civil discourse results in part from not naming a central problem. But if a central problem is not named or studied, how can we know whether the optimism of our progressive discourse is well founded?

For instance, to introduce an example of my own, Black Entertainment Television appears in a cultural context where no footnotes, definitions, or conceptual clarifications are needed in order to communicate what it is about. One way of understanding the network's naming strategy is to see how BET is not planning to be another *white* entertainment network. On the other hand, there is no WET or White Entertainment Television, because just as racialized discourse is often negotiated through strategic practices of naming, so also are contours of racialized discourse in part normalized through strategic patterns of silence. Both the named BET and the non-named WET serve to introduce an important feature of our shared discourse of race.

There is no need to name White Entertainment Television in today's United States, because WET is the default perspective that is assumed without anybody saying anything about it. The silence that animates the non-naming of WET is not to be confused with the shunning silence that Judith Butler talks about when she says that "one can be interpolated, put in place, given a place, through silence, through not being addressed, and this becomes painfully clear when we find ourselves preferring the occasion of being derogated to the one of not being addressed at all" (Butler, *Excitable Speech*, 27). Such silences might be found within programming patterns of white entertainment, when nonwhite characters remain undeveloped or peripheral. Yet this is not the same silence that neglects to name the presence of white entertainment as white entertainment.

In the racialized history of the United States of America, racialized naming is a pervasive folk tradition, continually fortified through social, political, legal, and sociological practices. As Butler argues, "Racist speech works through the invocation of convention; it circulates, and though it requires the subject for its speaking, it neither begins nor ends with the subject who speaks or with the specific name that is used" (Butler, *Excitable Speech*, 34). Such conventions of race include what Dykes would name as the white center: that which convention assumes as the nonnamed assumption of racialized normality.

Cultural pervasiveness of racialized meaning also allows literary artist Toni Morrison to report that her work as an American writer requires her to "free up the language from its sometimes sinister, frequently lazy, almost always predictable employment of racially informed and determined chains" (Morrison, xi). As she writes, Morrison works to rewrite racialized conventions. And yet, despite the long and obvious history of racialized discourse, and despite the underlying assumption of whiteness that animates the corporatized call to manage the challenge of diversity, one of the strange features of whiteness today is a common refusal by white people to name themselves, their institutions, or their scholarship as white.

Anthropologist Ruth Frankenberg studies the cultural contours of whiteness by analyzing the way white people talk. She argues that although many white folks will say that race is not something they think about very much, in fact the way they continue talking yields evidence that race exerts a gravitational field upon the language they speak. Frankenberg finds evidence of these conflicted practices even among feminists. Subtle clues add up, as people speak their assumptions about who they are and who they are not. White people—even progressive white people—who say they do not think of themselves as white continue to talk in ways that convey their whiteness.

Philosopher John Dewey was an early white ally in the struggle for civil rights, serving on the founding board of directors for the National Association for the Advancement of Colored People (NAACP). He thought of himself as white and he was careful to point out that prejudice is often experienced as something that involves no thought at all. If Dewey is correct about the unthinking nature of prejudice, then to say that one does not think of oneself as white is to make a claim that does not address the unthinking dimension of cultural conventions.

The findings of Dykes, Butler, Morrison, Frankenberg, and Dewey yield a few reasons to remain skeptical when white people say they do not think of themselves as white, say they have never discriminated against anyone in their lives, and tell stories about situations where they did not see themselves as acting racist at all. The testimony of theorists in communication, anthropology, literature, and philosophy suggests agreement that whiteness has been with us in such powerful and pervasive ways that it would be incredible to suppose that it has disappeared.

I.

If we do not believe that white people as such are born predisposed to racist habits, any more than we believe that Americans are born with cravings for cigarettes, then we need *not* believe that racism as we know it will always be with us, because habits can be educated and changed. If it is possible to reduce cravings for cigarettes, it may be likewise possible to reform the contours of white identification. In both cases, we understand how people's desires and attitudes are often manipulated through powerful symbolic enticements. And we understand how difficult it can be to change what seem like simple and obviously harmful conventions.

The approach here taken both agrees and disagrees with important arguments made by predecessors in the field of white studies. I want to agree for instance with social historian David R. Roediger when he argues that, "whiteness of white workers, far from being natural and unchallengeable, is highly conflicted, burdensome, and even inhuman." Yet I want to quibble with Roediger's further assertion that in order to "address not only racial oppression and class exploitation and even militarism, the idea that it is desirable or unavoidable to be white must be exploded" (Roediger, *Towards the Abolition of Whiteness*, ix). If being white is always and only to be an exemplar of the mode of whiteness that effects supremacy, then being white is undesirable and avoidable, as Roediger argues. But if being white is also and often to exemplify a particular heritage in literature, art, and struggle, then there is a mode of whiteness that is unavoidable and need not be in all its aspects undesirable.

Roediger's analysis not only emphasizes a historical context for the understanding of whiteness, but he also distinguishes between two terms that deserve careful reflection for our logic of analysis. The first term, *whiteness*, asserts a complex model of social actions and interiorities. The second term, *white*, asserts the existence of examples that populate the model. In the logical relation between these two terms, the term *white* first picks out a raw collection of persons or events who will be objects of study from which conclusions about *whiteness* will be drawn. In turn, conclusions about whiteness will be used to add new examples to the collection. To draw upon a logic developed by John Dewey, we may see how the collection of white examples in the first case is a raw beginning for inquiry, while the modified collection is a refined result of inquiry. While I want to agree with Roediger's moral condemnation of whiteness as we find it—because of noxious patterns of supremacist attitudes and behaviors—I also want to claim a preference for naming oneself or others white as part of the very process of struggling against supremacy. Here I want to suggest the tentative possibility of conceiving an ethics of whiteness that would seek to pluralize, hybridize, criticize, and thus reconstruct whiteness as we know it.

When inferences proceed from collections of white evidence to conclusions about whiteness, and furthermore to judgments about what counts as white, then whiteness may be carefully formulated in terms of *historical practices and ideologies that have been developed by certain white groups* (beginning perhaps with the production of Shakespeare's play, *The Tempest*). If we are careful about the relation between the logical moments of inquiry into the historical development of whiteness, then we may transpose whiteness from a realm of logically fixed necessities into a reconstructable field of struggle. Being white in the raw sense may be unavoidable for white folks who take ourselves to be objects of inquiry into whiteness, yet inquiry into raw collections of white objects need not yield a totalizing model of essentially undesirable social practices or subjectivities.

For thousands of years prior to the seventeenth century, people had been classified as white. Scholars who studied Aristotle were long familiar with the proposition, "Socrates is white." The logic of Roediger's own scholarship supports the claim that if Socrates was white, the meaning of whiteness was historically different then. (We may, however, argue that the whiteness of Socrates was never innocent, because Plato had already made meaning of the difference between two colorized horses: a white, rational horse, and a black, wild one—but the issue need not be settled here.)

By naming oneself white, we need not assert that whiteness as we have known it is either desirable or unavoidable. The act of naming oneself white may be understood as an effort within a critical struggle to transform the fates of a cultural heritage—fates that will not likely disappear more quickly through evasion or denial. In terms of the logic discussed above, to declare oneself white is to present one's own facts as evidence in a developing inquiry into the continuities and ruptures that constitute the contours of historical whiteness.

Keeping the terms of logic in mind that distinguish white from whiteness, one may name oneself white under contemporary circumstances as a strategic response to the power of white supremacy that hides within nonnamed domains. This preliminary justification for naming even our own white selves provides a strict construction that would not automatically extend into other contexts. Under this strict construction of self-naming, we may develop a critical ethic of self-identification from within a context where we are still wary of the ways that overt supremacist traditions continue to use named forms of whiteness in order to perpetuate hegemonies of white power. Traditions of white supremacy continue to count as heavy influences on all further meanings that follow from being or not being perceived as white. For this reason, an ethic of naming must proceed carefully and critically.

But if we agree that hegemonic white supremacy sometimes works through strategic silence, then the practice of naming whiteness, where we find it, can serve as a useful method for testing whether strategic silences are at work. Anyone who calls himself or herself white may do so in order to begin marking one's own location as a place to check for the strategic silences of supremacy. As Paul Kivel argues, "in our society being white is also just as real, and governs our day-to-day lives just as much as being a person of color. To acknowledge this reality is not to create it or perpetuate it. In fact it is the first step to uprooting racism" (Kivel, 12).

If, as Roediger argues, "race is given meaning through the agency of human beings in concrete historical and social contexts," and if whiteness is a category that is "constantly being struggled over and remade," then the fact that one names oneself white may well serve to situate a racialized agency within the ongoing struggles to reconstruct whiteness. By making this argument I am not insisting that others are obliged to follow this method of naming their struggle, but I am insisting that coherent terms of struggle must be found.

From this point of view, I affirm Roediger's crucial claim that "the central political implication arising from the insight that race is socially constructed is the specific need to attack *whiteness* as a destructive ideology" (Roediger, *Towards the Abolition of Whiteness*, 3). Roediger's call for the "creation of working class nonwhiteness" makes sense to me only if he is referring to a transformation that will be measured by studying white folks who are working class. If this is true, the white workers in question will have to be named "white" in order to verify their "nonwhiteness." If I am a white worker, I will therefore have good reasons to investigate myself as white.

White history has not yet exemplified a period when white people themselves have offered to put their own identity up for careful reflection, yet there are signs that such a period is now possible. It is otherwise difficult for me to see how critical reflection can proceed if white folks refuse to name themselves as the historically specific subjects of their own responsibility.

Philosopher Naomi Zack warns that she feels uncomfortable when white folks identify themselves as white in the midst of nonwhite companions. She says it feels to her as if the announcement conveys news of a privilege that cannot be shared.

On the other hand, activist scholar Gloria Anzaldua invites allies to join struggles against oppression. "Becoming allies means helping each other heal." Furthermore, says Anzaldua, "When you are doing alliance work it is very important to say who you are" (in Adams et al., 475). If saying one is white arrogates a positionality of relative privilege, as Zack suggests, such naming may be precisely practiced for the purpose of situating white privilege within a critical field of reconstruction and struggle. If one names oneself white under these specific circumstances, the naming can serve as an invitation to critical interrogation. Under such circumstances, the meaning of whiteness is transformed away from its history of prescribing its own privilege as a universal essence. The ally who names himself a white man may do so for the purpose of positing a particularity and a problematic—to invite discourse and practice that would heal.

Anzaldua's preference does not negate the value of Zack's misgiving, however, because Anzaldua has made clear where and when she finds it helpful that people name themselves white. It is still possible to misuse the occasion. To declare a preference for white self-naming, under specific circumstances for specific work, does not qualify anyone for immunity against the charge that a particular act of self-naming might have been unseemly, insensitive, or poorly timed. In short, a defense of some practices of racialized naming does not inoculate all naming practices against allegations of racism.

Persuasive historical reflection has demonstrated that forms of white identity have been long developed and deployed as tools of social, political, and economic control. Independent scholar Theodore Allen has done exhaustive work in this area, carefully tracing how the language of white identity began to emerge in public discourse and law just when white folks were organizing their conquest of areas now known as the United States of America. The legitimation of white power over nonwhite populations was enhanced through rationalizations that dehumanized nonwhite populations and bolstered an idea that white folks were supremely endowed to conquer, kill, and enslave whole other races of people as a kind of natural and divine right.

With the help of ideological tools, white children have been raised for centuries in accordance with cultural practices that conditioned them to respond with fear, disrespect, and contempt toward nonwhite racialized groups. Public practices in religion, politics, art, and education are still in evidence today that have the effect of perpetuating white presumptions and attitudes.

"Whiteness has a cash value," argues George Lipsitz. Legacies of discrimination in housing, education, and employment ensure that white populations accumulate advantages in wealth and power that will be passed along to future generations. Therefore, "white Americans are encouraged to invest in whiteness, to remain true to an identity that provides them with resources, power, and opportunity" (Lipsitz, vii). Under such conditions, the critical white subject today seems to fit Judith Butler's descriptions of a subject that "is neither a sovereign agent with a purely instrumental relation to language, nor a mere effect whose agency is pure complicity with prior operations of power" (Butler, *Excitable Speech*, 26). If this is correct, then the critical white subject may follow Butler's further claim: "The responsibility of the speaker does not consist of remaking language ex-nihilo, but rather of negotiating the legacies of usage that constrain and enable the speaker's speech" (Butler, *Excitable Speech*, 27).

Philosopher Lucius Outlaw, who has done much work to develop a morally satisfactory approach to black cultural nationalism, worries that the heyday of white racist backlash has not yet subsided. Hollywood has been warning us in films such as *Falling Down*, and *American History X*, that white consciousness remains easily susceptible to racist resentment and contempt. As demographic and economic trends move the United States further into a future where white men find themselves increasingly outnumbered and economically insecure, the temptations toward historical racist reflexes is not unlikely. The film *Black Hawk Down* offers a cultural marker for racialized presentations that seem not to problematize the nature of the racializations that still lie ready to hand. The "war of cultures" thesis that seems to animate American popular belligerence toward the Islamic world may also serve as evidence that terms of white supremacy are still constitutive of working principles in American foreign policy.

Fortunately, for optimists, the last decade of the twentieth century offered promising signs that white folks were beginning to confront the challenge of achieving a better self-understanding and reconstruction of white racialized identity. Self-proclaimed race traitors founded a New Abolitionist Movement in an effort to abolish whiteness as we know it. Meanwhile, taking cues from critical race theorists of the previous decade, scholars began exploring the possibility of critical white studies. These efforts were then added to prior groundwork in anti-racist organizing that had been energized during the movement for civil rights in the 1960s.

Although the development of abolitionism and white studies offers some hope for the future, when we view these trends in the larger historical context of white power, we have legitimate reasons to be worried about the volatility of these efforts. Progressive projects that begin with the best of intentions face dangers of co-option and backlash. These dangers increase in proportion to how effective they are perceived to be. The history of civil rights, integration, multiculturalism, and affirmative action offer cautionary tales of good intentions carelessly sown by decent people or plowed under by implacable powers. Is the new abolitionism as careful as it could be? Can we organize our research into white studies in such a way that we and it will survive?

Philosophers Chris J. Cuomo and Kim Q. Hall seek "a more fruitful direction for scholarship and activism that is antiracist." They argue that whiteness must be explored as a "historical, constructed, and dynamic category"; otherwise, they argue, we take the risk of "treating it as normal (rather than normalizing), uniform (not immeasurably variable), paradigmatic (instead of fundamental to racism), and given (rather than defiantly maintained)" (Cuomo and Hall, 3). But Cuomo and Hall worry how it will be possible to intensify our investigations of whiteness without intensifying the legacy of racism to which whiteness has been attached.

Responding to the question posed by Cuomo and Hall, philosopher Naomi Zack answers that it will be difficult for people of color to "completely believe that it is possible for whites to talk about whiteness in ways that are not racist against nonwhites." Zack cites specific difficulties with four emerging white ideas: "the idea of race traitors; the idea of white privilege; the idea of white guilt; the idea of white racial identity." Zack does think that white scholars can be more helpful if they will seriously address "individual obligations to not participate in institutional racism" (in Cuomo and Hall, 77–78).

We can begin to reply to the challenge of ethical whiteness by first responding to Zack's plea for ethical resistance to institutional racism. A sympathetic yet critical approach to anti-racism may urge redoubled efforts to make anti-racist education essential to literacy in white communities. The work of anti-racism must remain connected to the structural analysis that views white prejudice as not only tasteless but unjust. While anti-racism often encourages personal development in awareness and practice, it too often neglects the need for effective transformation at the level of institutions. To work against racism ultimately is to abolish what E. Nathaniel Gates defines as "a relationship characterized by the practical domination of racialized others" (Gates, vii).

Following a discussion of the need for ethical whiteness to resist institutional racism, the next topic of this chapter concerns programmatic reconstruction in the realm of education for the purpose of transforming the cognitive structure of our knowledge to better understand the history and moral evil of whiteness. Here is where the emerging field of critical white studies has powerful potential, if and only if it is critically and explicitly guided by the need to service an ethics of institutional and existential reconstruction. Given the volatile legacy of whiteness, there is little room to play with cute or ambivalent formulations of what critical white studies should be about.

As for neoabolitionism and its call to abolish whiteness, race, and white studies, I think that abolitionism against slavery has much to teach us about the challenges and opportunities that face white allies in the battles against white power, yet there is a danger of incoherence when neoabolitionists oppose anti-racism, white studies, and postmodern developments in analysis. I am sympathetic to the abolitionist cause, but I reserve the right to offer critical terms of engagement. Neoabolitionist historian David R. Roediger has argued that there is a "specific need to attack whiteness as a destructive ideology" (Roediger, *Towards the Abolition of Whiteness*, 3). But I argue that the coherence of such a project requires reconstruction. In the realm of metaphorical argument, American history serves to clearly warn against the dangers of abolition without reconstruction. As Hannah Arendt has argued, "abolition of slavery sharpened inherent conflicts instead of finding a solution for existing serious difficulties" (Arendt, 57). Likewise, I worry that abolition of whiteness, without reconstruction, may yield new formulations similar to old Jim Crow. For instance, a war on terrorism, if not regulated by a critical ethic of whiteness, presents us with the danger of a supremacist world order whose whiteness will not be named.

II.

> Racism is a polymorphous agent of death, premature births, shortened lives, starving children, debilitating theft, abusive larceny, degrading insults, and insulting stereotypes forcibly imposed.
>
> —Leonard Harris, *Racism*

As philosopher Leonard Harris suggests, the ultimate meaning of racism lies in its social effects; therefore, a meaningful reversal of the effects of racism constitutes the first urgent arena of struggle. Because racism is a complex and evolving social technology that institutes a particular form of group domination, then the first challenge of anti-racism is to produce effective counter-dominating effects. In terms borrowed from Harris, our most urgent challenge is to stop the deaths, thefts, debilitations, insults, and stereotypes. We stop them one at a time where we can, but we stop them also by recasting systems at their systematic levels of operation.

In this section of the chapter, I want to explore how racialized naming is helpful in disclosing patterns of racialized hegemony and may also be useful to guide ethical practices of institutional integration. By contrasting the concept of integration with the concept of hegemony, I am suggesting that integration can be asserted as something other than a superficial adaptation. *Hegemony*, *integration*, and *whiteness* are terms that each draw upon histories of contested usage. In each case, I am deliberately attempting to recast usages that will be more helpful as guides to ethical life. When speaking of integration, I only intend to problematize institutions that are now predominately white. I do not want to repeat the mistakes of assuming that pluralized institutions of black power should be dismantled or that assimilation should be the end in view.

As John Rex has argued from a slightly different foundation, "the problem of 'curing racism' becomes not one of correcting theory on the abstract level, but of dealing with these basic acts of aggression" (in Harris, 144–45). Using this approach we will certainly strive to correct theory at the abstract level, but only after foregrounding the kinds of practical results that we demand for our theory to serve. We do this also in agreement with Rex's diagnosis that "the most common approach of sociologists and politicians to resisting racism and racialism has not been based on the kind of analysis above"—a definition that, in foregrounding the aggressive nature of racism, compels the foregrounding of an activist response (in Harris, 145).

The indispensable scholar Herbert Aptheker, for instance, well represents the philosophical approach that I am not taking when he defines racism as "*belief* in the inherent, immutable, and significant inferiority of an entire physically characterized people, particularly in mental capacity, but also in emotional and ethical features" (Aptheker, xiv, emphasis added). Of course, it is possible to harmonize the "practical" approach to racism with the "belief" approach the more we theoretically connect our sense of what counts as practical with our sense of what counts as belief. For this reason, some recent approaches to racism define it as a "symbolic system," where the system in question becomes inclusive of activities that are continuous with systematic deployments of meaning.

Yet even here, the scholar E. Nathaniel Gates, who is a proponent of the "symbolic system model," argues very carefully that he does not want to confuse racism with "reactive emotional positions." For the model of racism that Gates has in mind, racist systems begin with "selected social actors and practices" that are then distilled into "essences" (Gates, vii). What this means requires fuller exposition, but for our purposes right now, the important claim to note is that the initial evidence foregrounds actors and practices rather than noxious attitudes. Once again, I note that if a symbolic-systems approach to racism begins with emphasis on practice, then so would a symbolic-systems approach to anti-racism begin with the same emphasis on what is to be done differently in practice.

Paul Finkelman's work in the early history of racist legislation, for instance, points to a 1662 Virginia law that mandates children to be considered free or slave depending upon the status of the mother. Finkelman's interpretation of the law fits well with the symbolic systems model, because, argues Finkelman, "this law should be seen for what it was, an attempt to regulate the emerging social and economic institution of slavery in a way that would be beneficial to the master" (in Gates, 21). Thus, Finkelman's emphasis on institutional practice is just the emphasis we wish to reinforce in our approach to an ethics of whiteness by first answering Naomi Zack's important question: how can white folks begin to resist racism in its institutional form?

Relentless integration of our workplaces would be a good place for many white people to start. This means producing integration at every level of representation. Wherever two or three white people are gathered together for institutional purposes, there is where the trouble begins. Why are we all white here and what can we do about it? The question begs not another rationalized account for why things have to be this way, but insists upon problem-solving analysis and proactive response. In order to notice we're white, we have to name ourselves. Naming, noticing, asking, resisting. These are the practices that begin to exhibit evidence that an ethic of anti-racist whiteness is emerging into view. An institutional ethic of whiteness would require that groups of white folks begin problematizing their own predicaments of whiteness.

For instance, a friend of mine has just been appointed to a college committee. The list of names indicates to him that the committee is all white. Now what does he do? To whose attention should he call the matter and what should he say? Yes, the question makes him uncomfortable. It is impossible to imagine a course of action that will be comfortable. He surveys the list of names and finds two people that he would be most comfortable talking to about the issue. E-mail is a handy vehicle for sending nonintrusive messages without delay. He e-mails a committee member asking for a chat, either in person or via telephone. He prepares himself to tell them that he wants to try a brand new thing called ethical whiteness. In a white cultural context, he knows they'll probably smile. But the method of approach discourages us from dwelling on emotional reactions at this point, no matter how predictable. Keep the practice moving.

Another friend, serving on a hiring committee, asked the chair of the committee to schedule an early meeting with the college director of affirmative action. They began their committee work with that meeting. It is never likely that such meetings, especially when all white, will be comfortable affairs. But the practice counts.

Troubling dilemmas arise in the face of more overt activities. For instance, another friend tells me that an Asian candidate was once referred to as being "not a good minority" during deliberations of a hiring committee. The very same candidate had been called an "affirmative action baby" during a previous search, and by the same party. The candidate was later deliberated out of the running, although his vitae exemplified the best qualifications among the finalists. The finalists were all white. Based upon further inquiry, my friend discovered that the candidate had not made a favorable impression upon a decisive administrator. To insist upon the candidate's inclusion among finalists would have had little practical effect on the outcome. Yet it was wrong that such a process went unchallenged. While one can understand rationales for not blowing whistles, in the end, such failures cannot be excused.

I suspect that situations such as those above are not unusual. "A racist society or polity functions like a private club," argues the historian George M. Frederickson (in Gates, 55). If such situations constitute the banality of institutional racism, they also form the foundation for ethical interventions.

The integration of our institutional experience need not be constructed as a process of bringing in, although the invitational approach is part of the solution. Integration might well be conceived in terms of going out, too. Every institution nurtures its external relations. These too, should be surveyed and reconstructed.

III.

> The problem of a method for breathing an inspiration into a people is quite a new one.
>
> —Simone Weil, *The Need for Roots*

White educators who work on anti-racism with white students acknowledge a need to speak of special problems. In the context of anti-racist education, white students tend to demonstrate low competence in critical acknowledgment and analysis of positionality as white subjects. This form of illiteracy inhibits multiracial dialogue. It is defensible, therefore, to argue that white teachers need to make room for developing a critical race consciousness among white students. Christine Sleeter sums up the situation nicely:

> Cross-racial dialogue about racism, which involves white people, however, is rare and difficult to develop and sustain. Dialogue requires that people be able to articulate some analysis of racism and one's own position in a racist structure, one's own feelings and experiences, and the choices one has for acting differently. Most white people do not talk about racism, do not recognize the existence of institutional racism, and feel personally threatened by the mention of racism. (from the foreword of *Making Meaning of Whiteness* by Alice McIntyre, x)

When Sleeter emphasizes a need to educate white students about their particular relationship to racism, she legitimates the exercise as a preparation for pluralistic dialogue across racialized boundaries. Such pluralistic centering begins to suggest a conceptual context for developing a normative legitimacy for the emerging discipline of white studies. In keeping with the ancient imperative, white studies can help white students to know themselves.

Given the normative challenges presented thus far—to name whiteness for the purpose of anti-racist work at levels of institutional, therapeutic, and cognitive reconstruction—a prospective discipline of white studies seems worthy of pursuit. In order to explore how such a discipline might be conceived, I use Lucius Outlaw's approach to "Africology" (Outlaw, 97–134). In fact, I think it is doubly helpful to emphasize Outlaw's approach through an act of re-naming.

Rather than speak of white studies, I prefer to indicate an "Africology of Whiteness." The emphasis here is doubly helpful because an Africology of Whiteness need not reinvent from scratch a general theory of disciplinary norms. Outlaw's work provides helpful parameters for building a humanistic discipline of study. Second, an Africology of Whiteness proceeds on the assumption that some self-inoculation against supremacy is a prudent first step. If we situate our project within a unified field of humanistic studies, then the study of white people is but one branch of the study of Africology. Future science may obviate some of the foundations for this claim, but for the time being, the state of the art evidence suggests an African origin for all humanity, white folks included. An Africology of Whiteness reminds us already that the would-be supremacist must first of all reckon with his or her own African heritage.

Mission statements and evaluative criteria for programs that pursue the Africology of Whiteness should clearly situate whiteness studies within an anti-racist ethic. Meanwhile, it is important that academic politics not be played in such a way that development of white studies will be pitted against other emerging forms of ethnic studies. Instead, critical white studies should press its shoulder toward the domains that have always been white but have never been critical about it. Philosophy qualifies preeminently as an example (and my own first love, American pragmatism, ranks high among such peers), but we wouldn't want to neglect literature, history, or any other field where the commonplace syllabus is predominantly discourse by, about, and for white people. By making what is hidden plain, the Africology of Whiteness can be an ally to ethnic studies instead of a rival. As Sleeter argues (cited above), a central reason for investigating whiteness is to prepare white students for pluralistic dialogue.

Outlaw's prefatory warning about Africology is indispensable advice for all future deliberations about the study of whiteness: "the 'best path' is a matter of *choice*, conditioned by experience and understanding. And the choosing can never be formalized into an algorithm that systematically secures the selection of a correct path with rigorous and absolute certainty" (Outlaw, 97–98). Just as I believe there is no absolute argument against the field, Outlaw reminds us that neither can there be an absolute formula for legitimation. Just as I have carefully argued for naming whiteness under certain conditions for certain purposes, I have also begun the argument for an Africology of Whiteness by stipulating a need to develop expertise that will be helpful to racialized reconstruction.

When Outlaw proposes a new generation of disciplinary studies in *Africology* that would serve as successor to *Black Studies*, he explicitly seeks a new "heuristic set" that would move away from "color" by choosing to identify peoples with respect to their continental heritage (Outlaw, 101). The recasting of colors and races into peoples of various continental heritage conserves the rich resources of racialized critical scholarship, yet recasts terms of inquiry in ways that insist upon historical rather than essentialized ontologies.

An Africology of Whiteness thus undercuts the temptation to posit for whiteness the kind of premature transcendence that often stands in place of connected historical heritage. In my own experience as a teacher who grapples with white identities in dialogue with students, I find that today's practical consciousness of whiteness begins with a polygenetic fantasy in which white people appear full grown in the vicinity of Europe, without historical debts to any human ancestors. This is the primal fantasy of whiteness, the subconscious structure of free-floating, pure, transcendental identity that an Africology of Whiteness would serve to deconstruct. A whiteness out of Africa is a different kind of whiteness indeed.

For Hannah Arendt, the term *race* accumulates its precise meaning "only when and where peoples are confronted with such tribes of which they have no historical record and which do not know any history of their own" (Arendt, 72). Peoples who are viewed as having no history become the perfect image of Hildegaard's "black man" who, because he has no history, is a pure creature of nature. As Arendt explains, "What made them different from other human beings was not at all the color of their skin but the fact that they behaved like a part of nature, that they treated nature as their undisputed master, that they had not created a human world, a human reality" (Arendt, 72). An Africology of Whiteness begins to fuzz the precision of such a racialized imagination by re-historicizing its own consciousness of relations between tribes and peoples.

Transcendental whiteness, by perpetuating a fantastic self-consciousness of people *not* mastered by nature, also escapes history through its assertion of *pure mastery.* Says Arendt, in the particular case of South African whites, "Their race consciousness today is violent not only because they have nothing to lose save their membership in the white community, but also because the race concept seems to define their own condition much more adequately than it does that of their former slaves, who are well on the way to becoming workers, a normal part of human civilization" (Arendt, 74–75). In other words, if *race* is the term that conveys identity when peoples have been imagined apart from history, then transcendental whiteness racializes its privilege as something already granted. And this is where Naomi Zack's misgivings about the idea of white privilege warn that the *idea* of privilege, unless rigorously connected to terms of history and injustice, is unlikely to have nonracist effects. The moral problem of such privilege cannot be conveyed in backpack imagery—it is not something that white folks carry around. White privilege is white supremacy triumphant, unchallenged, normalized, and thoroughly reenforced.

For Hannah Arendt, "Rootlessness is characteristic of all race organizations" (Arendt, 76). I agree that rootlessness is part of the fantasy life that sustains white supremacy. Therefore, an Africology of Whiteness situates racialized peoples in the particularities of their globalized heritage where contingencies of power are rigorously connected to historicized technologies. This is a deliberate attempt to produce the antidote to symptoms of racism that were diagnosed by Arendt: "contempt for labor, hatred of territorial limitation, general rootlessness, and an activistic faith in one's own divine chosenness" (Arendt, 77). The challenge posed by Arendt confronts the bourgeois condition, where neither lower incentives nor higher motives breach the inertia of ennui "in a society where nobody wants to achieve anything and everyone has become a god" (Arendt, 77).

Outlaw's conception of Africology formulates a research discipline itself as constructivist and interventionist—a site where historicized identity is in the making. Borrowing from the terminology of Gerard Radnitsky, Outlaw's Africology calls for a *praxiological* perspective, where critical practice engages critical practice, where culture ever encounters culture in the labor of reconstruction.

A wonderful example of what might count as a seminal text for the Africology of Whiteness is found in Stefan Helmreich's anthropological report on the Santa Fe Institute. In his 1998 monograph, *Silicon Second Nature*, Helmreich refracts the racialized discipline of anthropology back upon a community of white scientists in order to show how constructions of artificial life may be understood as replications of whiteness in pure algorithmic form.

Consistent with Outlaw's proposed metatheory of Africology, Helmreich presents his study as "a critical political intervention." In the scientific attempt to digitize nature, Helmreich argues that "conventional visions of life" are being naturalized (Helmreich, 15). "My argument is that Artificial Life scientists' computational models of 'possible biologies' are powerfully inflected by their cultural conceptions and lived understandings of gender, kinship, sexuality, race, economy, and cosmology and by the social and political contexts in which understandings take shape" (Helmreich, 11). Working with the artifacts of artificial life, Helmreich demonstrates how such constructions may be viewed as embodiments of cultural assumptions.

From the first pages of the book, Helmreich makes note of the white, male demographics that constitute the elite tribe of artificial life scientists, and he seeks to maintain a critical consciousness toward the effects of such cultural particularity. With specific references to Frankenberg's anthropology of whiteness, Barbara Flagg's legal theory, and Paul Gilroy's explorations of race, Helmreich wants to fog the lens of what Flagg calls the "transparency phenomenon," where whites tend not to notice what is most "white-specific" about their own methods and productions (Helmreich, 161). Helmreich argues that the white scientists at Santa Fe, like white populations in general, are blind "to the ways their images of kinship and primitivity are cultural constructions built on the foundations of a white cultural imagination. In many ways, the genetic algorithm is animated by this imagination, and the worlds it supports resonate with its logic" (Helmreich, 161–62). When we think about the emerging power of simulation, Helmreich warns of simulated whiteness as the very structure of our impatient projections.

If Helmreich is correct, his conclusions only exacerbate cause for concern that a white racist backlash is not only predictable, but may be thoroughly normalized and naturalized as the very logic of evolution itself. If white folks would be counted among progressive forces for social evolution, a careful ethic of naming can serve to keep critical movement alive.

As this chapter is being written, white-dominated cultures are once again producing headlines that exemplify the power of conventional racialized categories. Both in Europe and America, a reflux of anti-immigration sentiments affects a striking plurality. If the whiteness of such phenomena is not named, perhaps it should be. If the vocabulary of whiteness is not yet a critical vocabulary, perhaps it should be. A public discourse continues to pose problems animated by assumptions of a white center while the central assumptions pass unnamed and unstudied. While we may assent to the dream of a day when racialized categories have long passed, in our waking world of conflict, there is need for a critical ethic of whiteness still today.

Bibliography

Adams, Maurianne, et al., eds. *Readings for Diversity and Social Justice.* New York: Routledge, 2000.

Allen, Theodore. *The Invention of the White Race.* Vol. 1: *Racial Oppression and Social Control.* London: Verso, 1994.

———. *The Invention of the White Race.* Vol. 2: *The Origin of Racial Oppression in Anglo-America.* London: Verso, 1997.

Anzaldua, Gloria. "Allies." In Adams et al., *Readings for Diversity.* 475–77.

Arendt, Hannah. *Imperialism: Part Two of the Origins of Totalitarianism.* San Diego: Harvest, 1968.

Butler, Judith. *Excitable Speech: A Politics of the Performative.* New York: Routledge, 1997.

———. *Antigone's Claim: Kinship Between Life and Death.* New York: Columbia University Press, 2000.

Cuomo, Chris, and Kim Q. Hall, eds. *Whiteness: Feminist Philosophical Reflections.* Lanham, MD: Rowman & Littlefield, 1999.

Dykes, Pamela Y. Forcing the square pegs into the round holes: A phenomenological inquiry exploring how African Americans experience whiteness. Ph.D. thesis, Ohio University, March 1998. Ann Arbor, MI: UMI Dissertation Services, 1999.

Frankenberg, Ruth, ed. *Displacing Whiteness: Essays in Social and Cultural Criticism.* Durham, NC: Duke University Press, 1997.

———. *White Women, Race Matters: The Social Construction of Whiteness.* Minneapolis: University of Minnesota Press, 1993.

Gates, Nathaniel, ed. *Racial Classification and History. Critical Race Theory*, Vol. 3. New York: Garland, 1997.

Harris, Leonard, ed. *Racism.* Key Concepts in Critical Theory. Amherst, NY: Humanity Books, 1999.

Helmreich, Stefan. *Silicon Second Nature: Culturing Artificial Life in a Digital World.* Berkeley: University of California Press, 1998.

Kivel, Paul. *Uprooting Racism: How White People Can Work for Racial Justice.* Gabriola Island, BC: New Society Publishers, 1996.

Lipsitz, George. *The Possessive Investment in Whiteness: How White People Profit from Identity Politics.* Philadelphia: Temple University Press, 1998.

Martinot, Steve. "Racialized Whiteness: Its History, Politics, and Meaning." www.ocf.berkeley.edu/~marto/cws/semiohst.htm

McIntyre, Alice. *Making Meaning of Whiteness: Exploring Racial Identity with White Teachers.* Albany: SUNY Press, 1997. Introduction by Christine E. Sleeter.

Morrison, Toni. *Playing in the Dark: Whiteness and the Literary Imagination.* William E. Massey, Sr., Lectures in the History of American Civilization, 1990. Cambridge: Harvard University Press, 1992.

Moses, Greg. *Revolution of Conscience: Martin Luther King, Jr., and the Philosophy of Nonviolence.* New York: Guilford, 1997.

Outlaw, Lucius. *On Race and Philosophy.* New York: Routledge, 1996.

Perlo, Victor. *Economics of Racism II: The Roots of Inequality, USA.* New York: International Publishers, 1996.

Roediger, David R. *Towards the Abolition of Whiteness: Essays on Race, Politics, and Working Class History.* London: Verso, 1994.

———. *The Wages of Whiteness.* The Haymarket Series. London: Verso, 1991.

Sexton, Jared. "The Consequence of Race Mixture: Racialized Barriers and the Politics of Desire." www.ocf.berkeley.edu/~marto/paradigm/sexton.htm
Spears, Arthur K., ed. *Race and Ideology: Language, Symbolism, and Popular Culture.* Detroit: Wayne State University Press, 1999.
Weil, Simone. *The Need for Roots: Prelude to a Declaration of Duties toward Mankind.* London: Routledge, 1955.
Weir, Allison. *Sacrificial Logics: Feminist Theory and the Critique of Identity.* New York: Routledge, 1996.

5

Meditations on Postsupremacist Philosophy

Anna Stubblefield
Rutgers University, Newark

As a white person who specializes in Africana philosophy, I have (on a regular basis) my most profound, in-my-face experiences of awareness of my whiteness when I function as a philosopher (when I teach, when I write, when I present). In an academic discipline that is only just beginning to emerge from a history and tradition of expecting its white students to not think of themselves as raced—indeed, to not think of themselves as even being embodied—this is highly ironic. Nonwhite philosophers confront their ethnicity time and again as they function as philosophers (not too long ago, *black philosopher*, *Latino philosopher*, and similar phrases were oxymorons in this very racialized, racist discipline). And as a white woman, I experience my white womanness when I do philosophy (*woman philosopher* also used to be an oxymoron). (Pause here and ponder the phrases *black woman philosopher*, *Asian woman philosopher*, *Latina philosopher*, and *American Indian woman philosopher* and laud the audacity and courage of those few who have chosen this treacherous path.) If one is a nonwhite philosopher, female or male, one has no choice but to deal with the repercussions of being a nonwhite philosopher, and one has them regardless of one's area of specialization. It is similar for white women, so I have had to deal with that. But had I chosen to do more "traditional" European philosophy, or even chosen to specialize in white feminist philosophy, I would most likely be blissfully unaware of my race as I went about my philosophical business. Putting myself in a situation in which I am forced to reflect upon white supremacy and my own whiteness, however, has made me a better philosopher and a better person.

In this chapter, I offer a definition of *white supremacy* and argue that white people pressure each other to be "good" by upholding white supremacy. A "bad" white person is one who challenges white supremacy. Similarly, within the discipline of philosophy, there are pressures about what constitutes being a good philosopher and a bad (or not so good) philosopher, and some of these pressures have to do with raciality and ethnicity as well as gender, disability, sexual orientation, and class. I define *postsupremacist* philosophy as philosophy that challenges racial, ethnic, gender, ability, sexual orientation, and class supremacy. I argue that we should move philosophy in postsupremacist directions and that this requires looking at how we define our discipline, including the importance of valorizing interdisciplinarity and publicly accessible philosophy.

White Identity

As I have been writing about the nature and ethical significance of racial identity in response to debates within Africana philosophy, I have been thinking about my own white racial identity. In my recent book, *Ethics along the Color Line*,[1] I develop and defend a social constructivist theory of racial identity. The notion of race as a social construction has been criticized recently by both Clevis Headley and Lewis Gordon. Headley argues that many social constructivist approaches to understanding racial identity render whiteness and blackness ontologically identical, a failure to appreciate the very real differences between them. He also worries that social constructivist approaches to race lead too easily to the conclusion that "race" is an empty concept and to underestimating the continuing profound effects of race in our lives.[2] In an essay in the same anthology, Gordon shares the latter worry, although he approaches the issue from a different angle. His concern is that students who are taught that race is a social construction frequently interpret this to mean that race is not real, which in many cases does not reflect their lived experience of it.[3] My conception of race responds to both of these concerns, but it is not within the scope of this chapter to defend it, only to present it briefly as a backdrop to my discussion of whiteness and philosophy.

European elites (political leaders, scholars, religious leaders) created an essentialist conception of race in which the different races are understood as having deep differences in intelligence, moral capacity, and physical capacity and in which the races are hierarchized with whiteness at the top and blackness at the bottom and with brownness, redness, yellowness, and "shades" of whiteness in between. They did this to support practices of genocide, enslavement, and exploitation that served their imperialist economic interests, and they used the offer of the status of "whiteness" as an effective bargaining point in their dealings with nonelite whites. Thinking of race in terms of "essential" and hierarchized qualities is a social construction because there is no natural basis for the essentialist assumptions endorsed by white people (there are not "stupid" genes or "criminal" genes). Human beings might have come to think of differences in appearance between people in very different terms with very different social results. What we have to live with, however, is what actually happened. Every African and South American civilization demolished by European invaders, every black man lynched by a white mob, every job opportunity closed to black people by white employers being pressured by white workers, every American Indian murdered by a soldier in the employment of the United States government, every woman of color raped by a white man or forced to leave her children for long hours while she cleaned a white woman's house, every child of color poorly educated by a white supremacist school system or denied health care in a white supremacist, capitalistic medical system, or suffering from asthma due to the pollution of poor and primarily nonwhite neighborhoods, or suffering from hunger and malnourishment in the "land of plenty," or losing her parents at a young age because they lacked health care and adequate nutrition—all these crimes against humanity have made the social construction of race more real, more material.

Therefore, regardless of what students are often taught or pick up, saying that race is a social construction does not in any way entail saying that race is not real. It does not even entail that the logical ethical conclusion to be drawn from this description is that we should "get rid of" race (this is a part of what I argue in *Ethics along the Color Line*). I base these conclusions on the following conception of racial identity: belonging to a racial group means occupying a social location, based on your and others' beliefs about your appearance and ancestry, in which you experience particular normative expectations from others and yourself about how you should behave, about your values, your attitudes, and your motivations. I refer to these expectations as "social norms." It does not follow from the fact that someone has an expectation about you that you will conform to that expectation, however. The expectation puts pressure on you, and it means that the person holding the expectation will judge you by how much or little you conform to it. What it means to be a certain kind of person, to occupy that location, is that you have to respond to those expectations. You have choices about how you respond to them, but you cannot escape dealing with them. Even if you can hide from them by "passing" as someone different, *you* know you are passing. Passing is a way of responding to anticipated expectations, not a way of avoiding them.

No one is only "raced," however. We also experience social norms that relate to our gender, our age, our economic status, our ethnicity, our sexual orientation, our "abilities," our lifestyle, our work, and so on. These social norms are not additive. A middle-aged, white, lesbian woman who uses a wheelchair and works as a veterinarian, for example, does not experience social norms for middle-aged people *plus* social norms for white people *plus* social norms for women, and so on. The interaction of social norms—how they react with each other—means that she will experience social norms specific for middle-aged, white, lesbian women who use wheelchairs and are professionals. She occupies a location at which expectations converge. This does not mean that one does not share experiences of social norms with other people who share some but not all of the same social categories, however. The social norms for women overlap but are different for white women, black women, old women, young women, and so on. Social norms about race overlap but are different for men, women, heterosexual people, homosexual people, working class people, professional class people, and so on. In order to understand all of this, we should analyze the ways in which social norms relating to one category are similar to but also change in reaction with social norms relating to other categories.

In *Ethics along the Color Line*, I argue that social norms that white people overwhelmingly hold for other white people in the contemporary United States pressure them to engage in white supremacist belief and practice. The ideology of white supremacy is that whiteness sets the standard—whiteness is normative—such that anything that is symbolic of or associated with blackness is therefore deviant. By *whiteness* I mean white (Eurocentric) cultural products, including value systems and aesthetic ideals, and worldviews that stem from a white (Eurocentric) perspective. I want to stress that white supremacist belief need not involve conscious dislike for what is symbolic of or associated with blackness, but rather exists so long as a person takes what is symbolic of or associated with whiteness as normative. To invoke Maria Lugones's classic observation, even when well-meaning white parents try to teach their children not to be racist, they often tell their children that "black children are just like you." Lugones asks, however, why they do not say "you are just like them"?[4] White people who believe that common humanity should be *extended* from white people to all people are still establishing themselves as the standard and hence are still engaging in white supremacist belief and action, however well-intentioned they might be.

White people pressure other white people to uphold white supremacy by forcing them to choose sides ("either you're with us or against us"), by pressuring them to acknowledge and nurture relationships through acquiescence to white supremacy, and by constructing acquiescence to white supremacy as a demonstration of good judgment. In the face of these pressures, to challenge white supremacy is to side against your social group, to rupture relationships, and to demonstrate poor judgment. A "good" white person is a white person who upholds the norms of white supremacy, while a "bad" white person is one who defies those norms.

I want to distinguish my view here from the views of Noel Ignatiev,[5] David Roediger,[6] and others who urge the "abolition" of whiteness. Ignatiev, for example, defines whiteness in such a way that there is no good or positive way to be white. According to Ignatiev, whiteness is always negative because whiteness is the denigration of blackness. I agree with Ignatiev that socialization to whiteness (the development of white identity) occurs in our society by learning to differentiate oneself from blackness. The problem with his analysis is that he considers racial identity to be an attribute that can be negative or positive. Identity is not an attribute, however; it is a social location where norms converge. It is what you *do* at that site in response to those norms that determines what kind of person you are. If you conform to norms of whiteness that demand that you stigmatize black people, you uphold white supremacy. If you resist or respond creatively to norms of whiteness that demand that you stigmatize black people, you help to undermine white supremacy. Either way you are still white.

Ignatiev argues that white people should disavow whiteness. To disavow means to dissociate oneself from or deny knowledge of or association with. It also means to deny responsibility for. I worry that urging white people to disavow their whiteness will amount to urging them to deny their responsibility for what white people do in the name of whiteness. This will not help end white supremacy. As Malcolm X famously observed, anti-racist white people should take responsibility for the racism of other white people, not distance themselves from it.[7]

Challenging Philosophy as a Means of Challenging Whiteness (and Challenging Whiteness as a Means of Challenging Philosophy)

Charles Mills describes the "theoretical whiteness" of philosophy—the ways in which questions are framed and answered that completely ignore the position of black people within white supremacist European and American regimes. Some philosophers defend the discipline against the charge that it is "theoretically white" by arguing that European philosophy is the study of the most general and universalizable questions—the nature of reality, of truth, of justice—that concern all people. According to Mills, however, those who offer this defense fail to appreciate that insofar as "all people" are

> conceived of as having their personhood uncontested, insofar as their culture and cognitions are unhesitatingly respected, insofar as their moral prescriptions

> take for granted already achieved full citizenship and a history of freedom—insofar, that is, as race is *not* an issue for them, then they are already tacitly positioned as white persons, culturally and cognitively European, racially privileged members of the West.[8]

I want to take Mills's analysis a step further and discuss how it plays out in terms of normative pressures on white philosophers. The theoretical white supremacy of European philosophy, in both its analytic and continental traditions, has meant that nonwhite women and men who have chosen philosophy as their discipline have had to force themselves to swallow and master work that alienates and disparages them. Many struggle with feeling that they, themselves—their bodies, their experiences, their worldviews—are at best ignored and at worse seriously and harmfully misrepresented in what they have been taught as the philosophical tradition. They have had to invest their time and energy and self-definition (what does it mean to say "I am a philosopher"?) in an intellectual history that fundamentally denies them full standing and relegates their experiences to the margins of "particularity" in contrast to the center of white "universality." White philosophers, on the other hand, can easily avoid ever having to think about their racial identity in relation to their work. A white person in philosophy can be considered a well-educated philosopher and one who has made important contributions to the field without having to think even once about race, without having to think of himself *as* raced.

Furthermore, just as a "bad" white person is one who challenges white supremacy in everyday life (thereby failing to uphold standards of whiteness and thus demonstrating poor judgment), a philosopher who specializes in Africana or Latino or American Indian philosophy or in postcolonial feminist philosophy or in any version of philosophy that centers the experiences of people who are not white will be considered by most of her colleagues to be a "bad" (unaccomplished, not outstanding, not "top drawer") philosopher. She faces pressures to prove that she is an accomplished philosopher by not challenging the white supremacy of philosophy. I was once told, for example, "You're really very smart; why waste your time on all that black philosophy nonsense? Those aren't the *important* issues, they aren't the *big* questions."

These issues are tricky, because it is neither *only* what you specialize in nor *only* what your body looks like that makes you a "bad" philosopher. Certainly women of all races (and women of color even more than white women) and men of color and people who are visibly disabled have to overcome doubts and prejudices from their teachers and later their colleagues in order to have their authority recognized, and this is a lifelong battle. But there is at least some reward, even if your body is suspect (not white, not male, not "able-bodied"), in striving to be a "good" philosopher.

Challenging white supremacy in philosophy is a struggle that nonwhite philosophers should not have to take on by themselves. White philosophers should choose to be "bad" philosophers, too. White philosophers should put pressure on other philosophers, as many "bad" nonwhite philosophers have already done, to end white supremacy in philosophy. White philosophers should challenge themselves and each other to learn, not *about*, because that objectifies, but *from* people of color (particularly women of color, whose insights are nowhere near often enough acknowledged, even by men of color and white women, all of whom should know better).

It is not enough to challenge white supremacy in philosophy, however. We must challenge all the supremacies in philosophy. This requires investing in what I call "postsupremacist philosophy."

Postsupremacist Philosophy

As I argue above where I define white supremacy, to be "supremacist" is to believe that a particular group sets the standard by which everyone should be judged. During the twentieth century, we witnessed an explosion of challenges to many different forms of supremacy: white supremacy, male supremacy, heterosexual supremacy, able-ist supremacy. In many ways, previous challenges to class supremacy were lost in the shuffle, but they should be revived in conjunction with these other challenges. The discipline of philosophy has already been impacted by these challenges, but it is time for the discipline to move and grow and develop in response. Furthermore, this should happen in such a way that all of the challenges to supremacy of all kinds come together. We should move beyond philosophy that concentrates on any one of the issues of supremacy—race and ethnicity, gender, disability, sexual identity, and class—in ways that preclude the possibility of addressing intersection with the others. This does not mean that we should not concentrate on particularities; doing so is often an important way to work out crucial ideas. Our overall theorizing needs to make room for intersectionality, not block it. Also, we should assertively explore the possibility that the analysis of or solution to one supremacist problem may have already been nicely worked out by someone whose work we have not read because that person is not writing in "our" area. Furthermore, although many of the challenges to various supremacies in philosophy have been undertaken as critiques within the areas of social and political philosophy, ethics, epistemology, and philosophy of science, we should seriously consider and address continuing supremacies in other areas of philosophy rather than assume that some areas are, by definition, exempt. And even if an area of philosophy is not, because of its nature, susceptible to being theoretically supremacist, such as logic or the study of color, people who specialize in these subdisciplines should nonetheless be concerned with supremacy in the discipline of philosophy as a whole. In other words, there is work here for every philosopher to do.

These are metaphilosophical questions. We should look not just at supremacy within particular philosophical areas or traditions but at how supremacy affects the discipline of philosophy in terms of how we value different kinds of philosophical work, which work is seen as most important, who is doing it and who is not, and why they are doing it. This challenges notions, for example, of what counts as a complete undergraduate and graduate education in philosophy.

We should, as philosophers, worry about the lack of black students, American Indian students, Asian students, Middle-Eastern students, Latino students, and students from other underrepresented groups among those who pursue doctoral studies in philosophy. We should worry about the lack of women from these groups. We should worry about the climate for people with disabilities in philosophy. We should scrutinize who is getting tenure, who is not and why. We should scrutinize who is making full professor, who is not and why. We should examine who is teaching in graduate programs, particularly in the top graduate programs, and why. We should discuss how graduate programs are ranked, and whether a graduate program should be considered "top" if it does not encourage postsupremacist philosophy or if it is not a comfortable environment for members of traditionally underrepresented groups.

These are questions of academic freedom. They involve what one is required to study, what counts as being well-rounded, what specialties are considered crucial within philosophy departments (which determines what jobs are available), what is required for getting tenure, what articles are published in the top-tier journals, what makes a journal top tier, what makes a program top tier, and so on. Academic freedom for people who do postsupremacist philosophy also requires promoting people who do this work to the highest levels. In order for people who specialize in postsupremacist philosophy to get tenure, there must be enough high ranking professors who understand and value this work to be tenure reviewers. If a philosopher has difficulty getting tenure, not due to the lack of quality or quantity of her work but rather due to her area of specialization, her academic freedom is compromised.

Interdisciplinarity

In order to improve the climate for postsupremacist philosophy, we also must encourage interdisciplinarity among different areas and traditions of philosophy and between philosophy and other academic disciplines. In both these ways, philosophy has become less interdisciplinary over the course of the twentieth century than it was previously, when philosophers did not restrict themselves to single areas of philosophy but rather worked in metaphysics *and* epistemology *and* ethics *and* political philosophy, and were also scientists, anthropologists, and so on. One cannot do good postsupremacist philosophy without being what we now call "interdisciplinary"—without reading history, sociology, literature studies, and the like. The construction of what we currently accept as the differing academic disciplines is itself a social construction that was contingent upon various historical developments. The rigidity of current disciplinary distinctions artificially divides people who are writing from postsupremacist perspectives, who need to share and develop understandings of each other's work across disciplinary lines in order for all to be doing the best work possible. (Many philosophers of mind have, of course, already discovered this in relation to work being done in cognitive science.) Depending on who hires us for jobs and who reviews us for tenure, however, working interdisciplinarily will not necessarily help us advance in a still very rigid, discipline-defined academic setting, so this is another issue to which we must attend if we are to adequately challenge supremacy in philosophy.

In regard to the question of interdisciplinarity *within* philosophy, it is equally important for postsupremacist philosophers to not be restricted or restrict themselves to particular areas or particular traditions (e.g., analytic or continental or pragmatist). This becomes a question of graduate education and departmental self-definition, a question of how we train new generations of philosophers and what we consider to be a complete or well-rounded education in philosophy and a complete or well-rounded department. I share Lucius Outlaw's concerns that the discipline of philosophy has suffered from, rather than being moved forward by, "increasing specialization and the concomitant development of narrowness, overconcern with methodologies and other discipline-focused matters."[9] Outlaw argues further that in response to this problem, the goal of philosophizing should be "to share in the refinement and perpetuation of critical intelligence as a practice of life that has as its goal raising to consciousness the conditions of life, historical practices, and blocked alternatives that, if pursued, might lead to life experienced as qualitatively—progressively—different."[10] As I interpret Outlaw's argument, philosophers have, in many ways, become so engrossed in the details of figuring out how the world works and how people interact with the world and with each other that we are prone to forget *why* we are trying to find answers to these questions. The goal of philosophy should be to better understand the nature of our existence in the world *in order to improve it for all people.* The valorization of postsupremacist philosophy is crucial to meeting this goal.

Public Philosophy

In order to promote interdisciplinarity among different areas and traditions within philosophy as well as between philosophy and other academic disciplines, and as part of keeping in mind that the goal of philosophy should be to understand human existence in order to improve it for all people, we must make philosophy accessible. A result of overspecialization is that many philosophers write in such a way that even philosophers who specialize in other areas cannot follow what is being said. When we use technical terms that we do not define, when we assume that our readers have background knowledge of specific issues and debates, when we employ arcane vocabulary and grammatical structures, we become gatekeepers, excluding everyone but a handful of experts in our own narrow area from sharing our ideas and thereby disparaging everyone else as not worthy of partaking in our work. (Note that the word *arcane* comes from the Latin *arcanus*, meaning "secret.")

Philosophy—love of wisdom—should be about sharing ideas with anyone and everyone who wishes to share with us. We should cherish our readers, not flaunt our supposedly superior expertise in their faces. We can share rigorous philosophy with others who have different educational backgrounds, both within and outside of the discipline of philosophy, if we make it a primary concern to do so. This actually requires more careful writing than that using technical terms and references without explaining them, so it is not easy to do. Part of valuing postsupremacist philosophy is valuing those philosophers, in any area of the discipline, who make this effort.

There is a paradigm trap for philosophers with "suspect bodies" (white women, women and men of color, visibly disabled people of all races). If the paradigm of academic qualification is the supreme authority in a particular area, then people who have all too often been perceived as not capable of being supreme authorities frequently experience having their expertise questioned. To demonstrate that they are as worthy as anyone to be a gatekeeper of the halls of philosophy, they must prove themselves to philosophers who question them by proving their mastery of technical language and of particular methodologies and traditions at the expense of accessibility of their work. When they do so, however, their work falls short of being fully postsupremacist, because part of moving beyond supremacy must be moving beyond inaccessibility as a hallmark of excellent philosophy.

Some Final Thoughts

Specializing in Africana philosophy as a white person has made me aware of the pitfalls of white people specializing in Africana philosophy. The more accepted Africana philosophy becomes as an area of specialization, and the more people who specialize in it, the more that white people will be exposed to it, become interested in it, and choose to specialize in it. Greater acceptance for Africana philosophy is a good thing. But it is so easy for white people to end up taking over, sometimes intentionally, sometimes just by there being more of us around, which in philosophy builds upon racism in schooling, university education, admissions criteria, who gets jobs, who gets tenure, who teaches at the "top-ranked" programs, and so on. Maybe it is overly optimistic for me to worry that too many white people will be interested enough in Africana philosophy to want to specialize in it, but it is a catch-22. I want to conclude my thoughts on postsupremacist philosophy by stressing that, insofar as I am advocating that postsupremacist philosophy should play the shaping role in the continuing development of the discipline, this must be through the leadership of those people from whose experiences postsupremacist philosophy springs. To the extent that anyone chooses to specialize in the philosophy of what she is not, this must be a path tread lightly and carefully. She should follow in the footsteps and hear the words of those from whose experiences the philosophy stems, and take upon herself only the task of clearing the path for more philosophers from those groups who will come after her.

Notes

1. Anna Stubblefield, *Ethics along the Color Line* (Ithaca: Cornell University Press, 2005).
2. Clevis Headley, "Delegitimizing the Normativity of 'Whiteness': A Critical Africana Philosophical Study of the Metaphoricity of 'Whiteness,'" in *What White Looks Like: African-American Philosophers on the Whiteness Question*, ed. George Yancy (New York: Routledge, 2004), 87–106.
3. Lewis Gordon, "Critical Reflections on Three Popular Tropes in the Study of Whiteness," in *What White Looks Like: African-American Philosophers on the Whiteness Question*, ed. George Yancy (New York: Routledge, 2004), 173–94.
4. María Lugones, "On the Logic of Pluralist Feminism," in *Feminist Ethics*, ed. Claudia Card (Lawrence: University Press of Kansas, 1991), 41.
5. Noel Ignatiev and John Garvey, "Abolish the White Race," in *Race Traitor*, ed. Noel Ignatiev and John Garvey (New York: Routledge, 1996), 9–14.
6. David Roediger, *Towards the Abolition of Whiteness* (New York: Verso, 1994).
7. George Breitman, ed., *Malcolm X Speaks* (New York: Grove Press, 1966), 221.
8. Charles Mills, *Blackness Visible* (Ithaca: Cornell University Press, 1998), xv.
9. Lucius Outlaw, *On Race and Philosophy* (New York: Routledge, 1996), 24.
10. Outlaw, 29.

6

Racialization as an Aesthetic Production: What Does the Aesthetic Do for Whiteness and Blackness and Vice Versa?

Monique Roelofs
Hampshire College

RACIAL FORMATIONS ARE AESTHETIC PHENOMENA and aesthetic practices are racialized structures. A theory of the nature of race and racism, at macro- as well as micro-levels of social organization, as a matter of large-scale cultural forces as well as everyday experience, in the realm of the personal as well as the impersonal, must address the place of the aesthetic in processes of racialization.[1] Correlatively, a theory of the aesthetic as a philosophical category—a category of experience, production, and analysis—must account for the ways in which structures of aesthetic exchange channel racial passions and perceptions.

This chapter develops a philosophical framework for understanding the interconnections among aesthetic and racial formations. It also points to avenues for moving toward novel alignments of racial and aesthetic schemes that this framework brings into view.

In order to think through the links among aesthetic and racial formations, I identify two interrelated but nonetheless distinct lines of interaction among aesthetic and racial phenomena. The first line of interaction consists in a phenomenon I call "racialized aestheticization," which pertains to the ways in which racial formations support aesthetic constructions. The second line of interaction is "aesthetic racialization," which concerns the ways in which aesthetic formations support racialized constructions. While these phenomena are inseparable collaborators in the production of racialized aesthetic structures, for analytical and transformative purposes it is crucial to recognize the specific contributions each factor makes to the larger aesthetic and racial fabric.

I trace several forms of racialized aestheticization and aesthetic racialization in historical writings by David Hume and Immanuel Kant. These forms are not unique to the eighteenth century but are both replicated and resisted in contemporary works by Jamaica Kincaid, Agnès Varda, Franz Fanon, Paule Marshall, Angela Davis, and others. In readings of these historical and contemporary works, I make the complexities of the operative forms of aesthetic racialization and racialized aestheticization legible, by analyzing these phenomena as elements of a cultural system I call "aesthetic relationality." By this, I mean a dynamic network of aesthetically generated and aesthetically productive relationships that agents inhabit vis-à-vis one another and vis-à-vis artworks and other aesthetic objects and environments.[2] A perspective on culture in terms of aesthetic relationships recognizes that the aestheticized and aestheticizing dimensions of whiteness and blackness inevitably put into play the full gamut of social and subjective determinants, such as class and gender.[3] A relational theory of the aesthetic postulates a layered texture of interconnections among aesthetic forms of signification and modalities of cultural positioning such as blackness, whiteness, gender, ethnicity, colonial background, and class. More generally, it brings into view ways in which subjectivity, identity, and culture implicate aesthetic structures, and in which aesthetic structures implicate modalities of cultural positioning. At the same time, a theory of aesthetic relationality draws out possibilities for alternative constellations of aesthetic and racialized subjectivity. It exposes the aesthetic as a social technology that must be retooled, an art of constructing and deconstructing formations of whiteness and blackness, that reaches into the minutiae as well as the broader outlines of our racialized, gendered, and classed lives.

Through its structure and thematics, the present book explicitly invites white philosophers to speak and be read *as* white commentators on whiteness, and black philosophers *as* black analysts of blackness. My chapter interrupts this organization of authorial voices and its concomitant modes of reading, with respect to both the text's focus and its address to the reader. I have two reasons for this. One, I see whiteness and blackness in the most significant sense of these terms as social constructions that are inextricably intertwined with one another as well as other markers of social identity and difference. This means that theorizing whiteness involves theorizing blackness and vice versa.[4] A framework that has whites focus solely on whiteness and blacks on blackness is too restrictive. Whites have a theoretical need and an ethical responsibility to think about blackness, to understand theories and artworks created by blacks, and to comprehend ourselves and our white identities in relation to blacks.[5] In this discussion, I thus examine questions of whiteness as well as blackness.

Two, the work of critique makes it crucial that we venture to speak, analyze, and experience *across* the cultural positionings that have been mediated by already given social categories. This need not amount to a self-serving occlusion of one's positionality, an unselfconscious imposition of one's perspective, or a naïve flaunting of the limitations of one's situated condition, but must proceed in forms that are (1) explicitly de-naturalized, that is to say, distanced from authentication by mere testimony, (2) theoretically and politically driven, and (3) productive of progressive reconfigurations of the categories that are fundamental to our social positionings. It is such forms of knowledge production that I am after in this text's address. By elaborating philosophical interconnections between writings and artworks by whites and blacks, it is possible to do historically grounded conceptual work that I take to be central to a critical account of the intersection of aesthetics and race. The links between aesthetics and race have been so underexplored in philosophy that basic theoretical stage setting is in order, some of which I hope to undertake in this chapter.

I begin by examining the links that philosophers have traditionally forged between the aesthetic and whiteness/blackness.

1. Enlightenment Connections between Whiteness, Blackness, and the Aesthetic

Enlightenment philosophers such as Hume and Kant have implicitly aestheticized whiteness. They have enlisted the aesthetic in the service of white processes of cultivation and construed whiteness as an aesthetic achievement. They have mobilized aesthetic modes of creation, reception, and interaction toward white cultural goals, goals that have been defined against blackness. Conscripting aesthetic passions and modes of exchange in the project of white culture formation, and distancing these passions and modes of exchange from blackness, they have, then, articulated forms of aesthetic racialization. Correlatively, Hume and Kant have also established forms of racialized aestheticization. It is modes of creation, perception, and interaction that support white subjectivity that they have identified as aesthetic, and it is modes of creation, perception, and interaction that support black subjectivity that they have denominated as uncultivated and lacking in taste. Construing the aesthetic along lines that render it effective in light of white cultural goals and orienting it against blackness, they have racialized it as white.

In this section, I examine a pattern of historically influential connections that Hume and Kant forge between the aesthetic and whiteness/blackness.[6] These connections are primarily located in the conceptual structures outlined by these thinkers, rather than in their overt statements. It is the subtexts of Hume's and Kant's writings that provide access to their constructions of whiteness and blackness, constructions that have been shaped, among other things, as we shall see, with the help of ideas about gender, class, and heterosexuality. A detailed analysis of these constructions is critical to an understanding of the experiences and desires that bind the categories of race and the aesthetic. I begin with Hume who regards the aesthetic, understood on the model of "taste," as a civilizing force.

Race and Taste in Hume's Philosophy of Culture

Racialized aestheticization, in Hume, emerges in the first instance from the ways in which differentiating categories such as race, class, and gender affect the distribution, the structure, and the functioning of taste. Aesthetic racialization, in Hume, derives from the alleged civilizing effects of taste. Hume makes taste central to the individual's and the nation's entry into and level of civilization and humanity. That given, a further kind of racialized aestheticization emerges as the acquisition of taste is rendered desirable on account of taste's cultivating effects. Racialized aestheticization and aesthetic racialization thus turn out to collaborate closely in Hume, as I indicate below. Both phenomena have their philosophical origins in the connections Hume forges between taste and the faculty of reason and between taste and the appropriate management of the passions. Hume sees taste as drawing on and productive of adequate levels of reason and passion. I first examine taste's ties to reason and next consider its links with the passions, which, in turn, affect questions of rationality.

The connection between reason and taste gives rise to the following form of racialized aestheticization in Hume's philosophy of culture. For Hume, the exercise of reason is fundamental to the operation of taste ("Standard" 16–17; "Delicacy" 26–27).[7] A high level of reason, however, is the prerogative of white, middle-class European males. Hume considers black men and women, white women, and lower-class or "common" white men inferior in rationality.[8] Given the centrality of reason to taste, in Hume's scheme, deficient rational capacities translate into a diminished taste. True taste is then reserved for white, European, middle-class males who go through a requisite process of cultivation, involving practice, the making of comparisons, and a freeing from prejudice ("Standard" 13–17). Indeed, Hume labels aesthetic preferences and pleasures that he ascribes to peasants, Indians, workers, and middle-class women, among other things, "course," "vulgar," "disagreeable," "insipid," "obvious," "idle," "harsh," "uninteresting," and "trifling" ("Standard" 14; "Simplicity" 43; "Refinement" 55; "Essay" 38; "Study" 97).

The realm of deficient taste is not a homogenous field. Hume diversifies this domain by race, class, gender, and ethnicity. It is worth taking a brief look at the structurations introduced through the category of gender because this clarifies the complexly gendered and whitened structure the aesthetic acquires on Hume's theory. Hume accords "women of sense and education" ("Essay" 40) a restricted form of taste. Given Hume's deprecating views of blacks, upper and lower classes, and his appreciative views of France and Britain ("Refinement" 57; "National"), this designation seems to apply to French or British middle-class women.[9] While white middle-class men's taste is supposed to range over all sources of beauty and deformity, including in particular, artworks and other cultural achievements ("works of genius"), the taste of sensible and educated women is restricted to objects and practices in their immediate surroundings ("Essay" 38). These women's taste also takes on a different structure from white men's. Unlike white men's taste, white women's taste is not guided by rules ("Essay" 40). It is also sensitive to perversion by women's "tender and amorous disposition" (41), a disposition that, in Hume's view, can legitimately affect young, white men's aesthetic judgments ("Standard" 20) without betraying a distorted taste. In spite of the tendency of female taste to slide into degeneracy, white women excel in two limited aesthetic domains, namely, the genre labeled "polite writings" ("Essay" 40), which includes novels; and the conduct of the domestic sphere, which encompasses "the ornaments of life, of dress, equipage, and the ordinary decencies of behavior" ("Delicacy" 172, textual variant, 1741–1770 editions). Taste is thus intricately gendered and racialized. Taste's gendering is part and parcel of its specific racialized and racializing structure and its racialization is part and parcel of its gendered and gendering structure.[10]

While white women are able to attain a special, limited form of taste, black men and women do not seem to be allotted any level of taste and, furthermore, are denied the possibility of acquiring it. As is well-known, Hume considers blacks "naturally inferior" to whites. He declares that black nations have not attained civilization, arts, or sciences. He infamously dismisses the idea that a black man might qualify as "a man of parts and learning" ("National" 306n). Hume excludes blacks thus not only from taste but also from the possibility of aesthetic education. Taste is the prerogative of white, middle-class males, and in a diminished variety, of a narrow group of white women. Hume's racialized, gendered, and class-based distribution of reason leads to an unequal distribution of the propensity for taste, and more than that, to an implicit coding of taste in terms of racial, gender, and class difference. We encounter here, then, the phenomenon of racialized aestheticization. Grounding racialized aestheticization initially in the link between taste and reason, Hume carries it further by connecting taste with the passions, thus implementing a version of aesthetic racialization, in the following way.

Hume sees taste as a civilizing factor. One of the ways in which Hume takes taste to civilize the individual is by regulating the passions. In Hume's view, "delicacy of sentiment," which is the central ingredient of taste, enables one to put into order another kind of delicacy, namely "delicacy of passion," that is to say, a sensitivity to the "good or ill accidents of life," which include, for example, small injuries, favors, and good fortune ("Delicacy" 26). Hume holds delicacy of passion responsible for an excessive degree of emotionality, which he sees as interfering with "the right enjoyment" of things (25). For this reason, delicacy of passion must be kept in check. Delicacy of sentiment, and therefore taste, is the only and most proper means of curtailing delicacy of passion (26). Clearing away obstacles to "right enjoyment," taste thus takes on great importance in the formation of white, moral personhood, as imagined by Hume.

Through its effects on the passions, taste enters deeply into the formation of white moral personhood and social agency, for Hume. Hume envisions five specific ways in which taste enables one to appropriately organize one's passions, writing the aesthetic into the minute structures of an individual's existential stance. For Hume, taste (1) corrects the passions; (2) brings them under the agent's control; (3) intensifies a respectable form of happiness; (4) refines the passions; (5) promotes passions that render one sociable. Each of these effects on the passions are civilizing factors.[11] Because taste is distributed differentially, and civilizes the individual, civilized status is distributed differentially. Hume extends the racialization of taste, then, to the level of civilization. Taste supports the cultivation of white, middle-class subjects, and at a more general level, the establishment of white civilization. Racialized aestheticization (the racial exclusiveness of taste) thus contributes to aesthetic racialization (the racial exclusiveness of the civilized standing generated by way of taste).

By examining the ways in which taste is taken to effect an appropriate management of the passions, we can bring into view the aesthetic forces from which Hume imagines white civilized existence to emerge. Taste influences the passions in the following ways: (1) By "cultivating a relish in the liberal arts" the individual is able to strengthen his judgment. Equipped with "juster notions of life," the man of taste comes to withdraw his attention from "many things which please or afflict others" (27), and instead, to focus on what truly matters in life. Bringing a person's sensitivity in conformity with adequate insights into life, taste functions then as a corrective to an excess of passion. (2) Taste brings the passions under control as it enables the man of taste to take his happiness in his own hands. Hume believes "we are pretty much masters of what books we shall read, what diversions we shall partake of, and what company we shall keep" (26).

The exercise of taste allows, then, for a controlled form of happiness, a kind of happiness that accords the tasteful subject an optimal level of personal autonomy. (3) Taste enhances a virtuous kind of happiness. In Hume's view, the man of taste "is more happy by what pleases his taste, than by what gratifies his appetites, and receives more enjoyment from a poem, or a piece of reasoning, than the most expensive luxury can afford" (26). For Hume, this affective and conative shift produces a morally praiseworthy state of affairs, one which everyone would prefer "when everything is balanced" (25) and to which every wise man aspires (26). (4) In Hume's view, taste refines the passions: "[A cultivated taste] . . . improves our sensibility for all the tender and agreeable passions; at the same time that it renders the mind incapable of the rougher and more boisterous emotions" (27; see also "Rise" 90). Hume notes that the study of "beauties" (read: aesthetically good works of fine art and other cultural productions) improves the temper and provokes "a certain elegance of sentiment to which the rest of mankind are strangers. The emotions which they excite are soft and tender." Taste thus refines the passions. (5) More specifically, taste promotes passions that are productive of adequate social bonds and, in this way, works to refine social life. Hume claims that the perusal of, for example, poetry, music, and painting, produces "an agreeable melancholy, which, of all dispositions of the mind, is the best suited to love and friendship." In his view, taste inspires suitable social passions by enabling the man of taste to make precise and detailed judgments of other people's characters (26–28). The man of taste can thus be seen to combine a high level of delicacy of sentiment with an appropriately measured degree of delicacy of passion as well as a third kind of sensitivity, an enhanced social sensibility, which I will call "delicacy of socialization." Taste deepens love and friendship by "confining our choice to few people, and making us indifferent to the company and conversation of the greater part of men" (27). This results, again, in refinement, at the affective as well as social level.

> One that has well digested his knowledge both of books and men, has little enjoyment but in the company of a few select companions. He feels too sensibly, how much all the rest of mankind fall short of the notions which he has entertained. And, his affections being thus confined within a narrow circle, no wonder he carries them further than if they were more general and undistinguished. The gaiety and frolic of a bottle companion improves with him into a solid friendship; and the ardors of a youthful appetite become an elegant passion. (28)

Through its effects on the passions, taste instigates "appropriate" social bonds among individuals while eroding less suitable affiliations.[12] By allowing for an adequately managed and refined set of passions, as well as a proper social circle, taste enables the individual to reach a high level of civilization. Cultivation, for Hume, is thus an aesthetic process, one that is fostered by the faculty of taste. As we have seen, Hume has differentiated taste along racial, gender, and class lines. Implemented as an element of the cultivating process, taste inscribes these differentiations into civilization, its product. Cultivation, as an aesthetic production, is a racially exclusive attainment, that is to say, an arrangement that enables white, middle-class men of taste to seek out one another's company to their mutual satisfaction and edification. Racialized aestheticization (taste's racialized nature) can be seen to support aesthetic racialization (white civilization as structured and produced by way of taste). Both reach into the minutiae of an individual's psychosocial identity.

At this point, as suggested above, Hume is able to motivate the acquisition of taste and interactions with artworks by their role in the civilizing project. Aspirations to white cultivation offer a powerful motive for engagement with art and for the attainment of taste. We thus encounter here a further kind of racialized aestheticization, that is to say, a new way in which racial structures support aesthetic structures. Taste owes its importance, in part, to the white cultural goals it fosters. Hume renders the aesthetic attractive on account of its civilizing effects. Racialized aestheticization, for Hume, resides then, in the first instance, in the cultural differentiations built into the notion of taste (through the link with reason), and in the second instance, in the importance taste derives from its cultivating labors (its affective and social impact).

The whitening effects of taste are in fact more widespread for Hume than I have indicated so far. Taste's civilizing force transfers its effects from the individual to the national level, at which Hume takes taste to improve knowledge, productivity, pleasure, and social life. He considers matters of taste such as luxury, refinement, and progress in the arts necessary to the economic and political well-being of the state. Taste functions in Hume's theory to build culture and, more specifically, to produce what Hume calls "humanity." Accordingly, he institutes aesthetic racialization at the level of the nation. His reasoning is as follows.

In Hume's view, the arts of luxury and the liberal arts depend on refined taste or sentiment ("Rise" 83).[13] Hume attributes four humanizing effects to refinement in the arts and refinement in the gratification of the senses. I list each of these humanizing effects because they turn out to be carriers of aesthetic racialization. They also indicate what precise and deeply ingrained forms such racialization takes. One, refinements in the arts and in the gratification of the senses make humans more active and productive ("Refinement" 49–50, 59). They counteract laziness (an overdose of indolence, idleness, sloth, and repose). They enable individuals to derive more happiness from their work. They help to keep desire and gratification within the bounds of "true" and proper pleasure (50–51). Accordingly, they sustain the level of virtue that marks refined society. Two, refinements in the arts strengthen the faculty of reason.

They provide occasion for the exercise and refinement of reason (52), inspire curiosity, and invigorate the mind (49–50). Three, refinements in the arts encourage conversation, sociability, and interaction between males and females, which has the benefit of softening men's temper (50, 51). Four, initial refinement produces yet more refinement. Hume attaches cultivating effects to the "taste, genius, and spirit [. . .] of a whole people" (50). He postulates a "spirit of the age" in which the arts mutually enhance one another ("Rise" 75).[14] Refinement thus is a phenomenon that spreads (predominantly among those subjects who are genuinely capable of it, that is to say, white upper/middle class males, but also, in carefully guarded ways, among these males and their white, female, social companions). The result of these four interacting refinements is an increase in humanity, which, for Hume, is the mark that distinguishes polished or civilized societies from barbarous and rude nations ("Refinement" 51, 53, 55). Taste, for Hume, functions then as one of several factors that are productive of the form of humanity which he places at the heart of civilization. We encounter here aesthetic racialization at the level of a nation's culture and its alleged measure of humanity. At this level, as we have seen, aesthetic racialization implicates not only ideas about reason and the passions, but also questions about work, productivity, happiness, sociability, and heterosexuality. Hume weaves aesthetic racialization deeply into the fabric of cultural life, immersing virtually every parameter of human interaction in a practice of micro-aestheticization that is also a practice of micro-racialization.

We have seen that taste, for Hume, regulates the nature and the level of a person's activity, passivity, passion, and pleasure. Capacities for reason and social judgment are sharpened. Refined relationships emerge. Members of the white middle-class become socialized, cultivated, and humanized. The nation enjoys mounting levels of national productivity, happiness, virtue, and civilization. Appropriate forms of cultural production, exchange, and interconnection take shape.

The contribution of taste to the civilizing process amounts to a form of aesthetic racialization. Hume aestheticizes whiteness in the sense that he construes white civilization, in part, as an aesthetic achievement, a project to be attained through the operations of taste. As noted earlier, aesthetic racialization, initially supported by racialized aestheticization, at the present stage, feeds back into the workings of racialized aestheticization. Hume values taste in part on account of its civilizing labor. Taste functions as a conduit for passions for whiteness. Taste is racialized, that is to say, its acquisition and exercise are partially motivated by desires for whiteness. More than that, taste is structured so as to secure white cultural goals. Hume organizes taste in such a fashion that desires for whiteness, at the individual and national levels, can inspire the acquisition of taste and the engagement with art.

What shape does whiteness take, in this scheme? I have already indicated that aestheticized whiteness pertains to the "adequate" regulation of individual passion as well as to the "virtuous" and "pleasurable" intensification of human productivity. More needs to be said about the modes of cultural production, exchange, and interconnection that are instituted through the cultivating operations of taste. Taste is in the first instance called upon to establish homosocial cultural ties among tasteful white men who engage in cultivated and cultivating connections with and over artworks and other cultural objects. In the second instance, taste functions to institute heterosexual bonds among white men and women, who mutually civilize one another. Taste realizes this task in the following way.

Civilization and taste make different demands on differentially positioned social agents. White women are asked to extend their softening influence to the tempers and rational minds of white men ("Rise" 92). They are imagined to contribute to the realization of a tasteful society by entering into conversation with white men, which allows white men to develop their taste and manners, to connect with the world, and to warm their hearts.[15] It is white women's role to make their cultivating influence available to white men ("Essay" 38; "Refinement" 51; "Rise" 92; "Study" 97). In turn, white men are asked to extend reason, knowledge, and gallantry to white women.[16] White men and women's differential labors of taste collaborate in the process of realizing what is seen as civilized society.[17] Hume imagines taste then to support cultivation by fostering appropriate affective and aesthetic interactions and affiliations among white men and women.

Absent the cultivating company of tasteful white men and women, and absent, also, for Hume, the requisite level of reason, which as we have seen, is central to taste, blacks are excluded from the civilizing process taste makes available to whites. Black men and women are placed outside the aesthetic dynamic that is productive of civilization; they have no place in the white, heterosexual arrangement that exemplifies taste. Moral, epistemic, affective, and aesthetic refinement is circulated among white men and women. The labor of taste demands that blacks stay away from the relevant affective and aesthetic bonds.[18]

Hume has outlined a process of aesthetic racialization. He inscribes a racializing trajectory into culture that is driven by taste. The aesthetic is complicit in the specific form of racialization that amounts to white culture building. Hume construes whiteness, understood in the sense of white civilization, as an aesthetic achievement. White racialization is created and sustained through taste, which is acquired through the process of creating and responding to art and other cultural objects.[19] Besides a process of aesthetic racialization, Hume has also delineated a form of racialized aestheticization. In the

Humean picture, taste and art-appropriate experience work to satisfy desires for distinctive modes of cultural interaction among whites and to reward aspirations toward white civilization. Hume has the passion to act and judge in conformity with taste function as a passion to enter into cultivating affiliations with white men and women, and to place oneself at a remove from bonds with black men and women. I see here the formation of a network of racialized relationships that is supported by and conducive to taste.[20] Civilization is imagined as a web of relationships centered around flows of products and modes of exchange that are both racialized and aestheticized.[21] In short, culture, as theorized by Hume, emerges from the interacting labors of racialized aestheticization and aesthetic racialization.

Race and Taste in Kant's Philosophy of Culture

Immanuel Kant replicates some of the above strategies of aesthetic racialization and racialized aestheticization but, as I indicate shortly, he also adds an influential move of his own to the already existing techniques, thus substantially enriching the repertoire of whitened and whitening aesthetic tactics that we inherit from the philosophical tradition.

Kant's account of refinement in the *Observations on the Feeling of the Beautiful and Sublime* parallels the cultural arrangement in which Hume sees white, middle-class men and women generate and exchange moral, epistemic, and affective goods. Like Hume, he envisions differential, hierarchized, and collaborating moral and aesthetic trajectories for white men and women. White men are asked to offer nobility, sublimity, and insight to white women (95, 102n), who are marked by mental deficiency (94). White women make complaisance and beauty available to men, rendering them more gentle, polite, and refined (95–96, 102n). Kant closes this exchange off to blacks and to a lesser extent to other nonwhites. He considers the mental capacities of black people inferior to those of whites (110–11, 113) and finds them incapable of more than trifling feelings (110). Since he defines taste as a faculty of *fine* feeling (46), this strongly suggests that he imagines black men and women as lacking any measure of taste.[22] Kant's constructions of racialized aestheticization and aesthetic racialization in the *Observations* thus parallel Hume's.

Kant shares with Hume also an interest in establishing comparative aesthetic hierarchies across cultures.[23] In evaluating the taste of "the Arab," "the Chinese," and other ethnicities, Kant places himself unhesitatingly and without argument in the position of the person who is able to recognize true and false taste. His recognition of a variety of tastes is fully explicit: "If [. . .] we cast a glance at history, we see the taste of men [. . .] continually taking on variable forms" (114). While he indeed posits links between taste and culture, these links do not enter into his overt account of the conditions of possibility of taste.[24] The phenomenon of ethnic, racial, class-based, and gendered diversity of taste is not given an explicit theoretical role in the context of Kant's *critical* account of the conditions of possibility for true taste.[25] In the *Critique of Judgment*, Kant grounds the general validity of the true judgment of taste in the postulate of a common sense, that is to say, in a set of cognitive faculties that human beings are assumed to have in common (pars. 19–22; 40). He understands these faculties as *natural* rather than cultural dispositions. That they are not natural I take critics such as Pierre Bourdieu ("Historical"), Richard Shusterman (*Scandal*), and Sylvia Wynter ("Rethinking") to have argued persuasively. As these thinkers have indicated, Kant's theory of taste privileges appreciative conditions and values that must be associated with educated, leisured, white, socially quiescent, masculine, middle-class subject-positions.

The difficulty, however, is not simply the false or impossible universalization of such appreciative conditions. From the perspective of the interactions between aesthetics and race, a further ambivalent deployment of whiteness must be noted. On the one hand, Kant can be seen to rely on comparative cultural evaluations. He announces, for example, that aesthetic judgments guided by charm and emotion are "barbarous" (par. 13), that is to say, uncultivated, in a manner associated with a status outside culture. He suggests that the aesthetic attractions of Caribs and Iroquois are more motivated by sensation than those of observers at a higher stage of civilization (par. 41). He tendentiously deploys figures of non-Europeans as examples of individuals whose taste somehow fails, such as the "Iroquois sachem" whose aesthetic perception he denounces as interested, rather than appropriately disinterested (par. 2). Given the *schematic* nature of Kant's conception of aesthetic experience and the unclarity and underdeveloped nature of important theoretical concepts such as charm, emotion, interest, and disinterestedness, Kant's cultural examples and judgments cannot straightforwardly be dismissed as inessential. The theory simply does not offer enough specification of its basic concepts. Kant's crosscultural comparisons help to substantiate these concepts. However, Kantians are able to dismiss crosscultural examples and evaluations as incidental to the theory by reference to the postulate of the common sense.

The postulate of the common sense protects Kant from having to provide a reasoned account of the cultural preconditions that his version of the natural implicitly makes relevant or irrelevant to the determination of what counts as aesthetic. Consequently, his deculturalizing move stands as an open invitation to an uncritical channeling of cultural preconditions that are likely to go unmarked for the simple reason that they happen to be associated with cultural identities and behaviors that have been normalized in Western culture, in short, with white modes of being.

Kant implicitly appeals to cultural conditions while at the same time insulating the aesthetically relevant appreciative faculties from being understood to be affected by cultural conditioning. Precisely by overtly *decentering* considerations of culture, the *Critique* is able to rely on normative connections between culture and taste. Kant's cultural gestures make their effects because they are masked by an encompassing deculturalizing move. He makes white, middle-class masculinity effective by ostensibly rendering it incidental. Kant here takes advantage of a common feature of whiteness, namely its function as an unmarked basis of normativity. The invisibility of securely established, white, middle-class masculinity participates in the *modus operandi* of this subject position in Kant's aesthetics. It is on account of the invisibility of this position that Kant is able to ground the general validity of judgment of taste in a *sensus communis*, without being theoretically impelled to critically reflect on possible connections or disconnections between this universalizable cognitive disposition and the differential processes of enculturation that underwrite his comparative evaluations of varieties of taste.

In sum, Kantian aesthetics renders white, middle-class masculinity foundational aesthetic power by dismissing the relevance of cultural conditions. It is in virtue of the invisibility of normative whiteness that Kant's aesthetic system can appear to be founded on the postulate of a common sense without essentially seeming to implicate a series of unfounded crosscultural aesthetic hierarchies. Whiteness functions, in Kant's scheme, not as one ethnicity among others, but as an ethnicity that carries its normative status, cultural specificity, and existential content into his conception of art-appropriate faculties and perceptions.[26]

At the level of aesthetic relationships this plays out in the following two ways. One, Kant's (and Hume's) aesthetics have historically provided a theoretical basis for the influential view that takes art to have its home in the public sphere, and that construes aesthetic meanings as public meanings, that is to say, as meanings that are accessible through the operation of common appreciative faculties. The notion of the public that is hereby in effect is basically the notion of a community of subjects equipped with generalizable appreciative faculties.[27] However, as many have argued, what has *seemed* to be public or generally accessible is in fact not truly or possibly public or generally accessible; the concept of the public functions in many ways as a stand-in for white, male, middle-class subject-positions.[28] Given the Enlightenment heritage in aesthetic theory, the racialized and racializing substructure that deploys but at the same time *masks* white normativity has been transported into contemporary notions of art's public functioning, where it continues to underwrite patterns of aesthetic production and experience. Contemporary philosophy has built its views of art's place in culture around a precritical, racialized, and racializing aesthetic.[29] This has a wide-ranging set of effects that must be studied in detail.

Two, deculturalization in aesthetics stands as an open invitation for white people to imagine themselves as standing above their cultural needs, untouched by culture's interactive, material supports. When white culture becomes an invisible datum, an unmarked given, the cultures of those who are not normatively white, that is to say, of white people's "others," can acquire hypervisibility, as many have suggested. In the plane of crosscultural and intracultural difference, "other" people's cultural needs and supports are then easily dismissed as extraneous, incidental, a burden these people bring with them, or at best, a momentary aesthetic thrill. The sphere of normative culture is thus whitened. White people's various "others" can then be relegated to an ornamental status.[30] The appearance ensures that they are excessively bound to their specific cultural locale, powerless to transcend their specific conditions, unlike normative whites, who freely move in universal terrain. Aesthetic deculturalization facilitates these well-known cultural prejudices.

We encounter in Kant's writings structures of aesthetic racialization and racialized aestheticization that are masked under a conception of aesthetic universality. Kant enlists the aesthetic in support of white civilization. Grounding taste in the *sensus communis*, he renders the aesthetic normativity of whiteness invisible and decenters the hierarchized cultural standards underwriting his aesthetic system. Both Kant and Hume exclude white women, lower-class men, and nonwhite men and women from the ordinary developmental processes that amount to the cultivation of taste. They have formulated aesthetic systems on which the desire for civilization *de facto*—in virtue of its structural, though not necessarily fully conscious or intentional functioning—amounts to a desire for participation in an exclusionary aesthetic system. In short, they have delineated a network of relationships that is supported by interacting forms of aestheticization and racialization. They have thus written racialization and aestheticization into the heart of the notion of culture.

2. Contemporary Figurations of Aesthetic Racialization and Racialized Aestheticization

Contemporary cultures are organized around multiple, interconnected varieties of aesthetic racialization and racialized aestheticization. The present section traces several of these forms in work by Jamaica Kincaid, Agnès Varda, and Franz Fanon. These artists and writers, I argue, have each more or less explicitly emphasized the subjective and cultural importance of everyday aesthetic activities. They have expanded the spectrum of legitimately aesthetic agents as well as the scope of aesthetically normative modes of perception, creation, and interaction, as compared to Hume and Kant. This is a crucial step toward clarifying the workings of racialized aestheticization and aesthetic racialization. However, by implicitly imagining the aesthetic to follow cultural delineations produced through racialized aestheticization and aesthetic racialization, these thinkers and artists nonetheless underestimate the cultural possibilities the aesthetic holds in stock, and sidestep complex connections among aesthetics and race in ways that are reminiscent of Hume and Kant.

An Aesthetic Stand-off

Jamaica Kincaid's novel *Lucy* is the story of a young black woman from an unnamed Caribbean island, who arrives in an unnamed city in North America to take up employment as an au-pair in a white family. The family consists of a mother, Mariah, a father, and four children, who are put partially under Lucy's care. Written in Lucy's voice, the novel offers her observations on her friendship with Mariah and her developing relationship with her current and previous home countries. Kincaid depicts Lucy's consciousness as an *aesthetic* consciousness. Lucy's experience foremost takes an aesthetic form. It consists in sensory impressions of elements such as food, clothes, sounds, bodies, fields, the sun, and music—elements whose subjective qualities are shown to reflect her ambitions and dreams, her history, and her understandings of her new surroundings. Kincaid depicts aesthetic experience as Lucy's primary means by which she makes herself present in her new environment. Aesthetic experience is represented as the medium through which Lucy establishes meanings and negotiates connections in novel cultural terrain. The importance aesthetic experience holds for Lucy as well as Mariah, is evinced in a clash between Mariah's and Lucy's different, personal, and cultural structures of aesthetic desire and value. Lucy describes a conversation in which Mariah longingly looks forward to the arrival of Spring.

> She said, "Have you ever seen daffodils pushing their way up out of the ground? And when they're in bloom and all massed together, a breeze comes along and makes them do a curtsy to the lawn stretching out in front of them. Have you ever seen that? When I see that, I feel so glad to be alive." And I thought, So Mariah is made to feel alive by some flowers bending in the breeze. How does a person get to be that way? (17)

Instead of the affective resonance desired by Mariah, Lucy responds with critical distance. For Lucy, the image of curtsying daffodils carries less enlivening connotations. She recalls a successful recital of a poem at "Queen Victoria Girls' School":

> After I was done, everybody stood up and applauded with an enthusiasm that surprised me, and later they told me how nicely I had pronounced every word, how I had placed just the right amount of special emphasis in places where that was needed, and how proud the poet, now long dead, would have been to hear his words ringing out of my mouth. I was then at the height of my two-facedness: that is, outside I seemed one way, inside I was another; [. . .] [I]nside I was making a vow to erase from my mind, line by line, every word of that poem. The night after I had recited the poem, I dreamt, continuously it seemed, that I was being chased down a narrow cobbled street by bunches and bunches of those same daffodils that I had vowed to forget, and when finally I fell down from exhaustion they all piled on top of me, until I was buried deep underneath them and was never seen again. (17–18)

In withholding empathy from Mariah, Lucy disengages from the British colonial cultural project and distances herself from a projective relation with nature, celebrated in the poem to which I take the passage to allude, namely, Wordsworth's "I Wandered Lonely as a Cloud."[31] Kincaid ends Lucy's and Mariah's aesthetic confrontation by having each take a step back from the other (18–19).[32] As the novel proceeds, this gesture is followed by similar attempts at aesthetic sharing on Mariah's part, which repeatedly provoke distancing moves on Lucy's part, who ultimately leaves the family to pursue photography.[33] Aesthetic clashes in *Lucy* represent a stand-off between an aesthetic that is implicitly figured as North American, middle-class, white and one that is imagined as immigrant, Afro-Caribbean, middle-class, black. Kincaid juxtaposes two aesthetic worlds. Structures of aesthetic desire are suggested to coincide with structures of racialization. She depicts racialized aesthetic consciousness as central to Lucy's and Mariah's personalities, structures of desire, and existential stances. This centrality carries over to Lucy's and Mariah's friendship. Although Lucy and Mariah are described as loving one another, the aesthetic, in Kincaid's book, exemplifies a relational deadlock, limiting further negotiation of the friendship. Kincaid imagines the aesthetic then to follow the racial delineations set out in the novel. She accords the aesthetic the power to make present in a relationship profound cultural and personal experiences and differences, and to bring out a need for distancing. This is a significant achievement of the aesthetic and I find it an important strength of the book that it brings this out sharply. At the same time, this produces also a limitation for the notion of the aesthetic that the book implicitly articulates.

Kincaid has staged an aesthetic clash along sharply differentiated racial and cultural lines. There is little crossover or syncretism between Mariah's and

Lucy's aesthetic desires and perceptions.[34] However, aesthetic activities are capable of shifting and diffusing tidy racial categorizations.[35] Aesthetic systems do not simply line up with colonial divides, as discussions of hybridity in literary studies suggest. In matching distinct aesthetic systems with distinct ethnic, cultural, and personal identities, *Lucy* parallels the Enlightenment scheme that channels aesthetic passions along tightly delineated, ethnic paths. Although the book does not represent the clash between Lucy and Mariah as one between barbarism and civilization, like Hume and Kant's theories, it lines aesthetic passions up with cultural identities in an orderly way. Considered as a view of the aesthetic, this all too rigidly stratified system amounts to a diminishment of the powers and complexities of aesthetic racialization and racialized aestheticization.

The Aesthetic as an Aside

In two documentaries, *The Gleaners and I* and *The Gleaners and I: Two Years Later* (France, 2000 and 2002), Agnès Varda articulates a conception of the aesthetic as a form of gleaning. Both documentaries celebrate everyday aesthetic experiences and activities. Varda interviews gleaners of several classes and races, including poor whites picking up loaves of bread at the end of the market, African immigrants making a living by salvaging stoves, middle-class whites picking apples after the harvest, a restaurant chef collecting herbs, and the psychoanalyst Jean Laplanche who registers unintended turns of language. Among these gleaners, Varda also includes herself. We see the filmmaker, digital video camera in hand, gleaning images from paintings, fruits, her hands, her hair, other people, landscapes, and coincidences, such as a "dancing" lens cap. Both documentaries propose a notion of video making in terms of daily activities such as the seeing, touching, recording, gathering, recontextualizing, and assembling of everyday materials. The gleaner/artist playfully devises new functions for things considered to fall short of ordinary standards of usefulness, and thereby creates a new value for otherwise devalued elements.

Varda lends gleaning a double pleasure. She presents the urban and rural spaces traversed in the films as occasions for abundant aesthetic pleasure to those who encounter them with a fresh eye and an open imagination. The videos testify to the joys on offer in the domain of commodified produce and artifacts. But Varda does not simply celebrate the material world. Building on and redeploying aesthetic pleasures anchored in the world of production and consumption, the viewer, artist, and gleaner also encounter a pleasure that is imagined to *elude* institutionalized commodification procedures. Varda accords gleaning the attraction of a gentle subversiveness as it disorients hierarchies of significance that have been encoded in the objects. The double pleasure of bringing out an aesthetic that has already materialized, and of carrying this pleasure nonetheless into unexpected and disparate directions, which then modifies the initial pleasure, is part of the immediate visual delight of seeing old refrigerators refurbished as living quarters for playmobil families or as sites for demonstrations by playmobil activists. Varda also shows the limitations of such playful resignification. Aging and processes of material decay will not be turned about through imaginative redeployment.[36] Neither does Varda redeem current structures of consumption and production. Gleaning includes the rescuing of damaged birds after oil spills, the salvaging of delicious fruits and vegetables whose limited profit margin destines them to rot away as waste, and conversations with homeless individuals who have been dismissed from the work force. Varda's cinematography remains in a constant connection with the underside of socially sanctioned economic life. Nevertheless, Varda's visual study somewhat paradoxically idealizes the aesthetic.

Casting the aesthetic in the shape of gleaning, Varda models it as an aside, something that takes effect *after* an element's designated usefulness has been found lacking, in the margins of the institutions of the market, apart from standardized regimes of production and consumption. At the same time, she complicates the aesthetic's status as an aside by lending it existential centrality. Showing souvenirs collected on a visit to Japan, Varda observes that "it is what I have gleaned that tells me where I have been." It is through individual invention that the gleaner both deploys and counters disenchanting and dehumanizing dimensions of routine economic formations. The videos celebrate the gleaners' and thus also Varda's and the viewer's discovery and framing of aesthetic meanings. The double pleasure of gleaning thereby extends to the activity of artistic and aesthetic looking and making. Yet more broadly, Varda depicts gleaning as a stance toward the physical environment, vis-à-vis the passing of time, in relation to one's body and to other people. This means that the aside paradoxically takes up a crucial existential role. While the centralization of apparent asides, to my mind, plays a significant role in the formation of aesthetic experience,[37] as a picture of the aesthetic this scenario occludes problematic sides of the aesthetic.

The concept of free aesthetic play represents only one side of aesthetic activities and identities. Aesthetic energies are more fundamentally embedded in processes of consumption and production than the idea of gleaning, imagined as a centralized aside, is able to express. Market formations observe aesthetic norms and standards. Aesthetic needs and desires fully participate in structures of consumption and production. Overconsumption, environmental pollution, mass production, and wastefulness are supported by aesthetic passions for objects and experiences. Aesthetic energies are impulses toward consumption and production. These energies are fully complicit in making the world of consumption and production the world it is. While the image of gleaning brings out important life-affirmative dimensions of the aesthetic, it disregards an influential spectrum of aesthetic choices that motivate and maintain economical processes. Of special significance, here, in light of the structure of racialization, is that it renders invisible the formative force the aesthetic wields in the ongoing establishment of culture.

To see the aesthetic as an aside, that is to say, to position it as a dimension of life that is conducted at a distance from economical and political structures, is to set it apart from important aspects of its subjective and cultural labor.[38] It is to bracket the racial importance of the aesthetic and the aesthetic importance of race. It is to screen out the work of aesthetic racialization and racialized aestheticization in favor of a fantasy image of white people as situated outside of a whitened and whitening aesthetic. A notion of the aesthetic as a supplementary factor, a decorative epiphenomenon, housed in the margins of social life, implicitly takes for granted the trajectories of white subject and culture formation. It owes its plausibility to a vision that has already been immersed in these trajectories, one that has securely whitened itself, precisely by way of the cultural powers it is now safely able to overtly disregard. The dominance of whiteness manifests itself in this case, then, in the obfuscation of aesthetic forces that bolster white selves and support white cultural life, as well as in the occlusion of cultural forces that underwrite a white aesthetic. A philosophical perspective that sees the aesthetic as an after- or side effect of moral, political, and epistemic practices participates in a regimen that renders the aesthetic workings and production of whiteness invisible. This fantasy allows whiteness to function as an unmarked basis of normativity with respect to racialization and the aesthetic. Varda's proposed conception of the aesthetic as an aside parallels in this regard Kant's deculturalizing move.[39]

Varda's and Kincaid's appeals to aesthetic dimensions of everyday activities and objects, though different, thus both appear to adopt moves that are familiar from the Enlightenment scheme. The task, then, is to think the aesthetic in a manner that is able to register the full extent to which culture formation is an aesthetic process and to which the aesthetic is racialized.

Racial Oppression as Aesthetic Oppression

Franz Fanon has emphasized the importance of the aesthetic to processes of identity formation. In his view, popular cultural forms such as newspapers, books, advertisements, film, and radio tend to establish and sustain white identities (*Black* 152, 177, 179, 191–92; *Wretched* 209). They do this, among other things, by shaping white worldviews and by providing anecdotes and stories that endorse white myths about blacks (*Black* 111–12, 188).[40] They cause both white and black people to identify with white attitudes and perceptions (146–48, 152–53, 191–92). To counteract the effects of white popular forms on blacks and to give shape to a black voice, Fanon believes it is necessary to create magazines, songs, and history texts that support black modes of socialization (148, 153). Furthermore, he sees "revolutionary" art as contributing to processes of decolonization (*Wretched* 227–32). Aesthetic elements thus bear important cultural weight, on Fanon's analysis. However, Fanon's emphasis on the power of the aesthetic stands in contrast with a strand in his writing that curtails this power. Fanon argues that the colonial system obliterates the culture of colonized nations, destroying their aesthetic rhythms, habits, and artistic creativity (40, 93, 236–38). Accordingly, "[i]t is around the peoples' struggles that African-Negro culture takes on substance, and not around songs, poems, or folklore" (235). Fanon sees no room for new cultural departures under colonial domination (237, 244; *Black* 187). To the contrary, he considers national liberation a condition for culture (*Wretched* 233, 244–45). He notes that under colonial oppression, the struggle for liberation is the only available and exemplary form of culture and creativity (93, 244–45, 247–48). Only the emergence of national consciousness is able to reenergize culture outside of the struggle (36). In Fanon's view, aesthetic change can and will arise at an advanced stage of the anticolonial struggle (238–46).

Fanon has identified important sources of aesthetic racialization (popular arts as instrumental in the realization of white and black cultural goals) as well as racialized aestheticization (popular arts as reflecting whiteness; "the" anticolonial struggle as fostering vital forms of postcolonial culture).[41] While it is important, as Fanon does, to register the aesthetic effects of aesthetic oppression, and while aesthetic oppression indeed dramatically violates the effectiveness and impedes the realizability of specific artistic forms, I believe that such oppression, on the whole, cannot adequately be understood as a general destruction of aesthetic modes and possibilities. Fanon subscribes to an overly diminished view of the aesthetic under oppression, one that makes it hard to recognize powers of resistance that remain unharmed. We encounter here a tension in Fanon's account, for his notion of anticolonial resistance as a form of culture already suggests that certain forms of creativity are retained intactly under colonial oppression and must be made productive. By recognizing the cultural dimensions of resistance, Fanon makes it plausible that where given aesthetic forms are damaged, other aesthetic forms must and do indeed arise. Accordingly, I propose to understand aesthetic oppression, alternatively, violent and unjustifiable restructuring of the aesthetic, that is to say, as a problematic *transformation* of aesthetic rhythms, choices, and possibilities. Aesthetic oppression, so conceived, is not exhausted by its destructive dimension but can be seen to re-establish the terrain from which novel productive forms must inevitably emerge. Fanon's reading of aesthetic oppression as an extinction of aesthetic modes and capacities aligns the aesthetic too closely with a pure, unambivalently valorized national identity. It replicates in this regard Hume's direct alignment of taste and civilization.[42]

In reading aesthetic oppression as cultural obliteration, Fanon downplays the aesthetic energies inherent in fundamental affective, cognitive, and social capacities. Sidestepping these energies, he also misses an important repertoire of political powers and passions. I find it implausible that the anticolonial struggle is able to do the cultural and political labor that it is called upon to do in the absence of the aesthetic capacities manifested in songs, poems, and folklore.[43] I do not see how "the people's struggle," defined as culture, but depleted of aesthetic rhythms, habits, and creativity, could be capable of revitalizing art and culture. The culture of political action is not simply distinguishable from the culture of aesthetic forms (such as "songs"). The performativity, the humor, and the affective intensity of much of Fanon's own writing is testimony to the power aesthetic forms carry *as political elements.* This power does not reduce to aspects of the struggle but amounts at the same time to the power aesthetic forms carry *as aesthetic elements.*[44] Whether they are oppressive or liberatory, racialized processes of culture and identity formation participate in and draw on aesthetic capacities and activities that—for better and for worse—coincide with basic human abilities.

Kincaid, Varda, and Fanon each implicitly challenge aspects of the relational framework inherited from the Humean and Kantian tradition by expanding the spectrum of legitimately aesthetic modes of agency, relationality, creation, perception, and exchange. However, they each also replicate influential aspects of this tradition, underestimate powers and possibilities that are inherent in basic aesthetic capacities, and downplay complexities that attach to the cultural functioning of the aesthetic. Clearly, enlightenment conceptions of aestheticization and racialization are deeply entrenched in artistic and theoretical figurations of aesthetic passions and relationships. These conceptions have come to be anchored in art forms, artistic modes of address, and institutional arrangements. They have been determinative of such fundamental parts of our cultural being that it is difficult to step away from them. Yet, at the same time, outlines of alternative configurations of aesthetic passions and relationships are visible that must be elaborated. In the following section, I consider links between the aesthetic and blackness that, like tendencies in Kincaid, Varda, and Fanon, gesture toward different forms of aesthetic racialization and racialized aestheticization, but challenge whitened and whitening aesthetic relationships further on the points where these three thinkers, as we have seen, observe Enlightenment postulates.

3. Aestheticized and Aestheticizing Blackness and the Reconfiguration of Whitened and Whitening Aesthetic Relationships

In creating and analyzing artworks addressed to black existence, artists, critics, and theorists have given the aesthetic a central role in light of black cultural goals, thus implementing processes of aesthetic racialization. Working toward the establishment of modes of criticism, reception, tradition-, and canon-formation that are adequate to black aesthetic productions, many thinkers have established processes of racialized aestheticization. Others have formulated deconstructive approaches to structures of aesthetic and racial signification that establish a measure of distance from what I take to be entrenched patterns of racialized aestheticization and aesthetic racialization.[45]

This section examines forms of aesthetic racialization and racialized aestheticization that are implicit in what may be called "everyday" aesthetic capacities, identified by Alice Walker, Audre Lorde, Paule Marshall, and Angela Davis. These thinkers each describe aesthetic powers and passions that are inherent in human capabilities that are at work in the conduct of daily, material lives, such as storytelling, sensory perception, ornamentation, speech, and the integration of feeling and understanding. They articulate aesthetic relationships, productions, and interactions that have been ignored by the Enlightenment model of aesthetic exchange. As I indicate below, they also implicitly challenge this model at junctures where Kincaid, Varda, and Fanon have replicated Enlightenment conceptions of culture.

While Varda, as we have seen, puts into play the double pleasures of the somewhat paradoxical logic of a centralized aside, Walker and Lorde insist on the existential and political necessity of the aesthetic. Walker sees art, in the form of storytelling and growing flowers, as work her mother's soul "must have" ("Search" 241). This work, hence, was a daily part of her mother's life (241). She describes her mother's art as an example of the creativity that she takes to have sustained millions of black women (238). For Walker, the aesthetic, then, includes the making of meaning and value "in simple ways" (242), namely by tapping into creative and material resources that are able to energize life, despite prolonged hardship and oppression.[46]

Audre Lorde, likewise, points to the importance of a form of poetry that is grounded in fundamental faculties of thought, feeling, and experience. Poetry, so conceived, in her view, is essential to the survival of feelings that are otherwise kept from developing, due to oppressive social structures. Hence, it enables the kind of freedom that can attach to formulating "the implications of ourselves" ("Poetry" 39). She describes it as "a revelatory distillation of experience," that is to say, as material that is crafted from daily life, which it then also serves to illuminate (36–37). In combining thought and feeling, poetry, according to Lorde, allows feelings to develop into radical ideas, where they come to hint at the realization of new existential possibilities (37, 39). Lorde and Walker thus both insist on the affective and existential necessity of the aesthetic. Highlighting aesthetic media and capacities that they explicitly locate in the context of racialized, classed, and gendered cultural conditions, they implicitly identify sources of racialized aestheticization. Furthermore, in depicting the aesthetic as indispensable to survival, resistance, identity formation, as well as ordinary forms of life, they implicitly describe sources of aesthetic racialization. Paule Marshall and Angela Davis have articulated similar forms of racialized aestheticization and aesthetic racialization.

Marshall affirms the indebtedness of her own literary work to the artistic lessons and standards of excellence passed on to her by other poets, namely her mother and her mother's friends, ordinary, working-class, Barbadian immigrants in New York City, who used to gather in the kitchen after work to talk. Marshall highlights the artfulness of their language, its beauty, originality, irony, exuberance, insight, and wit. She portrays it as an oral art form, which, "in keeping with the African tradition in which art and life are one—was an integral part of their lives" ("Making" 6).[47] Marshall (and with her, Walker and Lorde) clearly take a broader view of the powers of aesthetic racialization than Fanon. As argued above, Fanon recognizes varieties of aesthetic racialization (popular arts' ability to socialize whites and blacks into white culture; the struggle's cultural importance) but considers the aesthetic diminished under oppression. Contrary to the latter strand in Fanon, however, Walker, Lorde, and Marshall each describe aesthetic powers that are crucial parts of life despite—and in some respects on account of—the realities of systemic oppression. This also goes for Angela Davis, who in a reading of Billie Holiday's music, moreover, makes a shift vis-à-vis Fanon and Kincaid on the point of the alignment of aesthetic and racial forms.

Where Fanon and Kincaid tightly align aesthetic divides with racialized divides, in Davis's reading, Billie Holiday achieved a politically effective combination of white and black musical forms. Davis notes that Holiday challenged the often trivial texts of the popular songs assigned to her by white producers, through a humorous, ironical, or, to the contrary, deeply serious mode of singing (*Blues* 163–80). Accordingly, by conjoining black and white forms in a style that operated in multiple aesthetic registers, Holiday's work, as Davis reads it, acquired the ability to speak to heterogeneous black and white audiences (166, 171–72). Through this intricate manipulation of complexly racialized forms, Holiday's music opened these diverse audiences up to its meanings, according to Davis. This enabled the music to provoke changes in these audiences' understanding of race and racial, gender, and class relationships

(170–73, 177–80). Davis's account of Holiday's music clearly loosens the rigid aesthetics-culture parallelism postulated by Hume and Kant, which allots distinct aesthetic systems to distinct ethnicities.[48] Identifying a form of racialized aestheticization (Holiday's music is marked by black and white racialization) and of aestheticized racialization (Holiday's music is able to affect black and white constructions of race and racial, gender, and class relationships), Davis brings out relational structures and capabilities that Enlightenment theories have implicitly discounted; perhaps most notably, art's power to mold a critical and emotional community across racial, gender, and class lines (36, 90, 118–19, 155, 172).[49] Racialized aestheticization and aesthetic racialization take yet a further form on Davis's analysis.

Davis connects the layered aesthetic structure of Holiday's singing with the layeredness of everyday African American speech, which she sees as "musicalized" through African American slave songs (167–68). In Davis's view, this speech is marked by a "decidedly aesthetic character" (166) that reflects, besides slave songs and its interplay of literal and aesthetic meanings, interdependencies between music and speech issuing from West African art forms (174). Davis thus finds important aesthetic passions and powers in daily speech. In addition to this, she sees blues women's music as thematically interwoven with working-class black people's daily lives (142, 159). She notes that Billie Holiday gave her life experiences aesthetic form (179). More generally, she reads "Ma" Rainey's, Smith's, and Holiday's work as expressive of the lived experiences of black working-class women (171, 173).[50] Thematizing questions of emotion, sexuality, love, and racial and gender violence and injustice that were part of ordinary life in black working-class communities, women blues performers, on Davis's analysis, produced critical representations of these subjects, and thereby made blues audiences aware of the importance and the possibility of social transformation. By reading "Ma" Rainey's, Smith's, and Holiday's music in terms of its mobilization of everyday experiences and forms, Davis, then, renders legible the sexual, feminist, and racial politics of this music, which has historically been downplayed and misconstrued.[51] In seeing these performers' music as inflected by racialized forms and identities, Davis has articulated a source of racialized aestheticization. Theorizing the social and political powers of this music, she has articulated a process of aesthetic racialization.

As I have indicated, Davis points to a wider range of aesthetic relationships than is typically recognized in philosophical aesthetics. I have already mentioned the point about the formation of a critical and affective community that transcends given class, gender, and racial lines.[52] More specifically, Davis sees Billie Holiday's work as "drawing from and contributing to an African American social and musical history" in which women's political and aesthetic agency mutually nurture one another (164). It is precisely this kind of synoptic perspective, one that interconnects aesthetic, racial, existential, and political questions, that is central to an understanding of significance of aesthetic racialization and racialized aestheticization. Walker, Marshall, and Lorde come close to this in emphasizing the existential and political centrality of the forms of racially inflected artfulness they have identified, and in outlining the impact of this artfulness on self, agency, and culture. For example, Walker conceptualizes the transmission of creativity in expansive existential and political terms, when representing her mother as having passed on to her a respect "for all that illuminates and cherishes life," and, more than that, "for the possibilities—and the will to grasp them" (241–42). She also claims that understanding the creative spirit that she takes black women to have inherited amounts to knowing "who and of what, we black American women are" (235).[53] Marshall, likewise, as we have seen, considers conversation in the kitchen an integral part of her mother's and her mother's friends lives, a part, moreover, that provide an affirmation that Marshall depicts as critical to their sense of themselves. Relatedly, Lorde's view of poetry as "not a luxury" clearly foregrounds poetry's indispensability. Davis, Walker, Marshall, and Lorde thus each accord pivotal existential and political powers to fundamental aesthetic capacities that participate in the conduct of everyday life. They give the aesthetic a basic role in enabling survival, sustenance, community formation, and the creation of meaning in the face of racial, gender, and economic oppression, while also locating aesthetic forms in the racialized, cultural histories that have helped to shape them. Like Hume and Kant, they implicitly posit collaborations among racialized aestheticization and aesthetic racialization, but unlike these philosophers, they thereby affirm links between the aesthetic and black subjectivity and culture formation.[54]

Walker's, Lorde's, Marshall's, and Davis's insistence on the existential and political centrality of fundamental, everyday aesthetic activities goes hand in hand with their emphasis on historically underprivileged aesthetic relationships. Each of these thinkers posits artistic transmissions and exchanges along black, feminine, and often matrilineal trajectories. For example, Marshall, as we have already seen, affirms the cultural legacy passed on to her in the "wordshop of the kitchen" (12). Lorde's image of "the Black mother within us—the poet" locates poetry's claim on feeling and freedom in a black, maternal lineage.[55] Walker's "daughters" are represented as actualizing the creativity their "mothers" handed down to them on their own terms, offering their mothers' works a legibility they would not otherwise have had.[56] Davis, finally, traces connections among women blues performers that included the borrowing, influencing, and transformation of aesthetic materials among them.[57] In examining what may be learnt from blues women that could not be learnt from feminist writers and activists (xiv, 24), she places "Ma" Rainey's, Smith's, and Holiday's music in a feminist historiography.

In sum, in taking a careful look at frequently neglected, everyday aesthetic forms, Walker, Lorde, Marshall, and Davis expand our explicitly recognized repertoire of aesthetic capacities and relationships. Their acknowledgment of "ordinary," often feminized aspects of daily aesthetic life illuminates dimensions of a more complex relational understanding of aesthetic productions, perceptions, and experiences that must be systematized. They bring out aesthetic relationships among black mothers and daughters; friends; artists; members of black, working-class communities; and members of black and white publics. They identify cultural arrangements, aesthetic forms, and modes of address that the Enlightenment model of aesthetic exchange ignores or undertheorizes. They emphasize the centrality of a mutual involvement between aesthetic resources and political and existential capabilities. In connecting aesthetic forms with racialized cultural conditions and in making the aesthetic central to black aspirations, they envision varieties of racialized aestheticization and aesthetic racialization that establish a distance from the patterns postulated by Hume and Kant, patterns that, to this date, perform structural roles in aesthetic theories and productions.

4. Aesthetic Relationality

In the above discussion, I highlight multiple varieties of aesthetic racialization and racialized aestheticization that enter into the composition of culture. We have seen that Hume and Kant implicitly portray civilization as a product of interacting strata of aesthetic racialization and racialized aestheticization. These thinkers have imagined a network of cultural relationships in which racialization and aestheticization mutually support one another. Culture, as theorized by Hume, includes racialized and aestheticized arrangements of creation and perception, labor and knowledge, passion and control, social affect and conversation, virtue and judgment, friendship, indifference and love, refinement and dispositions that are to be refined. Hume and Kant, I argue, have authorized a structure of relationships in which aesthetic modes of exchange are geared toward white cultural goals. The significance of the aesthetic is at least partially construed as the appeal of these goals, and more generally, as the desirability of whiteness, that is to say, the attraction of a white culture, distinguished by racially exclusive forms of cultivation and refinement.[58] I have indicated that it is a highly specific form of whiteness that is thereby being aestheticized, one that is structured by differentiations according to class, gender, and sexuality, and defined by its differences from specific kinds of blackness and other identity markers as are imagined to pertain, for example, to Native Americans, Muslims, and East Asians.[59] In aestheticizing whiteness and whitening the aesthetic, Hume and Kant have severely limited the spectrum of what counts as desirable intra- and crosscultural relationships. More contemporary artists, critics, and theorists, such as Walker, Lorde, Marshall, and Davis, however, take steps toward alternative schemes of relationships. These thinkers each foreground aesthetic relationships the Enlightenment scheme has bypassed, such as those among mothers and daughters, black, female, proto-feminist artists, members of black working-class communities, and among black and white audiences. Beyond that, they identify aesthetic powers and passions that to some extent elude cultural delineations attained through collaborating forces of whitened aestheticization and aesthetic whitening. Like Fanon and Kincaid, these writers also draw attention to aesthetic powers and passions that are supported by and supportive of black cultural goals. In attending to daily aesthetic detail, they bring out resources inherent in everyday aesthetic activities that tend to go unnoticed. Among other things, these artists and thinkers thereby take steps toward a reorganization of the relations between acts of aesthetic perception and creation and structures of affect, identity, and social and public existence, which must be examined in greater philosophical depth.[60] Although further analysis of the intriguing relational interventions made by the authors and artists canvassed in this chapter is much needed, I hope to have indicated that the cultural field manifests a wide range of divergent, but interconnected forms of racialized aestheticization and aesthetic racialization.

Throughout my argument, I have found the aesthetic to be central to whiteness as well as blackness and other modalities of subject positioning and vice versa. More generally, subjectivity, identity, and culture appear to implicate aesthetic structures, and aesthetic structures appear to implicate modalities of cultural positioning.[61] Racialization cannot be understood apart from its aesthetic supports and the aesthetic cannot be understood apart from its racial underpinnings. A failure to recognize their complex, mutual entanglements runs the risk of aligning the aesthetic too tidily with historically stabilized cultural demarcations, or of reinstituting whiteness as a basis of normativity in the fields of art and culture. While Kincaid's *Lucy*, Fanon's reading of cultural oppression as aesthetic diminishment, and Varda's studies of gleaning successfully loosen the hold of several Humean and Kantian strictures, they nevertheless turn out to replicate in these respects problematic Enlightenment tendencies.[62] The project of thinking through the connections between aesthetics and race in their full complexity is thus crucial to the attempt to change them.

Readers may notice that the concepts of aesthetic racialization and racialized aestheticization are hard to wrap one's mind around. I believe this is due to the fact that they brush against thoroughly sedimented philosophical, phenomenological, and artistic histories, histories that have been profoundly formative of current aesthetic needs and passions.[63] The cultivating trajectories outlined by Hume and the deculturalizing move inaugurated by Kant continue to this date both to enable and to protect aestheticized whiteness and whitened aesthetic theory. Philosophical aesthetics, of the European as well as the Anglo-American varieties, is thoroughly mired in whiteness, and continues to celebrate whiteness as this came to be anchored in proposed accounts of culture, aesthetic experience, and art. The ongoing reiteration and reestablishment of aestheticized whiteness and whitened aesthetics underscore the urgency of the project of creating newly aestheticized and racialized passions, modes of address, and patterns of relationality.

My argument points to a layered texture of aestheticized and aestheticizing dimensions of whiteness and blackness that inextricably implicate other social and subjective determinants, such as gender and class. Their entanglements reach into the miniscule elements of social existence, of our embodied interactions with one another, and the material world. No aspect of cultural life is thereby left untouched. Aesthetics and race are fundamental constituents of patterns of identity and difference at the same time as they remain profoundly problematic. Their centrality makes it imperative that we look *within the relational structures* that they have helped to establish and from which they draw their energy, for the resources that enable us to craft novel configurations of aesthetic and racial passions and modes of address. As subjects of aesthetic experiences and members of aesthetic communities, we participate in these relational structures. We keep these structures in motion. They are in an ongoing state of metamorphosis. It is crucial that white participants in aesthetic exchanges be aware of the positionings and structurations we continue to bring to this relational field. As white aesthetic agents, we must integrate our aesthetic feelings, perceptions, imaginations, creations, and interactions with an awareness of these positionings so that we can begin to own up to our cultural stances and to take responsibility for our cultural agency. There is no other way in which white people can hope to inhabit our cultures in a richly interactive, embodied sense. The price that we pay for inaction in this regard is momentous. White people have decided to live culture thinly; they have chosen to make do with a self-serving fantasy, incarnating a pseudo-aesthetic, rather than an intersubjectively achieved cultural field. If we desire to actualize the ethically promising ambitions that aesthetics and culture have held for us, we must own up to the conflicted, ambivalent powers of our aesthetic agency, and put these up for critical transformation. Ethical projects to live our racial (gendered and classed) identities differently will at the same time have to be projects of re-aestheticization and vice versa.

Epilogue

The objective of the above discussion is to create a conceptual disruption of our investments in problematically racialized forms of aestheticization and problematically aestheticized forms of racialization. I point to the need to take a critical look at our engagement with racialized, class-based, gendered, ethnicized, eroticized (and so on) aesthetic forms, and at our aestheticized experiences, identities, and values. All racialized subjects who are positioned in systems of aesthetic relationality face this challenge, that is to say, blacks, whites, Asians, Latinas/os, and so forth, in multiple mixings and disjunctions. This project places our aesthetic and racial positions at risk; it destabilizes our cultural agency; it shifts the grounds for normativity in aesthetics; it dismantles the protected status of forms of whitened aesthetics and aestheticized whiteness; it asks for a reconsideration of the bases of modes of blackened aesthetics and aestheticized blackness; and it recrafts the aesthetic and racialized tools of self-fashioning, culture building, and political action. With the above discussion I hope to create openings for newly aestheticized and racializing passions, modes of address, and relational structures. My intention is to point to the presence of embodied insights, affective structures, and imaginaries that become tangible at the level of everyday aesthetic experience but are not legible at other levels of understanding and sensibility. I do not believe that the aesthetic can ultimately be divested from problematic ties to forms of subjectivity and identity. It is too fully intertwined with everything else for this to be a live possibility. However, I find the project of putting into motion given constructions of aesthetics and race from a position within them, through the means they make available, theoretically and ethically crucial.

While the present book fosters an autobiographical voice, I have approached the particulars of aesthetic existence, which implicitly include the personal details of my own white, aesthetic life, through an indirect, impersonal form of address. My point thereby has not been to depict this mode as aesthetically or politically neutral, as offering privileged access to universalizable insights, or as excepted from the challenge of re-aestheticization and re-racialization. To the contrary, in theorizing the aesthetic as a racialized and racializing technology, I have wanted to bring out for critical analysis—among a number of other things—the particular cultural power I exert as a white, aesthetically trained, European woman, in the context of a broader system of aesthetic relationality. It is this power that I both use and resist in my cultural and cross-cultural interactions, my philosophical writing, my art criticism, my teaching, my personal life, my enfleshed dealings with the material world, and my aesthetic self-fashioning.

My reason for adopting the impersonal voice, as noted above, lies in the urgency of basic theoretical work in the undertheorized philosophical field where matters of aesthetics and race coalesce.[64] More than that, in light of the critical project outlined in the above, a number of questions arise about the effectiveness of personal testimonies in the study of whiteness: How do such testimonies resist already scripted aesthetic scenarios of heroization, narcissism, and self-confession that they inevitably activate? How does the personal mode dislodge questionable kinds of aestheticized and aestheticizing power? How does this form avoid casting white self-professions in a self-decorative, recuperative mold, offering the freshly re-aestheticized self a new epistemic and moral cachet it is not yet able to sustain? Writers in the personal mode face the aesthetic demand to make their testimony engaging, or, at least, publicly presentable. This requirement impacts any edited sequence of poignant anecdotes, feelings, insights, and silences.[65] I believe this can hinder the critical effectiveness of self-declarations. I am especially reluctant to draw philosophical mileage from a centering of a supposedly achieved "insightful," "sophisticated," "cool," "courageous," "humorous," "morally remediable," "humane" whiteness. I worry about the capacities of self-aestheticization to pass off my whiteness as more critical than it can be. While it is crucial that whites take on the job of critical self-reflection, and extend this job to their own racial selves, I am not sure how self-reflections in print can be as critical as they need to be. I am skeptical about the power of white self-declarations—which keep whites solidly ensconced in the center—to help decentering whiteness from the grounds of cultural normativity. Juxtaposing white and black personal testimonies by itself does not dispel this skepticism. Moreover, the difficulty arises also for testimonies by blacks: Which black lives are being foregrounded over and above other black lives? While I do not doubt that carefully crafted, intentional self-contextualizations and autobiographical statements can do philosophical work, I am afraid that a personal testimony on the part of my white self replicates a pseudo-relationality and a pseudo-reciprocity, that must be analyzed and exposed.[66] These concerns apply not exclusively to the personal voice, which is at the same time also always theoretical, but pertain more generally to the aestheticization of self that is implicit in all reading and writing. Conceptual work along the above lines is indispensable to the realization of a critical stance vis-à-vis questions of self-representation, the formation of experience, and the aesthetic fashioning of individual selves, mine included.

Notes

My thanks go to Elizabeth V. Spelman for crucial commentary on this essay.

1. Philomena Essed (*Understanding*) and Linda Martín Alcoff ("Phenomenology" 271–73, 281) emphasize the importance of considering the workings of race and racism

at these levels. See also the centrality of psychoexistential and phenomenological structures in Franz Fanon's writings (*Black* 12, 169) and Lewis Gordon's focus on the phenomenology of "lived reality" (*Majesty* 5, 85; "What Does").

2. I define this notion more extensively in my "Pearl's" and elaborate this concept in a book manuscript, entitled *The Cultural Promise of the Aesthetic.*

3. These effects work also in the other direction, that is to say, all social and subjective determinants put into play the aestheticized and aestheticizing dimensions of whiteness and blackness. That race, class, gender, and other categories of social identity are analytically interconnected, operate interdependently, and can neither function nor be apprehended apart from their interconnections and interdependencies I take to be argued persuasively by Elizabeth V. Spelman (*Inessential*).

4. Theorizing whiteness clearly involves also thinking about the positioning of Native Americans, Asians, Latinas/os, and so forth, and about the implications of categories such as class, gender, and so on. This chapter's binary focus on whiteness and blackness limits the depth of the analysis. At the same time my proposed move toward relationality ameliorates this limitation to some extent through its explicit engagement of a wide range of dimensions of subject-positioning and multiple forms of racialization.

5. In fact, aesthetic relationality cannot be theorized without considering what black writers have said on the matter and without analyzing the relational interventions made by black artists.

6. Hume and Kant have outlined a normative framework that continues to ground theory formation in contemporary aesthetics. For this reason, I consider their treatments paradigmatic of what I loosely call here "the Enlightenment model of the aesthetic."

7. Hume calls reason, in the specific form in which it is basic to taste, "sense," or "good" or "strong" sense ("Standard" 16–17). Reason as an ingredient of taste includes among other things, "capacious thought" and "sound understanding" (16–17). It is responsible for rational virtues such as a clearness of conception, exactness of distinction, and vivacity of apprehension. Hume calls on reason to check the influence of prejudice, to comprehend the different parts of a work of art, to compare these parts with one another, and to assess the suitability of a work's means to its ends. Reason is thus crucial to a critic's capacity for judgment, and in particular to the ability to "discern the beauties of design and reasoning, which are the highest and most excellent" (17).

8. For Hume's views on black intellectual inferiority, see "National" 360n. For his comments on the debased minds of poor and laboring classes, see "National" 114. On women's mental inferiority, see "Immortality" 163, "Study" 96, "Rise" 91, "Essay" 38 and 40, where a group of individuals labeled "the conversable," who incline toward "obvious reflections on human affairs" and have a limited "compass of knowledge," are mostly implied to be female. The masculinization of intellect in Hume is also evident in his insistence that a good writer's sense (see previous note) be "strong and masculine" ("Simplicity" 43).

9. Presumably the women in this sharply restricted group have a requisite amount of "strong" sense which allows for taste ("Standard" 17).

10. The cultivation that taste achieves is both masculinized and feminized in distinctive, racialized ways and it is racialized in gendered ways.

11. Hume makes this explicit in the case of the fourth and fifth effects. Because the first three effects contribute to the fourth and fifth effects, the refinement and "socialization" of the passions, it is clear that these three effects are civilizing factors as well.

12. Taste also has the effect of rendering the passions and the individual's social bonds aesthetically more pleasing, witness the "elegance" of passion in the last sentence of the above quote.

13. The closeness of the fine arts, refinement, delicacy, and luxury is also apparent in "Refinement" and "Commerce" 157, 161–63.

14. Besides a productive interaction among the arts, this spirit also fosters the emergence of individual geniuses ("Rise" 74).

15. Conversation with white women allows white men to develop civility and deference ("Rise" 85). It enables white male intellectuals to develop "liberty and facility of thought" and makes available experience, which they are able to "consult" in their reasonings. Without white women's civilizing force, white male intellectuals lack a "taste for life or manners" ("Essay" 39); their writings remain "barbarous"; their hearts "cold" (40).

16. It is white men's task to rescue women's talk from triviality ("Essay" 38, 41). Learned men are called upon to correct false female taste (41) and to offer women sincere affection, or "the substance," where others can provide only "complaisance," in other words, "the shadow" (42). White men are to meet white women with gallantry, a passion that improves both men and women at the same time that it affirms white masculine authority ("Rise" 91). Hume links such gallantry immediately with taste, observing that gallantry is "refined" by art (90), and in turn, is indispensable to refinement in the arts (92).

17. Hume postulates a mutually uplifting organization of relationships among white males and females. In Hume's view, men's and women's "*mutual* endeavor to please must insensibly polish the mind" ("Rise" 92; my italics). He considers properly managed, heterosexual *love* the source of all politeness and refinement ("National" 125). More than that, this kind of love is a natural foundation for the "sweetest and best enjoyment" of both sexes ("Rise" 91).

18. Furthermore, given colonialism and slavery, blacks are implicitly expected to function, alongside white women and lower-class men, as material supporters of the aesthetic bonds among white, middle-class men and among white, middle-class men and women, performing the labor necessary to protect the leisure and the intellectual productivity of learned, white males (see "Essay" 38 and "Rise" 83). In addition to this, blackness, as indicated earlier, functions as a limit-category against which these white bonds are articulated, that is to say, as the zero-point of reason, and hence of taste, and therefore of humanity and refined society.

19. Aesthetic racialization lies at the heart of a concept of culture, the applicability of which is contingent on the racial identity of the cultured subject. Unmasking the supposed universality attaching to conditions for entry into culture, Fanon writes "[n]o exception was made for my refined manners, or my knowledge of literature, or my understanding of the quantum theory" (*Black* 117).

20. This is not a matter of intentionality but of the way these desires work out in a broader system.

21. The racialized and racializing dimensions of the aesthetic and the aesthetized and aestheticizing dimensions of race, on my analysis, must be read as pertaining to this structure of cultural relationships. This structure, as we have seen, includes elements such as specific configurations of the passions; strictures on bonds of love and friendship, regulations of indifference and care; as well as commercial arrangements that qualify as virtuous and productive. It also includes regimens of beauty, vision, embodiment, and self-abstraction, whose connections with aestheticized whiteness have been developed by several thinkers. For example, Cornel West gives centrality to questions of beauty ("Genealogy"); Kalpana Seshadri-Crooks emphasizes regimes of vision (*Desiring* 2, 8, 19–21, 36, 38, 131), and Richard Dyer highlights constructions of disembodiment and self-abstraction and their parameters, such as absence, purity, and neutrality (*White* 4, 30, 38–39, 75). While these factors have important connections with whiteness, I do not see them as privileged loci of aesthetic racialization and racialized aestheticization. The history of aesthetics, to my mind, suggests that collaborations among aesthetics and racialization activate an inclusive range of existential, phenemenological, psychological, affective, and cultural dimensions, more extensive than is usually acknowledged. It is only by recognizing a highly intricate and elaborate network of collaborating elements and relationships that we can hope to account for the complex cultural constellations that populate this field, such as, for instance, the figurations of the white imaginary described by Toni Morrison (*Playing*). See also n. 59.

22. Since Kant's put-downs of black people's intellectual faculties are global and unspecific, pinpointing precisely how his theory invalidates their aesthetic judgments and tastes requires extrapolation. Blacks' said intellectual deficiency presumably hinders their ability to make judgments of so-called "dependent" beauty and to grasp aesthetic ideas, both of which Kant's theory renders crucial to the aesthetic judgment of what today are considered art works. Alleged intellectual deficiency most likely hampers judgments of the beautiful and the sublime in making it difficult to achieve and register the relationships among the cognitive faculties that underwrite these judgments. See also n. 24 on Kant's views about knowledge and moral feeling as preconditions for taste.

23. He informs us that Spain has an "odd taste" (108), that the Chinese privilege "trifling grotesqueries" (110), that the grotesque is of special interest to Indians as well, and that "the Arab" possesses an "inflamed imagination, which presents things to him in unnatural and distorted images" (109).

24. In the *Critique of Judgment*, Kant recognizes connections between taste and culture, among other things, by arguing that "a culture of the mental powers by means of those elements of knowledge called *humaniora*," and "the development of moral ideas and the culture of the moral feeling" are preparatory conditions for the emergence of taste (par. 60). Another connection lies in Kant's view of genuine taste as a mean between the "large-mindedness," "refinement," and "higher culture" of "cultivated" classes and the "natural simplicity and originality" of "uncultivated" classes (par. 60).

25. To my mind, the presence of crosscultural, transhistorical, racialized, classed, and gendered variety in the forms and qualities of taste strongly suggests that the phenomenon of taste bears *complex* relations to cultural conditions, such as the supposedly aesthetically relevant factors that Kant takes to differentiate "the Arab" from "the

German." These relations must be accounted for. However, at the surface level of the text, Kant simply sidesteps the complexities he has opened up by admitting culturally grounded variety in taste.

26. At the same time, characteristics ascribed to other ethnicities carry their specificity and content into Kant's conception of inappropriate faculties and perceptions, and by contrast, help to give shape to what counts as aesthetically appropriate.

27. An example of a recent approach to aesthetic value judgments in terms of common cognitive faculties that deploys the term *public* in this sense is Railton's "Aesthetic," see esp. 90.

28. Examples of this extensive literature are essays by Nancy Fraser and Iris Marion Young in Benhabib and Cornell (*Feminists*); by Fraser, George Yúdice, and Michael Warner in Robbins (*Phantom*); and by Jean L. Cohen, Joan B. Landes, and Marie Fleming in Meehan (*Feminists*).

29. In my "Aesthetic" I deploy the notion of "address" to theorize artworks' differential aesthetic meanings and cultural labors, which Enlightenment constructions of the aesthetic as public, and the public as the sharable, and the sharable as that which is accessible by way of common appreciative faculties are unable to capture.

30. See María Lugones' *Pilgrimages* 135–36 on the idea of Mexican and Mexican/American culture as ornamental in the eyes of white America.

31. For the less joyful side of daffodils that is vivid to Lucy but not to Mariah, see also 29–30. The narrator of Wordsworth's poem, on a walk in the country, sees "a host" of golden daffodils "[f]luttering and dancing in the breeze." He experiences these daffodils as twinkling and joyful company, "tossing their heads in sprightly dance." Accordingly, at times of emptiness and solitude, his heart "with pleasure fills [a]nd dances with the daffodils." Wordsworth's narrator's projective stance, which finds in nature what it desires to see, while ignoring everything else, echoes Mariah's sealed relationship with nature, which is imagined to celebrate nature's beauty and the memories it holds and to deplore its devastation, without including the slightest awareness of the implications of her own comfortable lifestyle in such environmental destruction (71–73). The narrator's stance also echoes Mariah's attitude toward Lucy, insofar as Mariah is depicted as needing Lucy to see things the way she herself does, and as disregarding their different perceptions and racial positions (32, 35–36).

32. In reaching out to rub Lucy's cheek, Mariah creates a rapprochement, but she shifts the terrain of engagement from the aesthetic to Lucy's "history."

33. Mariah hopes to share, for example, the spring sky and weather (19, 20), real daffodils (29), the look of a ploughed field (33) and of fish she has caught (37), the smell of peonies (60).

34. An exception is Mariah's liking of coffee with hot milk which she has learnt to make in France and which Lucy picks up from her. This, however, is an example of Lucy opening up her aesthetic world to Mariah. The converse occurs only during a moment of great, shared pleasure and closeness centered around the smell of peonies (60).

35. Notably, it is precisely daffodils which take up a destabilized cultural position in Edwidge Danticat's novel *Breath, Eyes, Memory*, a story of migration and mother-daughter relationships that takes place in Haiti and the United States. These "Euro-

pean flowers," which are loved "because they grew in a place they were not supposed to" (21), are here imagined to connote strength, limberness, and freedom to the protagonist, a young Haitian woman (29, 9). They provide solace (112, 155) at the same time as they figure in an image of a rain of dry leaves, and in frightening dreams (7–9, 28). In Danticat's novel, daffodils are seen as having "the color of pumpkins and golden summer squash, as though they had acquired a bronze tinge from the skin of the natives who had adopted them" (21).

36. I owe this point to Catherine Portuges.

37. The image of the aesthetic as an aside links up with its standing as a detail. Part of the logic of the aesthetic detail, I argue, is an aesthetic significance it acquires during a process of interpretation, which, paradoxically, reflects also an earlier insignificance (see my "Pearl's," 58 and 64–66). Interestingly, taste in Lucy (the taste of boiled over fried or baked fish in the story of Christ and the fishermen) is also figured as a "small detail," a detail that means a lot to her (38–39), and that represents another point of aesthetic difference between her and Mariah.

38. Varda's specific use of form and address (to the viewer, to other artworks and, especially in the second video, to aesthetic objects and relationships) complicate her treatment of gleaning and the aesthetic in ways I am bypassing here. For example, the notion of gleaning resonates with a long history that associates the aesthetic with a field of distinterested activities, in which concerns of ordinary utility are eluded. Accordingly, my remarks here are not intended as a full reading of her treatment of these themes.

39. I feel ambivalent about this argument because Varda's videos at the same time do a lot to counteract the unmarked presence of the aesthetic in the intersubjective experiences and object-relations that underwrite everyday existence. However, Varda's celebration of aesthetic life is limited in ways that are racialized. It is these racialized limitations on which my reading here has focused, rather than what I experience as a seductive, loving, and pleasurable celebration of the life that can reside in the collaborative, ostensibly incidental interactions with the world of objects with which we surround ourselves—aspects of everyday aesthetic life that Varda's video draws out poignantly. It is precisely on account of the importance of the social possibilities generated by such interactions with our environment and other individuals that the limitations of Varda's cinematic essay are so significant.

40. Another way in which these forms help to sustain white identities is by offering them outlets for collective aggression (145–46).

41. Fanon also indicates that white art and culture have been damaged and blinded by colonialism's violence (*Wretched* 215, 313; *Black* 202–203). His view of Europe's alienated humanity poses a challenge to the quality of European art and culture that must be addressed. I read Fanon as pointing to the problems of white aestheticization as well as aestheticized whiteness.

42. Fanon writes that "every culture is first and foremost national" and points to "realistic" developmental trajectories that are to make culture "fruitful, homogeneous, and consistent" (*Wretched* 216–67; see also 222–24).

43. This goes for the beginning as well as the later stages of the struggle for liberation. (As noted above, Fanon does acknowledge such a role in advanced stages.) In my

view, the political challenges of colonialism are not fundamentally different from the aesthetic challenges. Aesthetic oppression is at the same time political oppression and threatens "the struggle"; politics deploys aesthetic forms and energies at the same time as the aesthetic is political. I elaborate this view of the intertwinements of aesthetics and politics more fully in my "Aesthetification."

44. Gordon mentions the beauty and other aesthetic qualities of Fanon's prose, which he considers "a work of art" (*Majesty* 39, 230).

45. Examples of this form of aesthetic racialization, which we have also encountered in Fanon, are the appeals to the creation of artworks that address black existence by Amiri Baraka and Ed Bullins and other members of the Black Arts movement (see, e.g., Bullins, *Drama*). Other examples are Amilcar Cabral's account of the role of a cultural politics in the process of decolonization ("National") and Gordon's conception of art as "a worldview," which sees the aesthetic as a dimension of black advancement (*Majesty* 231). For the complexities of racialized aestheticization along the above-mentioned lines, see the debates over forms of black feminist criticism, among Barbara Smith ("Toward"), Barbara Christian ("But What"), Mary Helen Washington ("Introduction"), Hortense J. Spillers ("Afterword"), Deborah E. McDowell (*Changing*), and Hazel V. Carby ("Woman's"). For a deconstructive approach toward racialized and gendered structures of signification, see Ann DuCille, "Toy." To a certain extent, West ("New" 29–30) and Paul Taylor ("Malcolm's") also subscribe to a deconstructive dismantling of racialized meanings.

46. Walker sees her mother as "ordering the universe in the image of her personal conception of Beauty" (242). Walker and Marshall both find artfulness in media that did not belong to the traditions and canons of high art; that is to say, in the only forms that were available to their mothers ("Search" 239; "Making" 6).

47. Marshall comments on the imagination and skill with which her mother and her friends infused new life into old words. On her account, they transformed the English they had learnt in Barbados into "an idiom, an instrument that more adequately described them," creating their own rhythm, syntax, and accent so as to render the sentences "more pleasing to their ears" (8). Marshall describes the conversationalists in the kitchen as poets (4), as "oral artists," whose "guiding esthetic," in Joseph Conrad's terms, was "to make you hear, to make you feel . . . to make you see" (9). Through such parallels, she contextualizes these women's conversations in relation to white literary canons. She also locates them in the context of black literary oeuvres, such as Paul Laurence Dunbar's (10–11).

48. A similar move is made by Marshall, who depicts her mother and her mother's friends as bending the English they had learnt in Barbados to the aesthetic desires they experienced in New York. For more recent analyses of similar eclectic and syncretic strategies, see Cornel West's and Kobena Mercer's deployment of the notion of improvisational and critical bricolage in connections with questions about aesthetics and racial difference (West, "New"; Mercer, "Black").

49. It will be noted that the notion of such a community is reminiscent of the universalizing conception of the aesthetic public adopted on the Enlightenment model. The difference with Davis's notion is that Davis, contrary to Enlightenment thinkers, affirms rather than denies the workings of these differentiating factors. Davis is inter-

ested in an actual creation rather than a mere positing of such communities. Enlightenment aesthetic theorists, clearly, also aspire for community across certain differences but fail to think through how this may be established in other ways than by hierarchizing different constituencies and grounding what counts as "public" in alleged commonalities that are considered normative. See also n. 52.

50. Davis also considers the blues expressive of African American working class identities and community consciousness (xv; 142–44).

51. This politics has historically been downplayed, among other things, by critics who conceived of the blues as a personal rather than a social form, or a direct exotic expression of black nature, rather than a self-consciously fashioned aesthetic medium. Davis attributes other misreadings to an overly narrow construction of protest in terms of organized action, and to the failure to see beyond the songs' most obvious surface meanings (92–99; 142).

52. While Enlightenment thinkers make much of art's transcendent meanings and its place in a public (see the above discussion of Kant), as suggested earlier, they have failed to build a framework that could actually support a multilateral and reciprocal emergence of the communities in which such meanings might be grounded (see also n. 49).

53. Walker indicates that this is crucial. Given the determination to be a black woman artist, in spite of the impediments to this, and the low status it involves, it is necessary, she argues, to "identify with our lives the living creativity some of our great-grandmothers were not allowed to know" (237).

54. Davis, as we have seen, and also Marshall (see n. 48) distance the aesthetic from a rigid parallellism between aesthetics and cultural identity that is replicated in Fanon's and Kincaid's treatments.

55. This poet's demand for freedom, "I feel therefore I am free," whispered in a dream, supplants the white fathers' injunction, "I think therefore I am" (38). Lorde also points out that poetry helps to fashion a language for sharing feelings where this does not yet exist (37–38).

56. The mothers are said to have handed on "the creative spark, the seed of the flower they themselves never hoped to see: or like a sealed letter they could not plainly read" (240). Walker suggests that perhaps Phillis Wheatley's mother was also an artist, and that many mothers have handed on their creativity, in forms that they were not able to fully know, but that are recognizable in their daughters' lives and works.

57. See 138, 144, 165, 171, 197. Davis also theorizes Ma Rainey's, Smith's, and Holiday's blues as indebted, among other things, to challenges to cultural oppression implicit in daily speech (166), slave songs (111, 167), African American folk practices (154–60), the call-and-response structure of West African based music, and fluid boundaries between speech and music inherited from West African cultural traditions (54, 174).

58. Connections between the aesthetic and whiteness in the Enlightenment model clearly implicate connections with blackness and other forms of subject positioning. Hume and Kant can thus be seen to aestheticize not only whiteness but also blackness. See Morrison (*Playing* 90) for the notion of aestheticized blackness in the white imagination.

59. Historical work in aesthetic theory suggests thus that aestheticized and aestheticizing whiteness takes a more complex historical form than suggested by notions of whiteness as, for example, a mastersignifier (proposed by Seshadri-Crooks, *Desiring* 2–4, 25), a melancholic structure of identity formation (proposed by Ann Anlin Cheng, *Melancholy* 10–14), or a structure of disembodied self-abstraction (Dyer, *White*). While I believe that these structures are part of the story, I do not think they are able to acknowledge the specificity of the multiple varieties of whiteness to which the above discussion points. As indicated earlier, I propose to read different aspects of whiteness as dimensions of an extensive network of cultural relationships. This network includes a wide range of collaborating factors, ranging from figurations of the passions to allocations of property (Cheryl Harris, "Whiteness") and privilege (see, e.g., Peggy McIntosh, "White"), and many other elements (see also n. 21). Given the intricacy and layeredness of cultural existence, these different elements, to my mind, actively intersect with one another but manifest different "logics" and show no prospect of being reduceable to a set of basic factors.

60. This chapter's separation between, on the one hand, Kincaid, Varda, and Fanon, and on the other hand, Walker, Lorde, Marshall, and Davis in this chapter is artificial and is grounded in certain selective ways in which they do or do not resist Enlightenment aesthetics. I see each author's insights into everyday aesthetic elements as complementary rather than contrastive, and as offering a part of a picture of aesthetic relationality that must be told.

61. I develop this view of the connections among subjectivity and aesthetics more fully in my "Aesthetification." See my "Aesthetic" for a more elaborate discussion of cultural positioning in the context of art's aesthetic functioning.

62. This difficulty is to be expected in a situation where it is necessary to work within available forms of racialization and aestheticization. In outlining ways in which Walker, Lorde, Marshall, and Davis move beyond untenable Enlightenment views I have neither meant to suggest that their approaches represent a full response to the reality of problematic constellations of aesthetics and race, nor that all problems lie with the Enlightenment, or that Enlightenment paradigms stand in need of suspension across the board. I believe that many Enlightenment tenets, such as the links Hume forges among aesthetic sensitivity, the passions, and social identities, bonds, and judgments, resonate with deep-seated contemporary convictions, that can also be recognized in, for example, Lorde's and Davis's views, and stand in need of careful critical examination.

63. While these histories, as I have hoped to indicate, have influenced the aesthetic needs of whites as well as those of individuals of color, whose social and aesthetic histories are fundamentally interconnected with those of whites, the difficulties of thinking through racialized aestheticization and aesthetic racialization—the fact, for example, that it is hard to compute these words and hold them in mind—is part and parcel of what it is to be socialized and educated within the white theoretical and aesthetic systems this chapter has aimed to analyze. This difficulty is indicative of one of the ways in which systems of aesthetic racialization and racialized aestheticization have worked to foreclose reflection on questions of whiteness and blackness.

64. I would like to note that, notwithstanding the impersonal terms of my analysis, I take myself to have spoken as the white individual I am. In an important sense of the idea of "speaking as" one cannot fail to speak as the socially positioned individual one is. This is not a matter that is within authorial control. Intentional abstraction from the particulars of one's epistemic location, for example, does not undo this. Nor can it be avoided by adopting an authorial *persona* that deviates from one's social identity, or by taking on voices that ask to be read in terms of identities one does not instantiate, and so forth. In these cases, one writes as the socially positioned author one is, although one's articulations proceed through a complexly mediated voice, or through a personification of someone else. In analyzing structures of aesthetic relationality, furthermore, I have explicitly addressed important *particulars* of my own white, aesthetic life. Given that aestheticized whiteness and blackness, as I argue, pervade the minutiae of our lives, I also examine significant personal dimensions of my existence. Accordingly, I then address personal details of my own whiteness, as a white person, speaking in an impersonal form.

65. It applies also to self-declarations that become attractive by ostensibly refusing such attractiveness, or by actively undercutting straightforward models of seduction.

66. The fear is that rather than genuinely destabilizing white normative ground, public autobiographical testimony may supply whites with a new way of remaining in the center, one that sustains an appearance of critical self-analysis but in fact allows for a restabilization of whites' centrality, now under the guise of an intersubjective, reciprocal, relational gesture. I elaborate the question of aesthetic reciprocity further in my "Aesthetic."

Works Cited

Alcoff, Linda Martín. "Toward a Phenomenology of Racial Embodiment." *Race.* Robert Bernasconi, ed. Malden: Blackwell, 2001. 267–83.

Benhabib, Seyla, and Drucilla Cornell, eds. *Feminism as Critique.* Minneapolis: University of Minnesota Press, 1987.

Bourdieu, Pierre. "Historical Genesis of the Pure Aesthetic." *The Rules of Art: Genesis and Structure of the Literary Field.* Trans. Susan Emanual. Palo Alto: Stanford University Press, 1995. 285–313.

Bullins, Ed, ed. *The Drama Review 12* (1968).

Cabral, Amilcar. "National Liberation and Culture." *Return to the Source: Selected Speeches of Amilcar Cabral.* New York: Monthly Review Press, 1973. 39–56.

Carby, Hazel V. "Woman's Era: Rethinking Black Feminist Theory." *Reconstructing Womanhood: The Emergence of the Afro-American Woman Novelist.* Oxford: Oxford University Press, 1987. 3–19.

Cheng, Ann Anlin. *The Melancholy of Race: Psychoanalysis, Assimilation, and Hidden Grief.* Oxford: Oxford University Press, 2000.

Christian, Barbara. "But What Do We Think We're Doing Anyway: The State of Black Feminist Criticism(s) or My Version of a Little Bit of History." Cheryl A. Wall, ed.

Changing Our Own Words: Essays on Criticism, Theory, and Writing by Black Women. New Brunswick: Rutgers University Press, 1989. 58–74.

Danticat, Edwidge. *Breath, Eyes, Memory.* New York: Random House, 1994.

Davis, Angela Y. *Blues Legacies and Black Feminism: Gertrude "Ma" Rainey, Bessie Smith, and Billy Holiday.* New York: Random House, 1998.

DuCille, Anne. "Toy Theory, Black Barbie and the Deep Play of Difference." *Skin Trade.* Cambridge: Harvard University Press, 1996. 8–59.

Dyer, Richard. *White.* London: Routledge, 1997.

Essed, Philomena. *Understanding Everyday Racism: An Interdisciplinary Theory.* Newbury Park: Sage Publications, 1991.

Fanon, Franz. *Black Skin, White Masks.* Transl. Charles Lam Markmann. New York: Grove Press, 1967.

———. *The Wretched of the Earth.* Transl. Constance Farrington. New York: Grove Press, 1963.

Ferguson, Russell, Martha Gever, Trinh T. Minh-ha, and Cornel West, eds. *Out There: Marginalization and Contemporary Cultures.* New York and Cambridge: The New Museum of Contemporary Art and the MIT Press, 1990.

Gordon, Lewis R. *Her Majesty's Other Children: Sketches of Racism from a Neocolonial Age.* Lanham: Rowman & Littlefield, 1997.

———. "What Does It Mean to Be a Problem?: W. E. B. Du Bois on the Study of Black Folk." *Existentia Africana: Understanding Africana Existential Thought.* New York: Routledge, 2000. 62–95.

Harris, Cheryl I. "Whiteness as Property." *Critical Race Theory: The Key Writings that Formed the Movement.* Kimberlé Crenshaw, Neil Gotanda, Gary Peller, and Kendall Thomas, eds. New York: The New Press, 1995. 276–91.

Hume, David. "Of Commerce." *Selected Essays* 154–66.

———. "Of the Delicacy of Taste and Passion." *Of the Standard* 25–28.

———. "Of Essay Writing." *Of the Standard* 38–42.

———. "Of National Characters." *Selected Essays* 113–25.

———. "Of Refinement in the Arts." *Of the Standard* 48–59.

———. "Of the Rise and Progress of the Arts and Sciences." *Of the Standard* 72–94.

———. *Selected Essays.* Eds. Stephen Copley and Andrew Edgar. Oxford: Oxford University Press, 1998.

———. "Of Simplicity and Refinement in Writing." *Of the Standard* 43–47.

———. "Of the Standard of Taste." *Of the Standard* 3–24.

———. *Of the Standard of Taste and Other Essays.* Ed. John W. Lenz. New York: Library of the Liberal Arts, 1965.

Kant, Immanuel. *Critique of Judgment.* Transl. J. H. Bernard. New York: Macmillan, 1951.

———. *Observations on the Feeling of the Beautiful and Sublime.* Transl. John T. Goldthwait. Berkeley: University of California Press, 1960.

Kincaid, Jamaica. *Lucy.* New York: Penguin Books, 1991.

Lorde, Audre. "Poetry Is Not a Luxury." *Sister Outsider: Essays and Speeches.* Freedom, CA: The Crossing Press, 1984. 36–39.

Lugones, María. *Pilgrimages/Peregrinajes: Theorizing Coalition Against Multiple Coalitions.* Lanham: Rowman & Littlefield, 2003.

Marshall, Paule. "The Making of a Writer: From the Poets in the Kitchen." *Reena and Other Stories.* New York: The Feminist Press at the City University of New York, 1983. 71–91.

McDowell, Deborah E. *The Changing Same: Black Women's Literature, Criticism, and Theory.* Bloomington: Indiana University Press, 1995.

McIntosh, Peggy. "White Privilege and Male Privilege: A Personal Account of Coming to See Correspondences through Work in Women's Studies." *Critical White Studies: Looking Behind the Mirror.* Richard Delgado and Jean Stefanic, eds. Philadelphia: Temple University Press, 1997.

Meehan, Johanna. *Feminists Read Habermas: Gendering the Subject of Discourse.* New York: Routledge, 1995.

Mercer, Kobena. "Black Hair/Style Politics." Ferguson, Gever, Minh-ha, and West, *Out There,* 247–64.

Morrison, Toni. *Playing in the Dark: Whiteness and the Literary Imagination.* Cambridge: Harvard University Press, 1992.

Railton, Peter. "Aesthetic Value, Moral Value, and the Ambitions of Naturalism." *Aesthetics and Ethics: Essays at the Intersection.* Ed. Jerrold Levinson. Cambridge: Cambridge University Press, 1998. 59–105.

Robbins, Bruce, ed. *The Phantom Public Sphere.* Minneapolis: University of Minnesota Press, 1993.

Roelofs, Monique. "Aesthetic Reciprocity: Skepticism or Address?" *Jaarboek voor Esthetica 2002.* Frans van Peperstraten, ed. Tilburg, The Netherlands: Nederlands Genootschap voor Esthetica, 2002. 138–62. Published also at www.phil.uu.nl/esthetica/.

———. "Aesthetification as a Feminist Strategy: On Art's Relational Politics." *Art and Essence.* Stephen Davies and Ananta Ch. Sukla, eds. Westport: Praeger, 2003. 193–212.

———. "A Pearl's Perils and Pleasures: The Detail at the Foundation of Taste." *differences: A Journal of Feminist Cultural Studies* 14.3 (2003): 57–88.

Seshadri-Crooks, Kalpana. *Desiring Whiteness: A Lacanian Analysis of Race.* New York: Routledge, 2000.

Shusterman, Richard. "Of the Scandal of Taste: Social Privilege as Nature in the Aesthetic Theories of Hume and Kant." *Eighteenth-Century Aesthetics and the Reconstruction of Art.* Ed. Paul Mattick, Jr. Cambridge: Cambridge University Press, 1993. 96–119.

Smith, Barbara. "Toward a Black Feminist Criticism." *The Truth That Never Hurts.* New Brunswick: Rutgers University Press, 1998. 3–21.

Spelman, Elizabeth V. *Inessential Woman: Problems of Exclusion in Feminist Thought.* Boston: Beacon Press, 1988.

Spillers, Hortense J. "Afterword: Cross-Currents, Discontinuities: Black Women's Fiction." *Conjuring: Black Women's Fiction and Literary Tradition.* Marjorie Pryse and Hortense J. Spillers, eds. Bloomington: Indiana University Press, 1985.

Taylor, Paul C. "Malcolm's Conk and Danto's Colors; or, Four Logical Petitions Concerning Race, Beauty, and Aesthetics." *The Journal of Aesthetics and Art Criticism 57.1* (1999). 16–20.

Walker, Alice. "In Search of Our Mothers' Gardens." *In Search of Our Mothers' Gardens: Womanist Prose by Alice Walker.* San Diego: Harcourt Brace Jovanovich, 1983. 230–43.

Washington, Mary Helen, ed. with an intro. Introduction, "The Darkened Eye Restored: Notes Toward a Literary History of Black Women." *Invented Lives: Narratives of Black Women 1860–1960.* New York: Doubleday, 1987. xv–xxxi.

West, Cornel. "A Genealogy of Modern Racism." *Prophesy Deliverance! Towards an Afro-American Revolutionary Christianity.* Philadelphia: Westminster Press, 1982. 47–65.

———. "The New Cultural Politics of Difference." Ferguson, Gever, Minh-ha and West, *Out There,* 19–26.

Wynter, Sylvia. "Rethinking 'Aesthetics': Notes Towards a Deciphering Practice." Ex-Iles: *Essays on Caribbean Cinema.* Ed. Mbye Cham. Trenton, NJ: Africa World Press, 1992. 237–79.

7

"Circulez! Il n'y a rien à voir," Or, "Seeing White": From Phenomenology to Psychoanalysis and Back

Bettina G. Bergo
Université de Montréal

Introduction

THIS CHAPTER PROCEEDS ON A COMMONPLACE: seeing "white" as a racial category with a number of cultural, political, and economic associations emerged over about three centuries. The "becoming-visible" of white has a history that is different from Europeans' accounts of "seeing black," though the two histories depend on each other. Weaving historical instances of seeing "black," seeing "Jew," seeing "other" together with the question of seeing white, I begin with a phenomenological question: What does "seeing" mean at all? The limitations of classical phenomenology lie in its focus on intentionality and "logical grammar," which bracket all that which "I" do not intend to say, see, or think. But seeing color, seeing otherness—and so, seeing white—require that phenomenological "seeing" be supplemented by those emotions and conceptual associations that accompany, semiconsciously, our conscious perceptions. The emergence of "seeing white" must pass through a phenomenology of perception, which is always overarched by a linguistic or symbolic dimension. But "seeing white" requires that we have some access to the cultural associations that escape phenomenology. These have been explored by psychologies of colonization and authority. One of the more intriguing confrontations, between Franz Fanon and Octave Mannoni, shows the pitfalls of what "seeing white" meant for a Martinican psychologist and a colonial psychoanalyst in the 1940s and 1950s. From this psychology of cultural "seeing," I turn back to the question of seeing, this time as gaze and everydayness. Seeing white, I argue, takes on complexity under circumstances of "interruption," when a person in positions of symbolic or political dominance is obliged to see him/herself (partly) as "being seen," rather than simply seeing and classifying (others).

I. Seeing Color, Or: the Historic Sedimentation of the (White) Social Imaginary

The history of "seeing color" seems easier to write than that of "seeing white." Numerous histories of European and American characterization of others have produced a rich documentation of the rise of what has come to be called "scientific racism." Much of this history is rooted in clusters of concepts and practices of a near hallucinatory variety, from craniometry to phrenology to physiognomy;[1] from neurology[2] to morphology;[3] from sexology[4] to the "signs" of the "biogenetic law"[5] and of "neoteny."[6]

For obvious reasons, between the mid-eighteenth century and the beginning of the twentieth century, images of whiteness, like the studies of white societies, have been less popular and often perceived, by Europeans and white Americans, as lacking critical interest, a largely tautological repetition of the standard—except when one considers whiteness as a feminine characteristic; in that framework, white functions as a sign of refinement, purity, *or* diseased pallor, effeminacy, degeneracy.

Within the white paradigm of the European nineteenth century, alternate "essences" are posited in ways that reinforce the so-called normality of the European Christian mind and body. Among the British, for example, Francis Galton photographed dozens of Jewish high school boys and proceeded to superimpose three to four photographs at a time, with a view to adumbrating the "essences" of the "Jew" through his composite images. Indeed, social and "scientific" approaches to Jews in nineteenth- and twentieth-century Europe provide acute indicators of the impact of racist social imaginaries on *what* one perceives. For, Jews were alternately considered white *and* not-white, degenerate or infantile *yet* intellectually gifted, according to the strategies and goals of a particular discourse. A similar binaristic ambivalence is found toward Asians;[7] less ambivalence was evinced toward Africans.

For all that, in the nineteenth century whiteness remained a category less significant than those of health, character and its sexual markers, caste position, skull shape and physiognomy, criminality and its forensic "indicators," which crossed over neatly with some of the "attributes" of "savages."[8]

In all these cases, nonwhiteness is articulated around three basic signifying clusters: childishness or effeminacy; moral and physical degeneracy; and hypersexuality or perversity. All of these are anchored in a posited racial or national essence, itself determined generally by two of these three clusters. Yet essence—whether it is sought *within* the body (cf. the great popularity and painterly dramas of autopsies of prostitutes in the nineteenth century), or in the *expressions* of the face or its ossature (jaw lines, eyebrow bones, skull size and shapes, etc.), or in behavior—demands a verifiable (which tended to mean visualizable) anchor and vouchsafe, in the nineteenth century.

If much of this imagery is forgotten or the subject of derision today, it remains sedimented in the visual and rhetorical social imaginary of Western societies and is reflected with irony and satire in contemporary art,[9] *even as* it is reworked in some contemporary "sciences" and works like *The Bell Curve.* In its elaboration over two centuries,[10] the "visual" indices of European "normalcy" work by effacing themselves. There are at least two reasons for this. The first is that in debates about human natures and essences, the concern to present a gamut of qualities whose proper balance the European possessed, led to imaginative exaggerations of other ("colored") positions on theoretical lines that ordered excesses and deficiencies in body structure, in intelligence and maturity, and in facial and cranial architectures. Thus, concerns focused on visual depictions of the other *over* the acknowledgment of variations—related to class position, region, ethnic history, and so on—among the Europeans themselves, except insofar as the latter served the purposes of criminal anthropologies like that of Lombroso, or determinations of intelligence and character[11] (Darwin was, we recall, almost refused passage on the *Beagle,* given physiognomist concerns about his character, as voiced by the ship's captain). The second reason was the antiquated and romanticized image of Europeans: how many images of *Greek* or *Roman* profiles were employed as *the* paradigm of European humanity in these treatises, it would be hard to enumerate. Moreover, the essence of white, European masculinity was abstract: rationalist, detached but possessed of a socially validated scopic power to judge and to classify, the seer did not require being seen, except when it proved necessary to draw economic or psychiatric distinctions. What white then looked like was often a matter of the white woman, whose body and face were never points from which visual mastery could be deduced. That is, unlike European men, European women did not have the validated gaze; women were observed and at times responded in such ways that it was obvious they suspected the stakes of the game. This is clear in the images preserved of the (largely female) population of hysterics in France and England.[12] Thanks to performances elicited from them, poor women, whose lives were often at risk from spouses, employers, or pimps, found some safety in large urban psychiatric hospitals in nineteenth-century Europe. In return for this, they formed the exemplars of a vast literature on the essence of "feminine," psychosexual diseases.[13]

What then is there to "see" in whiteness? In the nineteenth century, and up to the first World War, this question could hardly be raised in a self-reflective, political analysis. The irony of this recalls the French police remark, directed against the curious in cases of immigration *razzias* or roundups: "Roulez, il n'y a rien à voir!" ["Drive on, there is nothing to see!"] This *rien*, of course, belongs to the operation of foreclosed paradigms, which efface themselves and their self-referentiality, in their effective deployment.

II. A Phenomenology (of Whiteness) Concerns Perception—When It Is Combined with Language

Let us step to the side of this question and ask what it means, philosophically, to *see anything*. In other words, what is "seeing" itself? We overlook this question often enough, supposing that it is too obvious to consider. Thus, seeing, or perception, is a constitutive mental act, which, along with understanding and recollection, presents us with perspectives on an object "out there" or an event that is "actual." Seeing holds the privilege of evidence *and* distance—that is, an event is witnessed with my own eyes, even if it is out of the range of tactile contact. The eyewitness is thus to be preferred over one who knows by hearsay. And the visual approach to a being or to a horizon is the one privileged by the "science" of what appears, *phaino-* [to shine forth, and by extension, to appear *clearly*] menology. Can phenomenology teach us anything about whiteness, as it appears or as it effaces itself?[14] I believe it can, up to an important limit. Beyond the limit one must turn to what Cornelius Castoriadis has called "social imaginaries"[15] and to psychology. I will return to the question of psychology for whiteness theory in a moment. For now, let us look at two paradoxes intrinsic to phenomenology with a view to understanding why, in the matter of seeing white, there may seem to be *rien à voir* outside of specific, extraphenomenological meanings.

IIa. The Contradictions of Phenomenology as a Philosophy of Perception

Phenomenologist Renaud Barbaras has characterized the challenge to classical phenomenology, so far as it claims to be more than empirical observation and seeks to accede to something like a science of the visible. He points out that:

> A philosophy of perception [here, phenomenology] is faced with two seemingly contradictory requirements. On the one hand, perception is openness toward reality: its object is given as residing in itself, as preceding the act that makes it ap-

> pear without owing anything to this act. Nevertheless, on the other hand, [our] access to this reality is dependent on its appearance; that which gives itself as being is nothing *other* than that which appears. This is how we translate the fact that it is someone who perceives, that is, that the being of the world [or of ourselves and others] is measured by my *power to make it appear.* Thus phenomenality [what is perceived] enfolds Being, inasmuch as there is no being which is not perceived; but Being in turn *embraces phenomenality,* since what is proper to the perceived is that it gives itself as something that always exceeds its manifestations.[16]

If we recognize that "openness toward reality" involves *more* than just passively perceiving whiteness, then we must also *historicize* the conviction that, as a quality supposed to have some "objective" value, whiteness may not precede the acts that *make it appear.* However, once the conditions of its appearance are socially and symbolically analyzed, whiteness will appear much the way other qualities appear that "precede the act that makes them appear"; that is, as constructed and sedimented rather than "given." A phenomenology of symbolic and cultural "facts" must approach its acts as open to the question of whether they are indeed other than that which can appear at different epochs or under specific circumstances. Nevertheless, to the extent that whiteness belongs to a perceptual field (visually, by audition as "white voices," or by other sensory means), it falls under a specific regional ontology (sociology, ethnography) within phenomenological research. Its grasp, however, will be related to the power of an "I," or society of "I's," to *make whiteness appear,* as Barbaras remarks.

According to the founder of contemporary phenomenology, Edmund Husserl, reality presents itself by sketches or profiles. These part-entities can always be assembled to determine at least simple essences, and this is what Husserl means by his first phenomenological technique called the *Wesenschau* (or essences-gaze). The idea of a constructivist approach to perceptual realities, which passes through the synthesis of perceptible "essences," is an old one for science *and* pseudo-science. It even recalls Galton's composite "essence" of the Jew, created through the use of photographs superimposed on one another.[17] While Galton's racist, pre-phenomenological quest for essences has little to do with the twentieth-century phenomenological enterprise, the passion for constituting simple essences is an intrinsic part of the phenomenological undertaking. It requires a technical apparatus consisting of "reductions," including an "eidetic reduction" (to essences) and a "transcendental reduction" (designed to uncover the activity of psychic life itself, as consciousness re-presenting itself to itself, or passing beyond itself to an intended object or *presence*).

To the question, "what do we 'see' in seeing whiteness?" we have to respond in a roundabout way. There is no doubt that we "see" whiteness as a quality of persons. It seems hard to deny that one's social, ethnic, and gender position will have an impact on how readily we see whiteness and what other qualities we attach to that of whiteness. This is related to the paradox Barbaras introduced above: it is there, but an "I" or group of "I's" must also *make* whiteness appear. It is also related to what E. Levinas and J. Derrida have observed about language in Husserl's first great work of phenomenology, *The Logical Investigations.* We must understand this before answering the question of seeing whiteness—because visual perception alone cannot tell us enough about how one sees color or "race."

IIb. Language Doubles Our Perception: Or, the Symbiosis of Our Perception and Our Concepts

Early phenomenology entailed the confidence that what-is (presence) is truly *available* to human consciousness, understood as intentionality. Intentionality means that all consciousness, for Husserl, is consciousness-of something, whether this is a (white) person or object, or a memory, or a state of mind. Intentionality, along with the "living present" that is consciousness present to itself, are two core suppositions of phenomenology. Both suppositions proceed on the confidence that our consciousness, as a dynamic movement able to go beyond itself or into itself, is able to perceive and to describe all objects it finds in its purview. Later, phenomenology encountered two halting points limiting its optimism: our death, which clearly escapes experience per se, and the encounter with another person, who also escapes our perceptual grasp, despite her or his resemblance to us.

Barring these two halting points, one could infer from these remarks that all the world can be a spectacle for phenomenology. And we could discern visible essences and qualities—fundamental ways of being—no matter what they were, *independently* of the meanings and values carried by the words attached to them. But that would be to underestimate the scope of Husserl's phenomenology. On reading Husserl's *Logical Investigations*, Emmanuel Levinas glimpsed the problem of the range and power of word meanings. While phenomenology begins as a description of lived perceptual experience, Husserl recognized that mental life, as "intentional," is experienced as much symbolically (i.e., in language) as perceptually. Thus, moving beyond the empiricism of "things seen," Husserl's phenomenology acknowledged that the domain of *linguistic meanings* itself "covers . . . the entire domain of intentionality, outside that of [our] immanent constitution of time," which is just consciousness as an unceasing flow. Levinas adds, in what is a counter-intuitive conclusion, "To understand that the word signifies something is to grasp the very movement of intentionality itself."[18] Thus, perception and discourse—what we see and the symbols and meanings of our social imaginaries—prove inextricable the one from the other.

Now, if this is the case, then ultimately phenomenology not only proceeds on a theory of perception as "meaning-giving" through intentional consciousness in the world, but phenomenology requires a theory of linguistic (social and historical) meaning. Most important, perception and discursive meanings prove so intertwined that if a word or sentence had no meaning for a subject, it would be hard to see how that sentence could be intentionally constituted as an object of consciousness. This, I suspect, is the case for whiteness in the eighteenth (and part of the nineteenth) centuries. The concept of whiteness per se had little discursive meaning for the European who observed and classified other races, outside of general claims about others as "nonwhite." Thus the history of what we might call the *becoming-visible* of whiteness has yet to be written. However, *that* whiteness, as a complex of visibles, or meaningful perceivable qualities, is (like countless other objects we overlook in their habitual appearing) a historically determined perceptual event is undoubtable. This is why Levinas's conclusion, "Thus the phenomenon of the signification of the word"—noteworthy here is a word like *white* or *whiteness*—"will remain *the key to this notion* [of intentionality]," is precious. Language, or the symbolic dimension of human experience, is not only intertwined with human social and psychological perception, it is a primary ingredient in the construction that is perception.

And yet a word is not an image. In fact, a spoken word is not symbolic per se. Just to say *white* is not necessarily to symbolize, because *white* is not perceived for itself. Levinas adds, citing Husserl, that the word "is like a window through which we look at what it signifies."[19] If words like *white* stood alone, we would have little reason to speak of a symbolic dimension at all. It is that a spoken word, so far as it points toward something, functions like a window through which we see, *at another level of perception*, what it signifies. But we rarely communicate with just one- or two-word utterances. The window simile must be complicated to grasp how we see *white* symbolically—that is, through our social and historical imaginaries.

IIc. The Conjunction of Phenomenology and Psychology: Derrida's Criticism of Husserl

The complication of Levinas's window simile is provided by Derrida's study of speech as expression and indication in his *Speech and Phenomenon*.[20] Agreeing with Levinas's commentary, Derrida explains that the famous reductions of phenomenology, designed to get to the bare facts of perceptual experience, cannot hold human language out of play because language is *the* mode through which our living consciousness is present to itself. It appears to be simple common sense that our consciousness is present to us, fully and dynamically, through our internal monologue, no matter how many "voices" may arise in it, no matter how clearly conscious we are of specific words used, at a given moment, in that monologue. Yet the common sense begins to break up when Husserl draws two important distinctions: first, between consciousness approached psychologically and consciousness *revealed* by the phenomenological brackets he sets on it; second, between words as said and all those indications that surround words and make linguistic communication possible—pauses, exclamations, tones, associations, implications, and so on.

Husserl's project is a philosophy of life and concrete things. This is the core of its value for the intersubjective experience of whiteness, whether as a social, a cultural, or a psychological phenomenon. But Husserl's project is this precisely insofar as language holds *life* and *ideality* (ideas and memories) together. We could not form ideas about things, construct or perceive essences, if we could not repeat words, in living speech within us or outwardly, as utterances. Thus the voice, as signification, "seems to preserve ideality and living presence *in all its forms*" (*Speech and Phenomenon*, 10).

This living presence of our consciousness to itself, with its images, words, pauses, affects, and so on, is *one* life—ours. Husserl's phenomenological goal is to unveil this life as the "purely psychic" by holding aside our assumptions about subjective states or objective things out there in the world. Despite Husserl's elaborate technique of holding assumptions aside (i.e., his phenomenological "reduction"), the psychic or "transcendental life" he lays bare is, in all things, identical with "psychological" life, *though he insists that these two, the transcendental and the psychological, are different.* Certainly, they are different epistemologically—one is unveiled by phenomenology, the other is explored in various psychologies. But, Derrida reminds us, the "difference distinguishes nothing, [it is] a difference separating no state, no experience, no determined signification" (*Speech and Phenomenon*, 11).

Derrida's point is this: even though Husserl's "transcendental ego" is different from his *natural ego*, the difference has no event or object to hold it fixed in its difference. Even if I can make myself a phenomenological spectator of my own psychic self, it remains me, my psychic self, which is in question. This observation is of extreme importance because it shows clearly that phenomenology not only can be woven together with psychology (and, as we will see, with psychoanalytic observations), but that phenomenology can be *filled out by psychology* in cases like that of seeing whiteness.

I am condensing the arguments in Husserl and Derrida for reasons of space and in order to come to the basic question about "seeing whiteness." We were following the claims about language as an order of meaning that is intertwined with all intentionality (i.e., of all consciousness-of things). The upshot is this: if there is a level of experience that *escapes* language as signification, then *either* we will not be able to speak about it (could this be the experience of seeing white, seeing black—and if so, up until what historical moment?), *or* we will have to distinguish words as ideal objects and historical products, *from* words that are somehow "more" than cultural and historical things. This is where Husserl's notion of the voice or "speech in its transcendental flesh"—the way inner speech lives embodied in us and for us—comes in (*Speech and Phenomenon,* 16).

You might wonder what relevance these complex investigations into the life of the self—made possible by the phenomenological reduction[21]—have for seeing whiteness, or blackness, or otherness. But we know already, from criticisms about color blindness to the abjection and cost of acts of "othering," that seeing color is not just an interesting historically and culturally rooted act of spontaneous cognition. This seeing (which also involves hearing, feeling, valuing) affects us precisely at the level of the sensuous and affective life most intimate to us. If phenomenology can afford us a glimpse into a pre-expressive stratum of our experience, then we will get a fuller understanding of what such seeing involves.

The difficulty posed by the interdependence of linguistic meaning (which Husserl takes in its form of *logical* grammar, not *psychoanalytic* grammar, thereby leaving out unintended acts, acts in bad faith, psychic symptoms, etc.) and the intentional life of consciousness drives Husserl to search for some presence *not* mediated by language. But this quest drives him toward the inner *voice* as basic apperception (perception of self by self), rather than toward pure seeing. Consequently, Husserl's pursuit of a pre-verbal layer of consciousness leads him not to a psychological pre- or un-conscious, but to a crucial distinction within language itself, between language made up of expressive and indicative signs *and* our inner language made up of pure expression. All communication between subjects, he argues, will be a combination of expression (words said) and their conditions of meaningfulness (indicative "signs"). An indicative sign is any tone or mark (or silence) that *does not express any idea or thing* "unless [it also] happen[s] to fulfill a meaning *as well as* an indicative function." (*Speech and Phenomenon,* 20).

Indicative signs, or "indication," fill up the gaps in our speech. They point beyond a particular expression, connecting meaningful words to the host of things that those words do not specifically say, there and then. In this respect, no interpersonal communication is conceivable without "indication." This is simply because the other person is not present to us the way we are present to ourselves. Their absence must be supplemented with references and substitutions *in order to pass, in thought, from one thing to another thing,* or from one sentence to the next. Indication works as a linkage. It links two consciousnesses. It also links actual consciousness to what is *not* present in our consciousness. Indication is thus our connections to culture, to historical sedimentations of meaning, to unstated beliefs, unreflected images, and so on—all those things that condition our seeing other or seeing white, whether they are half- or un-conscious.

However, by Husserl's argument, our inner monologue has no need for indication, because in inner monologue we are fully present to ourselves as living consciousness; so much so that we *never really communicate anything "new" to ourselves* in our pre-discursive monologue. This is true even though the inner monologue seems to speak all "by itself," without our willed intervention.

Now Derrida's insight, here, consists in recognizing a move that is more traditional to philosophy (*and* psychology) than Husserl realized. In positing the originality and immediacy of our inner monologue, Husserl divides absolute presence (to self) *not only from interpersonal communication using indication, but also* from re-presentation, that is, from re-presented memories, images, and signs. We find ourselves returned to a distinction between apperception (of self by self) *versus* perception (of things or as representations), and one typical of classical psychology between originary *versus* secondary mental presence. And yet, even if we insist, with Husserl, that what "I" say "outwardly" is not the same as what "I" say "inwardly," neither of these two directions really entail places at all. They are just movements, not places in some inner or outer world. Moreover, despite Husserl's insistence on "*logical* grammar," which excludes from his discussion of meaning all those things we *do not intend* to say (slips of the tongue, forgettings, grimaces, twitches, silences, and so on), it remains true that meaning as expression always indicates. Meaning is possible *because of* the gaps, forgettings, the indirect references, tones, pauses, and the like, which surround and make expression possible. We cannot bracket indication in intersubjective situations. But Derrida shows that we cannot legitimately "bracket" or reduce indication in inner speech, either. Now, Husserl had insisted on inner speech as our immediate presence to self—that inner voice which was not like everyday language because it dispensed with indication. For Derrida, when we speak to ourselves we are speaking metaphorically to be sure, but we are speaking all the same, since our internal monologue proceeds thanks to signifiers. And though those inner words may not be spoken aloud within us, there *are no other signifiers with which we communicate than words,* whether we are speaking with others or with ourselves. That means there is no pure seeing and no deep self that is not already determined by the language(s) it learns and by its society and history. What we see, like what we can think, is conditioned by the words and indicators we learn.

Derrida's argument does two things. It vitiates Husserl's dream of an immediate, prelinguistic dimension of our lived experience. Further, it *historicizes* what was supposed to be somehow prior to words, or deeper than their historical-cultural sense. There would thus be no beginning in ab-solute (i.e., not relative to words) presence (to self). And there would be no ultimate difference between real words and our imagined words (*Speech and Phenomenon*, 43). The absolute certainty of self-presence, via the inner voice, must be connected to the historical and cultural conditions already obvious in intersubjective communication.

If Derrida is right, then the historical mutations of words like *white, whiteness, blackness, yellow, feminine,* and so on are always interwoven with socialized indication and its networks of meaning—both binary and complex ones.[22] And, if there is no pre-originary—that is, no directly perceived *or* apperceived—perception or expression, then there is no immediate or primary experience of the other as white or black or other—that is, none without language.

This claim is both compelling in its historical power and confounding in that it seems to eliminate the immediacy of our experiences of otherness. Certainly the eighteenth-century European perceived not so much whites or blacks, but Frenchmen, Chinese people, Africans, Indians, or again, types: "the mad," "the beggar," "the syphilitic"—all of which are anchored by other signifiers. If nineteenth-century national, cultural, economic, and "nosological" typologies have become simplified with the perception of whiteness or blackness, they have also become complexified, differently, since cultural and economic perceptions have anything but disappeared. These perceptions accompany what is a more insidious range of *types* of whiteness, blackness, and of multi-racial perception at work in Western perception today.[23]

Classical phenomenology sought a level of psychic immediacy at which perception, in its purity (i.e., without everyday language) could be described. Astute commentators of Husserl, from Levinas to Derrida, have argued that language, words (including *white* and *whiteness*, etc.), cover the entire range of intentional life, all the way to our passive, that is, spontaneous, time consciousness as it flows along. But Derrida has argued, further, that that "other" immediate presence to self (not just time consciousness), that is, the living inner voice, is already a language that uses the same signs and the same *indication* as discursive language. The inner voice (however aware we are of "its" signifiers) is just language. It too is mediated through indication—through silences, implications, and associated meanings. Therefore, even our deepest presence to self is historically and culturally conditioned. We saw why this is compelling for seeing white in section one. In short, until the concept *whiteness* matured as historical and political, for Europeans,[24] there was nothing much there to see. "*Roulez, il n'y a rien à voir.*"

III. The Discourse of "Biological" Racism and its Symbolic Impact

By Derrida's arguments, we "see" whiteness as whiteness becomes a culturally meaningful signifier. How does whiteness become such a signifier? The question is historical, political, economic, and cultural. To answer it by tracing something like a linear genealogy would just drift back toward the illusion of absolute beginnings. "White" is already present, if indirectly, in what Gustav Jahoda calls "the shift in perspective away from the question of the relationship between humans and apes, and towards an ordering of human races according to their supposed degree of proximity to apes, [which itself] was indicative of a shift from Enlightenment values towards racial intolerance" (*Images of Savages*, 53).[25]

This shift, dating at least from Buffon (1766), contains a displacement in attitudes and presumably in language. Jahoda illustrates it dramatically with the figure of Anthony William Amo, who was brought from the Guinea coast to Holland in 1707. Amo was educated first in Holland, then at the University of Halle (1729), and thereafter at Wittenberg. He wrote a treatise, was duly respected for his intellectual gifts, and moved to Jena, where he taught philosophy. Jahoda points out, however, "A few years later he became subjected to what we would call racist attacks and was forced to return to Africa in 1747" (*Images of Savages*, 53). It is not clear whether, or when, Amo would have returned to Africa had he not been forced out of Jena; it is very clear, however, that in the eyes of his attackers, who "saw black," Africa was "where he belonged."

With respect to critical self-reflection, seeing white appears to postdate Europeans' seeing black or yellow or red. Even the radical materialist Julien Offray de la Mettrie (1709–1751)—for whom the idea of the soul (whether in Europeans or other humans) was just a bad metaphor for the hypercomplexity of the body and so lacked reality[26]—was given to "seeing other" on the basis of blackness, brownness, or bodies. In a section of his *Œuvres philosophiques* (1751), entitled "On savage men, called Satyrs," he observed:

> They [satyr-men] run fast and have unbelievable strength. In front of the body they have nowhere any hair; but on the back one gets the impression of a forest of black bristling hair, the whole back being covered with it. The face of these animals resembles a human face.
>
> [But] nothing is more lascivious, more shameless, and more disposed to fornication, than these animals. (*Images of Savages*, 42)

Having freed himself of the burden of attributing or denying to humans a metaphysical soul, de la Mettrie boasted that he had seen one such "animal" at the fair in St. Laurent. But what *was* it? Rather than attending to his own phantasmic lapses, he compares the creature to a mythical being, a satyr, presumably because of his "observation" of its "shameless" sexuality. But he also insists that its visage "resembles a human face." The Descartes-Buffon claim that linguistic competence is a sign of humanity (the presence of a soul) being irrelevant to de la Mettrie, we confront a signifying complex, in his work, of mythical creatures, apes, metaphoric satyrs, and "savages." Against this, as suggested by the metaphor of a "forest of black bristling hair" covering "the whole back," we have, implicit, a seeing of whiteness (which does not bristle, contains no black hairy forests, is not lascivious, etc.), of true humanity, and capacities for sublimation and virtue. All this is *implicit* in the fantastic claims he ventures. This example illustrates a small part of the perverse history of the subdivisions of humanity and animality in light of the entrenched conception of a Great Chain of being.[27] Needless to say, de la Mettrie's emphasis on sexuality in the satyr-animal[28] combined projective and fantasy elements with Enlightenment concerns[29] with classificatory logics.[30]

The proliferation of fantastic and conflicting classifications of *man* and of *races* in the mideighteenth century ramifies into and contaminates, in the nineteenth century, more recent logics of sexual types and pathologies, criminality, personality, and types of racial-biological "degeneracy." These logics accompany a cluster of diverse forms of racism.[31] From all this, which has been extensively documented, we can conclude that seeing white, like seeing black, seeing Jew, or seeing degeneracy,[32] is historically and culturally determined, and transmitted through expression and "indication"; that is, through things said, but also through the unsaid that makes them possible. Yet, paradoxically, thanks to this transmission,[33] seeing white and seeing black each carries with it *a perceptual immediacy* that both intertwines with received history, and *seems* actually to precede history at the psychological level. It is *as if we immediately "saw" white, or black, and all that these mean.* This immediacy concerns the phantasmic dimension in much of our perception, and the interconnections of fantasy, projection, and anxiety *with* perception. But that cluster, completely bracketed by Husserl because it was extra-intentional—when taken with Derrida's point that Husserl's transcendental ego is indistinguishable from the psychological "ego"—obliges us to look closely at psychoanalytic discussions of fantasy and personality.

IV. From the Interconnection of the Symbolic and the Perceptual to the Psychology of Culture

The obvious lesson of the *récits de voyage*, missionaries' and colonial administrators' diaries,[34] some eighteen "colonial exhibitions"[35]—not to mention the spate of Robinsonade literature about islands and exotic others, from Shakespeare's *The Tempest* through Jonathan Swift and Daniel Defoe—is that Europeans saw in the so-called nonwhite what they feared or loathed in themselves *and* that they were fascinated by the nonwhite so long as he or she remained a docile screen for their projections, erotic and idealizing.

It is at the level of fantasy and projection that psychoanalysis and psychohistory complement phenomenological inquiry into seeing color or seeing white. But psychoanalysis can be a risky tool when it overlooks political and economic conditions in its study of "cultures" or groups. The French psychoanalyst Octave Mannoni, in *Le Racisme revisité*,[36] argued after the Malagasy revolt (1947), what was made obvious thanks to the works of Fanon, Césaire, and others. "The Negro *is* the fear that the White has of himself." And, he asked, "in effect, where is the *Other in this self image* that foments phobia without diminishing hatred?"[37] Now, the work itself is in part dated; yet I want to discuss, here, why it has been reprinted from 1950 to 1999.

Julia Kristeva, Sander Gilman, and others[38] have analyzed at length a group's ability to secrete an abjected, untouchable part of itself, conceiving it as intrinsically *other than* itself. The literature on this is considerable. And, while Mannoni's work is flawed by Eurocentrism,[39] above all when he elaborates a "psychoanalysis" of the French-assimilated Merina, it caught my attention with two provocative insights into those elements of French (European?) values and structures of seeing (in light of "indication"), which took on relief within the institution of colonialism. Mannoni argues that the images and tales of colonial administration[40] promised the French colonial an escape from the economic and cultural demands of European society and prodded his nostalgia for something like the life of a petty noble. Second, despite well-documented limitations, Mannoni tried to bring to light the contours of intersubjectivity in colonial Madagascar, the colonial *Mitsein*—and this, on the colonists themselves. I would insist, from the outset, that of the psychologists concerned with colonialism, Fanon's analyses of Madagascar, like those of some recent scholars,[41] are more powerful, and truer in regard to the oppression and violence of colonial conquest. They are so because they do not proceed primarily from the micro (infancy, family life, socialization) to the macro-levels of colonial existence, as Mannoni often does. Paradoxically, Mannoni had spent twenty years in Madagascar (presumably in Tananarivo), while Fanon had spent little time there. Nevertheless, from his stance as a Martinican psychologist, Fanon was able to evince Mannoni's difficulties (defenses?) in imagining the existence of the colonized Malagasy. I think it is as he says: Mannoni was looking, above all, for explanations of the white colonial "gaze"; asking what lay beneath the colonials' (often-failed) pursuit of wealth (*Le Racisme revisité*, 302). In his best moments, Mannoni was trying to see white, looking into European fantasies about native innocence and magical isolation (their own). In short, he inquired about who entered colonial administration, and what emerged from latency once they were installed in a colonial environment. Obviously, the culture whose disciplines define the philosophical and political stakes of seeing and classifying will not become transparent to itself using its own devices. This became abundantly clear after the French massacre of some hundred thousand Malagasies in revolt against colonial rule in 1947. What I am interested in at this point is how Mannoni tried, using psychoanalysis, to see the cultural conditions that encouraged French men to become colonial administrators, and what aspects of their characters developed within the blind *Mitsein* in which they were engaged.

If we combine Mannoni's analyses with recent work on the visual technologies of empire, it is the everyday spectacles, the photographs, and the exotic tales that provided some Frenchmen with the conviction that they could escape from an economic and social system on the Continent in which they led lives, in the main, of mediocrity and relative powerlessness.[42] This manufactured dream encouraged projections that, for Mannoni, teach us more about how French whites saw people of color, and how white colonials came to look in the colonial *Mitsein*, than how Malagasies themselves perceived white men. I thus read Mannoni in two ways: first, to focus on his analysis of projection and fantasy; second, to bring out his own blind spot, which proved common enough to structuralist psychologies, and which accounts for the ease with which Franz Fanon and Aimé Césaire could break down his arguments about the Malagasies, even as they too had recourse to what were sometimes blanket psychoanalytic approaches (*Black Skin White Masks*, 61–62). My point is this: psychoanalysis confronts Husserl's bracketed "indications"; it could do so because it did not begin with a theory of the subject as subject-personality onto which "character predicates" or behavior were grafted.[43] As Edmond Ortigues argued, psychoanalysis pursues personality itself as a (or a multitude of) predicate in a history. This opens a space in which conscious and unconscious values can be explored within cultural contexts. That said, it was Fanon, Césaire, and others who showed that the ambitions of psychoanalysis are worthless without history and economics, without the history and economics of colonialism.[44]

Within a narcissistic economy (arguably, the root of *all* our psychic economies), the visibility of the other appears greater to the degree that it functions as a screen for our projections. This seems especially so when an individual or a group confronts others with whom they have little spontaneous identification. Thus the islander, the African, the *Ostjude* [Eastern European Jews], are the blacker—the more "savage," the more "Jewish," the more "child-like" or "degenerate"—when they function as the anti-ideal or obstacle to a positive narcissism, as conceived by the white position, which is doing the projecting.

Yet this tells us little about the view of the white from the side of the one beyond the projection screen. In fact, a host of views of whiteness surface during and after colonization and postcolonial reorganization. What seems invariable is that the narcissistic reflex of ab-jecting and projecting negative (especially fearsome or disgusting) qualities onto an other, to protect the self from itself, seems less universal among colonized others than among European (or American) whites. Can we accredit this just to political dynamics *or* differences of psychology?[45] More interesting is that the abjected or othered persons, *whatever they ultimately do with the projections foisted on them*, internalize the emotional force *and* the imagery of the projections, and this, over considerable periods of time and through political changes. This creates a shattered image of self and body, what Fanon called the corporeal schema doubled by a "historico-racial schema," provided by "the other, the white man, who had woven me out of a thousand details, anecdotes, stories."[46]

V. Why (Colonial) Whites Saw "Black" while the Colonized Saw . . . a Gaze

After decades of discussion and critique, social structuralisms and psychological history have shown their failings. Mannoni, like Tzvetan Todorov,[47] retains an interest as *a moment* in structural psychology because he attempts to "see white" psychoanalytically, using novels, biography, ethnographic studies, and his twenty years' stay in Madagascar. Moreover, he commits the error that social psychologies must confront: to want to explain too much, within one framework. Indeed, he comes to realize that he was writing in pursuit of his own *desire*, viz., that he believed he could explain *both* Europeanized Malagasies *and* European colonials. If his enterprise fails on the Malagasy side, it does so because he is convinced of the universality of psychoanalytic categories. It fails again because he does not reflect on what Fanon would call a "galaxy of erosive stereotypes" (*Black Skin White Masks*, 129). Yet his failure is an effective introduction to the difficulty of seeing white, because the gaps Mannoni and Fanon both address concern those that Husserl's phenomenology left open, with its focus on *logical* grammar rather than *psychological* grammar. What drives this work is ultimately the will to see the human personality as the dynamic unfolding of our encounters with others, with violence, and with economic and cultural institutions—a will that carries a political dimension with it. Indeed, the political question for the psychology of cultures remains: how to avoid what Bruce Mazlish called the "counter-transference" problem. It besets efforts at seeing white, in the form of defenses and unacknowledged ambivalence. It blinds intellectuals into believing they are seeing the other, when they are just seeing the other in her or his *Mitsein* or way of being-with, or being-under, the other's (the white's) regard.

This then is Mannoni's dilemma. But he was, I think, the first (white) European to study—with sensitivity *and* opacity—the white colonial and to ask why what French whites saw in the colonized other was *not* what the colonized saw. He thus asked a question similar to Todorov's when he studied the sixteenth-century conquest of Mexico: Why was there relatively little revolt against the white colonizers? Both men have been criticized for missing a point that Fanon, Césaire, and others emphasized: as total violence, colonization destroys the personality of the colonized, with the result that, as Fanon put it in his first book, "When the Negro makes contact with the white world, a certain sensitizing action takes place. If his psychic structure is weak, one observes a collapse of the ego. The black man stops behaving like an actional person."[48] Both Mannoni and Todorov observed this inaction. But Mannoni attributed it to the precolonial acculturalization to dependency (on ancestors), surviving among the Merina. In response, Fanon argued differently. He pointed out that there was resistance, dependence, *and* paralysis in Madagascar. But in so doing, he slid toward a certain inconsistency: the Malagasy "never thought of" the "foreigner . . . as an enemy" (*Black Skin White Masks*, 99). Although this may have been true when the Merina nobles ("Andriana," who themselves took control of much the island in the 1790s) received Protestant missionaries, it was not true when the French overthrew the Merina monarchy (1895–1896). Against Mannoni, he urged that colonization was what accounted for the so-called complex of dependency in the Merina. Of course Fanon's arguments are situated at different levels and historical moments. However, he did not spend years in Madagascar and his first concern was not to see white but to explore what seeing color had come to mean. This is why I am taking a calculated risk with Octave Mannoni, for his discussion of the French colonial psyche strikes me as what has survived best in his work on Madagascar. I hope to show that psychology can supplement phenomenology, provided psychology comes to terms with a *critical history* of the groups it examines. From there, I turn to an existential question: What does it mean to "decenter a gaze," and can we really see white without the experience of being under a gaze?

Mannoni's essay, known in translation as *Prospero and Caliban*, first appeared in 1950 (in English, 1956).[49] The argument sought to be systematic. Moreover, it was itself criticized by Mannoni in an Afterword that he published late, perhaps in response to Fanon and Césaire—although he does not mention them.[50] Before Fanon had published *Black Skin White Masks*, Mannoni was asking how and why it was impossible, from the beginnings of

French colonialism to its first "ends" in the uprising of the 1950s,[51] to see white the same way that whites saw black. Using this to supplement the phenomenology of seeing white, I now summarize his claims.[52]

We may suppose that the massive expansion of Western techniques, rationality, and values has rendered the psychology of cultures an artifact from the past. Are we not all subject today to globalization, postnational capitalism, accompanying utilitarian and instrumentalist values, and the fragmentation of communities? This was part of Fanon's arguments against Mannoni. Yet the latter's analysis of European culture touched an area to which Fanon would himself be drawn two years after. It pointed to the persistence of a Western *fantasy* of the good savage and a Western quest for gentler or more childlike cultures and psyches. Overlooking the violence of Galliéni's 1896 "pacification" of the island, Mannoni argued that the *Mitsein* created between the French and the (already somewhat *Anglicized*) Merina gave rise to patterns in their relationship. His arguments for Europeans' projection of their own difficulties adapting to technological and economic changes at home, their compensatory quest to dominate others, and their self-delusion about white identity are compelling and recall the work, contemporary with his, of the early Frankfurt School.

Mannoni started from the premise that, even if demythified, the subject *as a lived personality* is never wholly unified, though it will strive to integrate itself. Studying presumably the Hova (Europeanized Malagasy merchants and farmers, many of whom resisted French domination), he found such a will to integration in phenomena of cultural adaptation and bilingualism.[53]

Nevertheless, what Mannoni was most interested in were the differences. In the West, the differences between cultures are illustrated, fixed, and perpetuated by an expanding mass of images, from drawings to etchings to photographs, whether posed or "spontaneous." The images run the gamut from "savages" dressed up and posed with "whites" (*Images of Savages*, 212) to dignified photos of indigenous persons of rank,[54] to absurd theatrics like the photograph of Fijian "cannibals" from 1890 (*Images of Savages*, 113), to the French Hottentot Venus, a caricature of so-called "steatopygism" in African women (*Images of Savages*, 80). These images of blackness, exoticism, infantilism, and hypersexualization became indices of European (and American) projections, whose structure belongs to fetish-making, narcissism, and what I called the three binaries of the adult-child, male-female, health-illness structures. On the other hand, Mannoni, like Fanon, shows that the narrative images of the white in Malagasy stories[55] *also highlight perceived differences*; but they do so according to a noneroticized logic of ambivalence.[56] And Fanon points to their roots in fear and loss of subjecthood.

It is not clear where he spent most of his twenty years in Madagascar, presumably in Tananarive, the Merina capital,[57] far from the Africanized coasts.

But Mannoni's argument addresses the island like a single case, perhaps because he used extensive ethnographic material from the *Académie malgache.* His principal argument was that, prior to French colonial implantation, the Malagasy, no matter what their caste status was (noble, free peasant, slave), grew up inserted into a network of interdependencies that were rooted in the power and authority of their ancestors and in that of their fathers, who pronounced the will of the ancestors in elaborate rituals. Virtually all social relations were anchored in this socio-sacred and psychological interdependence, and they were non-nomadic—that is, they promoted no errancy or *anomie.*[58]

Characteristic of Imerina society was the presence and power of the ancestors. This conviction structured the Merina's religious practices and customs. Indeed, Mannoni observes, the notion of "custom" translates as that which precisely "*makes one live,*" according to some communities (*Le Racisme revisité,* 98). Thus the proverb: "the living are like the branches of a lemon tree, at the base there is but one branch" (*Le Racisme revisité,* 89). Custom and the ancestor cult promoted a personality structure that depended on absent "fathers," Mannoni concludes. Against this, Fanon countered, "Since Galliéni, the Malagasy has ceased to exist," working against much of the French ethnography of his time. Indeed, Mannoni had arrived already (1920) a generation after the French implantation. It is therefore hard to know what a Malagasy psychic substratum might have been. "There was no [European] addition to the earlier [Malagasy] psychic whole. If, for instance," Fanon parodies, "Martians undertook to colonize the earth men—not to initiate them into Martian culture but to *colonize* them—we should be doubtful of the persistence of any earth personality" (*Black Skin White Masks,* 95).

Fanon thus reminded Mannoni of his own project: "the Malagasy exists *with the European.*" That means, against Mannoni's thesis, that there is no for-himself structure intact beneath that *Mitsein.*

"I begin to suffer [dependence or inferiority]," writes Fanon, "to the degree that the white man imposes discrimination on me, makes me a colonized native, robs me of all worth . . . tells me that I am a parasite on the world . . . 'that my people and I are like a walking dung-heap that disgustingly fertilizes sweet sugar cane and silky cotton'" (*Black Skin White Masks,* 98). Now, no realistic appraisal of colonialism can ignore this. Yet both Fanon and Mannoni's positions owe their insights to a psychology of culture. And they are in deadlock. But we have to ask: what *happens* to memory and to its narratives? While Fanon's Madagascar almost resembles the Martinican situation, Mannoni has given us an indigenous psychic structure that passively *accepts* colonial rule. The irony is that each position has something right to it: Mannoni wanted to disengage the Imerina cultures he observed from the Western obsession with death, and from the (Western) universality of the Oedipal structure. Thus he argued that the Merina father holds authority over wife and children but remained subject to *his* father, whether dead or alive. In fact, once the father dies, his power grows—as authority but also as fecundity.[59] For this reason, as Fanon *also* noted, there seemed to be no Oedipal complexes within Malagasy culture. But the consequence, which Fanon denounced as locking in a presumptive and convenient dependency, was that the Western drive to overcome father figures, and the accompanying *guilt* that Freud observed in the wake of the internalization of the father (the murdered father), do not take shape in Malagasy culture.

Both analyses, Fanon's and Mannoni's, provide insight into seeing white and seeing color; both are rooted in psychoanalysis, though Fanon was more sensitive to economic dynamics in colonialism. What is more, regarding the question of death and mortality, Mannoni makes a striking point, writing lines that make us think of critiques of Nazi intellectuals. He argues:

> It is that Europeans believe *in death*, and death for them is but an object of troubling doubts and questioning. The Malagasy believe *in the dead* but not in death; this is why, having the [ancestor's body] with them, they have need neither of rites nor [other] decorations. . . . [Thus] to understand the situation of a Malagasy child in a family whose ancestors constitute its most important part, it would be necessary to imagine a European family in which . . . all the authority belonged to a grandfather stricken with paralysis. (*Le Racisme revisité*, 96–97).

Mannoni is justifying a social and psychological dependence as transgenerational for the Malagasy. But the argument carries a more compelling intuition into death in twentieth-century Europe. Given Fanon's understanding of the *political* reality of colonization, the worth of Mannoni's psychology here *turns* on the question: What happens to memories, to narratives, and to Imerina custom in the wake of colonization? Now, Fanon was justly infuriated with Mannoni, for the latter was no trivial apologist of colonialism or seeing black. Yet it is impossible to determine what remained of Imerina memory, stories, and custom, because it is part of a larger debate about colonialism as rupture and catastrophe, or as the interruption of a much longer history. It is not even clear to me whether Mannoni has stumbled, in his research, onto what George Clement Bond called "buried knowledge" or whether he had researched the Sakalava and Mahafaly (tribes of the Maroserana, the other "nation" that did not live with the Merina) culture[60] and benefited from those stories "to distance colonizer from the colonized."[61] The boundaries of psychoanalysis are economics, and history, so far as it is decidable.

The consequence—Malagasies' "complex of dependency" to which Mannoni refers arrogantly—is clear for us. There is more to seeing color than "native" dependencies.[62] There is more to seeing white than seeing a new instance of power (colonial rulers), supposed to take the place of the ancestors' power. This is the failed side of Mannoni's work.

Yet those arguments for the dialectical structure of personality, cosmology, and "civilization" were above all directed toward Europeans, with a view to showing how whites *could not see color* beyond their projections. The point Mannoni was groping toward concerned power. To the degree that power is not something one wrests oedipally from a dominant male figure, this is because power cannot be possessed durably, like an object. For the Malagasy, of course, Mannoni's intuition about the colonials could scarcely survive the test of the real; that is, forced labor, forced cultivation, and terror. But Mannoni reminds us that he is making another point about power: against Western missionaries' insistence upon Malagasy, and other indigenous peoples' childishness, the colonials' aggressivity bore, for the Malagasy, what Mannoni deemed a corresponding infantilism (*Le Racisme revisité*, 87)—and, I would add, a dangerous, compensatory one. If the experience of the Malagasy was dual, one of fear and perception of European infantilism, then how can we deny that different cultural patterns, different perceptions, did not underlie the weight of colonial domination? In any case, the Europeans' suppressed inferiority, their anxiety about the authenticity of their own freedom is only half the problem. Fanon insists that the Europeans (and it would seem to be true for white Americans) were unconscious of any inferiority. Be that as it may, Mannoni's extensive reflection on infantilism was also designed to challenge the interpretations of ethnologists like Lévy-Bruhl, who labeled "infantile" what they perceived as a generalized lack of gratitude or predictability among "blacks."[63] After Mannoni, however, Fanon provided a different explanation, using the experience of "Medicine and Colonialism:"[64]

> The first thing that happens is that the patient does not return. This in spite of the fact that it has been clearly explained to him that his ailment . . . requires that he be examined several times at given intervals. . . . it has been explained to him and re-explained, and he has been given a definite appointment with the doctor for a fixed date. But the doctor waits for him in vain.[65]

By some interpretations, this conduct amounts to "infantilism"; by others, it is tied to "native traditions," according to which a cure does not "progress little by little" but must be "assaulted . . . in a single swoop."[66]

Fanon's explanation thus begins with the tones of the old ethnography, only to veer toward its own analysis of power and ambivalence:

> Colonial domination . . . gives rise to and continues to dictate a whole complex of resentful behavior and of refusal on the part of the colonized. The colonized exerts a considerable effort to keep away from the colonial world. . . . In everyday

life, however, the colonized and the colonizers are constantly establishing bonds of economic, technical, and administrative dependence. Colonialism obviously throws all the elements of native society into confusion.[67]

Mannoni's analyses were thus mired in what Fanon called "patterns of conduct existing before the foreign conquest."[68] By his arguments, seeing white proves inseparable from seeing conquest, violence—and "capital," as Senghor wrote (*Black Skin White Masks*, 133). From several citations in his text, it is clear that Mannoni spent most of his time with the Malagasy free mercantile caste, or "Hova," themselves at one time a conquering power on the island. Now, the development of his perspective after the 1947 massacre—one hundred thousand killed by the French colonial power—is addressed in his essay "The Decolonization of Myself," solicited by the London periodical *Race* in 1966 (*Le Racisme revisité*, 317–26). There, Mannoni showed himself defensive and skeptical about everything tied to *Négritude.*

On the other hand, despite Fanon's polemical statement that French society is simply "racist society" (as was or is Britain, the United States, etc.), the French racial imaginary was a necessary but not sufficient condition for attending the Parisian École Coloniale, to join the Corps of Colonial Administrators. The question of who joined, and why, suggests a composite picture of cultural anxiety, romanticization, and quest for isolation and freedom—as well as the desire to dominate. Mannoni's insights here seem to be borne out by William B. Cohen's study, "The Lure of Empire," as well as by the work of Catherine Hodeir and Paul S. Landau on colonial exhibitions and imagery.[69]

At their best, Mannoni's arguments rejoin those of the early Frankfurt school, treating *bourgeois* individualism as a social regression.[70] For Adorno and Horkheimer, European modernity unfolds with a mechanistic understanding of causality, likewise engendering an atomized sense of self whose passage into late modernity is characterized by anxiety, myth, and nostalgia. The modern nexus brings the striving for a fantasized autonomy into tension with its possible realization. The predictable outcomes range from melancholy to aggressivity. Colonial racism itself brings this tension forth (*Le Racisme revisité*, 173). Seeing the Other thus carries with it the attempted actualization of colonizers' projections (from the aforementioned eroticization to variations on the binaries of adult-child, etc.). And this actualization relies upon a massive incomprehension of the culture into which the European has stepped. Of course, Mannoni is only partly correct, having set colonial conquest and domination largely out of the picture—perhaps his incredible *escamotage* of raw violence (which prompted Aimé Césaire to say that Mannoni just "has an answer for everything") was itself a psychic defense.

Ultimately, it is not surprising to find the silence here; and it was not unique to Mannoni's ethnography. The difference is that he later found himself shocked by it—retroactively?—following the 1947 massacre; shocked into attempting a "Decolonization of Myself."

Mannoni's best intuitions include his observations of the European "complex" and drive for isolation in the works Kipling, Defoe, Thomas Swift, and others (it is striking that his main authors are English and that he spends little time with Rousseau; but then, the impact of Kipling on French bourgeois youth was also striking).[71] He speaks of the "Prospero" personality and a Robinson structure:

> A first remark, of great significance, is that the [fictional] shipwreck victim is still less unhappy in [his] absolute solitude than when he is afraid of *not being alone.* We must insist on this paradox . . . man is afraid because he is alone, and this fear is the fear of others. The fear of solitude is the fear of an intrusion. (*Le Racisme revisité,* 157)

But the other is desired only on man's own terms; he "fears and desires" this other in the "ambivalence of a complex" (*Le Racisme revisité,* 157). And once this *Mitsein* is established, the personalities stand in tension to each other, to the obvious peril of the "colonized."[72]

It may be that Mannoni's discussion of the "Prospero complex" was what first interested Fanon in his work. Before beginning a respectful but thorough critique of Mannoni, Fanon writes: "When I embarked on this study, only a few essays by Mannoni, published in a magazine called *Psyché,* were available to me."[73] "I was thinking of writing to M. Mannoni to ask about the conclusions to which his investigations had led him" (*Black Skin White Masks,* 83).[74] Certainly it is Prospero who corresponds to Horkheimer's profile of the "civilized." Moreover, "Whatever the reenactment is directed against, however unhappy it may itself be—Ahasuerus and Mignon, exoticism which evokes the promised land, beauty which summons the thought of sex, the animal whose hint of promiscuity condemns it as repulsive—draws down on itself the destructive fury of the civilized, who can never fully complete the painful process of civilization."[75]

We hear the echoes of Horkheimer in Mannoni's diagnosis.

> C. G. Jung expresses it thus: "Seen from a certain distance . . . it appears that this little part of humanity (Europe) has projected its own mental derangement on people whose instincts are still healthy."[76] This sentence gives us the essential part of what happens; and, largely, the image that we create for ourselves of these peoples is indeed a reflection of our own internal difficulties [*difficultés intérieures*]. (*Le Racisme revisité,* 293)

But he adds, on a personal note: "it is not sure that such an attitude has a cathartic value; it inclines us a bit too readily to refuse interhuman situations" (*Le Racisme revisité*, 293). And in a real gesture of self-reflectivity:

> It is not a matter of finding a psychological explanation for the facts of colonization. It is a matter of knowing why we see them in a certain perspective that deceives us [*qui nous trompe*]. After all, psychology has nothing very useful to say to us about true perception, but *it alone can explain* to us *the illusions of meaning* . . . it can teach us almost nothing about a correct reasoning, but it alone is capable of giving some meaning to a delirium. (*Le Racisme revisité*, 293–94)

That is psychology's best hope for contributing to a phenomenology of seeing white or black. The question, in the matter of seeing white (if we can speak of "seeing" at all, since Derrida and Horkheimer both demonstrate that "seeing" is always a comprehension and categorization *without debate*, i.e., *without "the self-conscious work of thought"*), is to be clear about the limits of concepts like *Prospero* or *Caliban*, and to confront these with economics and politics. As George Bond put it, "the construction of individual and collective identities (for example, racial, ethnic and national) . . . [is] part of the process of *inventing traditions*."[77]

The ultimate irony is that Mannoni's two types, Prospero and Caliban, seem to come together, or exchange places, by the end of his study: the "dependent" personality recognizes the impossibility of depending on the colonial power and fights for autonomy; the autonomous spectacle engineered by the colonial shatters in his dependency on the colonized, and the preservation of this dependency covers itself in violence. Not a lot of calm roosts for returning chickens, one might say. Indeed, as Fanon points out, the dependency complex of the native just recapitulates Recapitulation theory (ontogeny reproduces phylogeny), which had already been transposed from embryology to civilization, and then was reimposed on cultures thanks to Spencerian social psychologies. As to the European dependency, abjured and projected though it is, it arises from "relationships between childhood impressions and the actual complaint [and creates a] behavior pattern, whose final configuration is subject to some few changes, but whose essential content, whose energy and meaning remain unchanged from earliest childhood, [it] is [thus] the determining factor, even though the relations to the adult environment . . . may tend to modify it." This time, it is Fanon diagnosing dependency, using Alfred Adler's work (*Black Skin White Masks*, 61–62). In each category, and sometimes in both writers' speculation, Horkheimer's "self-conscious work of thought" sometimes gets short shrift. Fanon realized that the work of thought required that one show the limits of psychology *in light of economics and history*. At times, Mannoni also perceived this, as when he penned "The Decolonization of Myself."

I have tried to show how Mannoni's fundamental insight about the interhuman situation and about crossed gazes that see nothing recalls Horkheimer's analyses of projection. The latter is worth citing when he characterizes the "paranoiac gaze," because it awakens what looks like paralysis to Fanon and dependency to Mannoni. "[T]he one that goes past you, the hypnotic and the disregarding gaze, are of the same kind: in both, the subject is extinguished. Because in both looks reflection is absent, the unreflecting are electrified by them. [And] they are betrayed . . . the self-encapsulated figure remains a caricature of divine power."[78]

This suggests a meeting point for Fanon and Mannoni. But where Mannoni drew back into his categories, Horkheimer and Adorno pressed on to show the relationship between "positivism," paranoia, and magic in European modernity. "Objectifying thought, like its pathological counterpart, has the arbitrariness of a subjective purpose extraneous to the matter itself and . . . does to it in thought the *violence which later will be done in practice*."[79] In the unintended rapprochement of his two complexes ("Prospero" and "Caliban"), Mannoni, it seems to me, *enacted the antinomy of psychoanalytic positivism.* Fanon and Césaire called him on his own gaze. Why he did not move toward the type of critique that was suggested *precisely by the failure of his two types to be either complementary, or opposed, or dialectizable*, is another question. It has brought me, however, to what I hope is a double claim: for the value of psychology for addressing Husserl's neglected "indications," *and for the danger of psychology* as "saming" technique and metalanguage "that has an answer to everything." I therefore propose a return to one philosophy of the gaze, in an existential and moral sense. My return does not *supplement* psychology, this time. That has to be the work of historians, cultural theorists, activists. It only explores how seeing white might begin in the unchosen decentering of the gaze.

VI. Seeing "White" as a Return of the (Sartrean) Gaze

As I argue above, seeing white is not really about seeing per se. Husserl's elaborate bracketing techniques, designed to "see" the *things themselves*, speak volumes for Horkheimer's conclusion that seeing is always also understanding, even if false understanding: seeing is categorical. Consequently, the leap that seeing makes, to give back to its object a plenitude commensurate with the sensuous excess that the object, that all objects of sight, gives to it—involves projection. Under political or racist circumstances, the danger and regressive potential of this conclusion is obvious. A critical psychology can bring some sense to "delirium" (and I stayed with Mannoni because of his resemblance to

Horkheimer and because he shows a deep culture side of modern, psychic whiteness, when read with Fanon). But psychology cannot stand wholly outside that delirium. How then can we interrupt the movement of delirium? Often, we cannot. Yet some kind of seeing white may occur (at least for the unconsciously white and those who identify as such . . .) if the delirium of a perspective (say, on "others") is interrupted. This is something Fanon and Césaire did for Mannoni.[80] Can we examine this interruption for its existential power?

Joan Copjec's use of Sartre's "regard" in *Being and Nothingness*, which she calls the "gaze," to separate it from the "look" of the voyeur, allows us to glimpse both what *happens* in Mannoni, only to be covered over by him—and what was excluded by Husserl's phenomenological bracketing of psychological consciousness. This incipience and this exclusion are indispensable to understanding, beyond the colonial epoch, what it might mean existentially to start to see white.

According to Sartre's example, a voyeur, looking intently through a keyhole, "is absorbed in his own act of looking" or seeing, "until suddenly he is surprised by the rustling of the branches behind him, or the sound of footsteps followed by silence."[81] Copjec writes, "At this point the *look* of the voyeur is interrupted by the *gaze* that precipitates him as an object, a *body* capable of being hurt."[82] Now, unlike Husserl's other who is constituted *by me as my alter ego*—Sartre's gaze combines danger and an anonymity so basic that "I" *cannot constitute it on any mode of an "alter ego."* The gaze shakes up my implicit conviction that the world is my spectacle and my script. It displaces my stance as a subject—the phenomenologist's subject as well as the psychoanalytic one. Yet, for Sartre, "I can be sure that others exist *because I encounter a gaze*" (*Imagine There's No Woman*, 209, emphasis added). Although the gaze destroys the hegemony of my private perspective (here, through the keyhole) and makes me into an *object* symmetrical with the one I was constituting *for myself*, I do not encounter the subject of that gaze, only the *trace* of that subject (through the sound of footsteps, rustling, etc.). Yet, despite its power to reverse perspectives, the gaze is an everyday thing, a visual or auditory event related to Husserl's "indications": concrete, recurrent, daily, and anonymous.[83]

Unlike Husserl's phenomenology of the other, which Derrida questioned; unlike the complexes merging in Mannoni's argument, the gaze freezes any possibility of symmetry or reciprocity between observer and observed. No ultimate recognition—whether in the medium of analytic understanding, in a "negotiation," or in a co-constitution of same and other—proves possible. Sartre writes, "'The Other [of the gaze] is inapprehensible; he flees me when I seek him and possesses me when I flee him'" (*Imagine There's No Woman*, 210).[84]

Seeing white begins—in a psychopolitical sense—when the keyhole watcher is threatened by a rustling or a step. Although the use of the term *white* for Europeans or Americans predates this, it seems to me that seeing white begins when, forced into him/herself, the looker experiences him/herself as a thing—the very thing she or he was constructing through his/her keyholes. However, this evidence that there are others *out there* also means that the watcher, the seer, is seen, put in question as seer, and constituted as a someone who has now become an object-for. This is why seeing color does not give us seeing white as a truly psychological or political act. This is also why seeing white means nothing much, so long as the conceptuality, and the sedimentation of memory and affectivity *within several cultures*, do not intertwine with the intentional life of phenomenological perception—all the way down to its passive synthesis. That is why seeing white erases itself up until a gaze constitutes the observer as a nonsubject. This is why seeing white abjures itself in the temptation to return to a certain universality ("after all, we are all really human"), or in returning the seer to the position of the neutral emitter of discursive judgments ("as philosophers, *we* shall explore how *an I* is made into an object by . . . "). The gaze that inaugurates a sort of apprehension—the same gaze that actualizes a "seeing white"—halts the pen of a writer like Mannoni, until he or she adds, "And I was soon obliged to realize that my book couldn't *not* be interpreted in a political sense." (*Le Racisme revisité*, 319). This is not enough. But it joins the political of the everyday that Holt, Hodeir, and (many) others have described. It joins the political of anxiety and indeterminacy and may unleash violent reactions. But I think it is there, in the turning of the gaze, that different seeing begins.

Afterword

The three moments in this chapter are moments important to me personally; they interlock, even if, at the same time, I have obscured my own sense of seeing white, being white, within them. The funny thing about phenomenology, so long as we (I, you?) realize that perception is covered by the words and ideas we (I, you?) use, is that it generates values. Reading Levinas and Derrida thrust me toward the question of "seeing Jew" and the history of anti-Semitism. Beyond that, reading feminist philosophy and working with groups of women in France and the States opened me to women's issues. I was part of Maoist movements in the seventies and beyond that. Nothing very unique in that. Psychoanalysis taught me that there are judgments and values that I hold—sometimes act on—without being able to bring them painlessly to consciousness. Some stand in silent but structural contradiction to those that I *want*, and to those I express. This is why philosophies of perception can benefit from the questions asked by (good) psychoanalysis.

Contradictory and unconscious (or semiconscious) beliefs and values are what contribute to exploitative or impossible *Mitseins*. These must be brought forth, for the "me" who holds them, or the group—and they are political, or a hybrid of political, cultural, and deep psychological factors. No reader of this collection needs me to repeat that the domestic *Mitsein* forged by now-"American" whites with people of color and through economic exploitation is the possible (because it's here) *impossible*—in the sense of unlivable. No reader of this collection needs (the) me (half-showing, half-hidden in this writing) to remark that the *Mitsein* the United States has carved into Iraq invites us (what us is this?) to say that "we just haven't learned"—about colonialism, neocolonialism, racism, and political action.

What is missing for a learning curve? I don't know. I do know that when something like psychoanalysis, or literature, digs deeper than the phenomenological examination of what we see and what we say—into the what-we-didn't-want-to-see-or-say—the unmasking must also provide some way of fostering the courage to see and to say.

I'm reminded of a man, long misunderstood, Ralph Ellison, who wrote an entire novel, it seems, to come, at the end of it, to the shattering remark, "Who knows but that, on the lower frequencies, I speak for you?"[85] (Only to see his subsequent novel's "speaking" destroyed by an arsonist in Massachusetts.) The present chapter speaks for me. But who is "me"? I am a first-generation white of vague background and an absent father. I am this because, when my white mother arrived in New York in 1946, her "Scandinavian" looks (she had not finished high school) landed her a job at CBS—and later, a white, well-to-do husband. No need to compare her fate with that of any other person foreclosed (by color, environment, by revolt . . .) from the sort of white performance of class, of "breeding," that my mother took up.

A story illustrates why seeing white is hard to bear (yet necessary, I believe; it is *how* to see white more consistently and more politically, that is the question). When Mannoni set out to write about racism, he took refuge behind psychoanalysis. I've seen (white) people, white philosophers, seek refuge behind a host of protective barriers whose purpose is to make speaking to others (white and nonwhite) something they *can believe they can do*. Mannoni—who wanted to show that there did exist *a* discourse with which to analyze relationships of dominance and perceptions of white and black—found himself astonished by charges that his discourse was *political*. He was surprised that his psychoanalysis carried romanticism and the circular logics by which intellectuals find, willy nilly, precisely what (they didn't realize) they were looking for. That was not his intent. And this chapter no doubt shows what was not my intent: the veils that protect me, so that I can speak; or hide me, so that I think and see, up to a point. To the story, then.

Around 1992, I arranged to meet a (white) friend for brunch. She was going to (a largely white) church and I agreed to join her before going to brunch. She gave directions to the church from her home. I lost the directions and went to a church near her apartment. I walked over to an old Boston Back Bay church and entered. The service had not begun; the organ was playing, the congregation numbered about one hundred fifty people, three of whom were white—not counting myself. I didn't see my friend, but I decided not to walk out from a strange mixture of feelings that combined guilt, decorum, curiosity, and a kind of "it's a good thing to stay." The service progressed, we took communion from little glasses which, when it came my turn to lift one, was difficult to raise because my hand trembled. The pastor placed his hand on my shoulder, I believe, to comfort me. He also invited me to return, at the end of the service. And I wanted to return.

I did not return. The moments in the service, for me, were those of the "white" constituted as other, this time under benign gazes without any one single source other than perhaps the pastor—hardly Sartrean, yet other. When I told a black friend about my shame over my inability to return and my suspicion that here lay the bottom line of my own racism, she laughed. She said, "You're just not used to having a color, are you?"

Seeing white is harder than taking on the academic or liberal talk of "white flight" or "that's a really white town," all of which have become cost-free to intellectuals. Seeing white means more than letting oneself be seen. Does it mean creating and staying in sites where white is a color, a class, and a shifting, adaptable system of power fragments? In Boston, I couldn't bear the "whiteness" . . . of me, although "me" is also not singular. . . .

And yet a seeing-white is in a sense happening—along with regressions, some of them terrible. "White" becomes "visible" as white loses its power to authorize its own norms and legitimate its own unconscious: demographically, politically, in the academy. Perhaps I have to ask, writing these words: What, or whom, do I think I want to see *change* while I sit at my desk? This question is, for me, the site of too many illusions.

I know of a few philosophers who have challenged the (philosophical) faith that "reason" can "teach" people (and who are these people?) that seeing color and not-seeing white must be open to criticism. Impressive in some of their pessimism, a pessimism historically justified, is that some of these philosophers also invest their time and their work in making white visible, in unveiling the strategies of othering. So their pessimism about "reason" does not hold them in immobility. A kind of acting against expectations, or against oneself.

The possibility of sustained seeing white in self must arise with the sense that one (one? I?) is not destroyed by the turning of the gaze upon oneself.

Even if this destruction is a fantasy—and it is. Gaining this sense concerns mediations—of all kinds: writing, discussions, groups, friendships. Even the conviction of the value of analysis, history, and the critical direction of something like Sartre's gaze, will not get one "back into the church" without a sense that the "self," as a historical predicate, is not threatened with destruction if it goes to the church or to where it can see itself as white. That is a process, and one wanders off, forgets, forecloses—because it is not a matter of just living with anger, shame, criticism, with seeing-white.

There is something else, too. Fanon and bell hooks have both written about it. It concerns something like love, or a passion—something that moves our "gaze" inward without shame and outward so that seeing white does not collapse or close up again in self-effacement strategies. Is such a passion born of honesty, of a belief that there is a truth, here, that must be made visible? Is this political honesty? I don't know if passion is born from honesty or honesty from passion. But it's not born from ourselves alone. I don't think I can be honest, can see white, alone.

Notes

This chapter owes its form and the best of its ideas to discussions with George Yancy, to whom I am enduringly grateful. "Roulez! Il n'y a rien à voir." "*Drive on! There is nothing to see*!"—a familiar expression of French police at the scene of shocking, urban immigration roundups, often conducted by stopping police vans at the intersections of large avenues and demanding identification from all drivers passing through. Here, "nothing to see" lies at the core of the problematic of seeing "white"—a problem rooted firstly in historical sedimentation.

1. In a well-documented history of the development of racism, literary and "scientific," from the Renaissance through the nineteenth century, Gustav Jahoda discusses these three "sciences" extensively. Popular with an array of audiences, and dating at least to eighteenth-century materialist thought, physiognomy established the degree of species development using, notably, Camper's famous 1760s "facial angle" that measured the angle formed by forehead, or ear position, in relation to the jaw. Among other things, it argued that the wider the angle the more "ape-like" the specimen. See Jahoda, *Images of Savages: Ancient Roots of Modern Prejudice in Western Culture* (New York: Routledge, 1999), cf. "Towards scientific racism," 63–74.
2. Jahoda reminds us that in nineteenth-century neurology inferior "races" were argued to have *thicker* nerves, whose density then interfered with higher levels of cognition, see *Images of Savages*, 58.
3. Nineteenth-century morphology, from Cuvier's "Hottentot Venus" (1814) to Charles Richet's "ape-likeness" etiquette for Africans (1919), compared size and position of the gluteal muscles, head shape, length of limbs, notably forearms, as well as

the shape of legs—and feet in the case of "non-white" Jews—to establish species differences, invariably along a scale of more and less evolved. See *Images of Savages*, 79–92; also see Sander Gilman, "The Jewish Foot" and "Are Jews White? Or, The History of the Nose Job" in *The Jew's Body* (New York: Routledge, 1991), 38–59, 169–93; and "Trauma and Trains: The Testing Ground of Masculinity" in Gilman, *Freud, Race, and Gender* (Princeton, N.J.: Princeton University Press, 1993), 113–68.

4. Extensive, often florid, claims about genitals' size and shape, in racist physiology as well as the incipient "sexology" brought what were then called "hermaphrodites" and "hemi-spades" together with "Negroes," all of whom possessed larger, or different (e.g., circumcised) genitals than those of Christian Europeans. The phantasmic quality of these claims is evident in the rapprochement between genital form, intellectual maturity, concupiscence, and sexual activity. Jules Virey (1775–1847), among others, who divided humans into fair and dark and argued for polygenesis (multiple origins of human beings), insisted that color determined every sort of entity in nature, including flowers. He expatiated on the moral deficiencies and sexual organs of "Negroes." See *Images of Savages*, 69. The sexologists' concern with character, ability, and genitalia persists through the famous Havelock Ellis's *Studies in the Psychology of Sex*; vol. III, "Sexual Selection in Man" (Philadelphia, Penn.: F. A. Davis and Co., 1926), discusses steatopygia and the attraction felt by "the men of the lower races" for "European women," 153.

5. Ernst Haeckel's (1834–1919) contribution to evolutionary theory, sometimes called "recapitulation" or the "biogenetic law" of morphology, whereby different races reproduce the phylogenetic development of animal species, some of which stop developing earlier than others, see *Images of Savages*, 164. Recapitulation theory overlaps with a curious, long debated theory called "telegony," according to which the race of a male coupled with a female—animal or human—would leave traces in the offspring of the same mother fathered by a *subsequent* father. The famous case of this was the "quagga" (a zebra-like pony) stripes found on a colt sired by an Arabian horse and born to a mare who had first been mated with a quagga. Here, race, in animals or humans, was conceived in light of blood and "mis-alliances"—a holdover from race discourse rooted firmly in "blood lines." The debate about influence or telegony lasted from the heyday of the Great Chain of being conception of natural species in the eighteenth century through Darwin's doubts about clear demarcations between species—discussion of the quagga's mark, famously called the story of "Lord Morton's mare," took place in 1820. Interesting for us, here, is that telegony combined the conception of females as physiological palimpsests (they were "infectable," or "saturatable") for masculine traits *with* an abiding anxiety—among the aristocracy *and* the middle classes—over pure blood, "race," and genetic decay. See Harriet Ritvo, *The Platypus and the Mermaid, and Other Fragments of the Classifying Imagination* (Cambridge, Mass.: Harvard University Press, 1997), 105–20.

6. On the theory of neoteny, nonwhite children, notably Africans, are said to be born well adapted to their environment, only to see their intelligence "dim" after puberty. See *Images of Savages*, 174–76.

7. The work of David Eng and others on Asians, assimilation to "whiteness," and the oppressive "model minority" paradigm in the United States opens a different

perspective onto the white social imaginary and its impact on "others," not to mention a less frequently studied strategy of othering, this time as the "good other"—although not in the sense of "good" or "noble" or "sensuously free savages." See David L. Eng and Shin-hee Han, "A Dialogue on Racial Melancholia," in *Bringing the Plague: Toward a Postmodern Psychoanalysis*, Susan Fairfield, Lynne Layton, and Carolyn Stack, eds. (New York: Other Press, 2002), 233–67. Eng and Han's approach is indebted to object relations theory and to Homi Bhabha.

8. Sander Gilman reminds us that the infamous British slayer of women, "Jack the Ripper," was, according to the official description, a "caricature of the Eastern Jew: 'age 37, rather dark beard and moustache, dark jacket and trousers, black felt hat, spoke with a foreign accent,'" see *The Jew's Body*, op. cit., 113. Popular German literature associated the "nature" of "Blacks" and that of "Jews" under various rubrics of disease in need of healing. German novels after World War I blamed Britain for taking their African colonies, where German health practices were better able to "heal" Africans of their essential and acquired deficiencies. See *Jew's Body*, 215ff.

9. See, for example, the work of Kara Walker, collected in a number of published works including *Presenting Negro Scenes Drawn Upon My Passage Through the South and Reconfigured for the Benefit of Enlightened Audiences Wherever Such May be Found, By Myself, K. E. B. Walker, Colored* (1997), examined by Joan Copjec in *Imagine There's No Woman: Ethics and Sublimation* (Cambridge, Mass.: MIT Press, 2002), 82–107.

10. Until the second half of the eighteenth century, European philosophers and men of letters evinced attitudes of benevolent tolerance toward "savages" who, some of them argued, were traveling through a stage of civilization that the Europeans had already surpassed; or again, certain French writers extolled the independence of Native Americans and the happiness and Epicureanism of South Sea Islanders they encountered. See *Images of Savages*, 49.

11. The obsession with establishing separate "races" among even English and Scottish "whites" reached impressive degrees in England (and elsewhere) in the 1850s and 1860s, thanks to essays such as S. Anderson Smith's "The Degeneration of Race" in the *Lancet* (February 23, 1861). See Ritvo, *The Platypus and the Mermaid*, op. cit., 127–29, 253. There, the Celtic and the Saxon "races" are distinguished, but "white" was otherwise visible as well, in the "white" of the Boston, the Lincolnshire, the Nottinghamshire, the Jute or Kent types, etc.

12. See Georges Didi-Huberman, *Invention of Hysteria* (Cambridge, Mass.: MIT Press, 2003). The photos and drawings from this and other hospitals show a theatrical "scene" in which many of the women subjects present similar postures and "symptoms," the most significant of which were detailed by the famous psychiatrist, Charcot, and displayed in large paintings in the amphitheater in which he delivered his lectures on hysteria to an international community of psychiatrists and other men of science, including in the early 1890s, Sigmund Freud and Pierre Janet. This is not to say that muscular spasms and contortions might not be part of acute posttraumatic disorders; in question here is *how patients were encouraged to make visual display of themselves as subjects of science*, and how this science perfected essences of disease as readily as essences of otherness like Jewishness or "Blackness." Hysteria, Charcot always argued, was demonstrably *a single, unified malady.*

13. On the other hand, in numerous essays, we find that "white" *colonial* humanity is rarely taken, for animals or less-than-human beings. Tzvetan Todorov, among others, has shown that the Spanish arrival in the New World corresponded with Aztec astrological predictions of incipient social upheaval. Consequently, the *Conquistadors* were feared, but not dehumanized. Jahoda points out, in his discussion of cannibalism and European observations of Africans, that "There is no evidence that any savages attributed animality to Europeans—if anything, they were perceived as supernatural beings. Similarly, it was only in exceptional cases, when Europeans tried to learn the skills of other peoples, that they were regarded as child-like." See *Images of Savages*, 109. I return to this point below, in my discussion of Octave Mannoni's study of Madagascar.

14. For an insightful discussion of the tragedies of "color blindness" in Western philosophy—notably in Kant's and Hegel's thought—see Arnold Farr's "Whiteness Visible: Enlightenment Racism and the Structure of Racialized Consciousness," in George Yancy, ed., *What White Looks Like: African-American Philosophers on the Whiteness Question* (New York: Routledge, 2004), 143–58. For a collection of seminal texts, from Kant through Fanon, and the phenomenology of race to the structuralist analysis of race, see Robert Bernasconi, ed., *Race* (Malden, Mass.: Blackwell, 2001).

15. In his essay "The Imaginary" (and elsewhere), the social philosopher Cornelius Castoriadis argues that "each society is a system of interpretation of the world" just as "each society is a construction . . . a creation of a world, of its own world." This creative-interpretive activity is not the work of one or many "subjects," Castoriadis likens it to an atmosphere or a "magma" that is "of such a complexity that it defies imagination and is . . . far beyond our grasp; but, more radically, 'subjects,' 'individuals,' and their 'groups' are themselves the products of a socialization process, for their existence presupposes the existence of an instituted society." Nevertheless, this "social-historical field is irreducible to the traditional types of being," what is in question here is, instead, a "social imaginary, or the instituting society (as opposed to the instituted society)," which is never a "'thing,' another 'subject,' or another 'idea,'" but rather their symbolic, floating matrix. See C. Castoriadis, "The Imaginary," in *World in Fragments: Writings on Politics, Society, Psychoanalysis, and the Imagination*, David Ames Curtis, tr. and ed., (Palo Alto: Stanford University Press, 1997), 8ff.

16. Renaud Barbaras, "The Movement of the Living as the Originary Foundation of Perceptual Intentionality," in Jean Petitot, Francisco J. Varela et al., eds., *Naturalizing Phenomenology: Issues in Contemporary Phenomenology and Cognitive Science* (Palo Alto: Stanford University Press, 1999), 525, emphasis added.

17. See above, 2; also see Gilman, *The Jew's Body*, op. cit., 66–68.

18. Emmanuel Levinas, "L'Œuvre d'Edmond Husserl," in *En découvrant l'existence avec Husserl et Heidegger* (Paris: Vrin, 19XX), 21.

19. Edmund Husserl, *Logische Untersuchung* II, 21. In English, *Logical Investigations II*, Denis Fisette, ed. (Dordrecht and Boston, Mass.: Kluwer Academic Publishers, 2001). Levinas cites Husserl in his essay "L'Œuvre d'Edmond Husserl" in *En Découvrant l'existence avec Husserl et Heidegger* (Paris: Vrin, 19XX), 21. In English, "The Work of Edmund Husserl" in *Discovering Existence with Husserl*, Richard A. Cohen and Michael B. Smith, trs. (Evanston, Ill.: Northwestern University Press, 1998), 47–87.

20. Jacques Derrida, *Speech and Phenomenon*, David B. Allison, tr. (Evanston, Ill.: Northwestern University Press, 1973).

21. That is, the reduction of the contents of our consciousness, as it puts world, or self *as* subject, "out of play"; in brief, as consciousness observes itself *living*, perceiving, and apperceiving.

22. I mean, by binary significations, those opposed pairs like black-white, natural-cultural, "savage"-"civilized," male-female, healthy-diseased. By branching significations, I mean those clusters of meanings that attach to a given concept and are related to but not governed by binary oppositions. One example in the nineteenth and twentieth century racist discourse includes: colonized-infantile-dependent-passionate-bellicose (and obedient)-unpredictable-irresponsible, etc. This cluster maps onto clusters of sexuality, gender, health, "hygienes," and "therapies," as well as political formations. All of these "cover" *how we perceive*, and there is no perceiving, Derrida shows, without signifiers (words), which invariably come with their own meaning-clusters, even (maybe especially, since there we censor ourselves less) in our inner monologues.

23. But not only Western; unfortunately, we have only to think of Mariama Ba's novel, *Une si longue lettre* (Paris: Le Serpent à Plumes, 2001), among others, which explores the caste and class perceptions of her Senegalais peers.

24. Although perhaps to a lesser degree for Americans and Latin Americans, since slavery involved a domestic colonization to which Europeans could remain, for decades, largely oblivious, which meant they could remain oblivious longer to the effects and contestation of their valuations of race and ethnicity.

25. We must also note, here, that before this shift in perspectives toward an ordering of races took place in the mideighteenth century, only to expand in the nineteenth century, the term *race* meant something quite different. Diego Venturino points out that, in the France of the *Ancien Régime* (i.e., at the beginning of the eighteenth century, prior to the French Revolution, and to the advent of "scientific" or biological racism), *race*—when used at all (as opposed to the human species or *espèce*)—referred to blood, which was either noble or common ("roturier"). Within the Christian "mono-geneticist" paradigm, since all "men" descended from a common ancestor, nobility of blood was historically acquired: one could become noble or nobler, "annobli." Discussion of noble versus common "races" is found preeminently in the historian Henry de Boulainvilliers, whom Annals School historian Marc Bloch called a "Gobineau before the letter." For Boulainvilliers, there was no "white" versus "black" or "yellow" paradigm per se (although for Foucault, Boulainvilliers may have been one of its inventors with his mythology of the Germanic race conquering the Gallic race). Blood for de Boulainvilliers was either pure, in its nobility, or impure, "vil," and pure blood meant "aptitude for virtue." This view persists in the nineteenth century's projective images of nonwhites—including Jews, who, given the spectacle of their bodies (e.g., Jews' "weak feet," etc.) or their characters (Africans' infantilism)—as incapable of managing their affairs well and by extension, entering into public or political life. Nevertheless, the notion of race that was anchored in "blood" was also a history-rooted notion. Thus, in his *Essai sur la noblesse de France, Contenant une Dissertation sur son origine et son abaissement* (Amsterdam, 1732), Boulainvilliers writes: "It is thus true that men are naturally equal in the part they have of reason and humanity; if some-

thing distinguishes them personally, it must be virtue or the proper use of this reason: but it would be a false consequence if we concluded, concerning this principle, that it is the sole distinction that should rule amongst men. The examples of the first time we just touched upon, teach us the age [*l'ancienneté*], the use, and the necessity of nobility, the perils and the disorders befalling a State when [nobility] ceases to occupy the first rank. And the same reason, which has made us understand what we owe to virtue, makes it palpable that it [virtue] is more ordinary [regularly perceived] in the good races than in the others." See D. Venturino, "Le paradigme nobiliaire," in Sarga Moussa, ed., *L'idée de 'race' dans les sciences humaines et la littérature (XVIIIe et XIXe Siècles)* (Paris: L'Harmattan, 2003), 31. Venturino cites a passage from Boulainvilliers first cited by the Belgian anthropologist, André Devyver, in his *Le sang épuré. Les préjugés de race chez les gentilhommes français de l'Ancien Régime (1560–1720).* However considerable the persistence of early eighteenth-century *value judgments about blood*—it is certainly evident in Nazi eugenics—the "scientific" framework contributed one essential thing to racist discourse and values: "genetic" or "biological" (read: essential) immutability of race, or whiteness and blackness. Crossracial marriage could thus only "pollute" biological "whiteness," while "whiteness" could only ameliorate "blackness" etc., virtue, warrior nobility, and other related "historic" values did not modify an essence rooted in the body and the psyche—once biological racism gained a foothold.

26. See de la Mettrie, *Man: A Machine*, Gertrude C. Bussey and M. W. Calkins, trs. (LaSalle, Ill.: Open Court Publishers, 1961), first published in 1748. For de la Mettrie, the body was a machine that wound its own spring, and that which we commonly call "soul" was something more like a personality, itself rooted in the body and its processes.

27. Both of which were only rendered more complicated by debates between monogenetists and polygenetists (one versus many origins of historical humanity) and by a non-Lamarckian evolutionism.

28. Compare this with Linnaeus's classification of man, before him, as essentially a quadruped animal like the ape and the sloth in his *System of Nature* (1735). See *Images of Savages*, 41.

29. Materialist scruples that give way, for de la Mettrie, to mythical ones; zoological scruples that gave way, for Linnaeus, to dilemmas of human origins and limits of development.

30. Thus Linnaeus, for his part, further subdivided "man" into the nocturnal "forest man" [*homo sylvestris*, the translation of the Indonesian "Orang-utan"] and *Homo sapiens*, his creature of day (*Images of Savages*, 41). This time, in the language of daylight versus darkness, "whiteness" is there—incipient but clearly understood.

31. A notable example is anti-Semitism, from the ancient, religious version (Jews as killers of Christ) to speculations about Jews as transmitters of syphilis through circumcision, as natural hysterics, and as anomalous in their way of thinking. See Gilman, op. cit., especially, "Jewish Madness and Gender," 93–168 passim. Also see Gilman, *Freud, Race, and Gender*, op. cit., 66ff.

32. Cf. for example, Gilman's remarks on Cesare Lombroso and Alexandre Lacassagne's criminal anthropology and studies of sadism, in *The Jew's Body*, op. cit., 117ff, 131ff.

33. "Thanks to" this transmission, but also *motivating* the continuation of transmitted associations with whiteness and blackness.

34. The greatest of the missionaries' accounts is probably Abbé Prévost's sixteen volume, *Histoire générale des voyages* (Paris: 1746–1759), a work whose last volume preceded the *Encyclopédie* by one year and was utilized by it. See Anne-Marie Mercier-Faivre, *La Danse du Hottentot: Généalogie d'un désastre* in Moussa, ed., *L'idée de 'race,'* op. cit., 73.

35. Catherine Hodeir reminds us that, between 1883 and 1958, there were *at least* eighteen colonial exhibitions (i.e., expositions in which "Africa" and "Asia" were featured as "figures" with pastiche or agglomerative constructions of "temples," living "specimens" performing "native crafts" (many of whom were not allowed to leave the exhibit or the makeshift dormitories constructed to that end), etc. The function of these "Universal" (1885, 1889, 1900, 1935, 1958) or "Colonial Exhibits" (1883, 1886, 1894, 1906, 1922, 1924, 1938—to list a few) was indoctrination. To the last, images and performances were caricatural; to the last, it was insisted these exhibits were designed for the edification of Africans—visitors and those being "taught" techniques like farming in the colonies. Powerful events that clearly predated radio and film, they formed the imagination of French, Dutch, and British children, some of whom would later join the colonial civil service schools. See "Decentering the Gaze at French Colonial Exhibitions," in Paul S. Landau and Deborah D. Kaspin, eds., *Images and Empires: Visuality in Colonial and Postcolonial Africa* (Berkeley and Los Angeles: University of California Press, 2002), 233–51.

36. Octave Mannoni, *Le Racisme revisité: Madagascar, 1947* (Paris: Editions Denoël, 1997; first published as *Psychologie de la colonization* in 1950). This is an essay on colonization and revolt in Madagascar, written between 1944 and 1947.

37. Mannoni writes, "L'image que nous nous faisons de ces peuples [non-européens] est bien un reflet de nos propres difficultés intérieures" (*Le Racisme revisité*, 42).

38. The debate about "transcultural psychiatry" has seen various avatars from Fanon's powerful critiques (1952) of Mannoni (notably his arguments about the Malagasy revolt in 1947 and the massacre that followed), Sartre, Caillois, to critiques of unconscious racism in works on "stress," "ego-boundaries," "guilt" among "Africans" in the anthropological literature of the 1970s. See, for instance, D. Paul Lumsden, "On 'Transcultural Psychiatry, Africans, and Academic Racism" in *American Anthropologist 78*, (Mar. 1976), 101–104. It continues, no doubt.

39. See Franz Fanon's chapter "The So-called Dependency Complex of Colonized Peoples," in Charles Lam Markmann, tr., *Black Skin White Masks* (New York: Grove Press, 1967; first published in 1952), 83–108. Fanon was initially interested in Mannoni's essays on Madagascar. However, when the latter's book was published, in the form of psychological profiles of both the Malagasy (mainly, the Merina) and the French colonist (as "complexes" of dependence and of "inferiority," respectively), Fanon realized that, although he spent some of the 1930s and 1940s in Madagascar, Mannoni had little sense of what French colonialism had done to Malagasy culture—i.e., little sense of the "roots" of the "dependency complex"—much less its caste and class dimension. As Fanon writes, "I have tried zealously to retrace [Mannoni's] line of

orientation. . . . The central idea is that the confrontation of 'civilized' and 'primitive' men creates a special situation . . . and brings about the *emergence* of a mass of illusions and misunderstandings that only a psychological analysis can place and define." Now, since this is M. Mannoni's point of departure, why does he try to make the inferiority complex [of the Malagasy, rooted in a "dependency complex"] something that "antedates colonization?" See Fanon, op. cit., 84–85. Also see Nigel C. Gibson's critique of Mannoni, using Fanon and Merleau-Ponty, in "Mapping Africa's Presences: Merleau-Ponty, Mannoni, and the Malagasy Massacre of 1947 in Franz Fanon's *Black Skin White Masks*," in George Clement Bond and Nigel C. Gibson, eds., *Contested Terrains and Constructed Categories* (Boulder, Colo.: Westview Press, 2002), 235–58; and Gibson, "Losing Sight of the Real: Recasting Merleau-Ponty in Fanon's Critique of Mannoni," in Robert Bernasconi and Sybol Cook, eds., *Race and Racism in Continental Philosophy* (Bloomington and Indianapolis: Indiana University Press, 2003), 129–50. Aimé Césaire, poet and member of the Négritude movement, has similar remarks on the political and economic reality of colonialism in *Discourse on Colonialism*, Joan Pinkham, tr. (New York: Monthly Review Press, 1972, 2000; first published in 1955), 41ff.

40. It seems that Mannoni is circulating in an upper-class universe in Madagascar. For a French man to become an "administrateur," and not just an "agent," required that he have passed his *baccalaureat* and that he attend the elite École Coloniale (f. 1885) in Paris. William B. Cohen has surveyed this group of men, and provides the statistics of their social origins from 1929 through 1936. (See "The Lure of Empire: Why Frenchmen Entered the Colonial Service" in *Journal of Contemporary History 4*, no. 1 [Jan. 1969], 103–16.) In the first year for which we have statistics of students enrolled, 42 percent were children of fathers in "High [French] Administration," 30 percent were the sons of men from "Liberal professions," 14 percent were sons of "Rentiers, small businessmen, *prioriétaires*," while only 1.5 percent of students were sons of "Workers." By 1936, 34 percent came from High Administration families, 17 percent from Liberal Professions, 10 percent from Rentiers, small businessmen, etc., 14 percent from "Workers" (Cohen, 106). Does this point to a class "flip-flop" among the administrators of the French colonies? Perhaps. Would this be why Fanon emphasizes that the colonizer embarked, above all, to make a fortune? I think there may be confusion of levels here: immense fortunes were made by colonial corporations, but "agents" (if they were not also extortionists or contrabanders) were so badly paid that some tried to enroll in the École Coloniale (Cohen, 105–6). The motivation of individuals becoming "Administrators" was, it seems, about wanting to live in their conception of a "restored status," craving culture-power (23 percent of the 400+ administrators Cohen surveyed gave as their first or second reason: "The desire to spread the grandeur of French civilization"; Cohen, 110). "As an administrator who entered the service in the late 1920s wrote [the time when Mannoni was, himself, in Madagascar], his choice was shaped by a wish 'to change the world.' To assume real responsibilities, to dispose of real powers of tutelage and protection" (Cohen, 110).

Finally, as the director of the École Coloniale wrote in the 1930s, "all the answers throb with the desire for freedom" (Cohen, 108). Freedom and false consciousness? Certainly. These men also listed "exotic women," but as Mannoni points out—and

Cohen seconds him—they were readers of Jules Verne, Pierre Loti, and above all Daniel Defoe and Rudyard Kipling in translation. "Many of the men who entered the Corps in the 1930s mention the Vincennes (colonial) exposition as having had an important influence" (Cohen, 113). Dreams of robinsonnades, thirst for power, and the false consciousness of "changing a world" not theirs corresponds to Mannoni's own profile first as colonial, then as psychoanalyst of white European values.

41. I am thinking of Nigel Gibson, who, among other things, reminds us that the "colonial revolt" in Madagascar, which shocked Mannoni while he was in analysis in France, and caused him to return to Madagascar, and to write an Afterword to his book, ended in a massacre of over 100,000 Malagasies. *This* Mannoni largely missed, along with Fanon's pertinent argument that the "ancient" Malagasy culture—if there had been a single such culture (debatable since Madagascar was virtually colonized before the French arrival, by a group they called the "Hova," who became landholders and held indigenous slaves)—then it had been destroyed with the implantation of General Galliéni, colonial invader and, from 1896, "Resident-general of Madagascar." Fanon writes, "since Galliéni, the Malagasy has ceased to exist," op. cit., 94.

42. William Cohen cites André Maurois on the impact of British writers like Kipling on French youths. "Between 1900 and 1920 Kipling influenced French youths as few French writers have been able to do . . . His legends and stories inspired the games and shaped the thoughts of French children. . . . I found . . . above all in his books (*Kim*, *Stalky & Co.*, and *The Bridge Builders*) a heroic conception of life. It was neither exclusively British nor exclusively imperial" (*Figaro Littéraire*, 28 October 1965, cited by Cohen, op. cit., 113). We can imagine that, during World War II and afterward, the heroic conception of life probably was better exemplified by the Resistance and the Communist Party. The *desire*, rooted in *ennui* and the sense of economic and international humiliations, *remained constant*. And intellectuals were *anything but untouched* by it.

43. For a discussion of this, see the remarkable work of Edmond Ortigues, author of *Œdipe Africain*, in "La Théorie de la personnalité en psychanalyse et en ethnologie" in CNRS, *Colloques internationaux du CNRS: La Notion de Personne en Afrique noire (Paris 11–17 octobre 1971)*, (Paris: Editions du CNRS, 1973), 565–71.

44. Beyond Fanon's serious engagement with Mannoni, a few reviews of his work came out in the 1950s; all of which recognized the absurdity of Mannoni's thesis that Europeanized Malagasies had developed a dependency on the colonists only to feel "betrayed" by them upon the introduction of post-WWII reforms. One review, by Kenneth Kirkwood, pointed to the interest of Mannoni's "assessment of the radically different cultural backgrounds and personalities structures" brought together by the colonization of Madagascar and how new structures emerged from this "encounter" (*American Sociological Review*, 1957). Another review acknowledged that Mannoni was trying "to lay bare the foundation of racialism and the sentiment of white superiority which many Western colonials display," despite its overgeneralization about the "responsibility-freedom dilemma" (see Bert Hoselitz, *American Anthropologist 59*, no. 5, 1957, 939). Bruce Mazlish's "Psychology and Problems of Contemporary History" argued that, while Mannoni makes the error of speaking of "the natives as if they were a homogeneous group" ("seeing black"), despite (or because of) his own "personal in-

volvement in the situation," the "one overpowering virtue [of the book is]: he places his colonialists and natives in a *direct psychological confrontation.* This is perhaps the crux of his special addition to psycho-historical inquiry." Moreover, after the Malagasy revolt, Mannoni acknowledged what Mazlish called, his own "'counter-transference' problem." See Mazlish, op. cit., *Journal of Contemporary History* 3, no. 2 (April 1968), 163–77. This seems to me why Mannoni's book carries a certain seduction (which Fanon called "dangerous," because its concentration on psychoanalysis obscured the political history of colonialism in Madagascar) and was reprinted repeatedly in French.

Although the purpose of this chapter is not to assess the colonial or postcolonial periods, it is clear that Fanon's and others' argument, that colonialization (from the end of the nineteenth century through the 1950s) represented a traumatic break in the history of the sites and peoples colonized. There is a large and old debate about whether this "rupture" was definitive, whether it destroyed cultures and prior traditions entirely, or whether one should view colonialism from the vantage point of a longer history of Africa cultures. This debate evinces the dangers implicit in psychological *and* economic history. If one respects the reality of colonialism by acknowledging that it created a decisive break with the African past, is one also assuming, thereby, a continuist model of history such that Europe went unmodified by revolution between 1890 and 1950? Can we hold together the rupture position with no reference to the "internal history of Africa and its peoples?" And what of adaptation to the changes brought about, or forcibly introduced, during the colonial period? I am summing up some of the questions raised by Euro- and Afrocentric perspectives; perspectives that R. Hunt Davis called the 'radical pessimist' perspective (which he dates from Fanon) on irreparable rupture versus a more 'continuous' perspective (credited to J. F. Ade Ajayi, Basil Davidson, and others for colonialism as 'one episode in the continuous flow of African history.'" See Davis, "Interpreting the Colonial Period in African History," *African Affairs* 72, no. 289 (Oct. 1973), 383–400. My interest is to highlight the suppositions in and consequences of each position.

45. This appears uncontrovertible: Malagasies may have "seen white" as strange, ugly (gray eyes and pimento beards), and dangerous. Power and colonial violence probably caused a breakup of the Malagasy's perception of self, as Fanon describes (for himself, as Martiniquais). However that may be, Fanon and Césaire asked why the Malagasies called the whites *Vazaha,* or "honorable stranger." They give us the following answer, which emphasizes the endurance of African civility: "Once again, I systematically defend our old Negro civilizations: they were courteous civilizations." See *Discourse on Colonialism,* op. cit., 51, and Fanon, *Black Skin White Masks,* op. cit., 99. If we hold this answer, we must then ask another, uncomfortable, question: have we ever known a civilization that was courteous but "*failed to* think of a foreign invader as an enemy"? In short, is there anything else we can learn about the performative "*Vazaha*" that *neither romanticizes nor pseudo-analyzes the Malagasy*? This was Mannoni's question, like Todorov and others. It failed because he too romanticized the Malagasy, *even as he showed how the French imagination romanticized the colonies.* Can such questions be answered without violence? Does it imply that the imagination of an oppressor is invariably more dehumanizing than the imagination of an oppressed

person or group? I suspect an answer has would have to do with what one can imagine under conditions of surprise and intimidation. For seeing white, Horkheimer has explored the paranoid personality structure and its projections.

46. Fanon, *Black Skin Whites Masks*, op. cit., 113ff. For a contemporary exploration of the "everyday" stories, images, and practices—within a theoretical structure that anticipates the "new historicism," see Thomas C. Holt's study of minstrelsy and "political correctness" in "Marking: Race, Race-making, and the Writing of History," *American Historical Review*, February 1995, 1–20. Holt brings Fanon and Du Bois discussion of racial "gazes" together in this chapter.

47. Todorov's *The Conquest of America: The Question of the Other* (New York: Harper and Row, 1984; first published in French in 1982) is a semiotic and psychological study of the Spanish conquest of the Mexico. It asks, and answers in light of tribal portents and prophesies, why there was ultimately not more resistance to the Spanish conquerors.

48. Fanon, op. cit., 154. With this, he agrees with Mannoni, that the fundamental Freudian structuring pattern of the personality, the Oedipus complex, "is far from coming into being among Negroes" (152). But this, Fanon claims perhaps romantically, is because "It is too often forgotten that neurosis is not a basic element of human reality" (151–52). From a structuralist perspective, Edmond Ortigues argues that the "Œdipus complex" concerns the introduction of a third "term" into the mother child fusional binary. In this *structural* sense, it is both necessary and unavoidable *and it does not matter*, according to Ortigues, what sort of notion of a "person" or "persona" it contributes to constructing, since whether Western or non-Western the "person" as subject of attributes, is a fiction, a doubling of the being as in-dividuum, a "soul" or a specter—whether of one aspect or many. See Ortigues, op. cit.

49. Mannoni, *Le Racisme revisité*, 71. His psychoanalytic perspective is hybrid. As he puts it in retrospect, he "used principally theories like those of Karl Abraham and Melanie Klein." In regard to his approach, Mannoni writes, "the cult of the dead such as it exists among the Malagasy (and among many other peoples) can be considered as relating quite well, albeit in the particular framework of collective myths and beliefs, in the psychological preservation of an internalized 'good object,' toward which one must make reparations. Such a cult, whose continuous nature distinguishes it clearly from the sort of mourning that we know and which is subject to temporal discontinuities according to certain laws, effectively insures both prophylaxis and the cure for melancholic depressions, though without have the same protective effect against persecutory anxieties. . . . [Thus] the 'wholly phantastic' world that Melanie Klein discovered in the infant, and which is that of persecution, is the same world that has been preserved among the 'primitives' in another manner than among us."

We return to the question of persecution and the gaze below, with our discussion of Copjec.

50. The Martiniquais poet of "*Négritude*," Aimé Césaire, published his *Discourse on Colonialism* three years after Fanon, in 1955. There, he too took issue with Mannoni, "who has an answer for everything," and cites his psychoanalytical apologetics, which turn on the "dependency complex." See *Discourse*, 59–62.

51. The move from demand for reform or willingness to "assimilate" on the part of the "*évolués*" or Europeanized colonials has no single decade of origin. But what one scholar called the "stagnant" interwar years gave way, after World War II, to clear demands for independence. This "began" in Algeria, arguably, with the Algerian Manifesto of February 1943, which De Gaulle tried to palliate with reforms. It continued with the declaration of the Indochinese Republic in March 1946, and the manipulative response it received from France led to war in that year. Forced labor and forced cultivation during the War contributed to the mobilization of rural populations, while rising prices of imported goods angered city and town-dwellers. War time loyalty to the Allies, while receiving precious little after World War I, moved toward clear demands for independence over reform or "civil rights" after World War II. The story is, obviously, not "one." See R. von Albertini, "The Impact of Two World Wars on the Decline of Colonialism," in *Journal of Contemporary History* 4, no. 1 (1969), 17–35.

52. Discussions of the "gaze" in colonial contexts are vast. Homi Bhabha has written about British colonial "seeing" and discourse, see *The Location of Culture* (New York: Routledge, 1994), 85–92. Also see his discussion of the perspectives of the "English gentleman" contrasted with the "new *national* modes of . . . interpreting and speaking the Negro" in "DissemiNation" in Bhabha, ed., *Nation and Narration* (New York: Routledge, 1990), 291–320.

53. "One adapts to two milieux rather like one adapts to bilingualism: one changes attitudes, and under this change subsists the uniqueness of the deep personality, which is not in question. To be sure, this personality is modified by this apparent duplicity, but without ceasing to obey a general law of evolution that applies to all persons. This law would that all the elements that can coexist in a certain manner be integrated into a unity, while those that are not compatible are repressed [*refoulés*]. Thus, each person is unified, but the unification is never absolute, given the repression. Persons who pass from one milieu to another, and who have preserved their unity through integrations and repressions prove to constitute particular cases of this law" (*Le Racisme revisité*, 65–66).

54. For a discussion of this "almost the same [as the English] but not quite . . . but not white," for the Indian colonial experience, see Bhabha, *Location of Culture*, op. cit., 89ff.

55. Not to mention his extensive studies of Malagasy children's dream images, which Fanon, justly, tears apart, on the basis of their direct or indirect experience of Senegalese soldiers used by the French as police and torturers. See *Le Racisme revisité*, 142–49.

56. Is erotic projection subject to gender differences? A spontaneous answer might well be: "of course!" Yet Fanon is precious, here, because he not only points out that the Martiniquais who traveled to France brought with him an eroticized and exoticized image of the French white woman (*Black Skin White Masks*, trs. Charles Lam Markmann [New York: Grove Press, 1967], 70ff)—but this, in a neurotic structure that, he shows, happens to be black under these circumstances (79). Moreover, he also unfolds the erotic projections in white women's fantasies about "Negroes," the most pathological of which was Mlle. B who "lying in bed and hearing [imaginary] tom-toms . . . virtually *saw* Negroes" (208ff).

57. The Merina are supposed to descend from settlers from South-east Asia and speak a language from the Malay-Indonesian group. They first occupied the central highlands, but consolidated into a kingdom in 1787.

58. Upon marriage, the Malagasy woman left her family, only to be integrated into the family of her husband who, himself, received thereby an extended family and additional ancestors. However, Mannoni remarks, of the European experience of marriage, "If we consider the European boy, we see that he must take care, at once, of two difficult problems when he marries: first, [he must] accept his independent situation, leave familial protection; and thereupon . . . find a companion [who is] such that she gives rise to no conflicts between his *anima* [ideal desired one] and his maternal *imago* [introjected, live "image" of the mother], whose affective charge is increased by the fact that he [the European boy] suffers and feels guilty for having left his family. . . . The Malagasy boy does not strike so clearly up against the same difficulties *because he does not feel obligated to break his ties of family dependence.* Thanks to the survival of dependency [ties], he spares himself a transformation; and it seems as though he were never disturbed by the maternal *imago*; it always remains unambiguously protective; and his sexuality thrusts him without equivocation toward a *socia* upon which he projects his *anima*" 174–75.

59. "It was till recently the custom of the Sakalva of the Morondava region to decorate their tombs with sculpted wood of a stupefying obscenity—all the more stupefying that the Malagasys are uniformly prudish. Yet these sculptures are present to recall and make visible (and perhaps accessible) the fecundity that resides in the dead" (*Le Racisme revisité*, 95).

60. See www.metmuseum.org/toah/hd/madg_1/hd_madg_1.htm.

61. See George C. Bond and Angela Gilliam, Introduction to Bond and Gilliam, eds., *Social Construction of the Past: Representation as Power* (London and New York: Routledge, 1994), 8.

62. To be just, Mannoni says, "This civilization [rooted in the cult of the ancestors and producing what he calls "dependence" on them and on figures of power more generally] extends from the Indian Ocean to Melanesia. . . . In Madagascar, one no longer finds more than vague traces of these ancient structures" (*Le Racisme revisité*, 90). The question is less about vestiges of an ancestor cult than the fact that the dependency he sketches makes the Merina, and any other of the eighteen Malagasy tribes literally *susceptible to, even helped by, colonialism.* This is what made the book dangerous. We have seen this kind of dullness among psychoanalysts before.

63. Mannoni cites Lévy-Bruhl, who provides a battery of tales recounted by English travelers, among which, the following story of one Dr. Mackensie, who cures a "native" with his medicine. "The cured patient says to the doctor, 'Your herbs have saved me. You are now my White [mon Blanc]. If you please, give me a knife.' And he adds, '*It is to you that I shall come henceforth with my demands.*'" (*Le Racisme revisité*, 83–84). Mackensie interprets this as "a very strange case of confusion in his ideas" and Lévy-Bruhl goes him one better with "the hypothesis that the treatment was not understood by the native" (*Le Racisme revisité*, 84). Mannoni counters that, manifestly, this is not the case ("Your herbs saved me"). What the Europeans could not *see* was the

dual absence of that European "inferiority," tied to social structures built on competition and autonomization, and the presence of a dependence, within whose framework "gratitude" entails turning to one's "benefactor" for one's needs—rather than setting about to rid oneself of the dependency by "paying him back" or thanking him once and for all.

In isolation and on first sight, this apparent *defense* of Malagasy behavior is beguiling. And Mannoni adds to it a critical observation on Western hypocrisy. He calls this the "*paradox* of Western gratitude": "The [Western] sentiment of gratitude [*reconnaissance*] thus supposes . . . a loosening of dependency. How shall we understand it and what perspectives does it open for us onto the structure of our personality? The vulgar and commercial conception, according to which gratitude should consist, above all, of an exchange of services and good sentiments is not acceptable—one promptly frees oneself [of it] *through a lack of gratitude, in order to owe nothing at all* in certain cases. Gratitude seems to be an effort to maintain what is at first sight a contradictory attitude: to preserve at the same time the sentiment that one owes much and that according to which one owes nothing. It supposes the *negation of dependence and yet the maintenance of an image of dependence* grounded upon a free will" (*Le Racisme revisité*, 86–87).

It should be clear from this that Mannoni was ambivalent about the very meaning of "dependency," given European hypocrisy about it. (It is not so much that it is negative per se, but that it is unbearable to the European psyche, which preserves only the appearance of it in order better to be rid of it—this suggest the paranoid structure of which Horkheimer speaks in "Elements of Anti-Semitism: Limits of Enlightenment.") Still, that Mannoni was *romantic* about "colonial dependency" is, however, obvious.

64. Franz Fanon, *A Dying Colonialism*, Haakon Chevalier, tr. (New York: Grove Press, 1965; first published in 1959), 128–33.

65. Fanon, *A Dying Colonialism*, 129.

66. Fanon, *A Dying Colonialism*, 129.

67. Fanon, *A Dying Colonialism*, 130.

68. Fanon, *A Dying Colonialism*, 130.

69. See Cohen, *Art. Cit.*, and Hodeir, *Art. Cit.* Also see Paul S. Landau, "Empires of the Visual: Photography and Colonial Administration in Africa," in *Images and Empires: Visuality in Colonial and Postcolonial Africa*, op. cit., 233–52. An extensive discussion of the breakfast drink "Banania" is found there. Fanon addresses the product's "slogan": "Y'a bon!" (a "patois" distortion of "c'est bon," set in the mouth of one of the famous Senegalese *tirailleurs*, transformed into an avuncular fellow). Also see Gibson's discussion of Fanon and Banania in "Aping Africa's Presences," op. cit., 239–41. Finally, compare with Thomas C. Holt's "Marking: Race, Race-making, and the Writing of History," *Art. Cit.*, 16–18, for a discussion of minstrelsy and its emergent figures from Aunt Jemima to Uncle Ben.

70. Max Horkheimer and Theodor W. Adorno, *Dialectic of Enlightenment: Philosophical Fragments*, Edmund Jephcott, tr., Gunzelin Schmid Noerr, ed. (Palo Alto, Calif.: Stanford University Press, 2002), 244.

71. See Cohen, *Art. Cit.*, 113.

72. Mannoni writes, after examining the correspondence, and a late text of Defoe, *Serious Reflections*, "Misanthropy, melancholy, pathological need for solitude, projection of one's faults on the other, culpability in regard to the father, repressed sentiment toward a daughter whose sex one wants to ignore, such is the case of Defoe in broad strokes. From there came Robinson, in the manner of a dream. And when this dream was published, *all of Europe realized that it was dreaming it as well.* For over a century, because of this dream, the 'savage' was but that minimum of reality on which the European, more or less infantile or, like Rousseau, incapable of adapting to the real, could project an inward image that a too precise, too well known reality thrust aside" (*Le Racisme revisité*, 161–62).

73. Of the five essays Mannoni lists in his bibliography, written by himself, the *Psyché* essay is not one.

74. Also see Nigel Gibson, "Mapping Africa's Presences," 244: "Fanon welcomed Mannoni's attempt to understand the colonial dynamic psychoanalytically," but (as Gibson points out clearly) the appearance of the book was a betrayal, Mannoni essentialized the colonized psyche as one of dependency (on ancestors, then on the colonial power) rather than seeing *how* dependency was engendered by colonial terror itself.

75. Horkheimer, "Elements of Anti-Semitism: Limits of Enlightenment," in Max Horkheimer and Theodor W. Adorno, *Dialectic of Enlightenment: Philosophical Fragments*, op. cit., 141.

76. Fanon makes a comparable point, and uses Jung and Adler.

77. See Bond and Gilliam, Introduction to *Social Construction of the Past*, op. cit., 13. We see this played out in essays like R. Hunt Davis's "Interpreting the Colonial Period in African History," *Art. Cit.*; even his "globalist interpretation" joins in, and helps create, an intellectual "tradition" in understanding.

78. Horkheimer, *Art. Cit.*, 158.

79. Horkheimer, *Art. Cit.*, 158.

80. In the "Decolonization of Myself," Mannoni ventures the incredible remark that his book could not fail to be read *politically*—even though *it was not a political exercise at all.* Of course, what is it to try to see "into" the personality structures of same and other in conflict, if not a political gesture of sophistication *and* self-deception? Mannoni sees "white" in his colonials and in himself. He cannot "see white" from the Malagasy position, because as Fanon has shown, he cannot see the screen of the Malagasy personality under colonialism (certain assimilated Malagasy could probably not see it, either, and Fanon is aware of this in the situation of the Martiniquais). The screen facilitates projections of Mannoni's analysis, and these projections have an epistemologically stabilizing effect. Mannoni can continue to believe that the French, *his* French colleagues, are among the least racist people in Europe. But that he could not see the comforting effect of his projections is the zero point of the "political" core of his work.

81. I am largely following Copjec's summary here; see J. Copjec, "What Zapruder Saw," in *Imagine There's No Woman: Ethics and Sublimation* (Cambridge, Mass.: MIT Press, 2002), 209.

82. Copjec, *Imagine There's No Woman.*

83. The gaze is "there," certainly: "I stumble on it as a surplus object *in the world*." I encounter it "*directly* through a chance meeting" that destroys "the infinitely receding [or multipliable] horizon of experience on which idealist philosophers place the Other" (*Imagine There's No Woman*, 210).

84. Copjec is citing Sartre's *Being and Nothingness*, Hazel Barnes, tr. (New York: Washington Square Press, 1992), 529. Note that the "effect" of the gaze relates to Mannoni's account of the challenge posed to the ancestors' power by the colonists. The "challenge" was *neither* desired, *nor* freely accepted. It had a complex structure that involved a kind of "haunting" even as the Vazaha "gibbered" absurdly "in their ships"—as though the regard of the ancestors was threatened by something like a gaze of the ones "from beyond the seas."

85. Ralph Ellison ends, "Being invisible and without substance, a disembodied voice . . . what else could I do? What else but try to tell you what was really happening when your eyes were looking through? And it is this which frightens me: Who knows but that, on the lower frequencies, I speak for you?" Does this express a moment of a gaze . . . avoided by "you," a "you" looking through, inured to or unprepared for a gaze?" See *Invisible Man* (New York: Random House, 1947, 1972), 439.

II

BLACK ON BLACK

8

(Re)Conceptualizing Blackness and Making Race Obsolescent

Clarence Sholé Johnson
Middle Tennessee State University

I. Introduction

> An oppressive polity characterized by group domination distorts our cognizing in ways that themselves need to be theorized about. We are blinded to realities that we should see, taking for granted as natural what are in fact human-created structures. So we need to see differently, ridding ourselves of [race], class and gender bias, coming to recognize as political what we had previously thought of as apolitical or personal, doing conceptual innovation, reconceiving the familiar, looking with new eyes at the old world around us.
>
> —Charles W. Mills, *The Racial Contract*

TO ADVANCE A NEW CONCEPTION OF BLACKNESS (or any other concept for that matter), as is implied in my use of the term *(re)conceptualizing*, implies that there is a certain conception from which I wish to depart or to which I take exception. That this is certainly the case is evident from a casual examination of how blackness has been conceptualized in Western intellectual history. That conception, arguably traceable to the Bible but that gained prominence in the European Enlightenment, identifies blackness with evil. In the Bible, in particular, blackness is identified with evils or natural disasters, such as blight, pestilence, famine, floods, darkness, and plagues. In contrast, whiteness is associated/identified with purity, salvation, cleansing, and the like.[1] Perhaps such representations of blackness in religious contexts were meant only to be metaphorical. After all, it might be said, the Bible is pregnant (or heavily laden) with allegorical meanings, for which reason it can be read as good literature even if not for its purported religious (or theological) value. Be it so. Yet one cannot ignore the fact that the supposed symbolic representation of blackness in the Bible and related religious texts later will be given literal meaning in the European Enlightenment. In Enlightenment writings, the attribute of blackness, when instantiated in concrete particulars designated (question-beggingly) "persons," unequivocally meant that the entities so designated ranked lowest in the Great Chain of Nature *because of that attribute.*[2]

My proposed aim, therefore, is to counteract such a negative conception and to advance a positive one that is aimed at de-centering whiteness. The conception I advance, if successful, will provide a framework for moving beyond race in our attempts to address sociopolitical matters that are currently conceptualized within a race discourse. In this respect, my proposed conception of blackness is both counterhegemonic and *color transcending.* I characterize my reconceptualizing endeavor as a political conception of blackness. Given that the proximate cause of my attempt to reconceptualize blackness in the manner proposed is principally the negative representation that permeated Enlightenment discourses and that has filtered down to us, it is therefore with such a representation that I commence my discussion.

II. Background: The Enlightenment Conception of Blackness (or, How Blackness Was Socially Constructed)

One need not explore the gamut of Enlightenment writings to have an idea of how blackness was represented in Enlightenment literature. Two authoritative sources of Enlightenment intellectual views of blackness, at least as this property was instantiated in Africans, are the French *Encyclopédie* and the *Encyclopaedia Britannica.* The *Encyclopédie* characterizes Africans as ugly and wicked because of the blackness of their skin. Similarly, the *Encyclopaedia Britannica* identifies the blackness of Africans with ugliness and vices such as idleness, treachery, cruelty, stealing, lying, and so on.[3] One of the chief architects of this view, however, was the French scientist François Bernier.[4] According to Léon Poliakov, Bernier was the first to undertake a "racial classification" and to use the term *race* in modern scientific discourse to characterize different groups of individuals, to use a philosophically neutral term (Poliakov 1974, 135). In his *Journal des Sçavans* (Paris, 24 April 1684, 85–89), Bernier wrote: "I have observed that there are, in the main, four or five races of men among which the difference is so conspicuous that it can properly be used to mark a division" (quoted from Poliakov, 143). After he had designated the various "races," Bernier then proceeded to assimilate the "Egyptians and the swarthy Hindus" to the Europeans, and to claim that "their colour is only accidental and is due merely to the fact that they are exposed to the sun," in contrast to the Africans, whose "blackness is essential." (Poliakov, 143) Drawing upon these observations, Poliakov concludes that Bernier "was a modern man . . . [who] divided mankind both according to skin-colour and other physical traits, and according to geographical or spatial considerations" (Poliakov, 143).

Bernier subsequently was followed by other Enlightenment figures such as Carl von Linneaus, Georg Louis LeClerc (also known as Count de Buffon), and others in this endeavor to categorize the varieties of men.[5] This is not the place to delineate a comprehensive account of the construction of blackness, and by extension race. But I provide this rather crude thumbnail sketch only to highlight the fact that the construction of blackness started out seemingly as a scientific project. It supposedly was to elucidate the source of the pigmentation of blacks. That black pigmentation called for an explanation at all presupposes that blackness was deemed a deviation from some norm, and that norm was white pigmentation. It was therefore in light of that presupposition that European scientists (and nonscientists) posited what they considered certain biological "facts" about blacks. However, this attempt took on special social significance when it became linked to European politico-economic aims. The conception of blackness that resulted identifies blackness with deficiency in nature: physical, cognitive, emotional, moral, and aesthetic as is evident in the *Encyclopédie* and the *Britannica* and also in the writings of some key philosophers and statesmen.[6] It is in light of this social significance that scholars have come to characterize the resultant conception of blackness in Enlightenment discourse as a social construction.[7] What this means is that the concept of the black *race* that presumably originated in science and disseminated through the humanistic disciplines was calculated to promote European hegemony and politico-economic aims post-Columbus.

There appear to have been three procedural elements to this social construction of blackness. First, the color, black, when instantiated in two-legged mammals, was not simply considered an inherent property of such entities, but also, and more importantly, those entities were generically relegated to the class of nonrational animals *because of that color*. What we have here is an opposition between blackness and cognition (or rationality) and thus the "animalization" of blacks in the sense that blacks are cognitively deprived. Bluntly put, to be black is to be an animal. Second, and as reinforcement, these two-legged, noncognitive black animals categorically were declared nonhumans, since being human entails being rational, and vice versa. We should here be reminded of Locke's admonition in the *Essay Concerning Human Understanding* not to confuse and conflate the identity conditions for being a man with those for being a person. Locke expressly tells us that the concept of a man is distinct and different from the concept of a person. Thus, that a thing is (re)identifiable as a man does not entail that it is also (re)identifiable as a person. This is because the capacity to reason and reflect is the defining attribute of a person, and this attribute is not necessarily instantiated in a man.[8] And we also should not forget Hegel's unabashed characterization of blacks (meaning Africans) as "animal man," as noted above. We thus have the explicit conceptualization of the black as a nonhuman entity. Third, given that of all nonwhite, two-legged, apparently noncognitive animals, blacks *seemed*, however, to make articulate sounds, even if incomprehensible to the European, as they also seemed to exhibit voluntary conduct, blacks therefore must belong to a different *species* from that of humans and other non-rational animals. It is through this speciation that blacks are conceived of essentially as a distinct *nonhuman racial category*.

The black race thus conceptualized, in terms of a necessary connection between color and (quasi-) cognitive deprivation, and being made the antithesis of the white race, was designated "inferior" to the white race and then ascribed a subordinate ontological status to the white. This is clear from the ontological hierarchy disseminated by Bernier, Linneaus, LeClerc and others, and defended particularly by philosophers such as Hume, Kant, Jefferson, and Hegel, among others. Among two-legged sentient beings, those presumably cognitively endowed were deemed superior ontologically, and hence socially, to those cognitively deprived, wherein cognitive endowment or deprivation was a function of pigmentation, and hence race. In the ontological arrangement thus devised, the black race was beneath the white but above other two-legged noncognitive animals.

For the purpose of the present discussion, I wish to note that the hierarchy of races created during the Enlightenment holds the key to explaining the existential realities of diasporic blacks dating back to slavery. First, we now have the ontological basis for slavery: Africans were deemed at best subhumans and at worst brutes. We should remember in this connection that during slavery in the United States, blacks constitutionally were declared three-fifths humans.[9] Moreover, among the various rationales given *against* the abolition of slavery was that black slaves were infantile; they were cognitively incapable of seeking their own individual welfare, so that they had to be enslaved for their own good.[10] Second, we have also the ontological basis for colonialism in Africa: Africans were considered inherently incapable of self-rule because self-rule manifests rational agency. A rational agent can originate and terminate change. She can act and forbear to act. Africans were not endowed with the cognitive capacity for rational agency and as such they were not agents in the crucial sense of volitional beings. Thus, as Hegel would go on to remark, colonialism would be good for them.[11] And third, we now have the ontological basis to explain black social oppression or the intense universal hatred for blacks in contemporary Western societies. The common denominator in all instances of overt or covert black oppression in contemporary Western societies is the pigmentation, black, that is instantiated in two-legged, speech articulate mammals. Black existential realities derive from no other source than their color. In particular, it is the source of the systemic discriminatory acts against them. It also is the source of the inequity they experience in the distribution of societal dividends and costs of which they invariably receive lesser dividends and at greater costs. We should consider here the appropriation of black labor without pay during slavery as well as the exploitative share-cropping system of farming during Reconstruction.[12] These are some of the *social and political consequences of blackness.*

Of course, the view that blackness in particular, and race in general, was socially constructed by Europeans essentially to validate Europeans and with certain politico-economic aims is not particularly new.[13] However, I have tried to bring out what I consider the procedural steps in the construction enterprise. In this regard, the social construction of blackness (and race as such) is analogous to that of any other human invention: social utility. It was causally efficacious for Europeans to construct blackness as Otherness, or as deviance, in order to advance European hegemonic aims. To adapt the words of Valentin Mudimbe, Europe "invented" blackness (Africans) in order to advance European politico-economic aims both in the New World and in the Old World.[14] It should not escape notice, however, that the Enlightenment classificatory categories applied only to *human beings.*[15] In other words, the terms *whiteness* and *blackness*, as category identifiers with cognitive, moral, and aesthetic implications, were not extended to animals and plants. Enlightenment thinkers did not characterize a black cat, for example, as ugly, stupid, and full of vices, and a white cat as beautiful, intelligent, and virtuous. Yet there is no denying the ontological givenness of color differences among cats and other natural entities, including humans. Why did they not apply such characterization to entities other than things that could be characterized as humans? The answer is obvious. These animals did not have the kind of social utility that could be exploited in the magnitude to which black labor was exploited for monumental economic gain.

III. Being or Becoming Black: A Reconceptualization

Given the foregoing observations about the social construction of blackness, what then might it mean to be (or become) black if there is no biological *essence* to blackness? Two approaches may be taken to addressing this question. The first and obvious approach is to identify blackness with skin pigmentation. In this sense one can be or become black only through some chemical procedure such as "reverse bleaching" (or tanning) to alter one's skin pigmentation. Bleaching itself is a chemical process to "lighten" the skin color/tone from a darker hue. Pop Star Michael Jackson, for example, is deemed to have "bleached" his skin color, thereby altering it from black to white. So, by "reverse bleaching" I mean a chemical procedure to *darken* skin color/tone from a lighter hue. In the present context, "reverse bleaching" would be the use of a chemical process specifically to alter a white pigmentation to that of black, contrary to what some may describe as "the practice" of alteration in the opposite direction. Undoubtedly, chemical alteration of one's pigmentation, whether in bleaching or what I have termed "reverse bleaching," may have sociopolitical consequences in that it says a lot about the aesthetic values privileged in the society and the effect of the valuation system on individuals. Yet this approach is not what I think is called for in the present context, for being or becoming black is not about altering skin pigmentation. This leads me to the second approach, and the one that I think is germane to sociopolitical discourse.

I begin by characterizing this approach as *being or becoming black in a transgressive counterhegemonic sense.* On this approach, to say that an individual is or becomes black is to say that the individual is or becomes conscious that the positing of racial categories itself was to advance and uphold certain power dynamics in society. Moreover, as a result of this awareness, the individual engages in some form of counterhegemonic activity aimed at dismantling the racial categories in question. Let me expand this view presently.

An individual's consciousness about racial categories in this transgressive, counterhegemonic sense consists in her or his awareness of the fact that to be black (in terms of a person's pigmentation) automatically translates into occupying a subordinate social position in society. By contrast, to be white (in terms of a person's skin pigmentation) automatically translates into occupying a position of power. The significant point here concerns the individual's awareness of *whiteness* and *blackness* as terms for racial categories that represent and reflect distinct and unequal social locations in society, wherein the criterion for membership into a racial category, and hence for entry into a given social location, is skin color.[16] Given this understanding, to be or to become black in the sense I am proposing is a two-step enterprise. First, it is to become aware of the social inequities that derive from social locations contingent on skin pigmentation. And, second, it is to undertake transgressive forms of activity aimed at dismantling the social hierarchy built on pigmentation and the notions that sustain it. Blackness in this regard transcends pigmentation in much the same way that (say) the concept of an Africana scholar cuts across categories of nation, race, class, and gender, among others.

Obviously, it does not follow from the fact that an individual is pigmentationally black that he also is black in the transgressive, counterhegemonic sense. Nor does it follow from the fact that an individual is pigmentationally white that she cannot be or become black in the counterhegemonic sense. To illustrate, some so-called self-hating blacks are not black in the counterhegemonic sense.[17] Sometimes, such individuals are materially successful, so they celebrate the status quo because of their success in it. However, they fail to see that material success does not necessarily entail social equality.[18] Or, more directly, those self-hating blacks fail to see that even as they are materially successful, they still occupy a subordinate social position in the society because of their pigmentation. It is in this respect, as I have argued elsewhere, that an individual may be oppressed even though he or she has not had any denigrating experience.[19] The individual's oppression is a function of her or his social location whether or not she or he has had the relevant experience of denigration. At best, then, such self-hating blacks are socially tolerated by the status quo. But social toleration is not social equality. On the other hand, there are individuals whose pigmentation is white and thus stand to benefit from the privileged social consequences of whiteness, but who nevertheless choose to be involved in transgressive, counterhegemonic activities to dismantle the norms and institutions that promote social inequities built around pigmentation and other variables.[20] On my analysis, such individuals choose to become black.

Some might perhaps object to the conception of blackness I have advanced, saying that it is condescending to those who are pigmentationally black. The very idea of choosing to become black is denigrating to blacks, the objection might go, because it tacitly upholds the existing social values ascribed to color and skin pigmentation of which black is cast as negative. On the view being proposed here, to become black is tantamount to saying "I am going to be like you people so that we can all join together to fight *your* oppression." But the idea of "becoming like you people" is offensive and condescending to blacks. Thus, the conception of blackness being advanced, if successful, will have achieved its aims but at great costs to blacks. It will have done so by subjecting blacks to further indignity as also by indirectly validating the very social hierarchy it had sought to dismantle.

What this objection highlights is the difficulty of attempting to rectify the discourse in which a whole group of people has been presented negatively while retaining fundamental terms in the discourse. To motivate the point of the objection, calling a child stupid, for example, affects the child psychologically and otherwise. So even if one alters the meaning of the term *stupid* after the damage has been done, such alteration of meaning still leaves intact the damaging effect of the prior use of the term. But unlike the state of affairs just described, it is not possible to eliminate the terms *black* and *white* from regular discourse, nor can we very easily change their meanings. This is because these terms are used at the very least to identify and designate different pigmentations of entities, and so their referents are real. In other words, the terms play a significant role in language. This being the case, there is no other sense to being black, white, red, or anything, except that already present in language. And there is therefore no sense to becoming black except along the same lines.

But this objection can be met. The objection seems to miss out a very significant element of my discussion, namely, that, insofar as humans are concerned, the very discourse of blackness and whiteness is sociopolitical in the sense that it is clothed in normative and other values to uphold a hierarchy that was socially constructed. The discourse is about social positioning of which skin pigmentation and the relevant referential expressions are a tool. Granted this claim, one can alter the normative use of whiteness and blackness by dismantling the sociopolitical framework within which it is embedded. One way of effecting this dismantling is to alter the conventional use of the terms of the discourse. It is such alteration of terms, and by extension the dismantling of the state of affairs to which they refer, that I am advocating by positing the concept of blackness as counterhegemonic. Far from discounting blackness and whiteness as descriptors of pigmentation, however, my view recognizes such uses of the terms. But it goes beyond them in suggesting a political use as well. The political use is one in which blackness is subversive of the status quo, viz. whiteness. Given this use, there is no incongruity in the idea of a person being pigmentationally white and politically black, or of a person being pigmentationally black and politically white. All it means to say that a person is politically black is that the person is anti-status quo; that she or he is ideologically committed to de-centering whiteness; that she or he is oppositional or counterhegemonic. Indeed, there is a historical precedent for the reconceptualized view of blackness I am proposing. The precedent is in the 1805 Constitution of Haiti that formally established Haiti as a sovereign state subsequent to the Haitian Revolution in 1803. The Revolution was by African slaves in what then was a French colony called Saint Domingue. Following the Revolution, a constitution was passed that, among other things, changed the colony's name from Saint Domingue to Haiti, thereby inaugurating a new beginning for the former slaves in a new state, both literally and metaphorically. In the context of this new beginning, the Constitution made some very significant stipulations, such as eliminating color differences among Haitians by characterizing all Haitians as black. Article 14 of the Constitution states: "All distinctions of color will by necessity disappear among the children of one and the same family . . . [and] Haitians shall be known from now on by the generic denomination of blacks."[21] This stipulation about color should be seen in the context of the provisions of Articles 12 and 13. Article 12 outlaws both the ownership of property and the acquisition of "title of master or proprietor" by white men. And Article 13 stipulates that such prohibition on property ownership in Article 12 shall not extend to "white women who have been naturalized by the government, nor on their present or future children." In this respect, the Germans and Poles are specifically mentioned.

Severally or collectively, these stipulations are highly significant. To begin, they show that the 1805 Constitution of Haiti deliberately excluded white men from having property rights and the title of master precisely because the twin characteristics of property owner and master were central to the institution and practice of slavery. White men considered themselves property owners, of which blacks, *qua* slaves, were included among their property. And white men also regarded themselves as masters over blacks. Since the revolution was by slaves, and its goal was to achieve freedom and end slavery, the "founding fathers" of the new state thus thought it fit to eradicate these cardinal features of slavery and black oppression from the new polity. They effectively accomplished this goal through the Constitution by making white men a depropertied class. In this way, the 1805 Constitution not only formally ended slavery in the former French colony of Saint Domingue, but it also sanctified a new beginning for the freed slaves in the very symbolic act of *renaming* the former French colony. More to my purpose in the present study, however, the 1805 Constitution of Haiti erased racial categories from the newly established polity in declaring that all pigmentationally and phenotypically white persons were from that day considered black. Although the Constitution specifically named the Poles and Germans, these groups are to be seen merely as examples of white people in the new republic. In any case, by so doing the 1805 Constitution of Haiti proposed what I have variously characterized as a political, transgressive, and counterhegemonic view of blackness. In light of this historical fact, therefore, the position I am advancing is not as far-fetched as it may seem at first. On the contrary, it provides a useful conceptual starting point for challenging the race discourse that we have been bequeathed by the Enlightenment, social policies that are framed within such discourse, and social injustice predicated on social location that in turn is driven by such discourse. Accordingly, the objection that my proposed conception of blackness subjects blacks to further indignity by upholding the status quo is seriously mistaken. The truth, on the contrary, is that my proposed transgressive conception of blackness undermines the status quo by transcending color, and hence race, in a way similar to the transracial coalitions of the 1960s. There is a significant difference, however, between the underlying concept behind the transracial coalitions of the 1960s and the transgressive concept of blackness I am advancing. The underlying concept behind the transracial coalitions of the 1960s was racial unity, whereas the view I am advancing is to dispense with race altogether. The term *racial obsolescence* thus better characterizes my position.

Still, some may insist that there is more to the concept of blackness than I have offered. What about a cultural conception of blackness that captures the ways of life of black people and a similar conception of whiteness for white people, it might be asked? The import of this question is that blacks and whites exhibit different forms of behavior, so such differences should be reflected in any reconceptualization project of the kind being pursued here. My response to this objection, however, is that it seems to be essentializing blackness and whiteness in the sense that it would have us explain the supposed different ways of life of blacks and whites as a function of different *essences.* But what might these essences be? Indeed, my endeavor to decenter whiteness in part by reconceptualizing blackness highlights the fact that the concepts *whiteness* and *blackness* are social constructions. They simply are associated with pigmentation and then arbitrarily ascribed different social values—normative, aesthetic, and psychological. This means, in other words, that there is no biological essence to blackness or whiteness. Indeed, what, if anything, we should learn from studies in the human genome is that the only essential characteristic of humans is chromosomal. The rest of human characteristics are accidental. So it suffices that a cultural conception of blackness, which implies that there is a black or white essence, must be rejected outright as erroneous.

Furthermore, a cultural conception of blackness would preclude the possibility of (say) a pigmentationally white child being *culturally black* even though the child is raised from birth in a black family and in a socially black environment. The same consideration would apply to a pigmentationally black child being raised by a white family and in a white environment. That is, on the cultural conception, such a child would be precluded from being *culturally white.* We know, however, that behavior is learned in a sociocultural context, and as such there is nothing anomalous in a pigmentationally white child growing up culturally black as also a pigmentationally black child growing up culturally white. This again shows that there is no (black or white) essence from which individual behavior derives, contrary to the claim implicit in the cultural conception of blackness. Thus, again, that conception of blackness should be rejected as false because it attempts to posit as essential personal characteristics attributes that otherwise are purely accidental.

IV. The Obsolescence of Races

I have distinguished two senses of blackness, the political and the pigmentational. The political is concerned with individual social location wherein social location is a function of skin pigmentation. The political is socially constructed. The point of my discussion is to show that, since there is nothing natural about social location, it therefore can be transcended. And a first move toward such transcendence is to overthrow the concepts around which social location revolves.

The pigmentational, on the other hand, is natural, having to do with the color of a person's skin. It is natural because a person's skin, like all other natural objects, is colored, and colors, *qua* colors, are value-free. Transcendence therefore does not apply. It is only when values are arbitrarily ascribed to colors, however, that the latter become socially significant. But since the ascription of values is purely arbitrary, such values as are assigned to any given natural entity can just as well arbitrarily be altered. It is precisely the valuation of a natural phenomenon, namely skin color, that I have sought to dismantle in the present reconceptualization project. The view I have presented is significant because it ultimately will erase all race-talk as meaningless, since no one race will occupy a privileged place in society. As noted, the terms *black* and *white* would still function as color designators; however, they will have been stripped of any social values.

It would of course be naïve and foolhardy to think that making race talk meaningless in the manner I am proposing would end racism.[22] On the other hand, my reconceptualization project should be seen as *a necessary first step* toward the elimination of racism. As in the Enlightenment when ideas were put to political use in shaping public policy, so the view I am advancing is intended similarly to provide a first step toward a policy of deracializing society. I recognize that there is a second, and equally important, step to end racism. This step consists in the political will of the society to undergo transformation. It is in this step that public policies are formulated. The ideas I have advanced are useful therefore only insofar as they are drawn upon in and by the second step in which public policies are formulated. Or, alternatively, unless there is the political will to have a deracialized society, my reconceptualization project will not be practically realized. Even so, the reconceptualization project could serve to indicate that it is conceptually (or theoretically) possible to end racism. And once the conceptual obstacle to eradicate racism is removed, the next step would be to overcome the practical obstacles. And that too, in time, is achievable.

My optimism, however, does not seem to be shared by scholars such as David B. Wilkins, Naomi Zack, and Lucius Outlaw, to name a few.[23] Wilkins contends that to eliminate race is to erase the contingent experiences of African Americans, experiences that are central to their history of racial oppression and consequently to the formation of a racial identity to defend against racial oppression. Embedded in this racial identity is a moral dimension, a moral outlook that is essential to the group ("Context of Race," 21–24). Zack calls into question the practical efficacy of resolving race issues by making race obsolescent in the manner I am suggesting. Characterizing all such positions as "racial eliminativism," Zack begins by contending that race, although a biological and cultural fiction, is a social reality that just cannot be dispensed with. It is a social reality in the sense that it is the medium through which the various racial groups see their respective identities as well as the identities of others. As she puts it, "The way that members of racial groups perceive their own and other races is also part of the social reality of race" (Zack, *Thinking About Race*, 12). And again, "The ways in which the social realities of race are described depends on the racial perspective of the person doing the describing" (12). And since different races—blacks, whites, Native Americans, and Asians—have different perspectives of themselves and others, the social reality of race thus reflects their varying perspectives. One important element of the social reality of race, Zack goes on to note, is that there is a dominant group (consisting of whites) and an aggregate of subordinate groups (consisting of all nonwhites). To eliminate race, therefore, is to eliminate the varying perspectives of these groups about this relation. But precisely because these perspectives represent, if not constitute, the vantage point (or lenses) from which each group perceives the relation, as the latter is anchored in race (or color), Zack reasons, those perspectives therefore ought to be retained. At the very least, those diverse perspectives reflect society's pluralistic outlook. And it is in such pluralism that the society can lay claims to being egalitarian (*Thinking About Race*, 16).

Using the optical metaphor, another way of seeing Zack's point is to say that, since it is impossible *not* to have a perspective on the relation between dominance and subordination, and since any given perspective is peculiar to each perceiver (read subject-group) because it is through that perspective that the perceiver *experiences* the world, it is therefore practically impossible to eliminate that perspective without also eliminating the perceiver's *experience*. But the perceiver's experience is real, being the medium through which she or he encounters the world of race. So it is necessary. By extension, therefore, the world about which the experience provides information is necessary and ought also to be retained even though that world is a fiction.

Unlike Zack and Wilkins, however, who grant that race is a fiction even as they appeal to the notion in order to explain the experiences of African Americans, Outlaw grounds race in the supposed *different biological features* of persons, thereby making race an ontological category. As he says:

> I shall use "race" to refer to a group of persons who share, more or less, biologically transmitted physical characteristics that, under the influence of endogenous cultural and geographical factors as well as exogenous social and political factors, contribute to the characterization of the group as a distinct, self-reproducing, encultured population. Thus, biologically transmitted physical factors, conditioned by and along with cultural processes and geographical factors, combine to constitute a "race." (*On Race and Philosophy*, 136)

And, using this notion, Outlaw proceeds to argue that social justice, in the sense of the fair and equitable distribution of societal benefits and burdens, requires that racial differences be taken into account especially "in societies that have continuing histories of racial and ethnic oppression" (*On Race and Philosophy*, 137). Indeed, part of the substance of Outlaw's argument in defense of race is that if race were to be eliminated, then all of the hard-won gains blacks have earned as a result of contesting racial oppression would be eliminated, and that would be yet another injustice against blacks. Besides, a significant percentage of African Americans are still under the throes of racial oppression, which means that they are at a disadvantage compared with other social groups. In short, for Outlaw, blacks are still experiencing *racial* injustice, the remedy to which has to involve race.

I have very grave reservations about all these conceptions of race even as I sympathize with their motivations. I shall therefore proceed to examine them beginning with Wilkins's. There is no doubt about the unique experiences of oppression that African Americans have suffered since slavery. These experiences comprise at least part of African American history and are pivotal in shaping African American identities. But to construe such identities in racial terms is highly problematic. There were blacks who, although born in slavery, chose repatriation to Africa after the Emancipation Proclamation of 1863. Specifically, they were repatriated to Liberia and Sierra Leone. The present (African) descendants of these blacks thus at least share part of the experiences of their forebears and hence part of the experiences of present-day blacks in the United States. Given that the descendants of the former slave returnees to Africa now live in Africa, should we then say that, because of the shared experiences they have with blacks in the United States, they too are a distinct "race" from other blacks in Liberia and Sierra Leone? Are they also part of the supposed African American *racial identity*? That uniqueness of experiences is not sufficient to confer supposed racial identity is very easily seen if we consider the similarities in the experiences of Jews and Rom people, the latter formerly referred to in a derogatory manner as Gypsies, in Nazi Germany. Both groups were subject to similar Nazi vilification, brutalization, and systematic state-sanctioned murder. Yet, if Wilkins's criterion of racial identity is sound, we should conclude that both Jews and Rom people comprise a distinct and particular "race." But what is this race? Yet we can identify *differences* between Jews and Gypsies.

When we turn to Zack, we see that her position is just as problematic as Wilkins's. First, Zack's argument commits her to reifying a fiction (race) or to give it an ontological status, and this is highly problematic. Notice that she recognizes that race is a biological and cultural fiction. So, by arguing against its elimination she is saying, in effect, that we should recognize this fiction in order to make intelligible the varying perspectives of groups. But do we need to make real that which we know is unreal, a fabrication, if only to make intelligible our varying perspectives? My appeal here is to Occam's Razor, the principle that we should not multiply entities unnecessarily, thereby populating our ontologies with strange and mysterious beings. No doubt, the varying perspectives are veridical, *for they are about the relation of domination and subordination.* But since we know that race, the props for the relation, is a fiction, all we need do then is to rid ourselves of it and we will have rid ourselves of both the relation to which it gives rise and the perspectives that in turn it occasions. In other words, the perspectives are no longer needed or necessary as sources of information once we get rid of the fictional foundation(s) upon which they are grounded and about which they supposedly give us information.

Second, I suspect that Zack was led into accepting the social reality of race because she mistakenly identifies and conflates skin color and race to explain the relation between dominance and subordination and how this relation impacts the distributive paradigm. She is aware that the relation of dominance and subordination is asymmetrical, and this asymmetry is usually unpacked or described in terms of the inequitable manner in which societal goods and ills are distributed among the various social groups. Since color (or skin pigmentation) influences the distribution mechanism, and color is real, race therefore must be real because it is identical with color. Besides, when groups describe the asymmetrical relation they do so from their respective perspectives, and those varying perspectives take into account each group's color and hence its situation relative to the dominant group. Given the reality of colors, and the supposed identity between race and color, race therefore must be real.

The seductive element of this (kind of) argument, however, is the supposed identity between color and race, an identity that I have been contesting. As I have shown, color and race are *conceptually* distinct and different, and they simply have been arbitrarily associated. Color is natural; it is real. Race is not natural. It is a human invention, an artificial construction deliberately set up and imbued with values to influence the distributive paradigm in society by privileging one color over others. Invested with values, therefore, *color has been made into* race. But the two are not identical. Because the societal problem is with race, or "value-laden color," and race is an artificial construction, race therefore can be eliminated like any other human invention. Put otherwise, there is no reason we should accept it as part of our social ontology. On the contrary, we should dispense with it and there will be no net loss to our social enterprises. If anything, society will stand to benefit considerably from its eradication. That is what I have been arguing.

Outlaw's position fares no better. It follows from his account of what constitutes a race that the Irish, Scottish, and English would be different "races," as also the Berbers from North Africa, sub-Saharan Africans, and African Americans. To say the least, the world would be full of races, and this is certainly bizarre.[24] As Amy Guttman has correctly observed, "Similar skin color and other discernible physical features do not a race, or subspecies, make" ("Responding to Racial Injustice," 113). But besides that Outlaw's biological concept of race populates us with races, his position is clearly retrogressive in that it takes us back to, and tries to legitimate, the once standard but now much discredited view of racial essentialism that was propagated by Enlightenment thinkers. It is to be remarked in this connection that, even despite arguments against this Enlightenment-originated racial essentialist thesis, there are those like Richard Herrnstein and Charles Murray who are still trying to resurrect it if only, in my judgment, to give apparent intellectual legitimacy to bigotry and prejudice.[25] For example, social, not genetic, factors explain why black and Hispanic students generally perform poorly on standardized tests compared with their white counterparts. Thus, by advancing the position in question, Outlaw ends up, perhaps unwittingly, aiding and abetting such a racist endeavor that underlies the work of Herrnstein and Murray. Surely, Outlaw could (or ought to) have seen that such a consequence follows from his position—unless, of course, he believes that both the Enlightenment view and its contemporary variants are correct!

But even despite the characteristics that Outlaw uses to define race, what he is describing in reality are *phenotypical and cultural differences* among groups, differences that are contingent outcomes of nature and that ought to be recognized in a pluralistic society and in social bargaining (*On Race and Philosophy*, 140–41). The politics of social bargaining that acknowledges and celebrates group differences is what Iris Marion Young refers to in the title of her book as "the politics of difference" (Young, *Justice and the Politics of Difference*, 1990). It is precisely such politics that Outlaw too wishes to advocate, hence he titles the chapter in his own book in which he discusses race, "Against the Grain of Modernity: The Politics of Difference and the Conservation of 'Race'" (*On Race and Philosophy*, chapter 6). But, surely, we can acknowledge these differences and advance a politics of difference without thereby implying that differences are signs of different *races.* The reason is that there is a moral dimension to race in which some supposed necessary connection is claimed to exist between race and morality. Revisit the racial classifications by Bernier, Linneaus, and others. It is precisely this feature of race that makes all race-talk dangerous, a point well noted by Guttman. As she points out:

> Race consciousness is the kind of consciousness that presumes the existence of separate human races and identifies race with essential natural differences between human beings *that are morally relevant.* Either phenotypical differences such as facial features and skin color are accorded moral significance in themselves or, more often, they are considered indicative of some deeper, morally significant differences between blacks and whites. (Guttman, "Responding to Racial Injustice," 163, emphasis added)

There is no doubt that Outlaw is aware of this insidious and pernicious feature of race (and race discourse), as is evident from his discussion of modernity (*On Race and Philosophy*, chap. 7). So why then would he insist in speaking of biological characteristics, subject to geographical, cultural, and sociopolitical factors, as entailing different races, with the (unwitting) implication that he allows for morally significant differences between different groups? The answer, as we have seen, is that Outlaw is drawing upon the brutal historical experiences of African Americans in the United States, experiences according to which race reigns supreme in the distribution of social benefits and burdens. So he thinks that social bargaining in the quest for justice has to be "racialized" if the different social groups expect to claim fairness. But Outlaw mistakenly thinks that *the argument for differentiated group equality*, which I take him to be advancing, requires the recognition of "races" to be effective. My position, on the contrary, is that it does not, nor should we subscribe to the existence of "races" in order to alter the distributive paradigm. Certainly, the present race- and gender-based affirmative action has been the paradigm of a distributive measure that attends to the contingent situation of the affected wronged groups. This distributive mechanism makes use (at least partly) of the concept of race. So it might be thought that this use of race validates Outlaw's biological concept of race. Not so, however. We should regard race in the present affirmative action distributive measure as a functional, not a biological, concept to enable the society to remedy the historical transgressions against the wronged groups, namely blacks and women. In this respect, the concept of race in affirmative action is fundamentally different from that in Outlaw's discussion. But even the functional concept of race has severe limitations. Despite the fact that it has been useful in modifying the distributive paradigm, it suffers from the inherent defect of being parasitical on the existing status quo of white male supremacy and has not done anything to demolish the status quo. And this status quo rests on the fiction of race. So, even as I have endorsed affirmative action and will continue to do so as long as we still have racial and gender oppression in the society, I do believe that we should aim for a society that will transcend the need for such measures.

The transcendence for which I am arguing requires that we dismantle the fiction of race. But failing to dismantle the fiction of race and hence the status quo, and pursuant to Outlaw's proposal, we would be left at best with a situation in which the various social groups involved in social bargaining will engage in appeals to "comparative victimology," to use an expression of Michael Lerner.[26] By this I mean that each oppressed group will seek "its own fair share of the pie" relative to others by claiming that its own oppression is more severe than other groups, so it should receive more of societal goods or special considerations in the distribution of social goods. Paradoxically, the distributive paradigm even in such a situation is dictated by the very race structure that is responsible for the oppression of the various groups in the first place. In other words, Outlaw's position entails that we accept and even reinforce the institutional structure within which black oppression is situated just so as to be able to claim benefits from the society. Yet if this is so, then the status quo cannot be as vile and oppressive as we have been claiming all along. It can be seen from this unsavory consequence of Outlaw's position why I reject his view and similarly all "realist" conceptions of race. The idea of race, to repeat, is a fiction that must be exorcised from the repertoire of our conceptual package if we desire genuinely to address the issue of social justice. I turn now to Naomi Zack's specific arguments against racial eliminativism.

V. Naomi Zack and Racial Eliminativism

Recall that the fundamental premise of racial eliminativism is that race in its multifarious forms—biological, cultural, or social—is a fiction that ought to be eliminated. And the elimination requires us at least to disseminate information about the myth of race. Zack describes this position as the argument from principle because of its challenge of the very idea of the reality of race. But Zack rejects this argument on two counts. First, she says that merely proclaiming "the truth" about race does not mean that the society will accept it. And the eliminativist cannot impose this supposed truth about race on others without violating their First Amendment Right that guarantees freedom of speech, thought, beliefs, and so on. Besides, she continues, "belief in races is part of the received opinion, [so] parents and even teachers would strongly resist an educational program to eliminate ideas of race" (Zack, *Thinking About Race*, 16). Second, Zack argues that the eliminativist's supposed "truth" about race cannot be enforced, again on First Amendment grounds. Consequently, re-educating the society about race "could not be done in this country" (16).

I take exception to Zack's defeatist position. There can be no doubt that the so-called received opinion about race is entrenched in the psyche of Americans. But does that mean we should desist from disabusing American minds of such a false concept? Should we relent in re-educating the society at large about this wrongheaded view of race? If Zack's reasoning is correct, then we simply should accept (say) the once "received opinion" about blacks posited in the Enlightenment, a contemporary variant of which is expressed, as already noted, in Herrnstein and Murray's edited volume, *The Bell Curve.* (See note 25, above.) Moreover, we should tell black children that the supposed Enlightenment "truths" about blacks describe a reality that cannot be contested. These are some of the damning consequences of Zack's position. We know, on the contrary, that scholars have been doing exactly what Zack says cannot be done without violating individual freedoms of speech and thought, namely, re-educating society by challenging received opinions. Specifically, by reconceptualizing race, gender, and the like, scholars have contested myths about various social groups—blacks, women, Asians—and posited "truths" about each of these groups. Of course, old mindsets persist in some, and that goes to show that the task of social transformation, beginning with the conceptual, is fraught with difficulties and obstacles. But that does not mean that it is an impossible task. Americans have been miseducated about race. Color differentiated groups have been psychologically and socially conditioned to see themselves and each other in so-called racialized terms. But if our collective quest is for social justice that sees color difference in value-free terms, then we are obligated to expose the lie about race in much the same way that we have exposed the Enlightenment deliberate lie about black (lack of) personhood. We should remember that the very basis on which rests the notion of black civil (read *human*) rights without incongruity is that blacks *are* human. And the proposition that blacks are human, we should remember, is contrary to the once received opinion of Enlightenment science.

What about Zack's contention about the difficulty of enforcing the eliminativist's "truth" about race? Unfortunately, Zack makes it sound as if social transformation of the kind being discussed requires an anti-Race Police for compliance. But society did not need a Gender Police to ensure that men treat women with respect and dignity. For the most part, education has helped to transform the male perception of and attitude toward women. Education about sexism, date rape, domestic violence, and the like is the means through which men and women are continually being transformed conceptually and socially. And there is little doubt that society has made considerable progress in this direction. Is there any doubt that education can do the same about race? If we can contest the so-called received opinion about race; if we posit the truth about race; and if the truth became part of our formal and informal curricula, then I have no doubt that society will have little choice but to respond favorably, even if slowly.

Consider, for example, that even whites now are contesting and repudiating whiteness to the extent that, as they have argued, whiteness has been used unfairly to acquire benefits that are undeserved and at the expense of nonwhites. For example, Iris Marion Young's discussion of social justice is premised on the assumption that whiteness has been, and continues to be, the major source of social injustice against nonwhites and other marginalized groups in society. I should note in this connection that, usually, when issues of race and racism are critiqued, it is by the victims who are mainly nonwhites. And such critiques often times are dismissed with the familiar refrain, "Here we go again." But, as if to preempt such a dismissal of her criticism of racial and other forms of oppression, Young calls attention to her being "a white, heterosexual, middle-class, able-bodied, not old woman," whose "political commitment to social justice . . . motivates . . . [her] philosophical reflection" (*Justice and the Politics of Difference*, 14). Young is saying, in effect, that, even from the vantage point of the social location she occupies, one that offers her and others similarly situated certain privileges in a racially stratified society, she knows that whiteness, among other things, is the source of those privileges, truth be told. Along similar lines, John Garvey and Noel Ignatiev, in their essay, "Toward a New Abolitionism: A *Race Traitor* Manifesto," call attention to a new journal, *Race Traitor*, whose cardinal aim is to abolish whiteness or, as they put it "the white race."[27] Two reasons motivate this abolitionist project: "First, that 'the white race' is not a natural category and, second, that what was historically constructed can be undone" (346). Furthermore, Garvey and Ignatiev note that *Race Traitor* "is intended to serve as a forum for discussion among those who recognize that whiteness is a social problem" (349). All this is evidence that there are serious attempts by white scholars to interrogate race, albeit whiteness thus far, and to do away with it in order to attain social justice. It is in the spirit of these aims that I am arguing that *all* forms of race are social problems to the extent that the very concept of race is a social construction. Thus, in the same spirit in which Young and others advocate the elimination of whiteness, so it is that I seek to eliminate *all* races. No doubt there will be resistance. But the goal is achievable.

Yet Zack advances a second argument, this time aimed at another variant of racial eliminativism that she characterizes as consequentialist because the argument emphasizes the good consequences that racial elimination would have for the society. According to Zack, the thrust of the consequentialist argument is that Americans are still trapped in nineteenth century ideas of race. Those ideas have structured the distributive paradigm in that they have created social/racial inequities in the distribution of societal goods and ills. To attain racial/social justice, therefore, we should eliminate those ideas of race. *The consequences of doing so would be good for the society.* Zack sums up the argument saying, "If Americans were unable to think in . . . racial terms or to speak the language of race, then they would be unable to behave unfairly on the basis of racial difference" (*Thinking About Race*, 17). Zack then proceeds to reject this argument on the ground that even if race were to be eliminated people would still select other criteria of difference to discriminate against others. And she concludes from this that race is not really the problem but human greed and cruelty (17).

Zack is right that people can discriminate against each other using whatever characteristics they deem important to mark out difference. Ethnicity, for example, is one such marker, and we saw its role in the recent conflict between Bosnian Serbs and Moslems in Yugoslavia. There, race does not apply. But in America and other Western countries, unlike Yugoslavia, we are dealing with societies that are racially structured in a hierarchy. In these societies, race is the most perceptible identity marker. I should call attention to Canada's official designation of nonwhites as "Visible Minorities." This designation underscores the point that Zack fails to see and that Canada got right, namely, that even though there are other forms of identity markers, in the societies with which we are dealing the visible (namely race) is preeminent. Is it any accident that the oppression in apartheid South Africa and Rhodesia (now postcolonial Zimbabwe) was race-based, similar to that in the United States? So, by virtue of the nature of the society with which we are concerned, namely, one in which race is central, Zack's argument against the consequentialist version of racial eliminativism simply translates into an irrelevant thesis.

Let us observe also that whites in the United States are not a monolithic group. Coming from various parts of Europe, they are ethnically diverse. But such diversity yielded to their being white when the society was trying to create a national identity. This national identity was founded in whiteness (see note 14, above). The significance of this observation is that all those who were *perceived* as nonwhites—blacks, Asians, and Native Americans—were immediately excluded from that identity. In short, race reigns supreme. So it is obvious that race is what needs to be targeted for destruction in the quest for racial/social justice.

But other than her unsuccessful attempts at rejecting racial eliminativism, what is Zack's own solution to overcoming the race issue? Zack suggests that we allow for more classificatory categories of race, beginning with mixed race. She thinks that opening up spaces for more racial categories eventually would nullify the concept of race itself. Her reasoning is that we know already that the concept of race "did not always exist historically, [so] it could pass out of history on its own without strenuous intellectual effort" (Zack, *Thinking About Race*, 17). Yet again I think Zack is wrong. True, the concept of race was made to exist by human intellectual effort and ingenuity. *But so has been its continuity and preservation.* Its dissolution therefore would require deliberate human intellectual effort and ingenuity. Indeed, as Zack herself acknowledges, race is not a natural but instead an artificial category. This being the case, and in light of human artifice to ensure its preservation and sustenance, what sense does it make to appeal to nature's course for its disappearance? On this natural course solution, race would disappear but only if the entire human race is obliterated from the face of the earth. And surely, this is not what Zack meant, for then the issue of racial/social justice is moot. So, her very concern with social justice requires, if anything, that we intervene rather than let nature take its course.

Finally, Zack's solution of opening up more racial classificatory categories is simply wrongheaded. Since we know that race is a fiction, it is unclear how populating our ontologies with more fictions will resolve the issues of racial and social justice. Again, I invoke Occam's Razor. But if Zack insists that we retain the concept of race, then she needs only to be reminded of the pernicious use of racial categories in apartheid South Africa. There the racial stratification consisted of whites, coloreds, and blacks, in descending order. And that structure legally upheld the putative inferiority of coloreds to whites and of blacks to both coloreds and whites. As we now know, the solution to South Africa's racial problem was not to populate the society with more and different shades of races, as would be entailed by Zack's suggestion. Rather it was to dismantle the very apartheid structure of racial classification itself. At least, *in principle*, we have a raceless South Africa. That is what we should be aiming for in the United States of the future.

VI. Enacting Blackness within the Present Status Quo

The focus of contemporary discussions on blackness, whiteness, and race, in essence, is how to address issues pertaining to the distribution of social goods, both locally and globally. By locally I mean in the United States and each of the other Western industrialized societies. And by globally I mean what is known in geoeconomic terms as the Northern and Southern Hemispheres, wherein the Northern Hemisphere consists of the industrialized nations that comprise the G8, and the Southern Hemisphere consists of the nonindustrialized nations of the world. It is no accident that, whether locally or globally, the distribution of social goods has favored whites, and thus the acquisition process itself somehow has acquired a normative force for whites over people of color. The counterhegemonic, political conception of blackness that I have proposed, therefore, is aimed at demolishing this norm by de-centering whiteness, at least locally. But whatever suggestions apply locally can be extended globally. My overarching goal is to demolish race itself and as such to effect a distribution system that is nonracialized. Because my proposed aim is futuristic, however, it is therefore only a prolegomenon to any future race-free and morally just society. Amy Guttman has anticipated me in this endeavor (See Appiah and Guttman, *Color Conscious*, 1996.) As Guttman so effectively remarks, it is one thing for oppressed people to identify and band together using color and phenotype, the very features on which their oppression is grounded, to challenge oppression. But it is an entirely different issue to construe color and other phenotypical differences as constituting different races. The former enterprise is understandable and hence justifiable. The latter is not. Yet by doing the latter, some members of oppressed groups unfortunately end up becoming victims to the lie about race ("Responding to Racial Injustice," 167). But probably this is because of the very pervasiveness of racism and racial injustice in the society, and the existing state of affairs. This now leads me to yet another issue. Given the present state of affairs, how then does one's blackness impact one as a professional philosopher in the United States? Or, alternatively put, how does one enact one's blackness as a professional philosopher and through the medium of philosophy?

It can be inferred from all that I have said above that, as a black philosopher, I embody the oppositional, counterhegemonic stance for which I have been arguing. The status quo that I am challenging is white hegemony. And I enact my contestational point of view through a very critical examination of the Western philosophical canons by bringing into sharp focus their Eurocentrism. For example, Locke's seemingly benign epistemological motivation in casually speaking of "savages," saying that the latter are cognitively deprived of so-called innate ideas and morals, does not seem so benign after all. For the question "Who are these savages anyway?" is not simply glossed over as is otherwise done in the routine way of teaching the Western canons. Rather, it becomes a subject of serious discussion. This is all the more so when one tries to understand Locke's view of slavery, as also his concept of a rights-bearer in his celebrated distinction between the concept of a *man* and that of a *person*. (I advance similar analyses to the views of other Enlightenment thinkers.) The point of my examination of these authors is to demonstrate that we philosophers often arrogantly pride ourselves as being concerned with justice, morality, and humanity. We even profess to speak on behalf of humanity. To that end, we tend to consider ourselves as cognitively superior to others in the humanistic disciplines, for we supposedly often interrogate the underlying assumptions that drive issues and bring out consequences of various points of view. Did not Plato even go so far as to suggest in the *Republic* that society would be better administered—that is, with justice—if presided over by philosopher kings and queens? Yet, even as we make such grandiose pronouncements and indulge in self-congratulatory gestures, we often are incapable of identifying our own intellectual blind spots, and hence our faults and foibles. Or else we think we have none? This perceptual and cognitive limitation should make us wonder whether, as philosophers, we indeed have the moral authority to critique others given our own practices.

It is to this problem of philosophers and the discipline of philosophy that Leonard Harris so effectively, even if hyperbolically, calls attention in his scathing, acidic critique entitled "Believe It or Not or the Ku Klux Klan and American Philosophy Exposed."[28] The essence of Harris's essay is that the virtual absence of blacks and other minorities in philosophy, either as faculty or as students, cannot just be accidental. Rather, it seems to be the result of a deliberate and well-orchestrated effort of the custodians or gatekeepers of philosophy departments to ensure that the discipline be white. In this respect, contends Harris, the mechanism of exclusion overtly or covertly employed by philosophy departments to preserve the face of the discipline seems analogous to the methods used by the Ku Klux Klan to exclude blacks from mainstream society. Among the chief culprits in this respect are the Ivy League schools and others that award the doctorate in the discipline. Harris's language may be deemed incendiary in likening the supposed exclusionary methods of the discipline of philosophy to those of the Ku Klux Klan. But what must one think when white males effectively dominate and run most departments of philosophy with the token black, Hispanic, or/and white female? White males are the cultural gatekeepers, the custodians and preservers of the status quo. If therefore the Ku Klux Klan's battle cry is white supremacy, then it seems to Harris that, even in their apparently silent walls and corridors, philosophy departments somehow loudly echo and heed this cry.

Regardless of how one views Harris's position, for me to enact blackness as a minority professional philosopher is to highlight some of the contradictions between the rhetoric of philosophy, its supposed noble quest for and on behalf of humanity (!), and the actual practice of both the discipline and its practitioners. And I exhibit these contradictions through an examination of, among other things, the typical philosophy curriculum. For example, my approach to teaching philosophy, especially the celebrated canons, is somewhat different from those of many of my colleagues. This is not to suggest by any means that all I look for in the canons are those features that may be deemed racist or sexist. Rather, as I investigate the oft-recited valuable insights of the texts I also call attention to their not so valuable insights. To illustrate, as I teach the nature of Hume's ethics or Kant's universality principle of reason as moral legislator, I also probe the criterion of membership into the moral ontology of each of these authors. And I do so against the backdrop of some of the notorious assertions of these authors about non-Europeans (or the Other). My goal in doing so is to show that philosophy and philosophers are neither race-less nor apolitical. On the contrary, they are every bit racialized and political, and there is ample evidence in both the canonical works and in the views of the canonical authors to demonstrate this claim. Yet, these authors were professing to speak of humanity! So, to de-race philosophy and society at large requires that one, as a marginalized Other in the discipline, critique the principles enunciated by practitioners of the discipline as well as the practices of the discipline.

I can say in this regard that over the years I have met with remarkable success in bringing to the attention of my students this aspect of philosophy and philosophers. Indeed, some of my students, the majority of whom are white because I teach in a predominantly white institution, have expressly told me that I bring to bear on both the canonical authors and the issues we examine a perspective that they have not had in any other philosophy course. Of course, this is not surprising.[29] The point here is that the venerated figures are taught in the customary way, that is, as Past Masters who shaped Western civilization. Very little attention, if any, is given to the wider social, political, and ethical implications of their views. In fact, there are courses called "Great Books of Western Civilization" that are usually taught in what I have described as the customary way. The subtext in this kind of approach is that Western civilization is all good, thanks to the ideas of the Past Masters. When one notes, however, that the epistemological endeavors of Locke, Hume, and Kant, for example, were largely preparatory for their social and political positions, it is thus beguiling that we sometimes teach those views in a highly sanitized manner and without attending to their social and political consequences. If the goal of each of these philosophers was to theorize ideas about the good society and to ensure the implementation of those ideas, then we need to look carefully at the practical consequences of the positions they advanced especially for people of color. Yet, this is scarcely done in the customary (or standard) way philosophy courses are taught. The perspective therefore that I bring to bear on teaching the Past Masters, as they are called, is one that shows, among other things, how these Past Masters contributed significantly to the social and political morass in which we find ourselves in contemporary society.

For example, talk of reparations for slavery presupposes grave moral transgressions against blacks, transgressions whose intellectual and political structures were the architectural designs and products of the Past Masters. So, while the standard manner of presenting and teaching the ideas of these figures is celebratory, even adulatory, the perspective through which I approach their ideas is one that brings out their aberrant and indefensible views. Students often are shocked when they encounter these views for the first time because, after all, they had been conditioned to seeing these figures as purists or intellectual demigods. Imagine being told about Locke's arguably indirect role in the subjugation of Native Americans or of his ownership of shares in the Royal Africa Company that was involved in the trans-Atlantic slave trade in the same breath as we read his "just war" theory. And imagine the shock when I commence my discussion of Locke's "just war" theory with the prefatory remark "Exterminate the brutes!" (from Joseph Conrad's *The Heart of Darkness*). Yet, this remark aptly captures the thrust of Locke's justification of slavery and the just war theory. My goal in doing so is not to demonize or vilify these celebrated philosophers. Rather, it is to advance my political conception of blackness, or blackness as a counterhegemonic discourse aimed at decentering whiteness. In the final analysis my overarching aim is to establish a deracialized society. But first, like an alcoholic who desires to be healed from the disease and so must confess to being an alcoholic, we first must confess to the sins of whiteness and of race in general as a social fiction. Thereafter, we can dismantle whiteness and race in their entirety, and advance toward social equity. And a catalyst for this confession (and hopefully purgation) is the political conception of blackness I have theorized. This, to me, is what it is to reconceptualize blackness.

Notes

I thank Tina Johnson, Harry M. Bracken, and George Carew for criticisms of earlier drafts of this study that I found very helpful, and, for help with the biblical references, my departmental colleague Jeanne Hoechst-Ronner and my aunt Mrs. Rebecca Cole (popularly known as Aunti Oni).

1. See, for example, *Isaiah* 9:2: "The people that walked in darkness have seen a great light: they that dwell in the land of the shadow of death, upon them hath the light shined." *Joshua* 10:13ff: "In Joshua where the sun stands still so good can conquer evil. So the sun stood still, and the moon stopped, till the nation avenged itself on its enemies." *John* 1:5: "The light shines in the darkness, but the darkness has not overcome it." See also *John* 1:3–19 and 3:19–21. *First Peter* 2:9: "But ye are a chosen generation, a royal priesthood, an holy nation, a peculiar people; that ye should shew forth the praises of him who hath called you out of darkness into his marvelous light." And *Song of Solomon* 1:5, 6: "I am black, but comely, O ye daughters of Jerusalem, as tents

of Kedar, as the curtains of Solomon. Look not upon me, because I am black, because the sun hath looked upon me: my mother's children were angry with me; they made me the keeper of the vineyards; but mine own vineyard have I not kept." Other citations are *Jude* 11–13 and *First John* 1:5–10.

2. I place the term "person" in quotation marks to indicate that, among Enlightenment scholars, the characteristic of personhood when applied to black sentient beings was debatable. Indeed, for some the expression "black person" would appear to be an oxymoron. G. W. F. Hegel referred to blacks as "animal man." See his essay, "The Geographical Basis of World History," in Emmanuel Eze (ed.), *Race and the Enlightenment* (Oxford, UK and Cambridge, MA: Blackwell Publishers, 1997), 127. John Locke distinguished between being a man and being a person in respect of blacks. See Book Two, chap. 27 of Locke's *Essay Concerning Human Understanding* (ed.) Alexander Campbell Fraser (2 vols.), vol. 1 (New York: Dover Publications, 1894). I return to this point below.

3. See Eze (ed.) *Race and the Enlightenment*, 91–94. Léon Poliakov states that since the fifteenth century, "Blackness, and with it a range of evil associations, was contrasted with whiteness, as was innocence with crime, vice with virtue, and bestiality with humanity." See *The Aryan Myth: A History of Racist and Nationalist Ideas in Europe*, transl. Edmund Howard (New York: Basic Books, 1974), 135. I thank Harry M. Bracken for directing my attention to this significant work.

4. Poliakov 1974, 143.

5. See Emmanuel Eze, *Race and the Enlightenment.*

6. See the following selections from Eze (ed.) *Race and the Enlightenment* for the respective views of Hume (chap. 3), Kant (chaps. 4 and 5), Jefferson (chap. 8), Georges Léopold Cuvier (chap. 9), and G. W. F. Hegel (chap. 10).

7. For some fairly recent examples, see K. Anthony Appiah, "The Uncompleted Argument: Du Bois and the Illusion of 'Race'" (in Henry Louis Gates [ed.] *Race, Writing and Difference* [Chicago and London: The University of Chicago Press, 1985]); also Appiah, "Race, Culture, Identity: Misunderstood Connections," and Amy Guttman, "Responding to Racial Injustice," both in *Color Conscious: The Political Morality of Race*, ed. Appiah and Guttman (Princeton, NJ: Princeton University Press, 1996); Paul Gilroy, *Against Race* (Cambridge, MA: Harvard University Press, 2000), chaps. 1 and 2; and Naomi Zack, *Thinking About Race* (Belmont, CA: Wadsworth Publishing Co., 1998).

8. Locke's view is found in Book Two, Chapter 27, of the *Essay Concerning Human Understanding*, his discussion of the subject of personal identity. I should note also Locke's attribution to a child in *Essay* IV.7.16 the view that blacks are not men because of their color. This suggestion does not mean that Locke thinks the idea of man and that of person are identical. I suggest that Locke did not attempt to critique or correct the child's unphilosophical view because he simply was using a nonphilosophical (that is, the ordinarily held, uninformed but empirically ascertainable) view about the external property a thing may be deemed to have to be considered man. In this case, the color white is that property. And since, on this view, white(ness) precludes black(ness) it is therefore impossible for a thing that is black to be man. On Locke's sophisticated/philosophical view, however, reason is the property that characterizes persons.

In any case, on either view, blacks are not humans. For a discussion of this issue, see Harry M. Bracken, *Mind and Language: Essays on Descartes and Chomsky* (Dordrecht-Holland/Cinnaminson-USA: Foris Publications, 1984), chap. 3, 54–55.

9. It really does not matter even if this declaration was for estimating the economic worth, in terms of assets, of slave owners. The point is that blacks were part of those assets; they were things, of sorts, and so less than human.

10. See Howard McGary, "Paternalism and Slavery," in Bill Lawson and Howard McGary (eds.) *Between Slavery and Freedom* (Bloomington and Indianapolis: Indiana University Press, 1992), chap. 2.

11. I attribute this view to Hegel based on his characterization of Negroes (i.e., Africans) as living in barbarism and savagery, and his further claim that slavery may help transform Africans from barbarism to some measure of civilization and culture. Since colonialism derives from the very presuppositions of slavery, it was thus an extension of slavery. To that end, Hegel thought that colonialism would be good for Africans. See his "Geographical Basis of World History" in Emmanuel Eze (ed.) *Race and the Enlightenment*, esp. 126–28. For a discussion of this aspect of Hegel's thought see also "Introduction" in Emmanuel Eze (ed.) *Postcolonial African Philosophy* (Cambridge, MA, and Oxford, UK: Blackwell Publishers, 1997), 7–10.

12. See W. E. B. Du Bois, *The Souls of Black Folk* (New York: Bantam Books, 1989), specifically the essay "Of the Dawn of Freedom," for a succinct account of such exploitive practices in the American South.

13. See, for example, Gilroy, *Against Race*, esp. 54–72; also Valerie Babb, *Whiteness Visible* (New York and London: New York University Press, 1998), chap. 1.

14. See Valentin Mudimbe, *The Invention of Africa: Gnosis, Philosophy, and the Power of Knowledge* (Bloomington and Indianapolis: Indiana University Press, 1988), chap. 1. Valerie Babb has very ably demonstrated that a similar invention and use of blackness significantly influenced the United States' construction of a national identity *in terms of whiteness*. Babb, *Whiteness Visible*, 31–45.

15. All the more reason John Locke's reason for distinguishing between the concepts *man* and *person* warrants very close examination. I have already hinted that the reason for this distinction is that Locke was trying to rationalize European classificatory categories and hence European hegemonic and economic aims. See my *Cornel West and Philosophy* (2002), chapter 6.

16. Of course, I am aware of the importance of phenotype, too, such as physical characteristics, hair texture, and the like, in the matter. However, since the focus of this study, and part of the focus of the volume, is on blackness, I do not emphasize phenotype as such. This much should be noted, however, that phenotype is subordinate to skin pigmentation. An individual may be phenotypically white but with a black pigmentation. For all practical purposes, such an individual would be regarded as black. It really does not matter how the individual wishes to classify herself or himself. Conversely, an individual may be phenotypically black but with a white pigmentation—e.g., Mick Jagger of the rock band The Rolling Stones—and such an individual is regarded as white. This shows the primacy of color in race issues.

17. These are blacks who are struggling with the social denigration of blacks and black modes of being. They sometimes attribute this state of affairs to putatively

decadent black culture and values, and consequently adopt a conservative political stand against so-called blackness. For a critique of this type of self-hating blacks, see Cornel West, *Race Matters* (New York: Vintage Books, 1994), chap. 4. Yet there is another group of so-called self-hating blacks. These internalize the aesthetic and other values of the dominant society and so engage in self-abnegation. Some would say that Pop Star Michael Jackson belongs to this category.

18. On the issue of the inverse relation between black material success, as reflected in their upward economic mobility, and their social denigration see my discussion in *Cornel West and Philosophy* (New York and London: Routledge, 2002), 71–78.

19. *Cornel West and Philosophy*, 88–91. See also Iris Marion Young, *Justice and the Politics of Difference* (Princeton, NJ: Princeton University Press, 1990), chap. 2.

20. See for example Iris Marion Young, *Justice and the Politics of Difference*, 13–14. Charles Mills has also sketched out a similar position in his book *The Racial Contract* (Ithaca, NY: Cornell University Press, 1997) but with a focus on whiteness. Elaborating some of the major tenets of the relation of global dominance and subordination of nonwhites by whites as constitutive of the racial contract, Mills writes, in response, that his position "distinguishes between whiteness as phenotype/genealogy and Whiteness as a political commitment to white supremacy." Accordingly, he continues, in light of this distinction his position thus allows for "white renegades" and "race traitors." Furthermore, Mills says that his aim in foregrounding and exposing the racial contract is "to eliminate race (not as innocent human variety but as ontological superiority and inferiority, as differential entitlement and privilege) altogether" (126–27).

21. See Sibylle Fischer, *Modernity Disavowed: Haiti and the Cultures of Slavery in the Age of Revolution*, Appendix A, "Imperial Constitution of Haiti, 1805" (Durham, NC: Duke University Press, 2004), 274–81. For an online version of the 1805 Haitian Constitution, see Uhhp.com: Haitian History: 1805 Constitution (from http:// Haiti.uhhp .com/historical_docs/Constitution_May_1805.html). My citations are to the version in Fischer. The significance of the Haitian Constitution of 1805 for, among other things, the issue of race, was noted by Anthony Bogues in a paper "Shifting the Geography of Reason: From Critical Reason to Radical Reasoning" and also by Clinton Hutton in "The Haitian Revolution and the Cosmological Roots of Haitian Freedom." Both papers were presented at the First Annual Caribbean Philosophical Association conference at Cave Hills Barbados (May 19–22, 2004). I gratefully acknowledge both scholars for the insights I obtained from their respective presentations and to Bogues in particular for directing my attention to Fischer's work.

22. I think this concern is *partly* what motivates Lucius Outlaw's critique of Kwame Anthony Appiah's view in Outlaw's essay, "On Reading W. E. B. Du Bois' 'The Conservation of Races'" (*SAPINA Newsletter*, Vol. IV, No. 1 [January-July 1992], 13–28). This work has since been revised as "Against the Grain of Modernity: The Politics of Difference and the Conservation of 'Race'" (in Outlaw, *On Race and Philosophy* [New York and London: Routledge, 1996]), chap. 6. Subsequent references to Outlaw's views will be to the latter work. I take up this issue in the next section.

23. David B. Wilkins, "Introduction: The Context of Race" (in Appiah and Guttman, *Color Conscious*, 21–24); Naomi Zack, *Thinking About Race* (Belmont, CA: Wadsworth Publishing Co., 1998), chap. 2; and Lucius Outlaw, *On Race and Philoso-*

phy, chap. 6. Essentially, each of these scholars, for varying reasons, argues that race is a social reality that ought not to be eliminated. For a contrasting view see Amy Guttman, "Responding to Racial Injustice" (in *Color Conscious*), esp. 163–78.

24. The view about the variety of races that is entailed by Outlaw's position is consistent with Du Bois's argument for different races but inconsistent with Outlaw's own project about social bargaining. (Outlaw's position, paradoxically, is advanced while defending Du Bois's view, articulated in the essay, "The Conservation of Races," against a criticism by Anthony Appiah.) In "The Conservation of Races," Du Bois felt compelled to make the case for black humanity, saying that the Negro race has as much to contribute to humanity as does the white race. (Du Bois echoes this view again in *The Souls of Black Folk.* There he speaks of the spiritual strivings of the Negro "to be a coworker in the kingdom of culture" [3].) It is in this context that Du Bois speaks of a variety of races, each of which has as much to offer humanity as the others. Given this historical context, therefore, Du Bois's position is understandable, as also is the fact that he did not interrogate the concept of race itself. He simply assumed, among other things, the biological foundations of race. Unlike Du Bois, however, Outlaw and the others, in their own present historical moment, are aware of critiques of the concept of race as a fiction, and their projects are situated in a historical context very different from Du Bois's. So, in my view, they cannot appeal to the objectionable and discredited notion of race to advance their projects without at the same time endorsing raciology as it was originally conceived by Bernier et al. For Du Bois's view, see "The Conservation of Races" in Philip S. Foner (ed.), *W. E .B. Du Bois Speaks: Speeches and Addresses 1890–1919* (New York: Pathfinder 1970). Anthony Appiah's critique of Du Bois is "The Uncompleted Argument: Du Bois and the Illusion of Race" in Henry Louis Gates, Jr. [ed.], *Race, Writing and Difference.* (See n. 7 for details.)

25. See Richard Herrnstein and Charles Murray (eds.), *The Bell Curve: Intelligence and Class Structure in American Life* (New York: Free Press, 1994).

26. Michael Lerner and Cornel West, *Jews and Blacks: A Dialogue on Race, Religion and Culture in America* (New York and London: Plume/Penguin Books, 1996), 73. I should point out in this connection that those who characterize affirmative action as "reverse discrimination" are appealing to this notion of comparative victimology. They are saying, curiously, that they are oppressed!

27. See Mike Hill (ed.), *Whiteness: A Critical Reader* (New York and London: New York University Press, 1997), 346–49.

28. *The APA Newsletters on the Black Experience, Computer Use, Feminism, Law, Medicine, Teaching, International Cooperation,* Vol. 95, No. 1 (fall 1995), 6–8.

29. I confess that one handicap of white colleagues teaching about racism and sexism in the Western canon is the fear of possibly being confounded with the proponents of racist and sexist views, especially when there are minority students. White colleagues therefore may be extremely sensitive to these issues and so entertain fears about being misunderstood. That is clearly understandable. But, as I said in a workshop-presentation on this subject to the 1994 conference of the American Association of Philosophy Teachers (AAPT), it is often better to risk presenting the material in a very critical manner than not to. (My presentation at the AAPT conference subsequently was published as "Teaching the Canons of Western Philosophy at Historically

Black Colleges and Universities: The Spelman College Experience," *Metaphilosophy*, Vol. 26, No. 4 [October 1995], 413–23.) The minority student is more likely to admire and respect a white faculty colleague for doing so than if the colleague tried to avoid these issues. If the colleague fails to make the student aware of the aberrant views of the canonical figures, and if the student finds out about these views independently, then the student may end up thinking that the colleague is protecting the culprits of those views. And that unwittingly would make the colleague a suspect, at least in the student's mind. Personally, it was Professor Harry M. Bracken who exposed me to the racist views of Enlightenment figures when I took his course in modern philosophy as a graduate student at McGill University, for which reason I have the ultimate respect and admiration for Harry. So, white colleagues may wish to take note and overcome the handicap I mentioned at the beginning.

9

Blackness as an Ethical Trope: Toward a Post-Western Assertion

Molefi Kete Asante
Temple University

The Parameters

IN THE INTRODUCTION TO HER BOOK, *The Afrocentric Paradigm*, Ama Mazama (2003) raises a profound question about Franz Fanon's understanding of the idea of blackness. What Mazama seeks to demonstrate is the fact that the brilliant Fanon, like so many black thinkers, had not thought through his own dislocation, although he had made a strong analysis of the effects of colonization on African people. Indeed, Fanon had been born in Martinique in 1923 and lived most of his life under the colonization by the French in the Caribbean and in Africa. Colonization was a preoccupation of his writing and he understood, as presented in his book, *Black Skin, White Masks* (1967), that it was possible for Africans to be deeply alienated from culture because of the violence of the colonization process. However much Fanon might have wanted to do so, he could not distance himself from the continuing predicament of Africans who had experienced self-hatred, self-rejection, and the pathological doctrine of white supremacy. Blackness emerged as an obstacle to unfettered injustice and became, in the moment of psychological terrorizing, the ethic of resistance.

Therefore, it is clear that to be black is not merely an issue of color nor simply the use of the language of black people, but to use it to express the most progressive political, cultural, and ethical interests that, in a racist society, must always be for human liberation and, thus, against all forms of oppression. Thus, it has become over the decades a trope of strong ethical dimensions with implications for a post-Western construction of reality.

A preacher from Jackson, Mississippi, went to Chicago to preach. He complained that the people did not respond to him the way they responded to him in Jackson. He said, "I spoke in the people's language, used the proper idioms, and they sat there like I was not talking to them." The preacher assumed that the mark of blackness was language alone or, at least, the ability to speak the idioms of the people. However, idioms represent only one aspect of the meaning of blackness.

What the preacher missed is the fact that to be black is to share the evolving political and social interests of oppressive people. The language is essential, but it must be devoted to the liberation struggle of oppressed people. Language is more than a personal skill, it is a commitment, a belief, an emotion. Thus, some people may have mastered all the technical elements of Ebonics and still not be considered "black" by those with sentiments born of political and social situations. There are therefore degrees of blackness as there are degrees of Ebonics. No one has ever come full grown into blackness; no one ever will. However, there are individuals who we say possess "charisma," but what does this mean in the sense of blackness? It means that the person has found a commitment to the emotional, political, and social interests of the black community and knows how to master the language of community ambitions.

There is a reason that African Americans felt that Malcolm X brought the persona of morality when he entered a room. The meaning of this is that he brought with him the full complements of blackness, the expected rhetoric against oppression, the optimism of victory over evil, courage to speak his mind, and the validity of struggle for a good cause. The reason it was often said that Malcolm X was the fulfillment of the culture of the African American was the fact that he was indeed immersed in an environment of consciousness to humanity. Every thought, action, and motivation appeared to be connected to the totality of the people's will and desire. This was his meaning; indeed, it was the meaning of black culture or rather he was the meaning of the culture, a cultured person. Malcolm understood the nature of blackness as a trope in the American consciousness and his persona was an explicit presence of its power.

Lewis Gordon (2000, 12) writing in *Existentia Africana* rightly claims that "race has emerged throughout its history, as the question fundamentally of 'the blacks' as it has for no other group." While Gordon is not here concerned with blackness as a trope, he is definitely interested in seeing how blackness operated within the context of a racist society. He knows that the question of Africana philosophy has been "the only situated reality that has been conditioned by blackness" (2000, 12). The fact of the matter is that race matters are not simply matters of "chromosomal makeup or morphological appearance" in Gordon's terms, but rather they are matters of "the values placed on what has been interpreted as given" (Gordon 2000,12).

Isolating a Perspective

Blackness is certainly not seen as a form of confraternity among all people who are black in complexion. If it were the basis of confraternity we could well argue that it had taken an essentialist turn. However, when I am in Paris and I speak to an obvious African by phenotype, indeed, a very black French-speaking African who is with a French woman, he is likely to ignore me with the implication, "We have nothing in common." Thus, blackness is not merely a phenotype phenomenon. It is more concretely a phenomenon of time and place. Mark Christian noted in *Multiracial Identity* that some black British spoke of blackness as a "belonging" (Christian 2000, 35).

I am dealing here with situation and history.

Frank Thorpe, my twelfth grade history teacher, had a profound impact on my conceptualization of the world. He was, however, most distinguished by his pedagogical method that might be described as a provocative inquisition of young minds.

"Why were some people made black and some made white?"

"Who is responsible for racism anyway?"

"Why are white people white?"

He would pound his fist on the desk and then say, "If you can't answer the questions leave the room and return with the answers." Sometimes he would leap out of his chair and shout, "What is blackness if it is not the color of the universe? If you cannot answer the question, you all know what to do." No one ever left the classroom and he did not intend that we should leave even if we could not answer his questions. The joy, in Thorpe's classes, was to be in pursuit of answers; it was the one activity from which no one escaped. Blackness itself is a pursuit.

I am in pursuit of the full complements of blackness in the context of twentieth-century foundations and twenty-first-century possibilities. Of course, I know better the foundations than I do the possibilities since I do not frame my inquiry as either a prophetic fragment or prophecy. I am much more realistic and ordinary in my objective. Yet I do not find this pursuit unfamiliar turf since as an Afrocentrist I have been convinced always by the arguments of history that African people have moved off of or been moved off of their own philosophical, cultural, economic, and political terms for a long time. Thus, the discussion of blackness itself as an attribute of a people is an unnecessary marginalization of what is a central philosophical and pragmatic action of our times. This should become clearer in the tension between blackness as taxon and as practice.

Taxon and Practice

The notion of blackness as taxon yields different results than blackness as practice. The first is based on an Aristotelian essentialism. It is therefore founded upon what we have come to call a Greek tradition. The second derives from an assertion of humanity that struggles against the chaos of domination. It is from the Kemetic tradition of the ancient Nile Valley, the classical home of African cultures. Both traditions have helped to advance science. Nevertheless, these two notions of blackness have been often confused in the literature and orature of proponents and detractors of blackness. Resolving this issue so that all the pieces are in place will require a step-by-step analysis.

One of my intentions, therefore, is to establish the fact that the Aristotelian patriarchy of taxonomic essentialism is responsible for much of the confusion surrounding the concept of blackness. In this way, I hope, in my discussion, to free the discourse from unnecessary attributions. This allows me to distance my discussion of blackness from Du Bois's entrapping attribution of "double-consciousness" (Du Bois 1903; 1982). I then demonstrate how blackness is itself a revolutionary praxis free of any essentialist taxons. The chapter concludes with a personal statement attesting to the legitimacy of a revolutionary blackness.

The Aristotelian Patriarch

Aristotelian essentialism has been correctly termed property essentialism (Jones 2005) because it seeks to define a thing by listing its qualities. Thus, one has various kinds of things in the world. There are many natural things, but we can know differences through attributes and characteristics of a thing. A dog is not a cat but neither is a man a dog. However, the taxons of the cat and dog are closer to each other than either one is to a man. This is the basic idea of property essentialism. If you wanted to define something you readily sought to discover its attributes and therein was the critical difference between that thing and something else.

One sees these Aristotelian taxons in a discussion of race where Western writers subsequent to Aristotle used various taxons to create the notion of race. One was said to be of a different race if one's hair was textured differently or one's complexion possessed more or less melanin than another. Thus, property essentialism was basic to establishing the unscientific idea of biological races. Much emphasis is placed on the German school of the von Humboldts as promoters of the taxons of race, but there are many Europeans engaged in the pedantry of race. Their legacy was to be found in the works of the greatest European minds. Furthermore, the influences of these European thinkers have penetrated the thinking of many African writers as well. The question of race is not an African question; it is preeminently an issue of European thinkers. No African writer espoused a doctrine of racial superiority. Indeed, it was neither in the literature nor the more generally available orature of African cultures.

The Illusion of Double Consciousness

The literary people among us have been trumpeting Du Bois's statement about double consciousness for the past twenty or so years to explain identity chaos or a sort of identity complication due to a racist society that privileges whiteness (Du Bois 1982).

However, there is no double consciousness. I announce an end to Du Bois's errant conclusion and I question the strength by which it is promoted by academic literary scholars who are often not in contact with the ordinary African person in America. The idea of "double consciousness" has fueled too many leaps into the abyss of meaninglessness and caused too many misconceptions about identity. Even if there had been a war of ideas, there is no longer any struggle between ontology and citizenship. "American" is not a race, it is a shared idea of society. It is not a static idea; it is nothing more than a citizenship. It is neither an ethnic group, nor a clan, nor a nation. To say the American nation is to talk nonsense; there is only the potential for an American nationality. It is socially constructed. There is no biologically structured American race. Furthermore, what Du Bois meant by "double consciousness" at the turn of the twentieth century has remained debatable for many decades.

Now Du Bois may have meant what he said, growing out of his own personal situation, and I am not suggesting that some Africans in America do not think they have the same personal issues, "two warring souls in one dark body," but as for me and my family we have only one consciousness; we are black. This is not a biological statement; it is an affirmation of consciousness. As is shown below, the biological question is another matter, one that has little bearing on the question of blackness in its full complement as an assertion.

The Nature of Consciousness and Identity

Consciousness can only be unitary anyway. It cannot be otherwise. One can be conscious of being conscious of conflict, one could have a tortured consciousness because one wanted to be something that one was not and the something that one wanted was perceived to be better than what one was. In such a case this is not double consciousness, but madness. It is stuck in the interstices of our existence because we have permitted a dysfunction between *who we are* and *who we are told we ought to be.* Clearly all of this comes from one's society, family, and peers. We know who we are and to whom we are connected by knowing our ancestors, physical or spiritual. The more fully we know our ancestors, the rounder, the more powerful our sense of identity. This is why it is acknowledged that the fundamental requirement for slavery was the theft of history and identity, simultaneously. One way to regain what was lost is to seek a reconnection to a sense of identity and historical consciousness.

One may have a tortured consciousness but one cannot have a double consciousness. Ordinarily nothing in the African's life in America creates a clashing of consciousness. Put another way, the black man or woman living in the Deep South of Georgia at the beginning of the twentieth century did not have the "doubleness" madness. In fact, most blacks do not have it now. The tortured consciousness, mistakenly called double consciousness, is probably the results of blacks being magnetized by white privilege and thus experiencing pangs of self-hatred. Thus, the root of the madness is not in the African but in the society. Whatever Du Bois meant was meant personally. There is no doubt in my mind that Du Bois was on a quest, like many African American intellectuals, for personal space. Lucius Outlaw points out in *On Race and Philosophy* that Du Bois's notion of "race" is best read as a cluster idea in which "elements are connected in an infinitely disjunctive definition" (Outlaw 1996, 154–55).

If you read Du Bois this way then it becomes clear that the postmodern turn on the question of race, that is, its fluidity, mobility, and fleeting characteristics, is much more an issue of what *stasis* occurs at a given time along a certain continuum of human reality. Race, of course, is one thing. Blackness is another thing altogether. Where one might say emphatically that race is constructed and means one thing, to say blackness is constructed at this moment in history is to mean something entirely different. That is why the notion of a cluster idea for race might have some legitimacy if applied to blackness. To say, for example, that blackness might consist of elements that are connected in an infinitely disjunctive manner may make some sense to many people. It is not to say that blackness is the same thing as race in construction, but rather to say that the cluster idea might give one a reason to look at different definitions of blackness. I am eager to see a revolutionary turn to this idea so as to annihilate the racist ideas that accompany even the cluster into the present era.

Blackness as a Trope

This brings me back to blackness. What is the meaning of blackness? Is it a color, biology, politics, race, or convenience? In one sense this is a perspectivist inquiry because the answer might depend upon where you stand. On the other hand, it is a rational examination of the evolutionary development of an American trope that represents in some primary manner and in some authentic way the maturity of the national idea.

At a recent party, attended by a multicultural group of individuals, but mostly people of African descent, the conversation took an unsuspecting turn toward identity. One of the guests, a white woman born in England, indicated that she was now an American citizen and that her husband "who is Hispanic" was a protestant preacher. At which point one of the guests asked her, "Where is your husband?"

The woman looked toward the dining room and yelled, "Oh Richard, come in here and introduce yourself." The large, round man appeared in the doorway, and almost in unison, but led by the guest who had asked "where's your husband?" the fifteen or so other guests said, "he is a black man." The fact that the woman had referred to him as Hispanic was a test for the trope of blackness in a truly American drama.

"No, I am not," protested Richard. "My real name is Ricardo and I am Hispanic."

"What makes you Hispanic?" a guest asked.

"I speak Spanish," said Ricardo-Richard, hoping to put an end to the queries.

"I speak English but I am not English," said the inquiring guest. "Furthermore," he continued, "just because you speak Japanese does not mean that you have become Japanese."

Another guest, a university professor, said, "My wife is Nicaraguan. She speaks Spanish but since she has not spoken tonight everyone assumed that she was black, just like they assumed you were black, by phenotype, that is, by physical traits."

Ricardo protested, "But you can see that I am *not* black; I have wavy hair."

"So does my mother and she is black," shouted an African American woman in a long colorful African dress.

"How did you so-called Hispanics get that wavy hair?" inquired a South African accountant.

"But I am Puerto Rican and everyone knows that we are Hispanics," Ricardo insisted.

"Where did your food, music, and Santeria come from?" asked a Nigerian psychiatrist.

Ricardo was in a quandary. He could not answer the questions to the satisfaction of the audience. His wife was embarrassed.

The guests did not allow Ricardo to leave until they had pummeled him with other questions about identity. The host intervened and said that Ricardo had been a good sport but obviously he did not recognize his African heritage.

As the battered and good-natured Ricardo and his wife were leaving the party, his wife thought that she had better put everything in perspective and said, "You must understand that when Ricardo was a little boy he was the darkest one in his family and his father used to call him the 'little Negro' and this was considered by him to be an insult. It caused him lots of pain and so now he wants to avoid any reference to being of African descent."

Regardless of Ricardo's phenotype the Afrocentrist would say that Ricardo was not black, perhaps un-black. Blackness is not simply genetics, appearances, or color; it is fundamentally a type of consciousness, a specific consciousness that Ricardo apparently did not have nor care to have. He had been influenced by the negative connotations of blackness within the society. Had blackness been accepted by him as a positive he would not have objected; indeed, he might have embraced the idea. More importantly, had Ricardo interrogated the history of Africans in America and followed the journey of liberation and the quest for a more humane society he might have arrived at a more ethical idea of blackness; one which he could have accepted. Unfortunately, for Ricardo, he was stuck with the dominant and hegemonically tarred and feathered image of blackness he had received from his education and the media. There is no doubt in my mind that the media, education, politics, and religion have conspired to demonize blackness as a color based on the negative images of Africa, enslavement, and ideas of subordination.

Chosenness

Implied in any discussion of consciousness is choice, one must choose to participate. There are situations where choosing not to participate could produce historical and psychological discontinuities. Say you know someone who is phenotypically black and whose grandparents were active in the civil rights movement or the Black Power movement but who now chooses not to identify as black; that person has chosen to change identities. It is highly unlikely in a white racial hierarchical society such as the United States that a phenotypically white person would choose to be black. On the other hand, a phenotypically black person could choose to be white, that is, to claim to be white. One could see the decision as possible because of the identification of whiteness with privileges. This is one more indication that decisions are often dependent upon context. The case of Homer Plessy in the late 1890s is instructive. Plessy pleaded his case before the Supreme Court arguing that when the conductor forced him to sit in the "Colored Only" section of the railcar he was denied "the reputation" that should have been his because he was only one-eighth black. Being seven-eighths white, by blood, should have given him the right to exercise the power of whiteness and sit in the "White Only" section of the railcar. Of course, the decision of 1896 in *Plessy v. Ferguson* underscored the American idea that "one drop of African blood made a person an African."

Apparently, in the United Kingdom, the term *black* is used to refer to either people of African or Asian, particularly Indian or Pakistani backgrounds. Thus, it is not confined as it is in America to the idea of Africans who have been enslaved. The notion of blackness in the United States is wrapped up with previous conditions of servitude. In Britain people are identified by their color. Thus, an Indian or Pakistani is black in Great Britain. In the United States the same people are called Asians. The nature of blackness is such that it becomes an unwhiteness in England.

Moral Identity

The African American through a long struggle against domination has established a moral identity that is indestructible in the context of historical injustice and national duplicity. The concrete factors in the formulation of a moral identity of the African American are the ethical themes, not biological tenets, of the American sojourn. There are profound implications for human relationships if the lessons of our fight for freedom are appreciated as international symbols for social justice. Thus, the Dalits in India, the First Nations of Australia, and the Maoris of New Zealand, among others, have found strength in the African American's insistent and persistent struggle to bring about a moral ideal.

Our history in America remains authentic, shaped by the exigencies, conditions, pretexts, subtexts, and dramas of resistance to enslavement, segregation, and discrimination. We are not an amorphous historical body waiting for a claimant; ours is a history told in the lives of Malcolm X, Du Bois, Garvey, King, Harriet Tubman, and Zora Neale Hurston.

What Is Blackness?

It is necessary to outline the argument that follows. In the first place, blackness is not merely a color in the Aristotelian essentialist sense. Yet it is engaged in America and, in a wider context in Europe, as a taxon of race. But race itself is problematic in ways that blackness is not, as we see below in this discussion. Furthermore, blackness is not discovered simply in the styles of dress, modes of language, or habits of a people. While one could make a case, not my intention now, for the position that certain markers do indicate an awareness of blackness through language, it will suffice to say that one cannot effect Ebonics to claim blackness. While the proper linguistic markers of black people may help to identify blackness, they are not sufficient. When the novelist Toni Morrison declared that President Bill Clinton was the first black president, she did not intend to convey anything about his biology or his speech, but about his sense of fair play in the racial arena. One could be soundly rejected as not "black enough" even if one spoke Ebonics.

The use of what one might refer to as a black idiom is not enough to count as blackness. One must also share thematic content, mainly substantive commitments to the political and social objectives of a defeat of the doctrine of white supremacy, in order to claim blackness. Thus it is a commitment more than a skill and it allows someone to say that Ward Connerly or Clarence Thomas is not black and mean that their commitment to overturning white supremacy is absent. Strangely, it opens the door for certain people defined essentially as "white" to be seen as participating in blackness. As we shall see, the emergence of the African American movement as opposed to the Civil Rights movement initiated the evolution of blackness. I have argued that a black perspective was necessary for the college curriculum, but such an argument was never couched in terms that meant a black person needed to be in the classroom (Asante 2003a), although a person with experiences in the black gene pool of America would most likely bring a black perspective. While I was sure that one could better the odds of having a black perspective by having a black person in the classroom, I was also aware that some phenotypical blacks were agents of white supremacy, and therefore, anti-black, meaning anti-fair play and anti-justice. Self-hatred as an abnormality of consciousness has the capacity to render people black in complexion racists against themselves.

Separation

What separates blackness from nonblackness is the fact that blackness does not have crimes against white people in the cupboards. To say we are black is to argue that we are not keepers of secrets of conquest over others. Blackness infers no hatred of other people and black people have no arguments against the freedom of Palestinians, Kurds, Irish, or other people fighting to be left alone to determine their destinies.

Blackness is thematically against all terror perpetrated on any people. To possess blackness is to have hands free from the exploitation of the First Nations of America, Europe, Australia, Asia, or Africa. While many people, groups, and nations may have been born of strife, conquest, and domination, blackness is born of a desire for liberation and the resistance to conquest. One finds blackness disproportionately among people who are phenotypically black because we have been at the most violent edges of white supremacy. Jack Forbes has written brilliantly about white adventurers referring to Native Americans during the sixteenth and seventeenth centuries as "blacks," indicating their status as people to be conquered. As in a Marxist sense, the workers' consciousness is unlike that of the capitalist, so the oppressed is different from the oppressor. Albert Memmi has pointed to this distinction in *The Colonizer and the Colonized* (Memmi 1991). Thus, blackness becomes the antithesis to colonization, slavery, discrimination, and exploitation.

Blackness Becoming: *Khepera* Syndrome

There are no Jacobins to enforce blackness despite the fact that there are people who believe that is the case. It is neither acceptable morally nor is it necessary politically. Like the ancient Kemetic scarab, *khepera*, the glyph for "becoming," the idea of blackness is persistent wherever you find negativity, chaos, and ill intent. Blackness *becoming* is the most authentic myth in the history of the United States, and possibly in the West during the past five hundred years.

In a penetrating article, "On Race and Revisability" (*Journal of Black Studies*, 2005), Richard A. Jones opined that if one understood what the markers of blackness were then one would not have to feel "a sense of failure in not being black enough" simply because whites could not perceive one's blackness. Some people, defined by society as black, are disappointed when whites say, "I do not think of you as black." This causes some black people to question their behavior, language, actions, attitudes, and choices, because they realize that if you are truly black, there should not be any mistaking your identity.

Contrary to the statements of non-Afrocentrists, there are no blackness police because no centralizing or policing force is necessary to bring it into existence. Occasionally, a pundit will say, "The brothers and sisters want me to follow their blacker than thou philosophy." This is nonsense. One is either black or not black. There is no enforcer. One either supports the struggle against racist domination or not. There are no postmodern gray lines here, you either stand with the oppressed and against oppression or you stand with the oppressor against liberation. The shading and fading into degrees of blackness is inapplicable, as I see it, to this problem. One chooses, decides, in a transformative state, to become, thus perfecting *khepera*, the becoming.

There have been writers who expressed a desire to see an end to blackness, but this is a hopeless wish. The myth of the end of blackness is like the wish for the rainbow to cease to exist. Whenever you have histories, oral and written, of resistance to enslavement, segregation, discrimination, national expression, and white supremacy, you will discover blackness. It is the one abiding American value against the murder of hope and optimism. Thus, blackness becomes the reality of our historical activities against domination.

Of course, blackness can be altered thematically by conditions, contexts, and customs but nothing replaces blackness as the core conductor of the war against racist white supremacy. If the resistance has been intricately connected to African Americans it is only that we have suffered the most from the promulgation of the doctrines of white supremacy. It is reasonable to assume that a major part for human liberation would be waged on the lines of Black people. However, the mistake frequently made by those who have assaulted blackness is to assume that there is some genetic relationship between the thematic of blackness and race. Such a thought may have originated in the dark recesses of the minds of the Europeans who first encountered Africans, as much of the literature suggests, but the maintenance and usefulness of this connection has long since run its course.

In every sense, blackness is a new type of value for the masses of the people. It possesses a political and social sensitivity and sensibility directed against all forms of human oppression. Therefore, a new people are created and by maintaining the critical themes of blackness they become the new blacks, new Africans, marked or typed by an identity rooted in their fierce opposition to all forms of domination: racism, sexism, classism, pedophilia, national terror, and white racial supremacy. These new blacks are discovered in every nation and among all ethnic groups. Indeed, I have numerous friends, not phenotypically black, who are black, indeed, blacker than some individuals who proclaim that they are genetically black. Conversely, there are increasing numbers of individuals who are of African descent genetically but who are morally white, that is, they have assumed the burden of whiteness in a world in a post-Western era.

One of my graduate students, not genotypically nor phenotypically black, ran into a famous Harvard professor at an annual conference and happily announced that she was studying "Afrocentricity with Molefi Asante at Temple

University." Whereupon the famous professor looked her up and down and exclaimed, "Now, I have seen everything, a white student of Afrocentricity." Of course, this student never claimed to be black, appreciated the fact that being black was not mere biology, and understood, what he did not, that Afrocentricity was an intellectual enterprise. If being black in color or by some genetic formula meant blackness, then Clarence Thomas would be blacker than most people in this country. But to call Clarence Thomas "black," in terms of the struggle for justice against racism and sexism, is to stretch the trope.

By now it should be easy to see that blackness cannot be mere biology because in that case almost no people defined as black in the United States would be black. The DNA of African Americans tends to be representative of ancestors from several continents, although the core is African. Blackness is fundamentally extrabiological.

To say that someone is not black is not to pass a judgment on ethnicity. When I say that Clarence Thomas is not black I am not saying anything about his complexion or his ancestry; I am rather speaking about virtue. By the same token, to say that Julian Bond, Adam Clayton Powell, or Walter White are some of the blackest men in our history is to express not an ethnic or complexion statement, but a moral judgment. Some individuals may even have "black consciousness" as in skin recognition and yet not be against white supremacy; this is one of the peculiarities of just announcing that someone is black without knowing the meaning of the term.

Blackness is a virtue, not unlike justice, differing only in the object of application. To do justice is to participate in correcting actions deemed to have transgressed civil, criminal, or commercial codes. To do blackness is to participate in an assertive program of human equality, indeed, affirmative behavior to eradicate doctrines of white supremacy. Thus, "not by color, but by their words and deeds you shall know them" might be a new axiom.

Is it possible that Picasso, in choosing the Grebo mask, in 1912, as a key to his cubism, or Modigliani, in using stylized Senufo standing figures and Dan masks, to develop a portrait style, might have been the first to leap at blackness as virtue? The aesthetic value of the art forms of Africa translated into ethical icons in a world stunned by the World Wars begun in Europe.

What is the rhetoric of anti-blackness if it is not anti-Africanism? What is the meaning of Jim Sleeper's argument against blackness?

Ultimately, anti-blackness represents the highest form of pessimism toward humanity since blackness has been posited as the post-Western trope best qualified to serve as an ethical measure of our social universe. George Sefa Dei has explored this in depth in his works on anti-racist education (Dei 1997). In fact, African Americans who participate only in Eurocentric views can easily become anti-black simply because this is the logical extension of a virulent Eurocentric imperialism (Asante 1998).

One only has to remember the age-old plot strategy where an author has a falsely accused person charged with a crime before the court, and a chorus of others not so accused shout in unison, "I am guilty." In the same vein we have achieved the purpose of the virtue of blackness as a response to white racial domination in Western society when the entire body politic, building upon an ethical plinth, adopts the strategy and says definitively, "I, too, am black."

Works Cited

Asante, Molefi Kete. 2003. *Afrocentricity: The Theory of Social Change.* Chicago: African American Images.

———. 2003. *Erasing Racism: The Survival of the American Nation.* Amherst: Prometheus Books.

———. 1998. *The Afrocentric Idea.* Philadelphia: Temple University Press.

Christian, Mark. 2000. *Multiracial Identity: An International Perspective.* London: Macmillan.

Dei, George Sefa. 1997. *Anti-Racism Education: Theory and Practice.* Toronto: Fernwood Publishing.

Du Bois, W. E. B. 1903 (1982). *The Souls of Black Folk.* New York: New American Library.

Fanon, Franz. 1967. *Black Skin, White Masks.* New York: Grove.

Forbes, Jack. 1993. *Africans and Native Americans: The Language of Race and the Evolution of Red Blood.* Champaign-Urbana:. University of Illinois Press.

Gordon, Lewis R. 2000. *Existentia Africana: Understanding Africana Existential Thought.* New York: Routledge.

Jones, Richard. 2005. "Race and Revisability," *Journal of Black Studies* 35 (August).

Mazama, Ama, ed. 2003. *The Afrocentric Paradigm.* Trenton: Africa World Press.

Memmi, Albert. 1991. *The Colonizer and the Colonized.* Boston: Beacon.

Outlaw, Lucius. 1996. *On Race and Philosophy.* New York: Routledge.

10

Tongue Smell Color black

Janine Jones
University of North Carolina, Greensboro

"Nobody is born black." Klor de Alva spoke these words during a conversation with Cornel West on black-brown relations. De Alva went on to say: "People are born with different pigmentation, people are born with different physical characteristics, no question about that. But you have to learn to be black. That's what I mean by constructedness."[1]

WHILE IT IS TRUE THAT SOME PEOPLE BECOME BLACK only after entering a territory where they are identified as black,[2] nevertheless, regardless of what blackness as a construct means to anyone, it is simply false that some people—some people in the United States, for example—are not *born* black. I was born black. I knew at least this much by age seven. I suffered the consequences of this birthmark to such a degree that I *demanded* of my mother, at what some would think is a rather tender age, an explanation for why she would have brought a black child into the world! Was she crazy? Selfish? Unthinking?[3] The problem was not that she had brought a child into the world who would one day learn to be black. I was black in her womb, as black as a slave child sold before air filled his lungs, as black as Dubois's son had been during his short safari[4] from cradle to tomb, a journey during which he had neither the time nor the presence of mind to learn about the particulars of his existential condition. And so when Dubois writes of his son, "Within the Veil was he born, said I; and there within shall he live—a Negro and a Negro's son," I do not interpret him as West does; that is, as refusing to "linger with the sheer tragedy of his son's death . . . without casting his son as an emblem of the race or a symbol of a black deliverance to come."[5] I read

Dubois as acknowledging that his dead son was born a black son, and as speaking truths about the kind of life his black son would have inherited as his birthright, had he lived.

Perhaps de Alva needs to distinguish between *being* black and *experiencing* being black. It is possible for people who are in fact black not to experience being black, for example, babies, such as Dubois's son, who die before they have consciously lived. Another example might be that of blacks who live in territories where they *are* identified as being black, but who *cannot* (for whatever reasons) or do not (for whatever reasons) *consciously* live with the fact of being so identified.[6]

In my reading of de Alva I also got the impression that he believes that we can just name ourselves as we please and call it a day. He writes:

> All identities are up for grabs. But black intellectuals in the United States, unlike Latino intellectuals in the United States, have an enormous media space within which to shape the politics of naming and to affect the symbols and meanings associated with certain terms. Thus, practically overnight, they convinced the media that they were an ethnic group and shifted over to the model of African-American, hyphenated American, as opposed to being named by color. Knowing what we know about the negative aspects of naming, it would be better for all of us, regardless of color, if those who consider themselves, and are seen as, black intellectuals were to stop participating in the insidious one-drop-rule game of identifying themselves as black.[7]

As William Shakespeare once told us, a rose by any other name would smell as sweet. Similarly, a black by any other name would be as black. Naming, in and of itself, does not fully determine how things are or how things are perceived as being, as de Alva suggests. It matters who does the naming and in what context the naming is carried out. We have only to consider Ludwig Wittgenstein's family, an intellectual-artistic-aristocratic family if ever there was one. They had not considered themselves Jews. When Wittgenstein's Cambridge friend, Maurice Drury, told him of Hitler's takeover, Wittgenstein, to his surprise, "did not seem unduly disturbed." Drury asked him if his sisters would be in danger. Wittgenstein replied: "They are much too respected, no one would dare to touch them."[8]

But regardless of how the Wittgensteins and Jews in their position named themselves they lived within a power structure to which they were subject: a power structure with its own ideas on the categorization and naming of Jews and non-Jews. The question as to whether Wittgenstein's sisters were *too respected to be touched* would be answered by Nazi race theorists in a manner different from the way the Wittgensteins may have wanted to answer that question:

> The answer lay in the *Mischling's* grandparents. Those with three fully Jewish grandparents were defined as Jewish. Those with two were Jewish only if they were also Jewish by religion or married to a Jew. However, this would not free any half-Jews from the Nazi terror. They were still non-Aryans, and not full German citizens. Labelled "*Mischlinge* of the first degree," they would face an increasing threat to their existence.[9]

By 1938:

> The family's only real hope [. . .] lay in the reservation that they had put forward in July: they would have to produce evidence showing that their paternal grandfather, Hermann Christian Wittgenstein, was not Jewish, so reducing the number of Jewish grandparents to two and opening the door to a reclassification as half Jewish.[10]

However, in the final analysis, "salvation lay in the Nazi authorities' research into the family's wealth rather than its ancestry."[11]

As we can see, the possibility of becoming and, hence, of being Jewish, lay in the Wittgensteins' origins, notwithstanding the Wittgensteins' ways of naming and perceiving themselves. But what is also interesting to note is that Wittgenstein, prior to Hitler's rise to power, had described himself as having "100 percent Hebraic" thoughts. Whatever Wittgenstein meant by this—and it seems that he meant something entirely negative[12]—somehow his experience had been shaped in such a way that he had *certain kinds of experiences* of being Jewish, in spite of his family's attempts to determine who they were and how they were perceived through naming themselves. Indeed, their naming-categorization process had not allowed Wittgenstein to determine how he perceived *himself*, for the process was carried out within a social-political-economic space that carried its own conceptions of how to locate and identify Jews within *its* space; and so strong was the current of that space that it permeated, invaded, if you like, Wittgenstein's own personal space.

So I say to de Alva, nothing happened *overnight*. A certain group of intellectuals naming themselves African American did not change the fact that they were black or that they had certain experiences of being black. I would like to believe that *they* were wise enough to know that.

My remarks on de Alva's comments are just preliminaries to the main topic of this chapter. I thought it necessary to address de Alva in order to undermine the view that we can just get rid of being black—if indeed we wanted to!—through some magical naming process. But what I really want to discuss is one crucial aspect of *being black*, which I believe crosses age, gender, class, and economic lines, though in different ways, depending on the circumstances: Being black seems to always involve the real *possibility* of being sought out by the gaze of the blind-sighted; that is, members of the white community or white institutions, decked in cloaks of *self-styled innocence*, shielded by compassion-proof capes of *pure curiosity*, who will take your very life (or your soul) if you are perceived by them as being black. It's simply their special way of *playing in the dark.*[13]

As Patricia Hill Collins observes in "Contemporary Black Feminist Thought," black women have a different view of themselves and their world than that offered by the established social order. "This different view encourages African American women to value their own subjective knowledge base."[14] In this chapter, I intend to do just that by recounting a *personal experience* that speaks to the issues of white innocence and white curiosity, two prominent features of the blind-sighted white gaze I and so many other black people have been subjected to. My story takes place at the University of North Carolina at Greensboro, where I teach.[15] But, actually, this story began long before I was born; it began long before the birth of Brenda Dixon Gottschild and her husband Helmutt Gottschild, who brought one of their stories, my story, *our* stories to UNCG, through performance art. For my subjective knowledge base is a shared subjective knowledge base.

Tongue Smell Color

Tongue Smell Color. "That's our jewel," Brenda Dixon Gottschild said, her eyes sparkling. At that moment, on Thursday afternoon, I knew I would attend the Friday night performance. Indeed, the Gottschilds' final performance was a gem to behold, if you managed to follow it with your eyes, your mind, your imagination.

But no mere ornament; for all its beauty, this staged dance of memories lived or remembered through the lives of others was not a gem to be held, except by those whose hands, already bruised and calloused, welcomed a memento of, a testament to the source of their encrusted wounds; or by those willing to let go of the keenest desire of their elusive hearts—that selfsame thing that killed the cat, nine times over. I am speaking of that awesome thing that some hands are accustomed to holding and keeping as a cherished, God-given right (bloodless knuckles white with clenching).

But as very few in that Friday night audience possessed singed hands or open palms, most people partook of the performance as many a child would a sumptuous meal. With dirt under their nails.

Sitting down to supper with filthy hands is a pleasure many children will not forego. Indeed, they may find the taste of grit, grime, and spices intriguing, as they lick the grease from their fingers. Tell them to wash their hands, and they'll tell you, "They're *my* hands!" Tell them that filth can lead to disease, to death, and they'll insist, "But it tastes good!"

And yet some would reply to this childish nonsense, smiling on those minion authorities as if they were angels on high, "How free they are of everything in their age of innocence!"

And so while it may be remarkable that a stone—precious as healthy blood, translucent as teardrops on the cheek of a dark-skinned child, hard as the beats of still-life hearts—had been cut and carved, using tongue, smell, and color as tools, with the intention of being given away, shared, it should come as no surprise that the gift, by most, was refused. For most of those present to receive the gift were white and not of a mind to accept it. Only the paper used to wrap the gift would be kept and coddled, unfolded and used to celebrate the wealth of diversity academia must claim to cherish.

Brenda and Helmutt Gottschild had been on the UNCG campus for a week. In pedagogy workshops they used their bodies as metaphors, as signs, to explore thresholds and disjunctions, bridges and continuities between people of different races, genders, and nationalities. Guilt, memory, and curiosity—the cat's fatal flaw—served as stethoscope, periscope, spyglass. Students and faculty were invited to peer through so many mirrors and reflections of mirrors, and bear witness to what they saw, if they dared! Auscultating chambers and cells within chambers, would we be driven to speak in tongues, or would we find the courage to speak with our tongues, to intone some echo of truth savored by our taste buds? I attended two pedagogy workshops prior to Friday's performance. But that final performance—Tongue Smell Color—was indeed a jewel. The bomb.

When I arrived for the performance the night was still young and black. Although the streets were already empty in this suburban mall-morass, a few stars did light the sky. The auditorium filled up quickly. Neighbors chatted with neighbors. Festive excitement sizzled in the air. The dean of arts and sciences was resigning. He had given a farewell speech (**Public Lecture**), which had received such enthusiastic applause that one professor had thought it *prudent* to call out, "We're applauding all the wonderful years of service you have given us!" (**Private Thoughts**) The night is young and black, indeed; and full of promise (I'm smiling too). All of life may be a play, with individual actors on a stage. But community life—so open, so public—conducts its work *dans les coulisses.*

I glanced at the program:

Opening
Lindquist Quote
Public Lecture—Private Thoughts

Curiosity—What's in a Name
The First Summer
Touch—Skin Memories
Childhood Memories—Letter
Venus Hottentot
The Doctor's Dream
Venus' Reverie—Revenge
Lips and Tongue
Smelling and Selling
Passports and Saxophones
Your People—My People
Curiosity and its Consequences
It Wasn't I
Epilogue
After the performance the audience is invited to enter and extend the discourse through verbal interaction.

The Hottentot Venus. My eyes closed in on the title.

> Several prints dating from the early nineteenth century illustrate the sensation generated by the spectacle of "The Hottentot Venus." A French print entitled "La Belle Hottentot," for example, depicts the Khosian woman standing with her buttocks exposed on a box-like pedestal. Several figures bend straining for a better look, while a male figure at the far right of the image even holds his seeing-eye glass up to better behold the woman's body. The European observers remark on the woman's body: "Oh! God Damn what roast beef!" and "Ah! how comical is nature."[16]

I had watched a film about Sara Baartman just a week ago. A young woman, a bride, the prize of her community. (The daughter of a chief; "Everyone wanted to marry me," she said.) And to think it was the light from the fire burning for Sara's wedding that gave her away. She was captured (Are we talking about a hunter and animals? or perhaps terrorists and innocent civilians caught in one of their big-game hunting parties?), forced into servitude, and offered a way out of her predicament, her newfound poverty, through the doors of the great cities of western civilization by those who found her less than human.

Passport to Civilization

In London, Sara would be dressed for success and displayed in a cage for the curious gaze of the general public and erudite thinkers. In return for giving her audience a broadside view of her prominent buttocks, Sara was promised half the booty, which would pay her passage home, where once again she would live free and secure.

Childhood Memories

But Sara was sold instead to a Parisian in 1814, and exhibited in Paris. Subsequently, she was loaned out to Cuvier and his crew for further genital exploration.[17] She died in Paris a year after her sale, of what, the consortium of doctors did not say, for their curiosity extended from her butt to her genitals and back again, but never went quite so far as to seek out the cause of her death.

Curiosity and its Consequences

Sara's genitals and brains, which remained on display in the Musée de l'Homme until 1985 (and to think that countries like France were called upon to help end apartheid in South Africa!), "were the objects of the scientific and medical research that formed the bedrock of European ideas about black female sexuality."[18] European ideas about my sexuality, and Brenda's, and Lavinia's, and Gloria's, and Lauren's, and Kellie's, and Dana's, and Pam's, and Paula's, and Keira's, and Vienna's and . . .

Curiosity—What's In A Name?

The lights lowered. We lowered our private thoughts; hushed our public voices.

OPENING

Brenda stood behind a podium, giving a lecture about Sara Baartman. Helmutt spoke too. His words intertwined with hers, laced hers, at moments blocking hers out, overpowering hers, so that all we heard was Helmutt speaking about the curiosity that had fueled his desire to know the blackness of Brenda, as opposed to desiring to know the woman now his wife. On the verge of taking us on a journey into his former jungled mind, a swamp teeming with wild things, where he longed to *taste* black woman, *smell* black woman, and color her white-man's jungle black, Brenda cut him off.

They were off and dancing: a spatial fugue in motion, voices in counterpoint. Tongues lashing out. Exotic tastes, exotic smells—the delusions of a deranged mind, bloated with itself, barfing up its heart of whiteness fantasies.

Brenda played Venus, and played her well. How could she not? with pieces of the Hottentot's brains and genitals lodged in her mind, in her womb. Venus's revenge turned Cuvier's curiosity back on him with the same power and urgency her namesake (by the last name of Williams) used to transform 80-mile-per-hour serves into 120-mile-per-hour returns that blew a Hingis mind and game right off the court.[19] In a fantasy-dream come to life on stage, Brenda-Venus strapped Helmutt-Cuvier on an examining table, opened his legs, and gasped at the implausibility of nature creating such a hairless, lipless, buttless, balding creature and calling it, *The Image of God.*

Cuvier couldn't take it. (Neither could Hingis. I recall reading somewhere that in a slight to Venus's and Serena's physiques, Hingis said defensively that if she was *that tall* and *that muscular*, maybe she would have more winners too. Yes, Hingis was on the defensive. But in the context of the history of the white gaze on black female bodies, Martina's tongue lashed out a winner with a white public. Everyone understood the *surround-text—These weren't the bodies of real women; these weren't real women's bodies (a Venus indeed!).* What's more, Ms. Hingis knew *what* she was speaking. She had the words to say it, just as sure as she was sitting there, Snow White, lily of the field.)

Cuvier wouldn't stand for it. Up he jumped from the table, outraged. How dare she! Even in her dreams! Dreams indeed! Dreams are Cuvier's alone to realize. Curiosity, his burden as a white man, he gladly bears alone. Revenge is *his* prerogative. Venus, heavenly body of evening and dawn, remain on the table *who* you are! Stolen, despised, a fallen star. Be the first to be seen, whether morning or night. Open your legs wide so that *mankind* in the flesh might plunder your twilight and sully it with its poisonous spew.

NEWSBLURB FROM THE OFFSTAGE WORLD:

> **"Yesterday Hingis displayed a blind spot, not so much in race relations but in compassion."** *[Can the two be disengaged in practice?]* **On Monday, Hingis is scheduled to testify against a man she has accused of stalking her. What if the Williamses were to dismiss Hingis's fear of being stalked as 'nonsense,' as a figment of her imagination? . . . as Hingis dismissed claims of racism directed at the Williamses [as] 'nonsense.' She said Venus and Serena had an advantage being African-American on the tour, because 'they can always say its racism or something like that, and it's not the case at all.'"**[20]

Helmutt took on the spirit of Cuvier, his own alter ego, a shadow of his former self, his doctor Hyde painted in hideous living color across his white, white face. Helmutt as curious Helmutt. Helmutt as curious Cuvier. (Helmutt as curious George, the dangerous ape who rapes and impregnates African women, according to the European, scientific, mythological mind.)[21]

One of those men, Helmutt or Cuvier, one and the very same man—Helmutt-Cuvier—peered out into the audience, out into the offstage darkness, and dared to asked, "Is my curiosity racist?" After all that we had seen and heard could there be any doubt? Could a head but nod "yes"?

They were off and dancing again.

don't wanna be your exotic
some delicate   fragile   colorful bird
imprisoned   caged
in a land foreign to the stretch of her wings
don't wanna be your exotic
women everywhere are just like me
some taller   darker   nicer than me
but like me but just the same
women everywhere carry my nose on their faces
my name on their spirits
don't wanna
don't seduce yourself with
my otherness   my hair
wasn't put on top of my head to entice
you into some mysterious black vodou
the beat of my lashes against each other
ain't some dark desert beat
it's just a blink
get over it
don't wanna be your exotic
your lovin of my beauty ain't more than
funky fornication plain pink perversion
in fact nasty necrophilia
cause my beauty is dead to you
I am dead to you
not your
harem girl   geisha doll   banana picker
pom pom girl   pum pum shorts   coffee maker
town whore   belly dancer   private dancer
la malinche   venus hottentot   laundry girl
your immaculate vessel emasculating princess
don't wanna be
your erotic
not your exotic[22]

Got that Moby Dick!

Helmutt moved across the stage, his nose attracted to his arm, which was attracted to his leg, which was attracted to his foot, which was attracted to his knee, which was attracted to

Brenda. She acknowledged it all, dancing in the foreground, in the background, behind Helmutt, with him, till a moment of still embrace brought them together, tongue on tongue, tongues talking together, tongues teaching together.

A spatial fugue in motion, voices in counterpart, voices intersecting. Tongues lashing out to strike each other down—No, nonono no more. Tongues taste tongues 'cause tongue taste tongue taste good. Exotic tastes, exotic smells (delusions of a dangerous mind sick not free!). What exotic? Who exotic? Nothing but familiar tastes, familiar smells. 'Cause "Come smell fuck!" Come smell eucalyptus trees.

The lights went up. No curtain hid Brenda and Helmutt from our view. They remained on stage bowing to the applause, ready to face cacophony. They had opened up to us, and now asked that we open up to them, to each other, to ourselves: not with the distance of a critical eye, but with a sensibility conferred by touch.

People are quiet at first. No one wants to be the first to speak. A man in the front row takes the baton. He tells us of his biracial grandbaby who recognizes the difference between black and white but loves both sides equally, responding to black and white with joy and joy because she receives love from both sides.

What, had this great big bearded white man already asked his grandbaby, a child who could barely speak, what she thought of *the difference*?

The infant eyes of a South African couple, for whom I once babysat in France, came to mind. I recalled his milky blue eyes, which could barely focus. He was about three weeks old, and I was the newest thing in his environment. Wavering, his eyes went to me. The parents exclaimed—astonished, proud, relieved: "He sees *that* you are black! He knows! He sees the difference!" (I could only shake my head to myself. Madness!)

I know by now that many upper middle-class white children are thought to be geniuses, but the conceptual capabilities of three-week-old white infants must be incredible beyond anything I had ever imagined! But seriously now, hadn't the parents of that baby willingly condemned their child—a child they would have claimed to love—to life in a patch of blue? I wonder whom and how many black people that child has dissected with his acquired blind-sighted gaze since that time when he lay in my arms, truly an innocent white thing, simply struggling to get a grip on the world.

The comment of the great white man fell flat. No one responded. It did not speak to what we had seen. Brenda and Helmutt had taken us on a trip, and, apparently, this man had remained where he'd been before he came in, so pleased with himself, his largesse.

It wasn't I!

A few more comments fell like glass plates on a cement floor. But then a white American man spoke with shaky words, trying to open his hands—talking about the contradictions in his life. How could he reconcile being white and teaching African American studies and still always looking at the black students in a particular way when he spoke of certain things—he didn't say which things—but not the white students?

Your People—My People

One professor, Paula Underwood, thanked Brenda and Helmutt for their testimony to the pain endured by African Americans. Brenda tried to speak, to respond, but began to cry, words quivering in her mouth: "Nations around the world have forced the German people to examine what they did, who they were, who they might be as a result. They live with that burden today. White Americans have never had to face up to the harm they inflicted on Native Americans, Africans, African Americans, and who *they* might be as a result of inflicting that harm."

Finally, I found my tongue and spoke about what I had seen onstage-offstage: the curious gaze, the crippling gaze, the gaze that kills and seeks to kill again. The gaze that looks for death on the Other's side all the while seeking fountains of youth in forests of tight, black bushes. The gaze that seeks to discover nonbeing in black faces, between black thighs, branded on black butts. The gaze that then grows hungry to see itself grandiose, reflected in pools of black blood. I could speak about that gaze quite easily because I'd seen it and felt it all my life. Brenda and Helmutt had been portraying variations on chapters from my life. I knew those scenes by heart. It's a wonder my heart hasn't failed me yet. (Then again, I never risked giving birth to a black child and sending it out into their schools, their workplace, their global village, where rumor has it that you reap what you sow.)

I talked about the white children who had wiped my skin, curious to see if *it* would come off; about the white French intellectuals whose curiosity *demanded* that I tell them what *degree* of negritude I represented, who insisted that I was exotic—inviting me to look in a mirror and see for myself; the German museum workers in Dresden, who grabbed hold of me and another black woman, Vienna. They held us, their very touch paralyzing us like a vice. They turned us round and round, slowly, while they exclaimed and exclaimed and exclaimed. From where I was standing I could see the tears dropping from Vienna's dark round cheeks. (Could the woman examining her not see those teardrops! Plump enough to drench her hands!) Although Vienna and I were the same age, it was like watching a little sister, a virgin, being raped. I had grown up with white people; nothing they sought to do to a black person surprised me anymore. Vienna had only begun to get a taste of what certain whites delight in at Yale University, where she was a student. But that taste had not prepared her for what it feels like to be served up as a white person's meal.[23]

I spoke of that moment during the performance when Helmutt-Cuvier asked the audience, a note of desperation in his voice, "Is my curiosity racism?" I let them all know that my head had had nowhere to go but up and down.

That's when the rain fell like ropes.

"But curiosity is a tool," they cried out. "We need it! How can we live without it? *Why* should we be asked to live without it?"

Cuvier's Dream

"But how about the innocent curiosity of the child? I was curious like that. We felt the blacks' hair and they felt ours." (Brenda kindly observed to *that* white embodiment of innocence that we mustn't forget that all this mutual feeling takes place in a context in which values have been set and acknowledged, if only implicitly.)

It wasn't I! It wasn't I!

"I'd never seen blacks till I was in high school, so I asked a lot of questions when I met them for the first time. And I offended people. But I was just curious. It's only natural." (Only natural. And I'd been hoodwinked into thinking that these people wanted, at the very least, to control the natural world, and, at the most, to transcend it.)

It wasn't' I! It wasn't I!

It wasn't I!, It Wasn't I! Cuvier's privileged progeny cried out—demanding justice, compassion, understanding, and equal rights for the right to kill.

I turned around in my seat and faced the people who spoke. I wanted to speak again, but everyone had to have a turn. I wanted to address the issue of their particular kind of innocence. How can white Americans and white American children remain innocent when even turpentine won't suffice to remove the stain of black tears from their pale palms? Why must everyone else be guilty and shamed by the very fact of their birth and origin, while enjoined to extend their hands to these people who haven't the common sense of Pontius Pilate?

It's probably a good thing that I didn't get a chance to speak again, because the innocent were killing me so softly with their song—***It wasn't I! It wasn't I!***—that I might have choked on my words or used my words to stab them dead in the eyes.

Disjunctions

I turned around. Brenda's eyes met mine from time to time as they wandered about the room. She smiled at me, knowingly. We shared a secret anyone might hear who cared to listen.

And then there were Helmutt's eyes looking into mine, his lips slightly parted. He seemed to be barely breathing. I understood what his gaze had meant as a young man. I saw it for what it was now as a mature, white man. A mensch. **Transmission-Transformation-Transmission-Connections-Transformation-Bridges-Transformation-Continuities-Circuits-Transformation-Regeneration-Transfiguration**

Wondering
Imagining
A glimmer of recognition

Epilogue

People dispersed. Friends spoke to me; strangers spoke to me. One white American man told me that even as a gay man *he* had never known such pain. He told me that when I had responded that Helmutt-Cuvier's curiosity was racism it was like a slap in his face. He had been *certain* that it couldn't be! He opened his arms, his hands, and asked for a hug. I didn't refuse him one. Now I wonder who he is. Who could he possibly be? After what we'd seen, how so certain?

Three days later a young, white, American woman approached me on campus: "Weren't you the woman who spoke at Tongue Smell Color?"

We talked for a while. I told her that I'd seen a documentary about Sara Baartman a week before the Gottschilds' performance. I told her that she should check it out. And as I spoke of Sara Baartman's life, of how she'd been taken, captured, displayed in a cage, sold, examined, and died—cause unknown (curiosity couldn't care less), of how her bones had only recently been returned to Cape Town—I saw this young woman's face wrinkle with shock, horror, concern. Amazement transfigured my own face, but the words were on her lips: "I was under the impression that the whole thing was a fiction."

When whites play in the dark perhaps to them everything that happens to you, a black person, is a fiction: first, your very being, and, consequently, your death as well. Given that so many whites are blind-sighted, those in their field of vision who such whites identify as black and who may therefore be black in that context, will most likely experience themselves as being black. But part of *this type* of experience of being black can involve the awareness that the gazers are indeed white. They are not just normal or neutral or numb. Though they may indeed be mad—a whole white world of them! Therefore, as it turns out, being black in such circumstances can offer great opportunities. For a black struck by the gaze of a blind-sighted white is in the position to take the initiative and tell that white: "I see you and know who you are. Moreover, if you want to play mirror-mirror-on-the-wall, I will sure enough tell you *what* you are! Fair? Not quite. So come here my little white friend and let me describe for you what I spied through your peep-hole, here in our shared social-political-economic space cast by the darkest corner of your innocent, curious mind."

In speaking one's black mind there's a chance that some small degree of knowledge might be gained, on the other side. But even if not, a black voice of one's own making will have been heard, if only by oneself. Thus, it is in speaking one's mind under such circumstances that a black person may find pieces of herself, through a process of self-recognition.

Notes

1. See "On Black-Brown Relations" in *The Cornel West Reader* (Basic, Civitas Books, 1999), 499–513.

2. See Charles Mills's article, "Red Shift: Politically Embodied/Embodied Politics," in *The Philosophical I: Personal Reflections on Life in Philosophy*, ed. George Yancy (Lanham, Md.: Rowman & Littlefield, 2002), 155–75, where Mills discusses the process of going from being a red man in Jamaica to becoming a black man in the United States. It is to be noted that the academy played no minor role in Mills's red to black metamorphosis.

3. My mother later told me that she had suffered a terrible depression when she gave birth to my older brother. The medical community thought that she was suffering from postnatal depression. But she admitted to me that she "knew what she had done." She *knew* that she had brought a child, born black, into a white racist world. What her black son would *learn* to become she did not know. And perhaps it was ignorance in this matter that afforded her some hope.

4. From the Arabic "safara" meaning "to travel."

5. Cornel West, "Black Strivings in a Twilight Civilization" (Basic, Civitas Books, 1999), 87–118.

6. Furthermore, it might be argued that it is possible for a person of non-African descent to experience certain forms of being black even it is not possible for them to be black. Irish who were identified as niggers by the British might fall into such a category. And I think it no sheer coincidence that the Palestinian poet, Suheir Hammad, chose to title one of her works, *Born Palestinian, Born Black,* for it seems that, the world over, people are able to grasp the fact that there are political, social, cultural, aesthetic, and economic implications of being black, where being black represents, across these parameters, being at the *very* bottom. Of course, there may be exceptions. For example, in some Latin American countries indigenous people might occupy this degraded position, as they do in the Kantian racist schema. Nonetheless, I find it more than interesting that Hammad did not entitle her book *Born Palestinian, Born Brown* or even *Born Palestinian, Born Arab.*

7. "On Black-Brown Relations," 502.

8. "Wittgenstein's Poker," David Edmonds and John Eidinow (Harper-Collins, 2001), 121–22.

9. "Wittgenstein's Poker," 125.

10. "Wittgenstein's Poker," 126.

11. "Wittgenstein's Poker," 130.

12. "Wittgenstein's Poker," 115–16.

13. I borrowed the expression *playing in the dark* from Toni Morrison's work *Playing in the Dark* (Cambridge: Harvard University Press, 1992), where she discusses the "Africanist" presence in the fiction of Poe, Melville, Cather, and Hemingway, showing the degree to which themes of freedom and individualism, manhood and innocence, depend on the existence of a black population that was manifestly unfree, and which thereby served white authors as embodiments of their own fears and desires.

14. Patricia Hill Collins, "Contemporary Black Feminist Thought," in *African-American Philosophy: Selected Readings*, ed. Tommy L. Lott (Upper Saddle River, N.J.: Prentice Hall, 2002), 178.

15. Below I use extracts from an unpublished story, *What the Gaze of the Blind-Sighted Seek.*

16. www.emory.edu/ENGLISH/Bahri/Hott.html.

17. "Georges Cuvier was born in Montbéliard (Franche-Comté), August 25, 1769. From 1784 to 1788, he studied at the Carolinian Academy in Staugttgart. In 1795, Cuvier was named teaching assisting in comparative anatomy to the Musée National d'Histoire Nataurelle (National Museum of Natural History). His work through the Musée National elevated him to one of the most honored scientists of his time. Cuvier created a zoological classification of animals as well as developed the science of paleontology. To name a few of his most notable contributions to traditional geology are the theories of 'revolutions' over time in the fossil record now known as catastrophism, and the existence of mass extinctions over geologic past. He is considered the father of comparative anatomy as well as the father of paleontology." (www.geocities.com/swsalley/go521/rep3.htm) Report 3: European 19th–20th Centuries, © S.W. Salley (2003).

18. www.frif.com/new99/hottento.html.

19. William C. Rhoden, *New York Times*, March 30, 2001.

20. Rhoden, *New York Times*, March 30, 2001.

21. See Tommy Lott's article, "King Kong Lives: Racist Discourse and the Negro-Ape Metaphor," in *Next of Kin: Looking at the Great Apes*, MIT List Visual Arts Center, Cambridge, 1995, 37–43.

22. Suheir Hammad, "exotic" in *Born Palestinian, Born Black*, Writers & Readers Publishing, October 1, 1996.

23. Interestingly enough, after this incident, the white women with whom Vienna and I were traveling in East Germany suggested that we all return to the United States. When I told them that I saw no reason for returning to the states they enjoined me to "Stop playing the martyr." Playing the martyr? Where and what did they think I saw myself as returning to? a home where I lived free and secure?

11

"Seeing Blackness" from Within the Manichean Divide

George Yancy
Duquesne University

> Blacks are often confronted, in American life, with such devastating examples of the white descent from dignity; devastating not only because of the enormity of white pretensions, but because this swift and graceless descent would seem to indicate that white people have no principles whatever.
>
> —James Baldwin

> Colonial power produces the colonized as a fixed reality which is at once an "other" and yet entirely knowable and visible.
>
> —Homi K. Bhabha

IN THIS CHAPTER, I EXPLORE "Blackness" from within the Manichean divide. Whiteness constitutes a bifurcated and hierarchical epistemic regime according to which white is deemed "good," while that which is nonwhite is deemed "bad." The aim is to uncover the dynamic of the white gaze, to reveal how "Blackness" vis-à-vis the white gaze appears as a historically constructed tertium quid; it is that which emerges as a kind of third element, between, as it were, my "Black" skin color, which is a natural phenomenon, and the white gaze, which is a pernicious psycho-historical, racist phenomenon. Within the context of this chapter, I also provide significant reflective moments or breaks, like in a jazz piece, which elaborate my conception of various trajectories of Blackness. These breaks function to capture the sociohistorically complex and generative dimensions of Black agency vis-à-vis the pernicious and denigrating impact of whiteness.

Being Black, Being a Problem

Telescoping the colonial dimensions of the white episteme, Franz Fanon notes:

> At times this Manicheism [dualistic dichotomy of black/bad, white/good] goes to its logical conclusion and dehumanizes the native, or to speak plainly, it turns him into an animal. In fact, the terms the settler uses when he mentions the native are zoological terms. He speaks of the yellow man's reptilian motions, of the stink of the native quarter, of breeding swarms, of foulness, of spawn, of gesticulations. When the settler seeks to describe the native fully in exact terms he constantly refers to the bestiary.[1]

W. E. B. Du Bois was very much aware of how whiteness constituted that axiological standard against which all nonwhites are to be judged and assessed. Du Bois also recognized the flexibility of whiteness, how certain people can *become white*, which points to the social constitutionality of whiteness. In this way, he realizes that whiteness is parasitic upon Blackness. Many white immigrants came from Europe and had very little power. Once in North America, however, they learned how to negotiate their new ("white") identities vis-à-vis Black people. Du Bois notes that America "trains her immigrants to this despising of 'niggers' from the day of their landing, and they carry and send the news back to the submerged classes in the fatherlands."[2] They soon learn about the deep cultural dimensions of North America's color-line. Because whiteness is beautiful, Blackness is ugly. Because whiteness is intelligent, Blackness is stupid. Because whiteness is pure, Blackness is impure. Because whiteness is innocent, Blackness is criminal. Concerning this last point regarding the "criminal" nature of Blackness, Du Bois writes:

> Murder may swagger, theft may rule and prostitution may flourish and the nation gives but spasmodic, intermittent and lukewarm attention. But let the murderer be black or the thief brown or the violator of womanhood have a drop of Negro blood, and the righteousness of the indignation sweeps the world.[3]

Du Bois's point here is that *Blackness*, from the perspective of white mythopoetic constructions, *is the problem*, not the crime committed.

The connection between Blackness and the concept of "being a problem" is central to Du Bois's understanding of what it means to be Black in white North America. Du Bois reveals how white folk engage in a process of duplicity while speaking to Blacks. They often approach the Black in a hesitant fashion, saying, "I know an excellent coloured man in my town; or, I fought at Mechanicsville; or, Do not these Southern outrages make your blood boil?"[4] Du Bois maintains that the real question that whites want to ask is: "How does it feel to be a problem?"[5] Du Bois also points out that as a Black, some whites greet you with a certain sweet comportment. They talk with you about the weather, while all along performing hidden racist scripts:

> My poor, un-white thing! Weep not nor rage. I know, too well, that the curse of God lies heavy on you. Why? That is not for me to say, but be brave! Do your work in your lowly sphere, praying the good Lord that into heaven above, where all is love, you may, one day, be born—white![6]

Notice with regard to the notion of being a problem, whites do not ask, "How does it feel to *have* problems?" The question is raised to the level of the ontological: "How does it feel *to be* a problem?" Also, note that the structure of this question does not apply to people who have at some point in their lives felt themselves to be a problem. In such cases, feeling like a problem is a contingent disposition that is relatively finite and transitory. When Black people are asked the same question by white America, the relationship between being Black and being a problem is noncontingent. It is a necessary relation. Outgrowing this ontological state of being a problem is believed impossible. Hence, regarding one's "existence as problematic," temporality is frozen. One is a problem *forever*. However, it is important to note that it is from within the white imaginary that the question "How does it feel to be a problem?" is given birth. "To be" human is to be *thrown-in-the-world*. To be human not only means to be thrown within a context of facticity, but it means *to be* in the mode of the subjunctive, to be able to negotiate the facticity of one's "thrownness." It is interesting to note that the etymology of the word *problem* suggests the sense of being "thrown forward," as if being thrown in front of something, as an obstacle. Within the white imaginary, to be Black means to be born an obstacle at the very core of one's being. To ex-ist as Black is *not* "to stand out" facing an ontological horizon filled with future possibilities of being other than what one is. Rather, being Black negates the "ex" of existence. Being Black has been reduced to facticity. It is not as if it is only within the light of my freely chosen projects that things are *experienced* as obstacles, as Sartre might say. As Black, by definition, I am an obstacle. As Black, I am the very obstacle to my own metastability and transphenomenal being. As Black, I am not a project at all. Hence, within the framework of the white imaginary, to be Black and to be human are contradictory terms.

Being "Just Me" within the Racist Divide

To paraphrase Du Bois, in North America no Black who has given serious reflection to the situational reality of their fellow Blacks has failed, at some point in his or her life, to pose the deep existential question: "What, after all, am I?"[7]

Being Black in white racist America, one is forced to come to terms with what it means to be Black. I have heard some Blacks claim, "But, I'm just *me*!" I have also heard some whites make such claims as, "Sure, I'm white, but when it comes down to it, I'm just *me*." In both cases there is a profound sense of self-deception.[8] After all, how can one live in a country where "Blackness" signifies criminality, inferiority, danger, evil, predation, and hypersexuality, and yet lay claim to a "just me" status? The utterance is belied by the fact that when such a Black person is profiled by whites (and even other Blacks) while "driving Black" or followed while "shopping Black" in a department store, the "just me" illusion is shattered. Try being "just me" within a racial and racist context within which one's Blackness is ontologically overdetermined. Try being "just me" where one's Blackness is preceded by social, political, aesthetic, cultural, and economic vectors that always already render one's identity problematic. If you are Black, try being "just me" while white racist police officers have you in custody. Try being "just me" while being pulled over by a Mark Fuhrman. Try being "just me" when going for a job interview. Try being "just me" when the white Charles Stuarts and Susan Smiths of America place the blame (murder and kidnapping, respectively) on innocent Black folk, people who probably look like you. Within the social space of white racist America, living one's life as if colorless can lead to profound disappointment. It is sheer nonsense to believe that the majority of whites suspend their racist beliefs—or perform the *epochē*—during encounters with Blacks at various levels of social complexity. In the everyday mode of existence, the Black is essentially *Black*, defined by a substance ontology that sees racial fixity and immutability.

When whites claim the "just me" status, they too engage in a process of racial elision. The point here is that regardless of intentions, their whiteness already confers upon them a status predicated upon normative values that help them to obfuscate the degree to which "just being me" is really "just being white." For Blacks, "just being me" translates into "not being Black." Whites, however, can claim a "just me" status in ways that Blacks cannot. It is easier to claim a "just me" state of being when you're white, because society reinforces a white's sense of normality, while one's whiteness, as a site of power, remains invisible. It is dangerous, however, for Blacks to make such naive claims. In fact, I would rather be recognized as Black. I would reject the title of "honorary whiteness" if offered. It is far too dangerous. I am a Black male living in the belly of the beast, who could very easily go from a nonthreatening and acceptable, intellectually hardworking Black male, indeed, a so-called credit to my race, to an exemplification of the Black stereotypes prevalent in *Birth of a Nation*. Despite the biological and anthropological evidence that denies race as a natural phenomenon, my Black body is deemed a *racial* given, indelibly marked as dangerous, inferior, threatening.

How can we, as Black people, fail to raise the question of who we are when white racist America constantly forces us to engage in existential and ontological self-interrogation? But this is the situation into which we have been thrown. I, personally, did not create the hyperracial and racist situation in North America. Like those who crossed the Middle Passage, I inherited this nightmare. Indeed, the whole issue concerning the so-called fact and meaning of my "Blackness" is a question grounded within a racist historical context. "What, after all, am I?"—when posed by Blacks who find themselves at the mercy of white definitional power—is an existential, ontological, and historical question that white supremacy solicits. This does not deny that "I" could have raised this question in a different *possible world* in which the question was not asked within the context of white supremacy. But then again, "I" would not be the same "I." After all, the question may have been motivated from a sense of existential meaninglessness unmotivated by the context and effects of racism. The "I" that I am, however, is the "I" that is trapped within a specific historical and cultural matrix. It is a historical and cultural matrix that "niggerized" me before I was even able to pose the question of my identity from a nonracist place of inquiry. In short, the question is not intelligible outside of the context of the historical accretion of white hegemony and white hatred. I might be able to choose when I die, but I cannot choose *that* I will someday die. So, too, I have some choice over how I will live my Blackness, but I had no choice over how my body would be raced, how it would be demonized, rendered savagelike. The process of niggerization was out of my control. In other words, the historical process that shaped the white imaginary and, hence, how I am seen, was beyond my control. This raises the issue of socio-ontological constitutionality; for the meaning of my "Blackness" is constituted through the medium of the white gaze, which is a historical phenomenon. Within the present context, then, the meaning of my Blackness is found within history. Indeed, the historicity of my "Blackness" places it within a narrative historical context that is open, not closed.

The naturalization of my Blackness qua inferior and bestial is maintained by white supremacist logic and bad faith. Beneath the subterfuge of the naturalization of racial kinds, there exists historical contingency, iconographic slippage, and the falsidical (as opposed to veridical) basis of the white gaze. Bear in mind, though, that Blackness is never limited or confined to the white gaze. It is protean, ever changing into historical reconfigurations.

Blackness as Protean

Changing like life, moving like water.
The space of Yemanja, vibratory motions.
Trans-phenomenal. Multiple shades.

Multiple trajectories along class, geography, attitude.
Making, remaking, meta-stable,
Moving back and forth, like a "tidalectic" cradle.
It's criminal to say that polygenetic theory is true.
So many historical lies tend to accrue.
The truth will set U free.
Africa functioned as a site of creative force.
Sometimes like the force of the sea.
It's all about improvisation,
Whether on the court, in the ocean, in space, it's bout Creation!
Ask Nana Peazant.
Ask Christophine.
U know her,
The one from *Wide Sargasso Sea.*
In the beginning was the word.
Nommo. Logos. Word up! Word!
The words of Malcolm X,
King (B.B.) dreaming of some moment yet to come.
But a change is gonna come.
Ask Sam. Cookin at the mic.
Play it again. Sam. Cook. Sam. Sharpe as a tack.
The Zoot suit functions as both sign and symbol of who we *be.*
Cultural, political, aesthetic disruptions, and reconfigurations.
Blue. Indigo. West African hues. Calling for Langston; He of the same Hughes.
New creations, but still continuity.
Toussaint L'Ouverture. Jean-Jacques Dessaline. Harriet. Tubman. Harriet. Jacobs.
Garvey's voice in the whirlwind.
Being and becoming.
Like life and music,
Black bodies move in undulations to the sounds of distant drums.
Vibrating back from some distant moment in our history.
WE are the sons and daughters of those who survived the Middle Passage,
Waiting to go supernovae as Prospero's army, with its missile-gods, marches on.

Seeing, *Not Seeing*

The issue of the white gaze that assigns the value of *being a problem* to Blackness, that renders Blackness evil, bestial, and so on, raises the larger issue of perception. As Sander L. Gilman asks, "How do we organize our perceptions of the world?"[9] This is a highly relevant question in terms of the structure of the white gaze vis-à-vis the Black body (or nonwhite body, more generally). One might argue that when I open my eyes, I see the physical world before me, unmediated and direct. The cup before me, for example, impresses itself upon my consciousness and I "see" the cup as it exists in space. The cup is revealed *directly* to me through my power to see, hear, taste, touch, and smell. On this score, the cup before me is not a measure of what I do to make it appear; rather, the cup is that which pre-exists my encounter with it. However, to do the work that is required for coming to terms with the white gaze, to make sense of the complex process of "seeing Blackness," a more complex account is required. To say that when I open my eyes, I "see" the world unmediated and direct, would give credence to the following: "To see" a Black body as lascivious, sexually promiscuous, apelike, physiologically primitive, and criminal, would imply "seeing" the Black body as *it is*. On this score, the white gaze is said to be a passive reflection of the "reality" that is intrinsic to the Black body. The white need only look upon a native African and his/her primitive nature is immediately registered. The Black body is an active object/thing waiting to be registered upon the passive European mind. The reality of the Black body, its truth *qua* bestial, is all there to see. One only has to open his/her eyes. What is *seen* is what is *known*, and what is *seen* and *known* is what there *is*. Hence, the argument is that perceptual, epistemological, and ontological claims work in conjunction, according to which objects are not distorted, but clear and veridical, devoid of extra-empirical influences. History (or historical consciousness) is believed to be but a quiet witness to the accumulated "facts" of nature. European sciences were believed to be in possession of a neutral perspective on reality, a perspective that delivers reality *simpliciter*. Whiteness, however, has the tendency to undergo a process of elision; it forgets or refuses to acknowledge the world that it has actually *constructed*, a world within which certain values are generated, morphologies created, and essences sustained.

For Kant, objects appear only under certain conditions. There are pure forms of intuition (space and time) that are necessary conditions for the appearance of objects. There are also, for Kant, universal and necessary categories of understanding that play an indispensable role in terms of grounding our epistemic claims. However, there are no *transcendental* conditions for the appearance of Black people as "objects of knowledge." Black people do appear, however, as "objects of knowledge" of the white gaze under certain historical, cultural, semiotic, mythopoetic, discursive conditions. This involves historicizing what and how we see the things that we do. Contrary to the supposed objectivist view upon which the European sciences of anthropology, physiology, and phrenology were based, these "sciences" were mediated by mythopoetic constructions, that is, they constructed "reality" from a historical and cultural *here*. Hence, the issue of whiteness as the transcendental signified and Blackness as an ersatz form of existence demands an exploration of the extra-empirical, that is, the historical, semiotic, political, economic, and cultural dimensions that have shaped the European imaginary. The European imaginary was backed by brute force and violence. Not only did the European imaginary have negative implications for those Africans brutally taken from Africa, but it also devastated those who became targets of Europe's colonialist adventures. But still we resisted.

Blackness as Maroonage

The Dismal Swamp.
Sites of resistance.
Only to strike fear in the heartless,
The cold, white plantation overseers.
We talkin insurrection, baby.
Leaving that plan-tation,
With its *plan* to keep Black folk down.
You know, on lock down by Prospero.
Uncle Charlie.
The Pol-*ice. Cold* runs through your veins.
Amadou Diallo had no chance to escape those missiles.
Those AfroMaroons had to learn, improvise.
They had to *become* mountainous,
Transmutational. This is what we do,
Navigating those mountains,
A protean, improvisational people.
Making a way outta no way.
Do you see? Sea. The *deep sea diving* act.
Required.
De-colonized minds. De-colonized bodies.
Bodies longing for freedom,
A place to be.
To be Akan.
To be a self,
In a world that denied yo Black self.
Akan. I kan. We kan. You can.
Make a difference.
Nanny of the maroons did.
Obeah Black sista.
She be takin no prisoners.
She be a National hero/heroine.
Ask Kamau Brathwaite. He knows she fit the bill.
She was a dynamo.
Believe the Hype.
The archive is written in invisible ink.
Ask Kamau.

Nanny. She be Sharpe, too.
They both takin a *stand.*
Resi*stance.*
To take a *stance.*
To *stand.*
Refusing to fall.
Except in love with yo Black self.
Pecola Breedlove missed out this round.
Someone forgot to remind her.
U gots to fight, baby. Baby fight.
Fight for yo peeps.
Your beautiful brown eyes.
The only blue you need is that indigo blue.
That Euro-Blue will steal yo soul.
Fight baby. Baby fight!
FIGHT. FIGHT. FIGHT!!!
St Domingue.
1792.
Not 1492.
We bees talkin counter-violence,
Not violence for the sake of violence.
Counter-violence for the sake of freedom,
For the de-plantation mentalities of our young.
You gots to fight for this, my sista/brotha.
And it ain't all bout physical confrontation.
There is another battle.
And the enemy is U.
Becoming marginal to yo self.
To strip away white knowledge of self.
Attacking yo self. *Guerrilla warfare turned inward.*
Aimé Césaire knows. Fanon knew. Kamau knows.
Sojourner knew.
She had to tell the TRUTH.
Yeah, Sojourner. Sojourn. Moving. Out. Way out from that Plantation.
That Euro-plan. That Anglo-plan. That plantation.

The Colonizer and the Colonized

Through the powerful colonial structuration of the white gaze, the Black body/self was codified and typified as a subhuman, savage beast devoid of language/culture. Consistent with Hume's belief that Africans spoke "a few words plainly," in 1884 J. A. Harrison held that African American speech was "based on African genetic inferiority."[10] For Harrison, much of Negro talk was "baby-talk."[11] Geneva Smitherman notes:

> Blinded by the science of biological determinism, early twentieth-century white linguistic scholars followed Harrison's lead, taking hold of his baby-talk theory of African American speech and widely disseminating it in academic discourse. The child language explanation of Black Language is linguistic racism that corresponds to the biological determinist assumption that blacks are lower forms of the human species whose evolution is incomplete.[12]

Furthermore, within the colonial order of things, Blacks and other people indigenous to their land were deemed *things.* Between the colonizer and the colonized, there is "no human contact," as Césaire maintains, "but relations of domination and submission."[13] When the colonizer and the colonized are face to face, Césaire sees only "force, brutality, cruelty, sadism, conflict."[14] Colonialism had embedded within it a racist colonial ethnography/anthropology (or theory of the *anthropos*). On this score, theories of the "human" are not far behind white empire building, if not fundamentally linked.[15] Césaire observes:

> Gobineau said: "The only history is white." M. Caillois, in turn, observes: "The only ethnography is white." It is the West that studies the ethnography of the others, not the others who study the ethnography of the West.[16]

However, despite the above, we countered this colonialist conception of the *human* (read: *white* colonizer). Despite our journey into the semiotic and physically brutal space of the *sub*-human, we remained connected, strong, reinforcing our Black *hue*-manity.

Blackness as Connective

Connections. We are a people loop-linked to each other.
Despite our breakage, our having been torn,
Our having to mourn night and day/day and night down in those dark places of death.
Smell the stench? The vomit. The blood. The feces. The piss. The piss. The feces.
The faces, the anguished faces of Black people.
The people of Hue-manity.
Don't forget.
Can you smell it? Can you imagine it?
The vomit. The blood. The feces. The piss. The piss. The feces. The blood.
The number of births dropped in that filth.
Delivered in the belly of those ships,
The belly of the white missilic beast.
Packed tight, chained together,

Naked next to your brother, your father.
Twisted connections. Feces-blood-and-urine-connections.
Check out Freud's *Civilization and Its Discontents.*
He spoke of being born *between* feces and urine.
Between? Yes!
Dehumanized by?
Bodies dripping with?
Noses filled with? No!
And, yet, we survived. And still we rise!
So the sista said. You know, Angelou. Maya.
We are a people whose connections are indomitable.
Connected over space and time.
Connections through retentions.
The tenacity of Africa's memory of itself.
Like Nana Peazant, perhaps there are things we should not forget.
Told to forget in order to move *forward.*
Or is it *backward*?
Nanna Peazant: A spiritual source of connectivity.
She had to recall.
Had the good sense to recall.
Loas. Orisha. Ancestral spirits.

The process of "thingification" is a dialectical process that negatively impacts both the colonized and the colonizer. For Césaire, dehumanization is not simply restricted to the colonized. His point is that:

> Colonial activity, colonial enterprise, colonial conquest, which is based on the contempt for the native and justified by that contempt, inevitably tends to change him who in order to ease his conscience gets into the habit of seeing the other man as *an animal,* accustoms himself to treating him like an animal, and tends objectively to transform *himself* into an animal. It is this result, this boomerang effect of colonization, that I wanted to point out.[17]

Albert Memmi was also aware of this boomerang effect of colonization and dehumanization. Memmi: "To handle this, the colonizer must assume the opaque rigidity and imperviousness of the stone. In short, he must dehumanize himself, as well."[18] On this score, the colonizer *becomes* a *thing.* To become a thing, the colonizer need not feel responsible for his/her actions. The colonizer attempts to repress the anxiety that accompanies his/her freedom either through the process of becoming a thing or making the colonized into a thing. Memmi provides an insightful phenomenological observation where he notes: "Whenever the colonizer adds, in order not to fall prey to anxiety, that the colonized is a wicked, backward person with evil, thievish, somewhat sadistic instincts, he thus justifies his police and his legitimate severity."[19]

In his preface to Franz Fanon's *The Wretched of the Earth*, Jean-Paul Sartre characterizes the colonizer as undergoing a process of transmutation from the for-itself to the in-itself. Sartre writes, "This imperious being, crazed by his absolute power and by the fear of losing it, no longer remembers clearly that he was once a man; he takes himself for a horsewhip or a gun."[20] This is the space of what Simone de Beauvoir calls "the serious man," a space of dishonesty that involves the process of ceaselessly trying to deny one's freedom.[21] On this score, the white colonizer attempts to blur the distinction between his/her own praxis and the putative "objective necessity" of colonialism.[22] In other words, the white colonizer attempts to hide from his/her racist practices and pretend that white rule, white supremacy, and white brutality are processes that are undergirded by teleological design. Elaborating upon Memmi's notion of how colonizers manage to engage in a process of "self-absolution," a process that involves an elaborate process of self-deception and bad faith, Sartre writes:

> How can an elite of usurpers, aware of their mediocrity, establish their privileges? By one means only: debasing the colonized to exalt themselves, denying the title of humanity to the natives, and defining them as simply absences of qualities—animals, not humans. This does not prove hard to do, for the system deprives them of everything. Colonialist practice has engraved the colonialist idea into things themselves; it is the movement of things that designates colonizer and colonized alike. Thus oppression justifies itself through oppression: the oppressors produce and maintain by force the evils that render the oppressed, in their eyes, more and more like what they would have to be like to deserve their fate.[23]

The white colonialist strategy is to get the colonized Black (or native) to undergo a process of epistemic violence, a process whereby the Black begins to internalize all of the colonizer's myths, to begin to see his/her identity through the paradigm of white supremacy/Eurocentricity. Indeed, the objective of the colonialist is to get the Black (or native) to become blind to the farcicality of the historical "necessity" of being colonized. The idea here is to get the native, and in this case the Black, to conceptualize his/her identity/being as an ignoble savage,[24] bestial, hypersexual, criminal, violent, uncivilized, brutish, dirty, inferior, and as a *problem*. In other words, the strategy of colonialism is to get the colonized to undergo a phenomenological process whereby he/she begins to experience his/her own body as something alien, but as natural.

Colonial whiteness is also procrustean. Procrustes, the son of Poseidon in Greek mythos, would force travelers into his bed by either stretching their bodies or cutting off their legs. Within the current context, the myth applies to the arbitrary exercise of power over the colonized by the colonizers. The colonialist will go to great lengths to get the colonized to *fit* into his epistemological order of things. This was known to be accomplished through either a series of negations of all things indigenous or by literally severing off of limbs, as was regularly practiced by King Leopold II of Belgium during his colonial reign of terror in the Congo.

Even after such physical and psychological ruptures and fissures, resulting from white supremacy, we survived in our capacity to reconstitute ourselves.

Blackness as Craft

Keep in mind: We ain't talkin bout crafty.
Not Trickery. Deception. Duplicity,
Tools of Prospero.
I'm talkin bout the force to create. To use what is found,
Transforming the found into the useful,
For our survival in the so-called New World.
Remember our chains,
Remember our backs, raised-skin,
Red blood.
Remember when the white gazer,
Decided to rape her,
Black body,
Young violated womb.
Not quite 15 years of age.
What was her name?
Celia! Yeah, that's the ticket,
Price of slavocracy.
Madness.
Why aren't we all just dead?
Even amongst ourselves, our erotic relationality often spells danger.
We be hurtin each other.
Do you hear that movement, though?
The resistance.
Not like Shakespeare's Caliban.
Did Caliban listen to Sycorax?
Movement.
That changing, that transmuting,
Pain into something called,
Spirituals.
Our spiritedness, Blackness as craft,
Helping us to create new spaces,
Spaces through which we kept *hour* Sanity.
From second to second,
From century to century.

Syncretistic spaces.
My God!
He's gonna set me free.
Hallelujah!
Hallelu-JAH. Rude Boy. JAH!
Bob Marley in the house.
"Get up stand up. Don't give up the fight."
Reggae Sounds.
Sacred-and-secular mix,
Remixed for yo listenin pleasure,
It's for yo body to let go of those tight,
Muscular tensions felt beneath that ship.
Like fire shut-up in my bones,
More muscular tensions,
Doin the cake walk,
Gettin happy,
Strutting all around God's house,
I can't help but shout,
There's a blue note in my throat,
Do U hear it?
Sometimes we be Speakin in tongues,
In the field we be hollerin,
In the church we be hollerin,
As the whip hit yo back, U be hollerin,
We be hollerers.
Moving up to some higher plane,
Meta (physical) plane,
Moving in circles,
Arms clamped tight,
Keepin the spirit in the circle.
Moving, crafting that anger into a Blues mode.
WE beeeees Bluessssss people,
Ask my man Baraka,
They use to call him Leroi,
Takin our pain and flipping the script.
In song, in Haiti,
In Brazil,
In Cuba,
In North America,
In the Southern part of North America,
On the streets,
Brothas be harmonizing,
Living in the belly of the beast,
Where U might get lynched,
Didn't I tell you: "Don't look at that white gal, boy!!!"

Consequences.
Loving memories for Emmett Till.
White man's "law,"
And disorder,
Yo penis stuffed in yo mouth,
Yo testicles rammed down yo throat,
Just(ice) for being Black.
U gots to improvise. Charlie Parker,
Style,
Even in yo walk, you gots to represent,
Brotha. Sista.
Stay cool. You got soul,
On Ice.
If we ain't jazzing,
We hip hopping and hoping to the rhythm,
Of the BEAT. Beat it.
MJ.
Can he beat that rap?
Taking all that aggression,
All that anger,
Through historical accretion,
We like a knot,
Not your Gordian type.
We like a knot,
A *not* of negation,
Rejecting all that shit,
They told us to be true.
We reject it in our craft.
We reject it in our bodies,
Hips moving to erase the false memories,
The Painful memories.
The tight spaces.
There is freedom in our craft,
Always moving to some "post" sound.
Always moving us just a little higher,
Just A little farther.
Further.
Closer to who we *be/becoming.*

The Anatomy of the White Gaze

What can be said about the anatomy of the white gaze, which is informed by the white imaginary? The white gaze vis-à-vis the Black/native/colonized involves a series of *negations*. What the colonizer *knows* about the colonized constitutes what the colonized *is*.[25] "Far from wanting to understand him as he really is," according to Memmi, the colonizer strips the colonized of any recognizable human form through "a series of negations."[26] The Black body, for example, is *not* beautiful, *not* civilized, *not* moral, etcetera. The colonialist logic is that what the colonizer/white *is*, the colonized/Black *is not*. The white gaze freezes the Black through a process of *mythopoetic* constructions. The white imaginary projects onto the Black body its own fears and thereby creates certain myths (the "Black rapist") to render its own fears relatively innocuous. These constructions are so powerful that it makes sense to say that the white fails to "see" anything else. The white imaginary also creates a system of *codification* through which white perception is shaped in predictable ways. Hence, the *Black* body is *coded* as a form of pathology; it is coded as evil, dirty, promiscuous, as something to be avoided. Again, these codes carry so much cultural and historical weight and are backed by so many agencies of power/knowledge (anthropology, medical discourse, etc.) until it is extremely difficult to create a slippage between "seeing" that the code is indeed a code as opposed to "seeing" what exists behind the code. "Seeing" the Black body through these myths and codes, the white will frequently engage in a series of *rituals* (a white woman grabs her purse on an elevator and avoids direct eye contact, a child whispers/screams, "Look mommy, a Negro!"). The above leads to a process of *ontologization*, a process where the *being* of the Black body (and the white body) undergoes a process of radical transformation. This involves the process whereby the historically and culturally contingent markings of the Black/white body are transformed into intrinsically natural eternal dispositions. The white gaze also involves a process whereby both the colonizer/white and the colonized/Black undergo a mutual process of *constructivity*. The social construction of the Black is dialectically linked to the construction of the white, where the latter occupies a superior place within the construction. In other words, the relationship is *asymmetrical*. There is also the process of *stereotypification*, that is, where both whites and Blacks (and, of course, "Others") become "solid types," indelibly marked by nature's teleological design. Then there is the process of *overdetermination*.[27] In this process, Blacks and whites are overdetermined from the outside, pre-marked in such a way that new knowledge of either body is always already epistemologically foreclosed.

Fanon, Ellison, and Du Bois

Fanon, Ellison, and Du Bois provide examples of how each found himself constructed from the perspective of the white looker/gazer. Franz Fanon writes about the Black body and how it can be changed, deformed, and made into an ontological problem vis-à-vis the white epistemic gaze. Fanon describes a scene where a young white boy sees a Black man and screams, "Look at the Negro! . . . Mommy, a Negro!"[28] Fanon:

> My body was coming back to me flattened out, disjointed, destroyed, mourning on that white winter day. The Negro is a beast, the Negro is evil, the Negro is mischievous, the Negro is ugly; look, a Negro, it is cold outside, the Negro is shaking because he is cold, the boy is shaking because he is afraid of the Negro, the Negro is shaking with cold, that cold that goes through your bones, the handsome boy is shaking because he thinks the Negro is shaking with anger, the white boy throws himself into his mother's arms: Mommy the Negro is going to eat me.[29]

The white imagery of the Black as a savage beast, a primitive and uncivilized animal, is clearly expressed in the boy's fear that he will be eaten by the "cannibalistic" Negro. The white boy might literally be said *to see* Fanon as a cannibal. Notice that Fanon talks about the experience of having his body "come back to him." What does this mean? After all, Fanon's body is forever with him. It never leaves. So, how can it return?

Ralph Ellison's invisible man also experiences a kind of "return of the Black body." He knows himself as embodied flesh and blood, but yet he is invisible. His body is, and yet he is not. The invisible man observes:

> I am an invisible man. No, I am not a spook like those who haunted Edgar Allen Poe; nor am I one of your Hollywood-movie ectoplasms. I am a man of substance, of flesh and bone, fiber and liquids—and I might even be said to possess a mind. I am invisible, understand, simply because people [in this case white people] refuse to see me.[30]

The reader will note that in Fanon's example, the Black body is hypervisible, while for Ellison the Black body is rendered invisible. In either case, though, the Black body "returns" in some distorted form. There appears to be a slippage between one's *own* understanding of the Black body and how others (whites) understand/construct that same Black body.

Du Bois also writes about his own lived experience of a slippage of sorts. He writes:

> In a wee wooden schoolhouse, something put it into the boys' and girls' heads to buy gorgeous visiting cards, —ten cents a package—and exchange. The exchange was merry, till one girl, a tall newcomer, refused my card, —refused it peremptorily, with a glance. Then it dawned upon me with a certain suddenness that I was different from the others; or like, mayhap in heart and life and longing, but shut out from their world by a vast veil.[31]

In this example, Du Bois suggests that he was in some sense similar to the other (white) children. In "heart," "life," and "longing" he felt a kindred relationship. But something happened. There was this sudden self-doubt, which presumably did not exist prior to this encounter. Hence, Du Bois undergoes a distinctive *process*. He moves from a sense of the familiar to the unfamiliar. He feels *different*. In this example, it is Du Bois's Black body schema that he is forced to come to terms with, a schema that he was forced to thematize in ways not typically required. He was, as it were, taken outside of himself and phenomenologically *returned*. Surely, Du Bois is the same self that he was prior to the glance enacted by the tall white girl. But is he? It is here that he begins to say, even if only unconsciously, "I am a problem!" As the tall white girl refused him, she sent a semiotic message, a message whose constructive meaning was immediately registered in the consciousness of the young Du Bois. Her body language, her refusal, involved a ritual that had tremendous power. The *ritual look* took place within a pre-interpreted space of racial meaning. Du Bois's Black body was already *coded* as different, as a problem, as that which should be avoided. Although young, the tall white newcomer had already become hampered and imprisoned by the *myths* of whiteness vis-à-vis the Black body. Through the performative act of refusal, though words were presumably never spoken, Du Bois became, even if unknowingly, "a damn nigger." Through her glance and her refusal, she reduced Du Bois to his Blackness [read: inferior], a mere surface, a *thing of no particular importance*, though important enough to reject and avoid. Du Bois underwent a process of phenomenological corporeal disjointedness. Du Bois was no longer within the group, but outside of it, left looking upon himself through the eyes of the newcomer. Like the Black colonized, Du Bois began to experience a disjointed relationship to his body. In short, he underwent a process of double consciousness. As with Ellison's invisible man and Fanon, there is a sense of disjointedness in terms of being one thing as opposed to another. It is as if there is an extrinsic social transactional process that throws the self outside of itself, only to return to itself with a different feeling, resulting from now seeing the self through the eyes of another. Even Ellison's invisible man needs light. He, too, has been invaded by some extrinsic power not of himself. It is this extrinsic power that makes him feel invisible. This is why he says that "light confirms my reality, gives birth to my form."[32]

Seeing Sarah Bartmann, Seeing Venus Hottentot

From the examples of Fanon, Ellison, and Du Bois, one can extrapolate the incredibly painful degree to which Sarah Bartmann, the so-called Venus Hottentot, must have undergone the experience of "seeing" her own body appear before her wrapped in white colonialist lies. One can only imagine the pain felt as she measured her body/self by the constructions projected upon her from the unconscious/conscious European imaginary. Consider the following:

> Oh, my god. Becky, look at her butt.
> It is so big. She looks like,
> One of those rap guys' girlfriends.
> But, y'know, who understands those rap guys?
> They only talk to her, because,
> She looks like a total prostitute, 'key?
> I mean, her butt, is just so big.
> I can't believe it's just so round, it's like,
> Out there, I mean—gross. Look!
> She's just so . . . black![33]

The above quote could have come from European discourse used to describe Sarah Bartmann. However, the introductory lines are from a rap video in which Sir Mix-A-Lot performs his famous release, "Baby Got Back."[34] The reader will notice the move from having a big butt, to being a prostitute, to being Black. This is precisely the interreferential semiotic space within which Bartmann existed. Within the context of French society, where Bartmann was put on display for five years (after being displayed in London) for the French public to gaze upon, to gaze upon her big butt, French spectatorship was not a benign passive process, but an active, constructive process that performed acts of violence upon Bartmann's body. One might argue, "But they were only looking." "The look" is itself a performance, an intervention, a form of marking, labeling as different, freakish, animal-like. It involves rendering violable the human right to inviolability. Hence, the very act of gazing is itself a form of visual penetration by the phallocentric hegemony of the colonizing gaze. As T. Denean Sharpley-Whiting argues:

> The gaze is always bound up with power, domination, and eroticisation; it is eroticizing, sexualized, and sexualizing. The indisputable fact that throngs of a predominantly male, French crowd paid to gaze upon Bartmann as the essential primitive, as the undeveloped savage unable to measure up to Frenchness, is undercut by her practically au naturel presentation.[35]

Bartmann became the extreme, the diametrically opposed, Black *Other* to the white male/female *same.*[36] Sharpley-Whiting writes:

> Black women, embodying the dynamics of racial/sexual alterity, historically invoking *primal fears* and desire in European (French) men, represent ultimate

> difference (the *sexualized savage*) and inspire repulsion, attraction, and anxiety, which gave rise to the nineteenth-century collective French male imaginations of Black Venus (*primitive narratives*).[37]

Sharpley-Whiting's work on Sarah Bartmann critically demonstrates how "seeing" Bartmann is inextricably linked to discourses of power, dominance, and hierarchies. She is aware of the dialectical movement that I indicate above, where whiteness (as pure, good, innocent) is linked to Blackness (as impure, bad, guilty). The French Africanism is tied into the perception of the French as racially superior. This dialectic is clear where Sharpley-Whiting argues that "geographically, linguistically, culturally, and aesthetically, France, the French language, French culture, and Frenchwomen are privileged sites against which Bartmann, and hence Africa, are measured as primitive, savage, and grotesque."[38]

Within the context of the French imaginary (a site where race, gender, and class intersect), "truth" about Black women, and Bartmann in particular, is manufactured to foreclose any possibility of knowing Black women other than as prostitutes, sexually dangerous, diseased, and primitive. Despite the historical reality that late nineteenth century science constructed all women as pathological, and that they could easily be "seen" as possessing the bestial characteristics of the Black female Hottentot, white women were still *white* and thereby not deemed the radical Other of whiteness (read: human). They were still superior to nonwhite women. At the apex of aesthetic beauty, "Hottentot maidens and Indian squaws are beautiful because of their comparability to Frenchwomen, the embodiment of beauty itself."[39] The process of ontologization of Bartmann's and Josephine Baker's bodies, despite the latter's ability to negotiate her embodied identity through the conscious manipulation of certain received images, a form of praxis that Bartmann appears to have lacked, is where Sharpley-Whiting notes, "Black females are perpetually ensnared, imprisoned in an essence of themselves created from without: Black Venus."[40]

It is the European who has created a Manichean world to buttress his/her own sense of who he or she is. The creation of "essences" has a way of justifying what the French "perceived" to be "true" about Bartmann, and, hence, "true" about themselves. She was reduced to a *thing*. Just as the Black male was constructed as a walking phallus,[41] "most nineteenth-century French spectators did not view her as a person or even a human, but rather as a titillating curiosity, a collage of buttocks and genitalia."[42] The prominent naturalist Georges Cuvier wanted to do a painting of Bartmann, just as a naturalist would want to get a better picture of the physiology and physiognomy of any other animal. The idea here was to create a kind of physiological cartography of Bartmann, to map her differences against the backdrop of the European subject. "To see" her "big butt" (her condition of steatopygia) and her other alleged hypertrophies (enlarged labia minoria and her large clitoris) was *not* to "see" her at all. As argued above, perception is not passive. From my "Kantian" perspective, Bartmann's body becomes the distorted sexual *thing* that "it is" in terms of the paradigm through which she is being "seen." Hence, the European power/knowledge position of spectatorship—mediated by certain atavistic assumptions, theories regarding polygenetic evolutionary development, the so-called sciences of medicine, biology, anthropology, ethnography, criminology, phrenology, physiognomy, travelogues, and philosophical "authorities" (Peter Abelard, Goethe, Hume, Kant, Hegel, to name a few)—gives rise to an historical accretion, making for the epistemic conditions through which Bartmann "appears." What is interesting is that the French viewed themselves as "seeing" differences that "meant something" to them. The visibility of the "difference," however, is always already "seen" within the context of the *same*, which functions to remain invisible; this is a feature of the power of the same. Hence, to "see" Bartmann's "differences," her savagery, primitiveness, barbarity, and grotesqueness, one had to "see" her within a certain cultural space of semiotic sameness (read: normative whiteness). To the extent that she does not approximate the norm of European identity, which is also always already "seen" and "always constituted within, not outside, representation,"[43] she is deemed ersatz, the femme fatale; her "differences" become hypervisible and placed within a normative hierarchical and *ideologically* structured framework.

As noted earlier, Gilman is concerned with the issue of how we "see" the world. Furthermore, Gilman ties perception, historical convention, and iconography together in relationship to the science of medicine, that science that helped to "uncover" the "reality" of Bartmann's inferiority/ primitiveness. Gilman writes:

> Medicine offers an especially interesting source of conventions since we do tend to give medical conventions special "scientific" status as opposed to the "subjective" status of the aesthetic conventions. But medical icons are no more "real" than "aesthetic" ones. Like aesthetic icons, medical icons may (or may not) be rooted in some observed reality. Like them, they are iconographic in that they represent these realities in a manner determined by the historical position of the observers, their relationship to their own time, and to the history of the conventions which they deploy.[44]

The (iconic) ideologically "seen" difference in the buttocks and genitalia of the Hottentot was very important "evidence" to justify drawing the distinction between lines of evolutionary development. Hence, autopsies were performed, differences were "seen," "facts" and "realities" suddenly "appeared" within the framework of a European discourse that came replete with its own conditions of emergence. Gilman:

> The polygenetic argument is the ideological basis for all the dissections of these women. If their sexual parts could be shown to be inherently different, this would be a sufficient sign that the blacks were a separate (and, needless to say, lower) race, as different from the European as the proverbial orangutan.[45]

Of course, within a larger context, Africa was deemed that mysterious exotic dark continent. It is "the light of white maleness [that] illumines this dark continent."[46] Of course, this same light (read: reason) illuminated Bartmann's dark body, creating a body schema that "recognized" her simian origins. Sharpley-Whiting:

> [Georges] Cuvier's description abounds with associations of black femaleness with bestiality and primitivism. Further, by way of contemplating Bartmann as a learned, domesticated beast—comparing her to an orangutan—he reduces her facility with languages, her good memory, and musical inclinations to a sort of simian-like mimicry of the European race. By the nineteenth century, the ape, the monkey, and orangutan had become the interchangeable counterparts, the next of kin, to blacks in pseudoscientific and literary texts.[47]

The comparison of Bartmann to an ape is central to the French imaginary concerning the bestial nature of Black women. The sexual appetites of Black people, more generally, were believed to have no end. Some French theorists even claimed that Black women copulated with apes.[48] The point here is that Bartmann became the site for an entire range of sexual "perversions." Bartmann's "anomalous" labia was linked to the overdevelopment of the clitoris, which was further linked to lesbian love. Hence, "the concupiscence of the black is thus associated also with the sexuality of the lesbian."[49]

This brings me back to the anatomy of the gaze. What becomes clear is that Bartmann existed within an imaginary space created by European xenophobia, and anxieties regarding their own sexuality, and so on. *Mythopoetic* constructions of Bartmann were designed to "discover" the hidden "truths" about Blacks. It was this putative knowledge that enabled the European/Anglo-American to repress many of its fears. Bartmann was *codified* as the very epitome of unrestrained sexuality. Through various rituals (medically mapping her body while dead or alive, voyeuristically peeping and peering), Bartmann was further "seen" as strange, a throwback to some earlier moment in evolutionary history. Bartmann *became* what her gazers wanted to "see." She was the victim of "a totalizing system of representation, that allows the seen body to become the known body."[50] Through the constitutive process of "looking," which we have come to appreciate as a powerful act of construction, Bartmann was *ontologized* into the Hottentot Venus. In "becoming" Hottentot Venus, Bartmann underwent a process of dehumanization. But this is feature of colonial whiteness. Colonial whiteness is fundamentally misanthropic. This misanthropy is also dialectical. The colonial white hates the Other, but loves itself. Hence, it is both narcissistic (the colonial white loves to see his/her own reflection, even if it appears in the form of an inverse image in the colonized) and solipsistic (only the colonial white really has being).

The Road Taken

In this chapter, it was not my aim to reach back into some distant and pristine past for a glorious pre-colonial African identity, to uncover my "true" African self, which has been said to be hidden from view by years of white (Anglocentric and Euro-centric) baggage. This, of course, does not deny the importance of various methodological approaches aimed at constructing and reconstructing our African heritage. Rather, my aim was to ground Black identity within the semiotic and brutal racist space of whiteness. After all, our Blackness[51] is structured through our historical agency, the narratives that we tell, and grounded within the existential crucible of white supremacy. What we have *become* is dialectically linked to (though not reduced to) the material, ideological, and physical manifestations of whiteness. Such was the *facticity* within which we sought various modes of *possibility*. Keep in mind, however, that this link does not *dictate* the terms of our imaginative possibilities, how we negotiate what it means to be "Black," how we envision new ways of expressing our "Blackness." The various breaks crafted within the body of this chapter were designed precisely to illuminate the complexity of how I understand my/our "Blackness." Through the use of breaks, my aim was to *perform* Blackness, to *historicize* Blackness, and to *valorize* Blackness, within/between the text. The breaks, modes of narrative and discursive solos, as it were, served to enact Blackness in its complexity, to uncover more than can be captured by a conceptual analytic focus on Blackness qua race as having a nonempirical referential status. The aim was to explode the conceptual in order to capture something of the historicity of the multilayered dimensions of Black people. As a people who have constantly had to defend their right to be, who have engaged in courageous agential forms of resistance and liberation, it is important that we locate their situated ex-istence. Struggle and agency only occur within sociohistorical contexts, concrete situations, sites that have great implications for challenging and consolidating various forms of human relationality. Blackness as an "essence," whether said to exist by whites or Blacks, is far too limiting and philosophically problematic. Therefore, it was necessary to reach beyond the "essential" and place Blackness within the midst of the existential and the historical.

While I claim, as many others do, that the concept of "race" is ontologically bankrupt, and that its genesis is linked to ways of carving up the world for purposes of white racist material domination, it does not follow from this that the experiential dimensions of living one's "Blackness" is somehow also bankrupt, though there are ways of living one's Blackness that can involve bad faith. Moreover, there are ways of valorizing one's Blackness that can lead to "imperialist" proclivities. If one negates Blackness qua race, one still gets a rich and complex history of a people who continue to have a profound sense of who they are, though the boundaries may shift, and other significant vectors (class, gender, etc.) may influence that self-understanding. (The point here is that *difference* is also an important marker of who we are as Black people.)

It is one thing to show that the concept of race does not refer to some "given" in the empirical world. The ontological groundlessness of race, however, did not save the life of young Black Emmett Till, whose face was beaten beyond recognition by white racists; it did not save Black bodies from being brutally lynched; it did not prevent the pernicious, systemic practices of Jim Crow. Some may argue that I am poking fun at Black eliminativists, but no matter how much I claim race-talk ought to be abolished or that race, taxonomically speaking, is not real, this will not save me from receiving a "Rodney King ass beating" by white racist cops, who continue to see me through the assignment of negative values that render my Blackness as criminal. Epistemic virtue ought to be encouraged; that is, knowledge-seeking practices, ways of avoiding error, specifically regarding the epistemic status of race, need to be taught and encouraged. However, despite such encouragement, it is important to acknowledge the weight of historically shaped attitudes, differential socioeconomic and political power, and institutional and systemic practices of white power that transcend matters of the epistemic adjudication regarding whether or not the concept of race has a biological referent. My white math teacher once told me—after I told him that I wanted to be a pilot—that I should be realistic and become a carpenter or a bricklayer.[52] Think of how his racist remark may have negatively impacted how I reoriented my understanding of my sense of internal possibilities, my sense of self-confidence. Think of how my Black body *came back to me*, even if only unconsciously, rendered a surface, an external sign that registered what I was really *fit* for in life. He, along with an entire episteme of white ways of "knowing" and being, helped to provide me with an arsenal of psychological weapons of Black mass destruction to be used against the enemy that I am: My own Black self. "Yeah, but race isn't real; it isn't real!!; *damn it, it isn't real!!*" Given the above, the reader will recall Malcolm X's early experience with his English teacher, Mr. Ostrowski.[53] Although Malcolm mentions that he had not given thought to it before, he says that he disclosed to Mr. Ostrowski that he wanted to be a lawyer. Ostrowski replied:

> "Malcolm, one of life's first needs is for us to be realistic. Don't misunderstand me, now. We all here like you, you know that. But you've got to be realistic about being a nigger. A Lawyer—that's no realistic goal for a nigger. You need to think about something that you *can* be. You're good with your hands—making things. Everybody admires your carpentry shop work. Why don't you plan on carpentry? People like you as a person—you'd get all kinds of work."[54]

Again, a conceptual analysis of race bent upon showing how it is empirically empty, while very important, is too thin for my aims, both within the context of this chapter and in terms of my own *lived project.* Again, this is why the breaks were so important within the chapter. They cleared a space, ventured into the "extra-conceptual," to grasp the multiple tropes of Blackness; the historical movement of Blackness; the pragmatic and utility value of Blackness; the constructive and generative myths of Blackness; the magical realism of Blackness; the spiritual legacies of Blackness; the aesthetic and poetic expressions of Blackness; the pain and joy of Blackness; the blood and vomit spewed from Blackness; the rape and denigration of Blackness; the *resistance* of Blackness. The existential reality of lived Blackness summons the power of the *performative* possibilities of language. Going solo. Break:

Blackness as Healing

Making whole what has been severed.
The body might be broken, but the spirit remains intact,
Healed by song, healed through dance, healed through ritual and memory.
They told my grandfather: "There ain't no Black man better than a white man."
Sanity sustained through so many modalities
Of Black expressiveness.
"I ain't takin this shit no mo!"
Say it loud: "I'm Black and I'm proud!"
Think of (thank for) the possibilities.
Who will tell the narrative of our historically lived trauma?
Permanently broken? Erased? Walking zombies?
Filled with/full of nihilism? Traumatized for life?
Black bodies in need. Standing in the need of prayer.
Love. Black love.
Faith. Black Faith.
Unity. Black unity.
Sufficed!

The Black body.
Cellular knowledge.
Deep-down-in-your-bones-knowledge.
Sometimes that knowledge is too much to bear.
Ask Ursula Corregidora.
And yet, like the cosmos, we keep expanding.
And yet, we continue to hurt. You got it!
The bolder rolls back down the hill once again.
But still we rise!
Strong. Determined. Resilient.

What and who I am—as *Black*—is partly defined by my own recuperative imaginative agency, and by the sociohistorically lived *interstitial* narrative space and time through which I am constituted. Blackness is both a *constituted* lived reality and a *constituting* lived reality. I sustain my Blackness by defining myself through (and by being defined by) interpretive and imaginative dynamics that are linked to a lived tradition, a tradition itself grounded within the imaginative, the linking of the past, present, and future.[55] As a *lived project*, my Blackness takes the form of a responsibility. As active homo narrans and homo significans,[56] I identify and critically engage the history of Black people, a people who have had to make a way out of no way. I construct my identity through the history of the Middle Passage, the whip, torn Black flesh, "Nigger" dogs and water hoses, forgotten ancestors and orally transmitted tales. With pain and dignity, I wrap/rap my identity in my mother's personal history of being forced to pay for magazines around the back of stores, and who sat in segregated movie theaters. I am both constituted by her history and proudly engage in constituting myself within this oppressive-resistance narrative. I also enact the agential dynamics of Black struggle. The very act of resistance can function as an act of affirmation; for to resist ("to take a stand") is already an announcement that one affirms the opposite of that which oppresses, dehumanizes.

Given the above, one would expect that my work in philosophy is inextricably linked to my lived project of Blackness. Being ensconced within a history of struggle that I did not create does not negate the freedom to choose sides, even if that freedom leads to moments of tremendous disillusionment. I chose the side of my Blackness, a narrative grounded within certain material conditions, a trope, a sign and symbol of *resistance*, a site of human effort to be more than the white gaze was capable of capturing, a site of productive efforts to keep alive a shared sense of fellowship. I chose the side of those forgotten and unknown African bodies that await proper burial at the bottom of the Atlantic. I chose the subaltern voices of my ancestors, just as they, in their hopeful spirits, may have dreamt of my future possibility, a future voice unashamedly gathering and sustaining their collective pain, sorrow, and joy.

Philosophy is just one of many sites where Black resistance can take place. For example, recently a prominent white philosopher at an APA conference said to me, after having read my "philosophical biography" in my book *The Philosophical i: Personal Reflections on Life in Philosophy*, that he enjoyed my chapter, but thought that I should have not used "*that* language," referring to my use of African American vernacular speech. After all, he said, "You speak English so well." He went on to describe another African American philosopher who shocked him because he spoke English so poorly. The implications were clear: To do really productive philosophy, one ought to use "Standard" English (or some other European Language). My chapter was deemed problematic because of my use of Black vernacular speech. Who was it that said that those who control the army control the language? He failed to see how the very enactment of Black vernacular speech was an act of resistance. To choose to write in the language of my nurture, a language that was constitutive of my identity and my larger linguistic community, made the point that philosophical discourse comes in various modes. More so, the point was that "Standard American English" was not adequate in terms of articulating the dynamics of my life as experienced and traversed within the belly of ghetto Black America. Again, it was a question of agency, though linguistic agency. For me, a major part of doing philosophy is a matter of critiquing and possibly destroying sites of oppression. Hence, philosophy, on this score, has a service to fulfill. One might say that my philosophical engagements are shaped and get articulated through my *lived* participation in a distinctive, though by no means an exclusive, history of resistance.

Blackness as Shango

The Orisha of thunder.
A thunderous applause for Black freedom.
A thunderous march toward freedom.
Shango. The warrior god. Insurrectionist.
Revolutionary.
Back in that Afro-Maroon space of Combat.
A hermeneutics of overthrow.
Of Prospero's power.
Careful, though.
There's always a Caliban in our midst?
But whose Caliban?
Shakespeare's or Césaire's?
Let's give a big shout out to Sh-an-go.
Go tell it on the mountain.
Freedom is ontological and political.
We need all the help we can muster.

Callin the Orisha.
Sh-an-*GO*,
wit yo Baaaaad selfffffffff.
Public Enemy: "We got to fight the powers that be."

Notes

1. Franz Fanon, 1963, *The Wretched of the Earth*, New York: Grove Press, 42.

2. W. E. B. Du Bois, 1995, "The Souls of White Folk," in David Levering Lewis (ed.) *W. E. B. Du Bois: A Reader*, New York: Henry Holt and Company, 465.

3. Du Bois, "Souls of White Folk," 456.

4. W. E. B. Du Bois, 1969, *The Souls of Black Folk*, New York: New American Library, 43–44.

5. Du Bois, *Souls of Black Folk*, 43.

6. Du Bois, "Souls of White Folk," 454.

7. W. E. B. Du Bois, 1995, "The Conservation of Races," in David Levering Lewis (ed.) *W. E. B. Du Bois: A Reader*, New York: Henry Holt and Company, 24.

8. I would like to thank philosopher Clarence Sholé Johnson for the following observation. Johnson agrees that there is something deeply problematic about whites who claim "I'm just me," particularly within a racist context where being white confers unearned privileges. However, Johnson maintains that when a Black person says "I'm just me" that such an utterance could function as a form of rejection, that is, "I'm just me" could mean: "I refuse to accept the negative images that have been imposed upon me by the history of white racism." "I'm just me," on this score, declares, "I am just a person in the world, like anyone else; take me as I am. Don't read me according to how white people have constructed me." Of course, a Black person could also mean something like: "I am an autonomous, atomic individual. I am not Black. I am just me, just myself." Psychologically, this last case could indicate a deep sense of Black self-hatred. Such a Black person could mean, "Please don't identify me as Black." In this case, claiming the status of "being just me" could conceal as form of fleeing, an attempt to "permanently" transcend one's Blackness, which constitutes part of one's facticity.

9. Sander L. Gilman, "Black Bodies, White Bodies: Toward an Iconography of Female Sexuality in Late Nineteenth-Century Art, Medicine, and Literature," in Henry Louis Gates, Jr. (ed.) *"Race," Writing, and Difference*, Chicago: University of Chicago Press, 1986, 223.

10. J. A. Harrison, 1884, "Negro English," *Anglia, 7*, 232–79. Cited in Geneva Smitherman, 2001, *Talkin That Talk: Language, Culture and Education in African America*, London and New York: Routledge, 72.

11. Harrison, "Negro English."

12. Geneva Smitherman, 2001, *Talkin That Talk: Language, Culture and Education in African America*, London and New York: Routledge, 73.

13. Aimé Césaire, 1972, *Discourse on Colonialism*, New York: Monthly Review Press, 21.

14. Césaire, *Discourse on Colonialism*, 21.

15. Jan Nederveen Pieterse, 1992, *White on Black: Images of Africa and Blacks in Western Popular Culture*, New Haven: Yale University Press, 222.

16. Césaire, *Discourse on Colonialism*, 54.

17. Césaire, *Discourse on Colonialism*, 20.

18. Albert Memmi, 1991, *The Colonizer and the Colonized*, Boston, Mass.: Beacon Press, xxviii.

19. Memmi, *The Colonizer and the Colonized*, 82.

20. Fanon, *The Wretched of the Earth*, 16.

21. Simone de Beauvoir, 1976, *The Ethics of Ambiguity*, New York: Citadel Press, 47.

22. Memmi, *The Colonizer and the Colonized*, xxvii.

23. Memmi, *The Colonizer and the Colonized*, xxvi.

24. Pieterse, *White on Black*, 79.

25. See my introduction, "Fragments of a Social Ontology of Whiteness," in George Yancy (ed.), 2004, *What White Looks Like: African-American Philosophers on the Whiteness Question*, New York: Routledge, 11.

26. Memmi, *The Colonizer and the Colonized*, 83.

27. To see how Sharpley-Whiting relates these last three constructs to "the Black Venus narrative" see T. Denean Sharpley-Whiting, 1999, *Black Venus*, Durham, NC: Duke University Press, 10.

28. Franz Fanon, 2001, "The Lived Experience of the Black," in Robert Bernasconi (ed.) *Race*, Malden, MA: Blackwell Publishers, 186.

29. Fanon, "The Lived Experience of the Black," 186.

30. Ralph Ellison, 1995, *Invisible Man*, New York: Vintage Books, 3.

31. Du Bois, *The Souls of Black Folk*, 44.

32. Ellison, *Invisible Man*, 6.

33. Cf. "Baby Got Back" by Sir Mix-A-Lot.

34. What is interesting here is that the white girls at the beginning of the video reiterate some of the same representational myths that came out of Europe. The reader will particularly note the inter-referential association of a big butt, prostitution, and Blackness. They could have been describing Sarah Bartmann. "Baby Got Back" at once functions as a counteraesthetic to certain European and Anglo-American values, and as an affirmation of the "Black female body." When Sir-Mix-A-Lot says that "I'm hooked and I can't stop staring," this is reminiscent of the French men who found it difficult to withdraw the gaze from Bartmann's buttocks. Sir-Mix-A-Lot's gaze, however, is unequivocal; it does not suffer from the oppositional forces of attraction and repulsion; he knows exactly what he likes. He says that "Cosmo ain't got nothin' to do with my selection." He also adds, "I'm tired of magazines sayin' flat butts are the thing." My sense is that there is a certain disruptive dimension to the rap and the video; it discursively and visually fractures the typical image of the white female "beautiful" body, slim, blond, and almost anorexic. In fact, many of the women performing in the video, which already has problems in terms of how certain performative images of Black women are literally funded and others are not, have very large buttocks, some even visually distorted/enhanced and exaggerated for effect. Of course,

one still wonders to what extent Sir-Mix-A-Lot re-inscribes the male gaze, reducing the Black female to a collage of buttocks. A feminist critique would not miss all of the sexual (copulatory) references that appear to transcend the aesthetic dimensions of having a big butt. But to what extent can the sexual/erotic and the aesthetic be separated? After all, it is not that Sir-Mix-A-Lot just wants to make a politico-aesthetic statement, he is "beggin' for a piece of that bubble." And if you're like Jane Fonda, "my anaconda don't want none." And if you want to role in his Mercedes, then you have to "turn around! Stick it out!" And admitting that he can't help himself from "actin' like an animal," he says "with that butt you got makes me feel so horny." Within the context of the politics of desire, one wonders if there is a "legitimate" space within which the Black male might praise/appreciate "the Black female body," even if it's her buttocks that he is praising, without the accompanying misogynistic implications often embedded within the position of male spectatorship.

35. Sharpley-Whiting, *Black Venus*, 34.

36. The reader will note that this does not deny the fact that Europeans had their own "Others" who were indigenous to Europe. Jews, Russians, Slavs, Irish, etc., at one time or another were constituted as "Others."

37. Sharpley-Whiting, *Black Venus*, 6.

38. Sharpley-Whiting, *Black Venus*, 37.

39. Sharpley-Whiting, *Black Venus*, 35.

40. Sharpley-Whiting, *Black Venus*, 10.

41. Pieterse, *White on Black*, 175.

42. Sharpley-Whiting, *Black Venus*, 17.

43. Stuart Hall, "Cultural Identity and Diaspora," in Patrick Williams and Laura Chrisman (eds.) *Colonial Discourse and Post-Colonial Theory: A Reader*, New York: Columbia University Press, 1994, 392.

44. Gilman, "Black Bodies, White Bodies," 224.

45. Gilman, "Black Bodies, White Bodies," 235.

46. Sharpley-Whiting, *Black Venus*, 24.

47. Sharpley-Whiting, *Black Venus*, 24.

48. Gilman, "Black Bodies, White Bodies," 231.

49. Gilman, "Black Bodies, White Bodies," 237.

50. Sharpley-Whiting, *Black Venus*, 22.

51. My use of "Blackness" should not be interpreted to mean that I believe that "Blackness" functions like a Platonic Form, residing in some metaphysical realm.

52. For the larger autobiographical context in which this event was described, see my chapter "Between Facticity and Possibility," in George Yancy (ed.) *The Philosophical i: Personal Reflections on Life in Philosophy*, Lanham, MD: Rowman & Littlefield, 2002, 140.

53. Bruce Perry notes that his real name was Richard Kaminska. See Perry's controversial book, *Malcolm: The Life of a Man Who Changed Black America*, Barrytown, New York: Station Hill Press, 1991, 42.

54. Malcolm X, with Alex Haley, *The Autobiography of Malcolm X*, New York: Ballantine Books, 1965, 36.

55. Clevis Headley, 2002, "Postmodernism, Narrative, and the Question of Black Identity," in Robert Birt (ed.) *The Quest for Community and Identity: Critical Essays in Africana Social Philosophy*, Lanham, MD: Rowman & Littlefield, 68.

56. For more on these terms and how they are conceptualized within the context of a philosophical anthropology that conceives of human reality as an "ability to be," see my "Introduction: Philosophy and the Situated Narrative Self" in *The Philosophical i.*

12

Blackness and the Quest for Authenticity

Robert Birt
Morgan State University

> [T]he black man should no longer be confronted by the dilemma, *turn white or disappear*; but he should be able to take cognizance of the possibility of existing.
>
> —Franz Fanon, *Black Skins, White Masks*

> The struggle against racism . . . is not aimed at self-obliteration.
>
> —Tsenay Serequeberhan, *Our Heritage*

WHITENESS, I ONCE ARGUED, IS A SPECIES of bad faith in the Sartrean sense. As a form of identity and consciousness, it allows of no authentic existence.[1] Must we draw the same conclusion about blackness? Can blackness coincide with existential authenticity? Or must it not also be an inauthentic form of consciousness and identity riddled with the poison of bad faith? I hold that blackness and whiteness are not equivalent, and that blackness (unlike whiteness) does not necessarily imply a denial of existential freedom. Blackness and whiteness are not equivalent because the *situations* of black and white people are not equivalent. The situation of the blacks is not that of a dominant people within our racialized society, nor is blackness the bad faith identity of the dominant. Abstracted from the historical, lived situations of the people themselves, blackness and whiteness are meaningless. Indeed human existence is not meaningful (or possible) void of the lived situations in which it happens. Perhaps we should ponder for a moment the existential notion of situation and consider the possibility of black authenticity within that context.

Human existence is freedom, but it is always freedom in situation. A common misinterpretation of existential freedom (especially among interpreters of Sartre) is that it is pure transcendence (or "radical freedom") void of the facticity of situation. Bad faith is then taken to be exclusively a flight from our transcendence. But for Sartre freedom—human existence—is always the inescapable facticity of situation *and* irrepressible transcendence and possibility. Denial or exaggeration of either dimension of existence is an expression of bad faith. Hence bad faith can also be a denial of our facticity. We might recall that "There can be a free for-itself only as engaged in a resisting world."[2] But I think a less ontological, more explicitly social description is more apropos for our discussion here.

To say that the human being is "defined first of all as a being in situation" also "means that he forms a synthetic whole with his situation."[3] As such, the human being exists within an ensemble of limitations (class, race, gender, culture, physical attributes, one's past, and so forth) which one does not choose, and by which one is conditioned. Moreover, the human being "cannot be distinguished from his situation, for it forms him and decides his possibilities."[4] Yet the very meaning of situation is not a given, but emanates from the free choice of oneself in situation. A situation must be *lived.* It is always lived in relation to others, such relations being an inseparable aspect of one's situation and of one's becoming the human being one becomes. In short, I *am* my situation which shapes and limits me, but which I also transcend by choices and attitudes that decide the meaning of my situation.

But if all humans are beings in situation, humans may also differ in situation and in their choices of themselves in situation. Differences and variations in situation may be due to many factors, including race. Moreover, the different choices of ourselves in situation, our varied ways of exercising situated freedom, can be *authentic* or *inauthentic.* And it is in light of these differences that we ought to consider the question of blackness and existential authenticity.[5] Insofar as blackness is the identity and consciousness of an oppressed people desirous of liberation, and expressive of their striving for the emancipation of their denied or *thwarted transcendence*, it can coincide with existential authenticity. It may even be an indispensable condition for authenticity. We need not deny that blacks can be inauthentic, nor accept Sartre's problematic assertion that the black "is *held* to authenticity."[6] An historic oppression within a racialized social hierarchy which, in Fanon's words, "forces the people it dominates to ask themselves the question constantly: In reality, who am I?" is bound to elicit both authentic and inauthentic responses to that question.[7] Franz Fanon's book *Black Skin, White Masks* is full of insightful philosophical descriptions and analyses of black inauthenticity, as well as Fanon's own passionate seeking for more authentic ways of being in the face of French colonial degradation.[8] And the literary traditions of black America from the early slave narratives to contemporary novels of Toni Morrison reveal the same pitfalls of bad faith and the same striving for authenticity. But the historical *situation* of Blacks allows the option of choosing blackness *and* authenticity, and even the embracing of blackness as a path of authenticity, which is not analogously available to persons ensconced in the prisons of whiteness. Let us consider some of the reasons why. But to do so we must reflect a moment on the meaning of authenticity.

If existence truly precedes essence, and if "freedom is impossible to distinguish from the *being* of human reality,"[9] then being authentic means (among other things) choosing to embrace the ambiguities of our existence—neither denying nor exaggerating our transcendence or facticity. This means I neither flee nor passively yield to the facticity of my situation, but regard it as the inescapable context wherein I begin the transcending project of self-creation. As I am not a mere object or thing, I cannot deny my transcendence as a free human subject. I am not *mere* facticity. Yet I *am* facticity as surely as transcendence; and rather than exaggerating my transcendence in denial of facticity, I must recognize the facticity of my historical and social situation as (in Arnold Farr's words) the indispensable "raw material of my existence wherein I begin my project of self-creation."[10] To be authentic means that we embrace our freedom and the exalting privilege of responsibility it entails. It means that we embrace the ambiguities of our condition and abandon the comforting self-deceptions of bad faith. For essential to authenticity is "having a true and lucid consciousness of the situation" and "assuming the responsibilities and risks that it involves."[11] Moreover, in relations between self and others, the authentic person acknowledges that "the existence of others as a freedom defines my situation and is even a condition of my own freedom."[12]

Now while the black is not "held to authenticity," it is at least possible to live the experience of blackness in ways that are authentic. It is possible (if not essential) to choose authenticity precisely through the creation and affirmation of a radical black subjectivity and peoplehood. Whiteness, on the other hand, is the bad faith identity of the racially dominant.[13] A "true and lucid consciousness of the situation" is not available from within the perspective of whiteness; nor can the "white" person qua white assume "the responsibilities and risks." Whiteness *is* self-delusion and the abandonment of responsibility. The bad faith of whiteness is the self-deception of dominant people within the racialized social hierarchy. One cannot *live* whiteness authentically as one might live blackness. To embrace whiteness is to embrace the bad faith of privilege. Whiteness is the privilege of *exclusive transcendence*, a transcendence whose exclusiveness tends to dim the white person's awareness of his or her facticity, and which is predicated on denial of the transcendence of an Other.

The usurping, imperial transcendence of the whites has meant for that Other the experience of being reduced to the status of an object, reduced to mere facticity. At least in America, that Other has been primarily the blacks. And this has been the case since slavery when blacks, then regarded as chattel, were numbered among the beasts. Was it not through the relegation of blacks to the status of beasts that the lordly whites elevated themselves to the status of divinity? It was through the invention of the Negro as a degraded race that whites invented themselves as an exalted race. And from this process a common white identity was born. This legacy of an exclusive white transcendence has endured, more insidiously if less overtly than in the past.

For this imperial white transcendence to prevail, blacks have always had to suffer "the misfortune of being situated in a *what* mode of being."[14] There could be no *existence in black*. This fixating of the black in facticity, in a *what* mode of being, was practiced most explicitly during slavery with the demotion of people to the status of beasts. Hence Frederick Douglass recalls that "We were all ranked together at the valuation. There were horses and men, cattle and women, pigs and children, all holding the same rank in the *scale of being*."[15] Within this scale of being there could be no transcendence; no subjects, only objects. This denial of black transcendence did not end with slavery. Thus W. E. B. Du Bois discovers that he is *problem*, not a human being with a human personality. And he infers in *The Souls of Black Folk* that the black is born into an American world "which yields him no true self-consciousness, but only allows him to see himself through the revelation of the other world."[16] As a black subject of French colonialism, Franz Fanon, who claims to have come "into the world imbued with a will to find a meaning in things," discovered himself to be an "object in the midst of other objects."[17] Objects are not thought to seek a meaning, but to have meanings imposed by a subject. The seeking of a meaning is an act of transcendence, but this is what the black is denied. When blacks internalize this denial there is a devaluation of self, a loss of self. Is this not what Dr. King had in mind when he spoke of a "degenerating sense of nobodiness" that afflicted millions of African Americans? Again, it is a matter of denied transcendence resulting from a racial caste system that "substitutes an *I-it* relationship for the I-thou relationship, and ends up *relegating persons to the status of things*."[18]

To be authentic, black people must resist this reification—this "thingification" as Aimé Césaire calls it. The reclaiming of our human status as *subjects*, the liberating of repressed black transcendence, is an indispensable condition of black authenticity. This, one may infer, is at least partly what Dr. Du Bois had in mind when he described the end of the "spiritual strivings" of the black people as an effort to achieve a more genuine self-consciousness, and "a better and truer self."[19] Bell hooks prefers to speak of the affirmation of black transcendence as "liberating subjectivity."[20] Without the affirmation of transcendence, without the earnest effort to liberate subjectivity, there can be no pathway to black authenticity—no deliverance from self-estrangement.

Now some may wonder why we need speak of *black* authenticity at all. Is not the quest for authenticity a quest to become more authentically *human*? Moreover, anyone who has made even a cursory study of contemporary literature on race must be aware of a virtual cottage industry of writings advocating or heralding the abolition of race and the "end of blackness." There are, of course, the unending debates over racial essentialism and the social constructivism of race. And there are those who might argue that blackness is necessarily an essentialist racial identity, and thus inconsistent with authenticity in the existential sense.

But the affirmation of black consciousness and identity, of black solidarity and community, requires no essentialism—and no flight from either transcendence or facticity. For what constitutes a people is not some transhistorical essence, but their historical lived experience and what they make of themselves in light of that experience. When in *Dusk of Dawn* African American thinker W. E. B. Du Bois ponders his kinship with other blacks in Africa and the diaspora, he ultimately finds the source of this bond in a common history, though it is a history that is largely tragic—one in which black peoples "have suffered a common disaster and have one long memory."[21] What is essential to what Du Bois calls "kinship" or common identity among blacks is a "social heritage." The emancipatory strivings whereby blacks have sought to assert their transcendence as human subjects has not as its primary concern the defense of some black "essence" or "Negro soul" but, as Tsenay Serequeberhan notes, to "help create and cultivate conditions for black freedom."[22] An insurgent affirmation of black transcendence implies no insistence on "natural" or essential properties as definitive of the being of the black. What is implied is the common praxis of a people's self-discovery and self-creation as existing individuals and as a transcendent sociohistorical community. This self-discovery and self-creation, so indispensable to existential authenticity is, in Césaire's words, a "*concrete* rather than an abstract coming to consciousness." To be authentic "we must have a concrete consciousness of what we are."[23]

But "a concrete consciousness of what we are" cannot be achieved by fleeing ourselves, or by endless promulgations of the end of blackness. Our common lived experiences as blacks cannot be evaded in order to lay claim to transcendence and authenticity as simply *human*. For the "avenue of flight" from our situation, from ourselves, is characteristically inauthentic. Sartre noticed this tendency among inauthentic Jews who "deal with their situation by running away from it" and who deny it "or deny their responsibilities."[24] He even found some "inauthentic Jews who play at not being Jews."[25] Having internalized anti-Semitic stereotypes, they often fled their despised Jewishness in a vain pursuit of the "human," that is, of an abstract concept of Man "which is neither Jew, nor Arab, nor Negro, nor bourgeois, nor worker, but only man."[26] This is an attitude well-known within the black experience also, an attitude Fanon critiques both in *Black Skin, White Masks* and *The Wretched of the Earth.*

Of course, the human being *is* transcendence, and in affirming a denied transcendence blacks are affirming humanity. But it is, and has ever been, *as blacks* that this humanity has been denied through the denial of our transcendence. We can hardly reclaim our transcendence through an escape from blackness, at least not without running the risk of inauthenticity. If it is as blacks that our transcendence is denied, then it is at first as blacks that we ought to reclaim our transcendence. And as this reclaiming of our denied transcendence is a most essential condition of our *being* authentic, it is wholly fitting to describe it as a quest for black authenticity, or at least as *existence in black.*[27]

Indeed it is our existence that we reclaim in our quest for authenticity. Yet we cannot reclaim it on the plane of the universal abstract. For it is rather in the striving, concrete existence of living men and women that the universal is to be found. Nor is there a question of wrapping ourselves in a delusional shroud of "ontological blackness." Such essentialist methods create a new prison in which the many and often *enriching* complexities and perplexities of black consciousness and identity are concealed and denied. We do not wish to make of blackness a tomb within which to bury ourselves. But to abandon our common identity as blacks, to forget the common history, struggles, and experiences that make us a people, is to deny our situated existence. And by denying our situation we undermine the prospects of actualizing our transcendence. Transcendence is also situated, or is realizable, only within a given situation. That is why the flight toward an abstract humanity is vain. It forsakes our concrete, lived humanity for a metaphysical phantom.

But if we take the idea of existential authenticity seriously, then we should feel at least as justified in speaking of black authenticity as was Sartre in speaking of Jewish authenticity.[28] Black authenticity would similarly mean choosing and affirming oneself as black, choosing and affirming solidarity and community with one's black sisters and brothers, and affirming our legacy of struggle and the universal worth of liberating values emerging from that legacy. And while this striving for authentic existence and liberated subjectivity must be a movement of *resistance* to dehumanizing reification and denied transcendence, resistance does not exactly exhaust our quest. It is also a question of expanding the sphere of possibilities wherein human creativity—

especially self-creation—can thrive. In her essay, "The Politics of Radical Black Subjectivity," bell hooks queries, "How do we create an oppositional world-view, a consciousness, an identity, a standpoint that exists not only as that struggle which also opposes dehumanization but as that movement which enables creative, expansive self-actualization?"[29] The quest for authenticity and the reclaiming of black transcendence must be more than an act of personal and communal revolt. "Opposition is not enough. In the vacant space after one has resisted there is still the necessity to *become*—to *make oneself anew*."[30] But what is this radical black subjectivity that expresses itself as *becoming* if not our denied and now reclaimed transcendence? And to "make oneself anew"—self-creation—is this not the most unique manifestation of existential freedom that constitutes the *being* of the human?

Yes, the quest for authenticity is a quest to become more authentically human. And the quest for black authenticity can certainly be no less. For in Cesaire's words, "as blacks . . . we are dealing with the only race which is denied even the notion of humanity."[31] But blacks cannot affirm their denied humanity without affirming *themselves*. We cannot affirm human transcendence or existence as such without affirming our own existence in black. Asserting our own existence need not mean negating the existence of others, or even our possible community with them. "The consciousness of self," Fanon reminds us, "is not the closing of a door to communication. Philosophic thought teaches us, on the contrary, that it is its guarantee."[32] To coexist we must exist; and we can hardly form community with others without creating community among ourselves. To form ourselves as subjects, to create a radical black subjectivity, is precisely to create the possibility of intersubjective community among ourselves as well as with others. The quest for black authenticity, for our transcendent *existence in black*, is a striving to create that space of *be-ing* where creativity can thrive, and a people so often sealed in a "crushing objecthood" can flourish and discover a world of possibility.

Notes

1. For my initial, tentative development of this thesis, see "The Bad Faith of Whiteness," in *What White Looks Like: African-American Philosophers on the Whiteness Question*, ed. George Yancy (New York: Routledge, 2004), 55–66.
2. Jean-Paul Sartre, *Being and Nothingness* (New York: Pocket Books, 1956), 620.
3. Jean-Paul Sartre, *Anti-Semite and Jew* (New York: Schocken Books, 1976), 59.
4. Sartre, *Anti-Semite and Jew*, 60.
5. The reader will note that while I speak of "blackness and existential authenticity" or "black authenticity," I do not speak of authentic blackness. The latter expression implies an essentialist conception of black identity, consciousness, and peoplehood

that denies freedom and obstructs the quest for existential authenticity. The *being* of the blacks, as humans, is such that "existence precedes essence." There is no "Negro soul" or transcendent black essence to fix or define a black identity. Rather there is a common history and situation, and hopefully a common quest for solidarity, freedom, and liberation as a people that binds us and allows a path toward existential authenticity. Neither white racism nor black essentialism should tempt us to a bad faith return to a version of what Fanon once called the "fixed concept of the Negro."

6. Sartre, *Black Orpheus* (Paris: Editions Gallimard, 1948), 15. My emphasis.

7. Franz Fanon, *The Wretched of the Earth* (New York: Grove Press, 1963), 250. I realize that some readers may think this reference inappropriate in so far as Fanon refers to European colonialism, not American racism. Nonetheless, it is arguable (and has been argued by many thinkers) that American racism is a form of internal domestic colonialism—with features that resemble neocolonialism in our post-1960s era.

8. I find the first three chapters of *Black Skin, White Masks* especially insightful as analyses of the varied temptations to bad faith and inauthenticity often ensnaring Francophone blacks, while Fanon's fifth chapter on the "lived experience of blackness" (unhappily translated as "The Fact of Blackness") reveals an eloquent and passionate existential quest on the part of Fanon for more authentic ways of being in the face of a racist French colonialism.

9. Sartre, *Being and Nothingness*, 60.

10. Arnold Farr, "Racism, Historical Ruins and the Task of Identity Formation," in *The Quest for Community and Identity: Critical Essays in Africana Social Philosophy*, ed. Robert E. Birt (Lanham: Rowman & Littlefield, 2002), 21.

11. Sartre, *Anti-Semite and Jew*, 90.

12. Simone de Beauvoir, *The Ethics of Ambiguity* (Secaucus: Citadel Press, 1991), 91.

13. This argument is more fully developed in "The Bad Faith of Whiteness." That essay also includes a brief exposition of the Sartrean concept of bad faith, and an analysis of whiteness that shows how it fits the description of bad faith.

14. Lewis Gordon, *Bad Faith and Anti-Black Racism* (Atlantic Highlands: Humanities Press, 1995), 6.

15. Frederick Douglass, *Narrative of the Life of Frederick Douglass* (New York: Penguin Books, 1983), 89–90.

16. W. E. B. Du Bois, *The Souls of Black Folk* (New York: Bantam Books, 1989), 3.

17. Fanon, *Black Skin White Masks*, 109.

18. Martin Luther King Jr., "Letter from a Birmingham Jail," in *A Testament of Hope: Essential Writings and Speeches of Martin Luther King, Jr.*, ed. James H. Washington (San Francisco: Harper/Collins, 1986), 293.

19. Du Bois, *The Souls of Black Folk*, 3.

20. bell hooks, *Killing Rage, Ending Racism* (New York: Henry Holt and Company, 1995), 240–50.

21. Du Bois, *Dusk of Dawn: An Essay Toward an Autobiography of a Race Concept* (New York: Schocken Books, 1971), 117.

22. Tsenay Serequeberhan, *Our Heritage: The Past and Present of African-American and African Existence* (Lanham: Rowman & Littlefield, 2000), 15.

23. Aimé Césaire, *Discourse on Colonialism* (New York: Monthly Review Press, 1972), 76. My italics.

24. Sartre, *Anti-Semite and Jew*, 92.

25. Sartre, *Anti-Semite and Jew*, 96.

26. Sartre, *Anti-Semite and Jew*, 55

27. Since this is the second time I have used this phrase, it is only right that I mention that this is the title of an anthology edited by black philosopher Lewis Gordon. The full title is *Existence in Black: An Anthology of Black Existential Philosophy.*

28. See especially *Anti-Semite and Jew*, 136–37, for Sartre's discussion of the meaning of "Jewish authenticity." While I do not wish to conflate the distinct historical situations of two historical peoples, I do see some meaningful parallel in the matter of what the choice of authenticity might mean for oppressed peoples—especially oppressed minorities.

29. bell hooks, *Yearning: Race, Gender and Cultural Politics* (Boston: South End Press, 1990), 15.

30. hooks, *Yearning*, 15. My italics. I agree with bell hooks that "opposition is not enough," but I wonder if there cannot be creative moments within resistance rather than a "vacant space" preceding the making of ourselves anew. Cannot the transcending movement of "expansive self-actualization" coincide with, even partly emerge from, the transcending movement of resistance? Perhaps transcendence as self-creation is coterminous with transcendence as resistance. Human transcendence always involves *becoming*, but self-creation for an oppressed people whose transcendence is denied often finds its founding moments in resistance.

31. Cesaire, *Discourse on Colonialism*, 79. I invite the reader to explore my own reflections on this theme in chapter 16 of Lewis Gordon's anthology *Existence in Black.*

32. Franz Fanon, *The Wretched of the Earth* (New York: Grove Press, 1968), 247.

13

Act Your Age and Not Your Color: Blackness as Material Conditions, Presumptive Context, and Social Category

John H. McClendon III
Bates College

Transcendence or Affirmation

WHEN I WAS GROWING UP AS A YOUNG STUDENT at a predominantly Black public school a teacher, who was Black, once said to us (we were a group of ten and eleven year olds in the fifth grade) at a time when we were rather disorderly in class that we should act our age and not our color. This injunction clearly said more about our teacher's view about Blackness than it did about our behavior as fifth graders. Here was a situation when young Black kids were acting like most other ten and eleven year olds and in spite of this reality, for our teacher that day, our Blackness became the point of departure. For our hapless teacher, disorderly conduct signified the dreaded nature of Blackness and not the vast energy of fifth graders whose attention span sometimes failed to keep pace with the class lesson in the time period allotted.

Consequently, in virtue of the teacher's admonition, the universality of our actions (which signified what educators often identify as age appropriate behavior) was overridden by the material actuality that we were Black children. For our Blackness, in this teacher's estimation, was more than a racial description; it was in fact a severe indictment of our humanity. It was a manner of casting our identity within the racist framework of the negative connotations widely associated with being Black in a white supremacist country. The teacher's comments were ostensibly aimed at restoring order in the classroom; however, this declaration's substantive utility was more decisive and hazardous than maintaining an orderly classroom. The instruction not to act our color was congruent with the reproduction of racist social relations; an imperative to cease being who we were; a wretched proposition, which ultimately meant the reduction of cardinal principles about philosophical anthropology to the depths of racist conceptions about us as Black people. Simply put, we were to view ourselves (in our Blackness) as something negative and shameful. Acting our color, from our teacher's perspective, was therefore far more harmful than acting our age.

Of course, at the heart of the commandment, to act our age, was the absurd belief that non-Black ten and eleven year olds were not disorderly in school. Moreover, acting our color was synonymous with disorderly conduct; a mysterious quality that emerged as if it was something actually embedded in the very nature of our racial makeup and being. After all, for this teacher, Black behavior ranked as the epitome of disorderly conduct. And, I am sure that in this teacher's eyes, there was ostensible evidence and indeed proof of this basic racial characteristic; perhaps all we needed to do was examine the extensive record that demonstrated how so many Black folk had been arrested, time and again, for disorderly conduct. So therefore the message was loud and clear: if we wanted to be orderly, namely uphold one of the *sacred virtues* associated with really being good boys and girls, then we must make the effort of not falling into the trap of being *Black* children.

Malcolm X once said that the real danger in racism was not only that white people hated Black people, but moreover had to do with the destructive psyche that we obtained when they taught us to hate ourselves.[1] No doubt, our teacher was a victim of racial self-hatred and now was predisposed to teach us to hate ourselves. If this teacher had had a positive view of Blackness the opportunity to present a lesson in race pride was immediately there for the taking. Instead of exhorting us to reach the standards of excellence attained by previous generations of Black people, our pathetic teacher reasoned that it was better for us to be a ten or eleven year old shorn of our racial identity. Since our teacher was implicitly a virtue ethicist via the philosophy of education, we could have heard about the prominent examples of Black academic achievement that we might emulate, yet this teacher decided to denigrate our Blackness.[2]

Therein during the early stages of my life (not fully comprehended, yet in a real sense a nagging issue for me) I had to face a formidable challenge to my very sense of racial identity. In actuality, this formidable challenge later emerged as a daunting philosophical question about how to view my Blackness. In a nutshell, the question I was to confront as philosopher was simply, "Is Blackness something I must *transcend* or was it something I must embrace and *affirm*?" Now as adults, how should my former classmates react to this test about their own sense of Blackness? And in what way would I communicate to them, and others like them, why the choice I had made was the final alternative—the affirmation of Blackness?

My road in life led me to the latter option and I eventually became a teacher of Black history and an active theorist and philosopher working in formal school settings, informal community networks, and in neighborhood meetings and forums. The basement at home, the Afro-American Culture Center, Dunbar High School classroom, Central State University's Upward Bound Program, and the venues at various colleges and universities across the country were my avenues for traveling down the road to affirming Blackness over and against the ruthless assaults of white supremacy. Affirming Blackness included the fight against racism and hence my audience incorporated not only Black people but white people who were willing to listen and learn.

When I began to pursue the meaning of Blackness (as philosopher, scholar, and activist), it became clear that the aim of transcending Blackness (in effect the negation of Blackness) would stand in stark contrast to the principle of affirming Blackness. In this society, which is predicated on white supremacy, Black identity actually enters into a contested zone where we observe that the antithetical concepts of transcendence and affirmation are in constant struggle. Many times I have witnessed some famous Black personality as literary artist, musician, actor, intellectual, public official, entertainer/performer, journalist, or in other kinds of celebrity status, emphatically proclaim, "I just want to be considered as an literary artist, musician, actor, intellectual, public official, entertainer/performer, or journalist without consideration of my being Black." And indeed many commentators and pundits with the intention of presenting complimentary remarks, thus simply pronounce, "X is not *merely* a great *Black* artist but X is a great artist." Or even worse, in my estimation, they would say that "X is not just a Black artist but a great American artist." The latter statement actually goes beyond the abstract universalism in the former case and replaces the particularity of race with the particularity of a putative national identity as "American."

Malcolm X presents a powerful critique of such thinking. "He [the Uncle Tom Negro] wants to be an American rather than to be Black. He wants to be something other than what he is. And knowing that America is a white country, and he knows he can't be Black and an American too. So he never calls himself Black. He calls himself an American Negro—a Negro in America."[3] I say more on the issue of national identity and Blackness later in the chapter.

Today, as I gathered my thoughts on the question of Blackness as a philosophical object of inquiry, I reflected back on the fact that at one point, not long ago, Black philosophers debated over whether there could be intellectual (philosophical) merit to such an undertaking. Some years ago, Professor William Banner of Howard University, whose area of expertise was ethics, took a stand against adjoining philosophy in any way to Blackness.[4] Other Black philosophers—particularly Professors William R. Jones and Francis

Thomas—challenged Banner's position, and Jones brilliantly countered the notion that philosophy transcended race (and specifically Blackness) in his classic essay on "The Legitimacy and Necessity for a Black Philosophy: Some Preliminary Considerations."[5] Jones argues that the problem about the concept of "Black" in Black philosophy centered on the confusion of the meaning of "Black." Where "Black" is thought of as "exclusively a *racial* designation and, accordingly, race is the necessary organizing principle of a black philosophy . . . however . . . 'black' connotes an ethnic or cultural—not a racial—grouping. The experience, history, and culture are the controlling categories for a black philosophy—not chromosomes."[6] He further adds:

> This confusion regarding the connotation of "black" would quickly evaporate if we adopted the nomenclature of "Afro-American" instead of "black." That is not to say that an Afro-American philosophy will totally avoid a discussion of race. One must recognize that precisely because of their situation in America as an oppressed *racial* minority, the history and culture of blacks has been marked by the factor of race. For this reason it is materially impossible to comprehend the black experience and ignore the racial factor, but this is a consequence of the historical context rather than an inner logic of a black philosophy.[7]

Jones claims that given the fact that Black connotes ethnicity as well as race, then just as there is the public recognition of something called "Greek" philosophy, surely we must recognize the legitimacy of a Black philosophy. Jones asked, how was it possible to talk of Greek philosophy and not acknowledge that the universality of philosophy cannot be abstracted from concrete particularity? Black philosophy was another instance of the concrete particularity that in fact grounded philosophy in all of its universality.

Jones's marvelous piece, first published in 1977–1978, has tremendous value for us even today and ought to be mandatory reading in all courses focused on the philosophy of the Black experience and the philosophy of race. Not to mention that this essay has an acute value for those courses where the concern is with the history of African American philosophers and the philosophy of African American studies.

The great significance of the polemics about how philosophy is related to Blackness inexorably led some of us to higher philosophical ground, viz., what portends as the philosophical exploration into the very nature of Blackness arises to become a most pressing concern. Jones's and Thomas's efforts to establish the link between Blackness and philosophy were crucial initiatives for me. For if there is no tie between philosophy and Blackness then notions about a subfield dubbed *the philosophy of the Black experience* merely transpire as a moot question. At the very least, we would be hard pressed to justify a newsletter under the sanction of the American Philosophical Association and its Committee on Blacks in Philosophy called *Philosophy and the Black Experience.* Over the course of the past two years, I have joined with George Yancy to continue the efforts of other (previously inclined) Black philosophers to accent how the philosophy of the Black experience is one of the anchors in the intellectual thrust to diversify the doing of philosophy as well as to illuminate theoretically the struggle for Black liberation.

From the vantage point of our prior historical development to our present stage of contemporary problems in the discipline of philosophy, Black philosophers have wrestled with the philosophical meaning, import, and consequences of being Black in a racist society. Both professional and nonprofessional philosophers alike, of African descent in this country, have taken the traditional problems surrounding ontology, epistemology, axiology, and other subfields of philosophy and viewed them in light of the social predicament of being Black while living in a white supremacist society.

Although there are those who would call such inquiries an exercise in a *Black philosophical perspective*, I think of this mission as a philosophical quest to comprehend the *Black experience* in all of its ramifications. The difference between a *Black philosophical perspective* and *the philosophical comprehension of the Black experience* is a matter about how one ought to conceive of the Black condition and its relationship to philosophy. Is Blackness a particular philosophical perspective or is it the object of investigation?

Black philosophy, in my estimation, is more a question of a philosophy that engages the Black experience and condition than a case of representing a unitary philosophical view, which is shared by all or even most Black people. I have critiqued efforts to claim a monolithic Black/Afrocentric perspective in my articles, "The Afrocentric Project: The Quest for Particularity and the Negation of Objectivity" and "Black and White Contra Left and Right? The Dialectics of Ideological Critique in African American Studies."[8]

Given that the thrust and substance of those articles was directed primarily at the pitfalls of what Remi Fani-Kayode calls "Blackism" or of what Molefi Asante dubs "Afrocentricity," one should not conclude that my critique is on a par with Banner's attack on the philosophical import of Blackness.[9] Far from it: what is at stake is the locus of Blackness in both its subjective and objective dimensions. Therefore, we uncover the dialectics of a cognitive process in which Blackness serves as both our experiential starting point and the object of our investigation.

This is why my critique over the nature of Black or African American studies is not in concert with Banner's wholesale rejection of Black philosophy as a species of Black studies. Black studies or African American studies is not the source of the problem; in fact, I submit, it provides the solution to it. Intellectual work on the question of Blackness (I take this to be what is generically claimed for the scope and substance of Black studies) encompasses a host of disciplines including philosophy. In substance, the perspective adjoined to *Black* studies was a matter of carrying out *studies* on and in *Blackness* and surely philosophy was critical to this project.

Indeed, we ought not overlook the fact that the contemporary pursuit of the philosophical investigation into Blackness grew out of a larger movement to systematically engage the Black experience as an intellectual enterprise. This movement was initially labeled Black studies, and Black studies proponents faced opposition from those like Banner who insisted that Blackness was something we must overcome rather than affirm. But this affirmation of Blackness at a popular/mass level via the Black Power movement penultimately gave rise to the need for the intellectual and philosophical justification for its (Blackness's) very existence as a material condition and as a presumptive (conceptual) context. However, the sight for launching the philosophy of the Black experience was not the professional philosophy department in higher education. It was quite evident that philosophy departments were havens for nurturing the old classical notion of higher education (read: white and Western orientations toward formal study). Nonetheless, Black studies advocates confronted this philosophical bias about history and culture along with its adjoining Eurocentric traditions in the curriculum of higher education.[10]

Black studies called into question the reigning ideology of white supremacy, and the great number of lily-white philosophy departments found Black studies as much a threat as they found Marxism to be during the 1950s—McCarthy—era.[11] Therefore, it came as no surprise that the academic pursuit of Blackness within philosophy departments oftentimes considerably lagged behind Black studies programs and departments. The contemporary emergence of the philosophy of the Black experience owes more to Black studies than it does to philosophy as a professional field of study. With a few exceptions, the journals that initially published works in the philosophy of the Black experience were more often than not in Black studies as opposed to philosophy. This general condition (Black studies nurturing the philosophy of the Black experience) no doubt had an impact on my own evolution as a student and scholar of philosophy.

Although I took a number of philosophy courses under Dr. Thomas at Central State University, I made the choice to major in Black studies (along with political science) and this enabled me to search intellectually into how my life had been shaped by the Black experience. I had lived in a Black community and attended predominantly Black schools, and the overwhelming number of my significant others were Black people. Now with a major in Black studies, at the HBCU Central State University in Wilberforce, Ohio, my academic work was congruent with my life experiences. It became clear that what usually passed off as a universal education was in fact a false universality that either through the sin of omission or by wanton distortion relegated the Black experience to a marginal position and to an inferior status with reference to the white historical and cultural experience.

Black studies established an intellectual space for scholars and even for that handful of philosophers (both inside and outside the ranks of professional philosophy) so that they might offer us significant insights into the multiplicity of ways that philosophical inquiry into Blackness would ignite a new dynamic engine for intellectual exchange. Black studies opened its door to intellectuals who were not professional philosophers to engage in different aspects of the philosophy of the Black experience. The contributions of Percy Johnston, for example, are an important yet neglected chapter. This Black philosopher (without portfolio) was dedicated to erecting a foundation for the philosophy of the Black experience. He not only wrote articles and books but also launched the only Afro-American journal of philosophy.[12]

Furthermore, it was not a philosopher that pioneered the advancement into the philosophy of African American history; instead it was the late Afro-American historian Dr. Earl Thorpe who gave expression to *The Central Theme of Black History*.[13] Additionally, I remember how I became intellectually stimulated by the work of the Black historian Lerone Bennett who wrote one of the seminal essays on the philosophy of Blackness. His (1970) paper, entitled "The Challenge of Blackness," captured my critical attention. Moreover, the Institute of Black World, an African American think tank in Atlanta, Georgia, published Bennett's paper in a manner that amplified the affirmation of Blackness. So bold was this foray into Blackness that the paper carried the additional moniker of "Black Paper No. 1."[14] This obviously stood out in contrast to the more traditional notion of the "white" papers that were the usual stock of think tanks.

Reading the likes of Bennett and Jones and studying with Thomas were invigorating encounters that not only brought a certain academic rigor to my philosophical evolution but also enhanced my personal concerns about my own identity and being Black in this country. My Black education was directed at Black liberation and subsequently my own racial identity and its development was part and parcel of my future philosophical work.[15]

On Capturing the Philosophical Meaning of Blackness

From my studies, I concluded that *Black* was an adjective that described a people in racial terms. In one sense, *Black* simply replaced the name *Negro* in its function as a racial category. Consequently, I do not use *Black* as a noun or in the lower case rendering. The transformation of the adjective *Negro* into the noun *Negro* symbolizes the negation of Black humanity. The transformation meant, at the presumptive level, that Black people were less than fully human. This change in nomenclature was not just a matter of language. For when the word *Negro* was in vogue, we discover with regard to the material conditions of white supremacy, there was an intense push to reduce Africans into things or what is more basically the reification of social beings. In its linguistic usage, *Negro* as noun openly reflects the material reality of this reification of African American human beings into chattel, that is, things to be bought and sold as commodities. Bourgeois democracy simply meant that white workers sold their labor power in the form of a commodity, while Black people were reduced to commodities. Therefore, I do not refer to Black people as *Blacks* which is the equivalent of the former nomenclature *Negroes.* Hence I only employ *Black* as an adjective that describes people, persons, men, women, children, or humanity and I do not use *Black* in abstraction from some noun, which substitutes for the noun's capacity of denoting human beings or social institutions, for example, the Black church or the Black family.[16]

Moreover, I capitalize the word *Black* in view of the history to capitalize the term *Negro.* In the nineteenth century and far into the start of the twentieth century, *Negro* was generally not given caps. I argue that if *Black* is a replacement for the adjective *Negro,* and capitalizing *Negro* was the standard, then it follows that *Black* must be so written. Why is this a matter of significance? It is because the fight to capitalize *Negro* was a battle over the dignity of Black people's identity; a war waged over the presumptions dominant in a racist society about Black (Negro) people. Although it is true that *negro* derives from the Spanish term for *black,* nonetheless the word *Negro* does not signify just another name for a given color but it is a term that indicates for us what is a determinate racial identity. So therefore we must give the same consideration to the term *Black.*[17]

It is quite interesting that a number of scholarly journals, publishers, and editors often call attention to the use of sexist language and bar, for example, the employment of *man* as a generic word for humanity. Yet they fail to insist that *Black* also be capitalized and some even persist in the lower-case presentation of *Black.* Ironically, most insist on this given their own presupposition that *Black* acts only as a designator of color. Sometimes you can find statements that indicate the identity for specific groups such as Asian American, Native American, and even African American where upper-case letters are usually presented. However, "black" people also signify a similar type of identity, although lower-case letters are generally operative. Beyond the issue of the capitalization of *Black,* however, along quite similar lines, a considerable number of academic journals and publications still allow the use of terms such as *blackball* and *blacklisted*, which means they do not recognize that such terms are forms of racist speech.

Blackness is the Motivation Not the Orientation of My Philosophy

Given the aforementioned concerns, I want to continue my emphasis on how Blackness (as a predication of racial identity) plays an instrumental role in my life and why and how it is linked to the more philosophically (rigorously) considered definition I have of Blackness. In fact, I must admit that one major challenge for me, as a Black person who does philosophy, is to draw on the multifarious ways and modes that Blackness as a central aspect of my being in the world actually shapes the manner of my philosophical thinking. There is a sense in which there is this objective/subjective dialectic, where Blackness functions as the object of philosophical investigation as well as the existential grounds of my very personhood as subject. Hence, Blackness as an object of philosophical inquiry is intimately linked to who I am at the most fundamentally conceivable personal level. Of course, who I am is in part that of being a philosopher but I do not attempt, or even think that it is necessary, to try to initiate a separation between my role as a philosopher and the fact that I am a Black person. Dr. Charles Leander Hill, the philosopher/theologian and one-time president of Wilberforce College, gives voice to the spirit of my conviction about Blackness as a motivation for philosophical, and more generally, intellectual work. Indeed, Hill thinks our Blackness confers on us a special duty. Hill posits:

> [W]hile the scholar who is a Negro must devote to an objective, dispassionate search for truth like any other scholar, he would seem to me to be confronted with the additional responsibility of making known to the world of scholarship, any great mind that was lodged by accident of birth in a black body [sic]. This special or additional responsibility I gladly accept, and the results of the assumptions of this duty, you will read in the following pages.[18]

I only demarcate the concept of Blackness—as specified philosophical orientation—from Blackness as an object of philosophical inquiry. When Blackness is our object of philosophical investigation, the meaning of Blackness becomes a matter of discovery and is not a presumed given. If the meaning of Blackness is presupposed then it follows that Blackness should mandate how we actually do philosophy, that is, it is foundational to our philosophical orientation. Thus, we see that the Afrocentric approach to philosophy and Black philosophy are one and the same. Here we have Blackness/Africanity operating as an a priori orientation to philosophy. This is due to the presumption that Blackness (Africanity) is in effect an ideology or worldview.

In my own case, given my materialist philosophical perspective, there is no accepted or given meaning attached to Blackness. This is because the materialist conception of philosophy actually provides tools for comprehending the meaning of Blackness. It is the case that Blackness provides my motivation (for doing philosophy) but not my (philosophical) orientation, that is, my specified philosophical perspective. For me, the issue is not about *thinking* in *Black philosophical* terms; rather it is to *think philosophically about Blackness.* So, therefore, even though I disagree with the Afrocentric notion that one must think in terms of Black or African modes of philosophizing, I do not accept William Banner's position that Blackness is outside of the concerns of philosophical thought and investigation. What it means to be Black is a philosophical question and my Blackness cannot be separated from what motivates and informs my philosophical research.

One thing that struck my interest when reading some of the interviews in George Yancy's *17 Conversations* is the fact that there were a number of Black philosophers who thought that being Black was incidental and thus marginally important to their philosophical work. I, in turn, strongly contend that what it means to be Black in this country is decisive as to what comprises and represents my philosophical projects.[19]

Blackness as Material Conditions and the Problem of Capitalism and Racism

This position, on how Blackness fits into the equation of my philosophical practice, becomes even more important given my philosophical orientation. I am a Marxist-Leninist and I am aware that there is the mistaken viewpoint, on the part of some, that race is incidental and marginal to Marxism-Leninism. Many reach this conclusion due to their failure to grasp how the Marxist emphasis on class and class conflict is congruent with the analysis of racism. However, in spite of this prevailing assumption, the Marxist materialist conception of history with its accent on class contradictions, particularly those (contradictions) connected with capitalism, does not render race and racism as marginal or incidental. Instead, I argue that historically it was capitalism that gave rise to racism. You cannot fully comprehend racism in all of its complexities without an understanding of capitalism, which is the material basis of racism. The critique of capitalism provides an illuminating perspective on and context for the critical study of racism.

The history of the slave trade, slavery, and colonialism is a manifestation of capitalism. I will not undertake the task of outlining that history here. What is necessary, from the standpoint of a philosophical justification, is that given the history of capitalism, and the ancillary development of the slave trade, slavery, and colonialism, it was racism that provided the ideological basis for legitimating the exploitation of African people. To justify the ruthless exploitation and oppression of Black people, racism served as an ideological weapon and also as the material conditions on which white supremacy became all-encompassing under capitalism. While race is not reducible to class, nevertheless it is true that racism is grounded in determinate (bourgeois) class relations. A thoroughgoing class analysis of capitalism must of necessity include a critique of racism and its function within the ensemble of social relations. This ensemble I term as the material conditions for race, racism, and Blackness.

In my view, what constitutes the meaning of Blackness cannot be abstracted away from the history of racism. In fact, I can say without hesitation that racism is in the foreground of all my discussions about Blackness. This is because the very concept of Blackness derives from a definitive set of material conditions and a presumptive context of competing ideas, ideals, and values. The combination of material conditions (the ensemble of social relations, institutions, and practices) and the presumptive context (ideological forms) in which Blackness gains a measure of expression are rudimentary sources for uncovering the nature of Blackness. I use the concept "material conditions" to include capitalism as a mode of production. However, the material conditions of racism also incorporate the material manifestation of racism, which is over and beyond strictly bourgeois relations of production. My notion of presumptive context is an articulation of Marx's concept of ideological superstructure.

I first offer a definition of racism that highlights both the presumptive context and materiality of racism. Next I outline what is the definitive set of material conditions composing racism under bourgeois hegemony and then explain the dynamics of the presumptive context adjoined to this set of material conditions. My definition of racism, something I have taught for over thirty years, includes not only recognition of racist attitudes and beliefs (presumptive context) but as well takes into account the role of behavior and institutions (its materiality).

> Racism is not just the attitude or belief that there exist superior and inferior races but more importantly it is behavior (social practices) and institutions that give material support to such attitudes and beliefs by the actual (material) suppression of the supposed inferior group.

The above definition of racism accounts for racist attitudes (feelings that lack consciously derived justifications) and beliefs (consciously established justifications) and yet we see that they are not the necessary conditions for the existence of racism. White people who just feel that they do not like (or even more strongly hate) Black people but cannot explain why they have such feelings are attitudinal racists. When we observe whites who hold certain beliefs about the inferior character of Black people, what we witness are overt explanations that justify such beliefs.

In both cases we have forms of racism that are consciously articulated. But, from the materialist perspective, consciousness does not ultimately determine social being—the material conditions that harbor racism. Although racist attitudes and beliefs cannot exist without the requisite material conditions, racism can exist without conscious aims and purposes. This is particularly evident when racism assumes an institutionalized character. Here what is important is not racist *intent* but rather the *impact* of racism.

The institutional impact of racism (systemic racism) does not require conscious intentions or aims, but only those institutions and social relations that perpetuate the actual (material) suppression of Black people. This is why much of the legal discussion around affirmative action often gets bogged down when the matter of demonstrating intent is presupposed as salient. Here it is accepted that racism requires a motive or intention in order to act in a racist fashion.

Yet, institutional racism overrides the notion of social atomism and methodological individualism, where individual action is thought to be at the source of racism as social practice. The power vested in institutions has a cumulative impact and where the material relations of racism (white supremacy) are predominant then those relations need not immediately originate around goals of white supremacy. Where attitudinal and belief forms of racism are preeminent, then conscious articulation of racial differences is most pronounced. It appears as if such articulations are themselves at the basis of racism. Some people reason that only in relinquishing talk of racial differences can the possibility arise for eradicating racism. The presumption is that the solution to racism is at root a matter of color blindness.

This is why the color-blind thesis is often used as the justification on the part of both conservatives and liberals to deny the need for race-based solutions to the persistence of racism. For the former (as well as the latter) the process of transcending race (as a social category) is equated with eradicating racism. Given that attitudinal and belief forms of racism require a conscious acknowledgment of race and racial categories and in turn institutional racism does not, it follows then that the elimination of public recognition of race as a social category fails to uproot institutional racism. In effect, we have an ostrich head approach to racism.

What this means for me is that when a white person gives an argument to the effect that I am not seen as a Black person, but rather seen as a generic person without the "baggage of Blackness," then color blindness negates Black existence. Far from having a satisfactory solution to racism, we really have the perpetuation of racism under the guise of color blindness. Color blindness presumes that racial differences are stubborn anachronisms that have failed to make their exit from this country. The presumptive context for race and thus Blackness on such grounds as color blindness is a back-door approach to ignoring the material conditions that sustain institutional racism. Here the arid abstraction of false universality is not just the old sin of omission, where white people in their particularity are assumed to be what is universal, but also where particularity of Blackness is thought of as an occlusion to universality. Here the cry is to dispense with all forms of particularity in the name of universality. Subsequently, if we return momentarily to the Banner/Jones polemic we discover that the heart of the matter was whether or not the instantiation of the universal mandates the concrete particular as a logical necessity. If we answer the question in the affirmative then my own humanity (universality) is thus grounded in my Blackness (particularity). To deny my Blackness is to deny my humanity and not as the color-blind presupposition holds—as a measure to affirm my humanity.

Yet, if we follow the logic of my thesis about capitalism and racism then it follows that Blackness originates from racism. To justify the exploitation of African people, racism affixed derogatory meanings on the racial category of Blackness. One could ask, since the very definition of Blackness originates in racism does that mean we must dispense with Blackness as a form of identity on the grounds of its origins? Are the racist presumptions about Blackness solitary and static, especially given that they are reflections of the material conditions of racism? And does not the Marxist materialist approach uphold the idea that the presumptive context is derivative of material conditions?

Yes, it is true that the presumptive context is ontologically dependent on material conditions. In the case of racism, the presumptive context—ideas, ideals, and values concerning Blackness—is derived from the fact that racism is always under contention, thus Blackness is not static and solitary. Racist ideas, ideals, and values have always been contested and this is due to the fact that the material conditions of racism were constantly fought over through the course of history.

From the very first slave insurrections on slave ships crossing the Atlantic via the Middle Passage, the material conditions of racism were under assault. The resistance to racism (in terms of the various forms of social institutions, relations, and practices) is reflected in the presumptive context of contending ideas. The racist presumptions about Blackness were resolutely challenged from the start. Slave revolts, Maroon communities, the Underground Railroad, the invisible institution, and slave songs were both open and disclosed forms of resistance to the definitions affixed to the racist conception of Blackness. Although supporters of the subordination of Black people to white rule are advocates of racist concepts about Blackness, Black people themselves have not quietly and passively accommodated to such thinking. Blackness has always been contested and struggled over and the heroic history of Black resistance demonstrates this point. So now we can explore my efforts to launch a definition of Blackness.

Toward a Minimalist Definition of Blackness: Social Category or Social Construction

I want to offer what I call a minimalist definition of Blackness (MDB). The purpose of a minimalist (in contrast to a maximalist) definition is that it leaves open the option to add on to the defining terms that are initially given. Although a minimalist definition does not exhaust the full spectrum of possibilities, it can serve as a sufficient and adequate starting point. However, a minimalist definition of Blackness—although not exhaustive—must nevertheless meet specified criteria of an adequacy test. The first specification centers on the problem of how to develop a broad enough classification that encompasses the antithetical aspects of Blackness as a contested zone between negative and positive views on Blackness. The trick is in providing enough space to include the fact that the presumptive context is always a contradictory one. And we must constantly keep in mind that the ubiquitous movement of contending ideas, ideals, and values that characterizes the presumptive context of Blackness requires an all-inclusive category, which must not at the same time fall into the trap of trying to transcend Blackness as such.

In other words, it is not enough for my minimalist definition to take one or the other side of the antithetical ideals, ideas, or values under contention about Blackness. However, this all-encompassing scope is not the same as holding a neutral position with respect to the battle of ideals and ideas concerning Blackness. The function of the minimalist definition is to offer a broad enough (sufficiently adequate) account so that the dialectical contradiction comprising the very dynamics of the presumptive context of Blackness is under the minimalist regulative domain. If we grant there is more than a solitary and static definition of Blackness, we have to at least attempt to capture it in its motion, change, and development. So how is it that we can do this?

An initial condition is the presupposition that the definition of Blackness in its particularity derives from the material conditions of this country. Given that we have other white supremacist areas of the world, this clearly suggests that Blackness is also global as well as particular. For now, our purpose is to focus on the particularity of this country. Given this initial condition, we can then proceed on and make two primary assertions. I must point out that while what follows are ostensibly assertions, they are not without some form of implicit justification.

The justificatory measure here (in terms of the minimalist definition) is more a matter of drawing from history and material conditions surrounding the idea of Blackness than the formulation of an explicit a priori principle. Given a certain understanding about the history of African Americans, white supremacy, capitalism, slavery, and colonialism, we can establish an implicit justification on historical grounds. In other words, the justification of the minimalist definition is driven more by history than abstract logical (ahistorical) considerations. This is why the minimalist definition of Blackness is at root and branch—materialist.[20]

In stark contrast to such a materialist and historical approach, an explicit principle of justification can be derived from a strictly analytical process and precisely in an a priori manner. For example, an idealist (a priori) principle that is self-sufficient need not require any reference or accommodation to history. An example of this would be framing an a priori principle for the claim that the essence of Blackness was a matter of consciousness or mind. Here history in its ruthless, brutal, and ever-present reality can be ignored in the fashion of a kind like Stoicism and one could claim that Blackness was in its essence a matter of culturally (consciously) returning to ancient Africa. Although this idealist approach appears to be at core historical, nonetheless, in its full ramifications, it is ahistorical, since in essence what is considered as Blackness/Africanity ignores the historical reality and material facts surrounding various Black people's departure from Africa (via slavery in the diaspora) and that this marks a qualitative change from (a negation of) what is more appropriately African historical reality. Let us now turn to the two historically derived assertions on which the minimalist definition of Blackness rests.

The first assertion is that Blackness is negatively constituted such that a Black person is one who is not a white person. (Blackness is a particular form of being nonwhite. Keep in mind that Blackness does not exhaust the category nonwhite; it is only one of its many particular forms.) Let us call this our negative pole.

The second assertion centers on identifying a positive pole, which asserts that Blackness derives from African ancestry. Black people are African descendents in contrast to other dark people who are descendents from other parts of the world. So our complete answer translates into the composite assertion that Blackness indicates the presence of a nonwhite person of African descent.

This composite definition directs us to a racial identity rather than a form of national identity. Hence, while all African Americans (a form of national identity) are Black, not all Black people are African American. Ghanaians, Kenyans, Nigerians, and Ethiopians are Black on this account, but they are not African Americans. When we say that the African American is a Black person, we have in this instance what amounts to "is" as predication and not what is more properly an "is" of identification. What is most apparent given our MDB are not the antithetical positions, at the presumptive level, concerning the question of whether Black people are nonwhite people of African descent. All parties actually agree that Blackness is based on these two criteria. Thus the source of contention within the presumptive context is not the MDB.

What is under contention, in the presumptive context of Blackness, cannot be our two poles—nonwhite and having African descent. Who are Black people is not at stake in the contest between racists and anti-racists over Blackness. This accord is based on the fact that our racial distinction between Black and white is not merely a presumption but furthermore is a material condition. Those who are slaves, or oppressed under Jim Crow laws and later de facto segregation, are the oppressed because they are nonwhite and of African descent, in a word, which results from their Blackness. So if there is this agreement about the definition of Blackness, what is under contention?

Well, I think the point of conflict resides in the respective valuations and judgments that each side affixes to Blackness. The MDB is adequate precisely because it is not the definition of Blackness under dispute. Nevertheless, Blackness is a social category and all social categories have adjoining valuations. And in societies where there are conflicting social relations there are contested valuations, which are contested both at the level of material conditions and presumptive context. The former addresses the real (life and death) issues of material existence and the latter is the ideological struggle over identity, meaning of life, culture, values, and ideals.

The racist perspective on Blackness entails a negative judgment about people who are nonwhite and of African descent. And the antithetical position (affirming Blackness) embodies a positive evaluation of those that are nonwhite and are of African descent. Blackness is a social category that rest on two key components. One is what I term phenotypic description and the other I call genotypic classification. The need for the former grows directly from the material conditions that demanded a way of justifying the exploitation of Africans as slaves. Slavery, unlike indentured servitude, took an absolute racial form. All slaves were Black people. Although some Black people were not slaves, all Black people faced racism. Since slavery was restricted to Africans, now racially designated as Black, the minimalist definition of Blackness facilitated dividing the population on racial grounds. Nonwhite became a matter of phenotypic differences between Africans and those of European descent. Skin color was the most obvious difference; hence, Black skin was decisive. Nevertheless, since miscegenation, primarily through the rape of Black women held as slaves, resulted in a group of people of African descent that were phenotypically quite similar and in some cases indistinguishable from whites, identifying those of African descent became increasingly important to racist power relations in slavery and on until the present. This is where the practice of genotypic classification filled the gaps and loopholes of phenotypic description.

When phenotypic description proved ineffective in differentiating who was Black, then African descent, whatever the degree, was the telling factor. If nonwhite proved to be beyond visible description, then African descent would be the dividing line. Demarcating Black and white people was foundationally subject to how race was played out in the prevailing material relations, initially in slavery and then later under Jim Crow segregation laws. Descent from the mother was the determining factor for African descent. If your father was even Thomas Jefferson, and your mother was a Black woman (Sally Hemmings), then you were a Black person. Race in its function, as social category, clearly followed and reflected what were the (objective) material relations governing Black existence.

Now it may be apparent that I do not refer to Blackness as a social construction and instead I have called it throughout a *social category*.[21] I differ from the social constructionist viewpoint around three key issues. First, I think one of the chief concerns for (some) social constructionists is the question of the reduction of race (especially in view of its social character) to that of a natural disposition or category. The reduction of race to matters of nature facilitated scientific racism, which drew upon Social Darwinism and the natural and physical sciences as proof of the inferiority of Black people. Today the evidence shows that such "scientific" racist claims amounted to pseudoscience. Nature cannot explain the meaning of race, racism, and Blackness; and for that matter it fails to explain Whiteness. Since phenotypic description and genotypic classification were prominent as means for deciphering race among the pseudoscientists, then the quantitative measuring of physical indicators of race presented a certain veneer that made race/Blackness become a matter of physical/natural scientific computation. This concern about the naturalistic fallacy of race and Blackness is a legitimate issue, yet one that is incorrectly addressed.

At the heart of the matter, I think, is a certain propensity toward voluntarism, where reality is open ended and people can even construct their own reality, their own identity, and even their own racial categories without restriction. However, on the one hand, we have already seen that the presumptive context of Blackness derives from determinate material conditions and these conditions set limits on our categories. Social constructionism, on the other hand, is a form of activism that defies the static naturalism associated with racial categories à la natural categories. The *nature* of Blackness, social constructionists argue, is not *natural* at all. I want to respond by saying that it is true that racial categories are social and not natural categories. However, given that all social categories derive from social practices, institutions, and relations, then the additional use of the term *construction* adds nothing to the table. There is, as Ian Hacking points out to us, a certain redundancy. To be a social category is to result from social practices within the sphere of social relations and institutions.[22]

Social categories result from people acting as social beings who are wedded to determinate social relations. Social practice, of which labor is the most fundamental, transforms nature. We as natural beings actually transform ourselves in social activity. Why then insist that Blackness is a social construction since being a social category entails social practice? I think that my second point about social constructionism is instructive here. This is where the problem of essentialism becomes paramount for social constructionists.

When reality is classified in terms of natural categories then the idea of natural kind looms prominently in the picture. Natural kind contra social category speaks to something called essence or essential difference. The nature of a tree is essentially different than a horse and, indeed, the nature of a horse is essentially different from a zebra. Since in nature (with natural categories) we have essential differences, our social constructionists fear not only the naturalist reduction of Blackness, but also essentialism. Once committed to voluntarism, to a protean world without objective material constraints, then essence itself is problematic.

So therefore we must ask, are there essential differences that are social and not natural in kind? The social constructionist response is to reject all of forms of essential differences under the rubric of essentialism. But quite obviously there are social categories that are essentially different than one another. Most notably, in light of our discussion above about the word *Black* as noun and adjective, human beings are essentially different than the social "things" in the world. Reification conflates the difference and reduces humanity from its proper locus in the world. What about essential differences among human beings?

Now what is trivially true with regard to humans and things cannot suffice for different groups of human beings. The essential differences holding between groups of human beings are not natural but social in character. Essence derives from the social content ancillary to social relations, institutions, and practices. Capitalists hold an essentially different position in bourgeois society than workers. What it means to be a capitalist and what it means to be a worker exhibit essential differences that often times are a matter of life and death. The same holds for race and Blackness. What it means to be Black in a white supremacist society manifests some essential differences from what its means to be white. Essence as a category is necessary to making distinctions in the social as well as the natural world.

Do the essential differences between Black people (nonwhite people of African descent) and white people mean there are no commonalities? Are we going down the road of Black separatism or Black nationalism, where we assume that there is a condition such that there are sun people versus ice people and the like? Our MDB is not an abstraction away from history; it results from concrete, dynamic, changing conditions encompassed within the process of history. Indeed, people make history but not as they would always like for it to be. They are born into history, material relations and conditions of which they had no part in determining. This is what social constructionism misses in its dissertation on Blackness. Black people are not only a part of racial social relations but also are themselves divided into classes. And many working-class Black people and some bourgeois Black folks share in essentially the same class interests as their white counterparts.

Colin Powell shares more in common with George Bush than the multitude of Black and white soldiers, most from the working class, who fought in Iraq. Our MDB does not deny that Collin Powell is a Black man; he is a nonwhite person of African descent. But race as a social indicator is only one part of our social identity. Class positions are decisive in any analysis of Blackness. We cannot argue that Powell is not *really* Black; to do so would be to abandon our MDB criteria. If we would say that he was not "really" Black, we would have substituted for our objective measurement, a subjectivist version of Blackness, one that rested on some notion of what it is to be in terms of "authenticity." No, Powell is a Black man and he is not acting his color, instead he is acting out his bourgeois class interest.[23] We cannot use race as a basis to critique him. Black people have fought in every war this country has been engaged in; lest we forget that Ben Davis and Chappie James are too a part of Black history? Therefore, we must put Blackness into its concrete context and we must continue to affirm it in view of racist assaults. Yet we must not romanticize it and cast it as an abstract virtue that stands apart as an entity in itself and of itself. To be Black is a necessary but insufficient condition to evaluate Powell's political stance. Blackness is one of several important social categories that we must seriously bear in mind.

Notes

1. See Malcolm X, "Twenty Million Black People in a Political, Economic and Mental Prison," in Bruce Perry, ed., *Malcolm X: The Last Speeches* (New York: Pathfinder Press, 1989), 32.

2. Later, in my education, Mr. George Galloway, one of my history teachers at Dunbar High School in Dayton, Ohio, introduced us to Lerone Bennett's *Before the Mayflower*. We not only studied this text every week but also had a Negro History Week program in February. Via his Association for the Study of Negro Life and History, Dr. Carter G. Woodson institutionalized the idea of Negro History Week in 1926 and by the 1970s it became known as Black History Month. In 1977, I was involved directly with Dr. Woodson's organization as a co-author in a collaborative publication with J. Rupert Picott et al., entitled *Afro-American Studies: A Guide for Teachers*, which was designed for using in Black History Month programs and published by the Associated Publishers.

3. Malcolm X, "Twenty Million Black People in a Political, Economic and Mental Prison."

4. William A. Banner, *Ethics: An Introduction to Moral Philosophy* (New York: Charles Scribner's Sons, 1968). William A. Banner, *Moral Norms and Human Affairs* (Gainesville: University Press of Florida, 1981).

5. For an account of Dr. Francis A. Thomas's influence on my philosophical development, please consult John H. McClendon III, "My Tribute to a Teacher, Mentor, Philosopher and Friend: Dr. Francis A. Thomas (March 16, 1913 to September 2001)" *APA Newsletter on Philosophy and the Black Experience* V. 3, n. 1 (Fall 2003), 36–37. In this same issue of the *APA Newsletter on Philosophy and the Black Experience* there are tributes from several others outlining Dr. Thomas's various contributions. They include tributes from Professors William R. Jones, Leonard Harris, Jeff Crawford, and Ms. Cheryl D. Marcus. Dr. Jones's article first appeared as William R. Jones, "The Legitimacy and Necessity of Black Philosophy: Some Preliminary Considerations," *The Philosophical Forum*, V. IX, n. 2–3 (Winter-Spring 1977–1978), and was republished in *Yours in the Struggle: Celebrating the Devotion to Freedom, Special Collection of Works by Dr. William R. Jones* (Tallahassee: The FSU Foundation, 1999). All subsequent citations are to the *Yours in the Struggle* republication.

6. William R. Jones, "The Legitimacy and Necessity of Black Philosophy: Some Preliminary Considerations" 2, a-b.

7. William R. Jones, "The Legitimacy and Necessity of Black Philosophy: Some Preliminary Considerations" 2, a-b.

8. John H. McClendon, "The Afrocentric Project: The Quest for Particularity and the Negation of Objectivity," *Explorations in Ethnic Studies* V. 18, n. 1 (January 1995). John H. McClendon III, "Black and White or Left and Right?: Ideological Critique in African American Studies," *APA Newsletter on Philosophy and the Black Experience* (V. 2, n. 1), Fall 2002.

9. Remi Fani-Kayode, *Blackism* (Lagos, Nigeria: privately printed, 1965). Molefi Asante, *Afrocentricity: The Theory of Social Change* (Buffalo: Amulefi Publishing Co., 1980).

10. Instances where the debate entered into philosophy journals included when the African American Berkeley Eddins responded with Berkley Eddins, "Philosophical Perennis and Black Studies," *The Southern Journal of Philosophy* V. 9, n. 2 (Summer 1971); and also Paul Olscamp, "How Ought Philosophy Departments Respond to the Demand for Black Studies," *The Southern Journal of Philosophy* V. 9, n. 2 (Summer 1971).

11. On McCarthyism, see John McCumber, *Time in the Ditch: American Philosophy and the McCarthy Era* (Evanston: Northwestern University Press, 2001).

12. Percy E. Johnston, *Afro-American Philosophies: Selected Readings from Jupiter Hammond to Eugene C. Holmes* (Upper Montclair: Montclair State College Press, 1970). Johnston's journal was the *Afro-American Journal of Philosophy*. He was the editor in chief and I served in 1982–1983 as an associate editor of the journal.

13. Earl Thorpe, *The Central Theme of Black History* (Durham: Seeman Printery, 1969). Also see Earl Thorpe, *The Desertion of Man: a Critique of Philosophy of History* (Baton: Ortlieb Press, 1958). Also see Percy E. Johnston, "Black Theories of History and Black Historiography," *Dasein* 1969.

14. Lerone Bennett, "The Challenge of Blackness," *Black Paper No. 1* (Atlanta: Institute of the Black World, 1970).

15. For a treatment of the philosophy of liberation see Lerone Bennett, "Of Time, Space and Revolution, Beyond Either/Or: A Philosophy of Liberation," in Lerone Bennett, *The Challenge of Blackness* (Chicago: Johnson Publishing Co., 1972).

16. For a critical look at Negro and Black as concepts in racial identity, see Malcolm X, *Malcolm X on Afro-American History* (New York: Pathfinder Press, 1974), 14–18.

17. Richard B. Moore, "The Name Negro—Its Origin and Evil Use," in W. Burghardt Turner and Joyce Moore Turner, eds., *Richard B. Moore, Caribbean Militant in Harlem* (Bloomington: Indiana University Press, 1988).

18. Charles Leander Hill, "William Ladd, The Black Philosopher from Guinea," 20–21.

19. George Yancy, *African American Philosophers: 17 Conversations* (New York: Routledge, 1998).

20. My materialist conception of identity theory and African American Studies is also given in John H. McClendon III, "From Cultural Nationalism to Cultural Criticism: Philosophical Idealism, Pragmatic Illusions and the Politics of Identity," in Carole Boyce Davies, *Decolonizing the Academy: African Diaspora Studies* (Trenton: Africa World Press, 2003), 3–26.

21. For another treatment that I present on social constructionism, see John H. McClendon III, "Black and White or Left and Right?: Ideological Critique in African American Studies."

22. Ian Hacking, *The Social Construction of What?* (Cambridge: Harvard University Press, 1999), 12.

23. I have also addressed the question of Powel's class position vis-à-vis his Blackness in John H. McClendon III, "On the Nature of Whiteness and the Ontology of Race: Toward a Dialectical Materialist Analysis," in George Yancy, ed., *What White Looks Like: African American Philosophers on the Whiteness Question* (New York: Routledge, 2004), 211–26.

14

Knowing Blackness, Becoming Blackness, Valuing Blackness

Kal Alston
University of Illinois, Urbana-Champaign

When I teach courses to nonphilosophers that have philosophical content (which constitute almost all my courses teaching teachers), I have found it is good to give them three "half dollar" concepts with which to work. I suggest to them that, as educators, there is no press on them whatsoever to "become" philosophers, but that it does behoove them to think about their educational practices philosophically. Part of what I am seeking to exhort them to engage in is a more rigorous regime of self-examination; another part is to use philosophy's analytical functions to beef up whatever critical and interpretive skills they may already have. The idea that they really only have to concentrate on learning three conceptual frameworks and (this is the part they like) applying them to what happens in their classrooms keeps them calm and focused. True, it is not precisely accurate to say that they only have to learn three concepts, but as that great philosopher Walt Disney suggested through Mary Poppins, "A spoonful of sugar. . . ."

What are these three conceptual frameworks? I tell them on day one that philosophers (in the West) have been very interested in epistemological, ontological, and axiological approaches to enquiry about the conditions and problems of humans. Feel free to disagree, but these three rubrics really work in education and learning the half dollar words allows them to impress their friends. We are concerned in those classes with knowing, being/becoming, and valuing as these frame societal, cultural, and educational enterprises.

One of those enterprises comprises American race and racism, which remain entrenched stumbling blocks to the realization of education's full potential—whether as an essential public good or as a mechanism for developing democratic citizens or even as a sorter for the economic good of the nation. The invitation to contribute to this book as a black philosopher resonated immediately as calling for an extension of the ways that I have simplified some of the themes of philosophy for my students. Using these three frameworks will, I hope, illuminate both the convergent and divergent workings of race in general and blackness in particular.

Knowing Blackness

As a graduate student in philosophy, other black graduate students (in the respectable fields of sociology, literature, and biology) shook their heads at me. What possible good could it do for black people to study dry-as-dust tomes by the deadest, whitest men in history? I admit to having no ready or satisfactory answer; I simply loved the hermeneut's life and Aristotle into the bargain. I like to think that I could do better with that question now. Two primary reasons for that new confidence: first, that there are the livest, non-whitest philosophers (Lucius Outlaw, Charles Mills, Lewis Gordon, Leonard Harris, and others) whose work is at the same time original, responsive, and recuperative; second, the proclivities of philosophers to make distinctions, to analyze concepts, and to interpret values mean that it should come as no surprise that race crops up in eighteenth- and nineteenth-century Europe as a site bringing to bear Enlightenment understandings of the human condition.

I would not presume to do here in a very few pages what others, such as Outlaw, Mills, and Gordon, for example, have done so elegantly in the long form.[1] That is, I cannot tell a history of race and racism that draws out the many times and places in which philosophy as a field and as a practice have been implicated. From the very taxonomies of the human soul to analyses of the essence of "species," philosophy can be found in the very heart of racial formation, both in fact and in discursive form. From philosophy of mind to the notion of alterity to the use of philosophical tropes in critical race theory, there is no place that race is that philosophy is not.

But instead of focusing on that important history, I speculate briefly here on the significance of the specificity of the black philosopher in the production of racial knowing at the so-called "end of race." In this context, I refer to racial knowing as a knowing about race and the consequences of that knowledge for responding to racism and for living in blackness. If one is the least bit epistemologically inclined, it seems clear that philosophy's contribution to racial knowing would have to be something like producing sites in which knowledge about race as a category and phenomenon could be taken up with a genuine interest in the means of producing, reproducing, distributing, and interpreting that knowledge. One would perhaps be somewhat skeptical about how the identity of the knower connects (or doesn't) to the knowledge at hand.

Feminist philosophy has tangled with the thorny issues of essentialism and essentialist epistemological positions around sex—in which "women's ways of knowing" folks clash with the constructivist or rationalist groups—sometimes productively and sometimes not so much. Interestingly, the idea of sexual essences is being troubled by the science around sex, gender, and trans-identity. The same roiling water surrounds the "sciences" of race, perhaps to an even greater extent at present since one would be hard pressed to find a student of race who would deny the historical and social construction of race as we "normally" conceive of it in the contemporary U.S. context. Nevertheless, whether we have reached "the end of race" or the value of saying so—even if it may be true—continues a debate in many venues. For example, at the same time that biology is being used to disprove race as a heritable set of phenotypes, one hotly contested public policy issue that arises would be the question of whether it is racist or simply good science to try to create racially specific drugs for conditions like hypertension.

So one question that philosophers might contribute to discussing could take the form, "How much distance between different forms of knowledge and truth (say biological facts about DNA distribution in world populations and social facts about the identity politics embedded in the U.S. electoral system) are we as knowers comfortable sustaining?" Or, alternatively, "Are some forms of racial knowledge (like those epidemiological data) simply irrelevant because the social and historical frames in which the concept of race itself makes sense are themselves delimiting?"

In both those kinds of knowledge/knowing questions, there are some generalizable themes about the relation of knowers and knowledge and the viability of asserting warrants for certain kinds of claims at all. Does it, however, make sense to press forward with a claim that relies on the identity of the knower—either at the time of the creation of the racial knowledge or at the time of its philosophical appropriation? Is there philosophical knowledge of race that is somehow changed by the presence of knowers who are conscious of their racialized selves or by the presence of blackness itself? I imply above that there is something specific about this moment—a moment in which it no longer seems inconceivable to talk about a postrace human condition—that means something in philosophical terms. One way in which philosophers might contribute specifically to this moment is to remind us that knowing is not untethered, that understanding precisely requires a Gadamerian sense of the horizon. What can be known, that is, apprehended, is contingent on the direction of the view. Or, from a different tradition, to challenge us to translate racial knowledge into forms of praxis, that is, into the executive and judicial forms of action that require but are not completed by an accumulation of knowing that "x."

Admittedly, "knowing blackness" is a more specific form of knowledge and understanding than the more general case of racial knowing that I have focused on in this section so far. And knowing blackness presumably means something different to me from the philosopher's seat in which I sit than from the sociologist's chair or the psychologist's chair. I want to resist the easy assertion that philosophy is the "queen" of the disciplines, home of meta-analysis, tempting though that is. Instead, I want to suggest that the very manner in which I separated my sections constitutes the "agony and the ecstasy" of philosophy. On the one hand, those categories (knowing, becoming, valuing) cover so much real estate in human enquiry that philosophy gives one the space to frame problems in a multitude of ways. On the other hand, the idea that these streams are genuinely separable in some meaningful way—especially, although not exclusively, with this kind of knotty issue—is at best just a convenience, a rubric.

Knowing blackness (for the black philosopher) implies a recognition of self, a relationally derived epistemology, and a will to recuperation—all of which are simultaneously autobiographical, historical, ideal, and material. Knowing blackness is an opportunity for all philosophers to apprehend blackness or not-blackness, to invoke alterity, to become a knower and what is known, to enact and to evaluate practices. Knowing blackness is a space (like knowing love or knowing beauty) that is being created already admitting the possibility of being displaced by absence.

> For us black folks who would philosophize, that is to say, who would live *life conditioned primarily by the activity of critical, dialectical thinking,* [emphasis added] a very first task is to bring this activity to bear on the practice of "philosophy" today to the extent that we are to have any contact with the traditions and practices of philosophy in the academy.[2]

Outlaw goes on to propose a series of goals for the activities of black philosophy, goals that entail attempts to transform an academic discipline as well as practices in the "real" world. His characterization of philosophizing as concerned with specific forms of life and thinking is embedded in the conception of racial knowing articulated above. Knowing blackness is always bound up with "critical, dialectical thinking." Although there is nothing implied in knowing blackness that speaks directly to professional obligations, the transformation of a discipline—or an institution, a relationship, individual constraints of thought and action—is the kind of activity that ought (in Outlaw's view and in mine) be a consequence of thinking and knowing blackness. In his outline of goals for black philosophizing, Outlaw makes clear the necessary connection, temporal and spatial, between knowing, becoming, and valuing blackness.

Becoming Blackness

I have become black many times in my life. Linguistically, I think the first time was about 1968. Before that, I was mostly a Negro, occasionally (before moving from North Carolina to Pennsylvania at age five) colored, and, only twice that I can remember, a nigger. My parents were able to inoculate us effectively from the potentially degrading effects of the last by convincing us that "nigger" was not something any of us could actually become. It was a category of accusation that made no statement about our guilt (or innocence) but rather an unpleasant expression of a sentiment ("I hate you" or "I fear you") that had only to do with the psyche of the accuser, not the being of the accused. I am not certain whether this very encouraging explanation would have stood up to more numerous assaults, but it was intellectually and emotionally sufficient for our particular conditions of life.

I remember rather liking being a Negro. Having desegregated our suburban Pennsylvania neighborhood, my parents imbued us with a sense of moral triumphalism. We were in fact the foot soldiers in their version of a "new" American Dream. They made a political decision that had profound implications in the phenomenal experience of their children, including the move from an entirely segregated world to one in which negritude transformed either to a completely intimate/familial being or a completely public/performative being. When Pearl Bailey or Sammy Davis Junior or Civil Rights news came on the (pre-1968) television, my younger brother and I would run screaming through the house, "There's a Negro on TV! There's a Negro on TV!"

This jubilant cry was part recognition, part celebration, and part reminder. That identification with the "Negro on TV" was exciting for us precisely because of the absence of the "Negro" on the street. That phenomenal absence, though, provides a memory of the calmest period of myself as a racialized being. If I was colored in the South, where my mother was weeping over the fates of other colored children turned away from the closest (white) hospital in Greensboro and my father was anxious about the political high profile of one of our neighbors in relation to safety for children playing on the block, turning Negro signified a different time in my childhood. I enjoyed the benefits of my parents' racial struggles without having to engage in very many battles on my own behalf. When Patty told me I couldn't play in her yard because it upset the neighbors, I turned the other cheek and invited her around the corner to my house (where the fences constructed, when we moved in, protected the delicate sensibilities of our neighbors). Most days I don't remember being anything racial in particular. It seems strange to me now, but while I am sure that the white children and parents and teachers around me were aware that there was a Negro in the room, most of the time I looked out onto the white horizon without considering the disruptive possibilities of my brown skin. My parents succeeded in their color-blind dreams with us—precisely because there was rarely any blackness to see in the world around us. For them, lives of living among colored folk cleared a different sort of phenomenal understanding; they were the vanguard. For my brother and myself our position at the tip of a wedge disconnected us from those others for whom we were supposedly clearing the way.

1968 changed everything. The assassination of Martin Luther King was experienced in my house as a sharp and painful loss that was not only the end of a single leader's life but also the end of a time of belief in the inevitability of "overcoming." The anti-war movement, Bobby Kennedy's assassination, changed the mood from passive resistance to a more aggressive assertion (ironies notwithstanding) of the demand for liberation and peace. The suburban haven my parents sought for us was rocked by the changes in the outside world. The ideals of color blindness that made sense to my parents who grew up completely, and in every moment, aware of their color suddenly seemed inadequate as either social or intellectual preparation for the world their children would face. So they began to make sure more intentionally that we knew our black history, that we knew about the fires burning in the inner cities of America, that we knew to "Say it Loud! I'm Black and I'm Proud!" along with James Brown. We expanded the range of our cultural capital, going to New York to see *Purlie* and *The River Niger* in the theater and listening to the Last Poets on the stereo.

> When the revolution comes
> When the revolution comes
> some of us will catch it on TV
> with chicken hanging from our mouths
> you'll know it's revolution
> because there won't be no commercials
> when the revolution comes
> (Last Poets 1970)

So I became Black. Instead of the curse of previous generations, it was the mark of the free individual, claiming an identity that had been degraded but was now proud. Black could be integrated with white without the help of a melting pot. My parents were also amply prepared for the turn to African American—they led tours in West Africa and we had the dashikis and silver filigree jewelry and worked leather several years before Alex Haley brought us our roots. But if the (re)turn to Africa, like my very proper, three-piece-suit-wearing papa getting down with the "bad words" everywhere in the Last Poets, signaled a shift in my experiential identity, there was a sense in which it was primarily felt as an aesthetic booster shot—so I could love Bessie Smith along with Bonnie Raitt and Joni Mitchell—or an intellectual's fuller understanding of history, politics, and literature. I was still a child the first time I became Black, and I basically took my father's word for it.

The second time I became Black was at the end of college. At Dartmouth in the late 1970s when I was a student there, I embraced a deep sense of transcendence. In point of fact, the three-hundred-odd Black folks on the campus were the largest black community I had ever lived in, not that anyone could have experienced the campus or the town as filled with a black presence. For four years, I suppressed race as any kind of obstacle to my life—academically, socially, or personally. I was not attempting to become not-black, but I was pretty successful at imagining college as a realm of pure being, where the fact of being black was fairly inconsequential. I was able to be successful in this construction of fantasyland because almost every incident of explicit racism I encountered was imbricated in the fact of my femaleness as well, and every one of those incidents was outnumbered by two or three incidents that were only about sex and gender. Because I was in the fifth class to have been coed from the beginning, and because my father really looked upon my going to Dartmouth as my chance to integrate (sexually) an institution as he had done racially in previous decades, I saw my work clearly laid out in front of me. I was to fulfill my academic and personal potential and become a woman of power and accomplishment who could not be belittled because the world had once been ruled by men.

So my racialized becoming was subsumed under "objective number one," and I was faithful to the program. I avoided identity politics and social groupings. I was "naturally" part of only one group: the Class of 1980. Every other association or accomplishment was achieved through the application of personal interest or the dedication of talent.

After graduation, I became an admissions officer at the college, and my private little fantasy had to come tumbling down. Just in the nature of my work, interviewing applicants, interacting with alumni, coming to understand a complex institutional process, exposed me to a different college than the one from which I had just graduated. I was no longer a recipient of the environment created by the work of others; I was, in my own little corner, responsible for making that environment better for others. That process of recognition led me to join the Black Caucus, which was a very small group of faculty and administrators. There was no radical platform by any means, but the effect of the size and the lack of critical mass had a radicalizing effect on me nonetheless.

So I became Black at Dartmouth for the first time in four and a half years. By which I suppose I mean that I understood that my very presence as a Black person, as a Black woman, had significance beyond my phenomenal experience. In one sense I gave up the adolescent narcissism that made race a purely psychological construct and began to see myself as part of a network of institutional and community relationships. In another sense I could transform a vague sense of "representing" the race (a weakly felt responsibility that mostly manifested itself in encounters with individuals) into an understanding that representing the college as a person of color had implications for the history, the politics, and the future of the place.

For the first time I could begin to think in a nuanced way about Affirmative Action—removing it from my personal anxiety that someone might think that I did not get in "on my own merits" and seeing how institutions rely on that anxiety and others to maintain the status quo. I was liberated from my own dignity concerning race: dignity that kept me from "looking for racists under the bed," but that became blindness about racism. Now I could see that blackness was a confounding feature in the life of an institution that I loved and in the lives of the children I was meeting in high schools (private/public, urban/suburban, rich/poor) on the eastern seaboard of early 1980s America. That was the beginning but not the end of my final becoming.

Valuing Blackness

Naomi Zack begins and ends her recent examination of race and science[3] with a query of what difference understanding race as a social, as opposed to a biological, construction makes. This is the conundrum in philosophy about race, but also simply an illustration of the distance between what we know and what we do—that is a permanent problem in ethics. Outlaw's invocation of critical thinking reminds us of our ethical and political obligations; thinking and reflecting is not enough. The specificity of knowing and becoming blackness is contained in valuing and its consequent actions. Valuing is the antidote to the reflex of racism that is embedded in "what we know" and the possibility of self-loathing that is attached to becoming.

Philosophy can take up the challenges of valuing blackness with any number of strategic discourses. Here I elaborate two: anti-racism and visibility, with attention to two levels of analysis and engagement: self and polity. Anti-racism as a strategic discourse comprises a series of responses that, despite the very oppositional signal given immediately by the "anti" formation, cannot afford to be simply responsive. Almost because racism is often the expression of a very minimally rational reflex in viscera or in affect (I hate this!/I don't like this loss!/I hate you!), anti-racism needs to work as more than a rejoinder, equally bereft of thought (That hurts!/I hate you back!). Even the racism that comes either passively or actively from a reliance on history or white privilege can run the gamut of reliance on unconscious or cloned rationales (There must be a reason for your subordinate status and my superordinate one; my privilege is, therefore, justified in the history of slavery/capitalism/rap/last week). Most anti-black racism does not call its own name and so cannot simply be "hailed" by its subjects; however, changing material conditions necessitates destabilizing both the barely and the insistently rational justifications for racist practices. Any claim that the successes of anti-racist politics, movements, or practices could/should rely on philosophy as a guiding light falls far short. As Harris concludes the postscript in his edited volume, *Racism*:

> Destroying racism will require more revolutions. They may be violent revolutions or they may be nonviolent, direct-action movements, based on philosophies of pacifism and the power of conscience. In either case, power concedes nothing without demand, compulsion, expropriation, and radical redistribution of control over the resources that make life possible.[4]

Philosophy's contributions will play out, however, in the development of that will to demand, to combat the understanding of blackness as "abject, wretched, and inherently inferior."[5] Arguments about valuing blackness and (re-e)valuating its significance in relation to what is not-blackness will necessarily be part of an active engagement with the world. Valuing cannot sustain itself simply as a consequence of assertion (Black is beautiful). Certainly in the industrialized West, hegemonic power structures are fantastically adept at converting deep expressions of self-love and valuing into banal and commodified presence in the marketplace: for example, the challenge of the Panthers to American history converted into the sales of Afro-Sheen, dashikis, and distorted nostalgia for the "Motherland." Those new commercial values do not necessarily translate into social/ethical value. The contemporary appropriation of Hip Hop culture (read: urban, black) into the marketing of everything from Eminem to Hilfiger to "bling" to "wigger" dress codes has stopped neither racial violence among youth nor negative cultural stereotyping of the purveyors of these cultural signs. Renegotiation of the value of blackness will cross boundaries of practices, and its success (and the successful contribution of philosophy) will rest on its capacity to inspire and mobilize the revolutions of thought and action that will disable both the naturalized and rationalized practices of internalized, public, institutional, structural, and intellectualized racism.

The potential frames of discourse surrounding visibility are incredibly rich. Visibility on its face may seem passive, but I want to suggest that it is a site of resistance and a jumping-off place for more aggressive self-assertion. To remain visible, in the face of erasure, is to act against the juridical comforts of color blindness or the aesthetic comfort of assimilated familiarity. Visibility on this account is not simply a matter of allowing oneself to be an object of perception for others, but of shaping a visible subject. Part of the difference between the two is contained in valuing. The constraint of visibility as a strategy is its obvious limitation as a means of directly changing the value assigned to "blackness visible" by the perceivers. Its possibilities are, rather, contained in the challenge that blackness visible poses to the processes of assigning value and the possibility of intervention in naturalized assignments of value. The claim of visibility asserts the need for something other than what has been—a new horizon, different lenses, a reformed prospect. Visibility is dynamic; it may directly and immediately precede a new form of invisibility. For example, one black child in an all-white school will be visible, that is, distinguishable, in a way that she may seek to mitigate. That visibility as an object is turned to one of a different sort as the school's population moves toward a critical mass. That first child becomes "invisible" as an individual, while participating in the evolution of the visibility of the black subject—in which blackness potentially becomes more variegated and the very meaning of blackness is differently apprehended, valued, and experienced from the inside and from the outside.

Philosophy provides a context for strategic visibility to mark the persistence of valuing blackness in ways that may or may not comport with embodiments of cultural legibility. An example of this derives from the "taxicab in Manhattan" story that Cornel West tells in *Race Matters*, although it seemed that every black guy in the 1990s with a nice suit also told this story on a talk show, in a public lecture, or in a classroom: Nattily turned out black man attempting to catch a cab uptown left catching cold on the streets of NYC. This is intended to be a story about the racist assumptions of cabdrivers (who stand in for regular Joe America) worried about the possibility of being forced to drive to the outer banks of Harlem or (gasp!) the Bronx with no return fare and no tip. While I feel for Danny Glover and his cohorts, I actually think this is a story with a different twist. That is, the cab encounter pits the visibility of blackness against the assertion of the (il)legibility of class. I always heard in that story a complaint that their legible bodies could not contain enough text to counteract their racialized visibility; that blackness visible held an overdetermined amount of value to the passing driver. So it seems to me that the philosopher is thereby called upon to ask how what is visible can be legible in a way that transforms value. The call is not to get ever more expensive suits (or to abandon cabs for a Puffy-style limo) but to interrogate the possibilities of asserting something about the value of what is visible that is different from what can currently be seen or read—whether from close up or far away. The responsibility for visibility rests with those who can work from the visible subject position, turning racial knowing and being into value and valuing anew blackness—known, experienced, undergone, transcended, released, and celebrated.

> Poetry is black
> Black rhythm
> Words floating on black rhythm is poetry
> Poetry is black words floating on black rhythm
> Poetry is black people moving and grooving
> . . . .
> Groovy fast rhythm
> and
> Slow and mellow rhythm too
> . . . .
> Black poetry is black
> So groove on black people[6]

I believe that philosophizing is a very specific and contextual way of life. I fundamentally embrace Outlaw's formulation of the basic tenets of embracing critical and dialectical thinking; that thinking takes place in bodies, in time, in space, and in practices. This chapter was an opportunity to mobilize a rubric I have used to conceptualize my interests as a teacher and a thinker. In writing it I began to see on the page that being and becoming are literally central to my projects, linking what and how I know to the willingness to evaluate and to value. Although it is a personalized writing, I hope that others will be able to recognize and render it legible for their own purposes.[7]

Notes

1. Lucius T. Outlaw, On *Race and Philosophy* (New York: Routledge 1996); Charles Mills, *Blackness Visible: Essays on Philosophy and Race* (Ithaca: Cornell University Press, 1998); Lewis R. Gordon, *Bad Faith and Antiblack Racism* (New Jersey: Humanities Press, 1995).

2. Outlaw, *On Race and Philosophy*, 30.

3. Naomi Zack, *Philosophy of Science and Race* (New York: Routledge, 2002) 8, 116–17.

4. Leonard Harris, "Postscript," in ed. Leonard Harris, *Racism* (New York: Humanity Books, 1999), 448–49.

5. Harris, "Postscript," 448.

6. David Nelson, "Poetry Is Black," *The Last Poets: Right On* (first released as a soundtrack in 1970; CD remastered on Collectibles Records, 1991).

7. There are many people in my life, personal and professional, who have helped me with the life that constitutes this chapter. I want to thank them all, but two by name: Lewis Gordon and Ralph Page, colleagues whose wisdom and friendship have enabled much of my knowing, becoming, and valuing.

Index

About the Contributors

Kal Alston teaches philosophy of education and gender/women's studies at the University of Illinois at Urbana-Champaign. She is the editor of *Philosophy of Education* (2003) and has published work in *Educational Theory*, *Journal of Sport and Society*, and *Studies in Philosophy of Education*. Her interests in ethics and education led her to investigations of the cultural constraints on young adolescents, particularly for girls, as well as the intersections of race, gender, and class in youth popular culture.

Molefi Kete Asante, a professor at Temple University, teaches Afrocentric theory, ancient African history, and African American culture. He is the author of fifty-five books, including *Erasing Racism: Survival of the American Nation*. His articles have appeared in *Black Scholar*, *The American Scholar*, *Journal of Communication*, *American Political Science Review*, and twenty-seven other journals. He is the editor of the *Journal of Black Studies* and co-editor of Sage's *Encyclopedia of Black Studies*.

Bettina G. Bergo is an assistant professor of philosophy at the Université de Montreal. She has written on Emmanuel Levinas, psychoanalysis, and feminist thought. She recently translated *The Unthought Debt: Heidegger and the Hebraic Heritage*. Bettina is working on a short history of "anxiety" in nineteenth and twentieth century philosophy and psychology.

Robert Bernasconi taught at the University of Essex in England before coming to the University of Memphis in 1988; since that time he has been the

Moss Chair of Excellence in Philosophy. He is the author of *The Question of Language in Heidegger's History of Being* (1985) and *Heidegger in Question* (1993), as well as a number of articles on Hegel, Sartre, Levinas, Derrida, and political philosophy. He has worked extensively on the history of race thinking, editing three multi-volume sets that document that history: *Concepts of Race in the Eighteenth Century* (2001), *American Theories of Polygenism* (2002), and *Race and Anthropology* (2003). He has also edited *Race* (2001) and with Tommy Lott *The Idea of Race* (2000). Most recently, he edited with Sybol Cook *Race and Racism in Continental Philosophy* (2003).

Robert Birt teaches philosophy at Morgan State University. His research interests include Africana philosophy, critical theory, existential philosophy (especially Sartre studies), and philosophical anthropology. He is editor of *The Quest for Community and Identity: Critical Essays in Africana Social Philosophy*. His articles have appeared in *International Philosophical Quarterly, Philosophy East and West, Man and World, Social Science Information, Quest: Journal of African Philosophy*, and in the anthologies *What White Looks Like* and *Existence in Black.*

Chris Cuomo is an activist, artist, professor of philosophy and women's studies and Obed J. Wilson Professor of Ethics at the University of Cincinnati. She is the author of *The Philosopher Queen: Feminist Essays on War, Love, and Knowledge* (2003) and *Feminism and Ecological Communities: An Ethic of Flourishing* (1998) and coeditor of *Whiteness: Feminist Philosophical Reflections* (1999).

Clarence Sholé Johnson is professor of philosophy at Middle Tennessee State University (MTSU) in Murfreesboro, Tennessee. He earned his doctorate from McGill University in Canada, specializing in the philosophy of David Hume. In addition to his research and teaching in modern philosophy, Johnson also works in the areas of ethics, epistemology, social and political philosophy, and Africana philosophy. Johnson is author of *Cornel West and Philosophy* (2002), and has also published articles in a variety of major scholarly journals such as *The Journal of Social Philosophy, Social Philosophy Today, The Journal of Philosophical Research, DIALOGUE: Canadian Philosophical Review, Metaphilosophy, The Southern Journal of Philosophy, The Southwest Philosophy Review*, and *The Journal of Thought*, to name a few. He has also contributed chapters to a number of books as well as entries in a forthcoming *Encyclopedia of African Religions and Philosophy*, ed. V. Y. Mudimbe (Kluwer).

Janine Jones teaches philosophy at the University of North Carolina, at Greensboro. Her areas of interest include philosophy of mind, metaphysics, philosophy of language, and epistemology. Her current topics of interest are imagining and conceiving. Her published work has appeared in philosophical journals including *Philosophical Studies*, the *Journal of Speculative Philosophy*, *Philosophia*, and nonphilosophical journals including *Travelers' Tales America*, *Travelers' Tales Danger*, and *Travelers' Tales Ireland*.

John H. McClendon III is associate professor of African American studies and American cultural studies at Bates College in Lewiston, Maine. McClendon is editor of the *American Philosophical Association Newsletter on Philosophy and the Black Experience* and is the author of *C. L. R. James's Notes on Dialectics: Left Hegelianism or Marxism-Leninism*. He also has a forthcoming text entitled *Marxism in Ebony: A Materialist Philosophical Perspective on African American Studies*. His most recent articles have appeared in journals such as the *Journal of Speculative Philosophy*, and in *Socialism and Democracy*. He has chapters in several recent anthologies including George Yancy's *What White Looks Like: African American Philosophers on the Whiteness Question* (2004), Carole Boyce Davies's *Decolonizing the Academy: African Diaspora Studies* (2003), and Jacob U. Gordon's *The African Presence in Black America* (2004).

Greg Moses is author of *Martin Luther King Jr. and the Philosophy of Nonviolence* and editor of the *Texas Civil Rights Review*. His article on King's approach to affirmative action was selected as among the best of the first decade by the editors of the *American Philosophical Association Newsletter for Philosophy and the Black Experience*. And his essay on Alain Locke's concept of reciprocity may be found in Leonard Harris's collection on critical pragmatism.

Monique Roelofs is assistant professor of philosophy in the School of Humanities, Arts, and Cultural Studies at Hampshire College. Her areas of interest include aesthetics, the philosophy of art and culture, feminist philosophy, and the philosophy of race. Roelofs's articles on visual representation, aesthetic address, feminist theory, and racial formations have appeared in journals such as *differences: A Journal of Feminist Cultural Studies* and anthologies including *Art and Essence* (2003), *Religion "nach der Religionskritik"* (2003), and *Richard Wollheim on the Art of Painting: Art as Representation and Expression* (2001). She is currently at work on a book entitled *The Cultural Promise of the Aesthetic*.

Crispin Sartwell is visiting associate professor of political science at Dickinson College. His weekly opinion column is distributed by Creators Syndicate. His books include *Act Like You Know: African-American Autobiography and White Identity* (1998), *Extreme Virtue: Truth and Leadership in Five Great American Lives* (2003), and *Six Names of Beauty* (2004).

Anna Stubblefield is an assistant professor of philosophy and affiliate of the Afro-American and African Studies Department at Rutgers University-Newark. Her doctoral degree is from Rutgers University, where she studied with Howard McGary, Jr. She is the author of *Ethics along the Color Line* (2005). Her work has appeared in journals and anthologies including the *Journal of Social Philosophy, Social Theory and Practice,* and *Socialism and Democracy.*

George Yancy has written numerous articles and reviews, which have appeared in *The Journal of Speculative Philosophy, The Review of Metaphysics, The Journal of Social Philosophy, Philosophy and Social Criticism, Radical Philosophy Review, Hypatia: A Journal of Feminist Philosophy, Encyclopedia of Feminist Theories,* the *Western Journal of Black Studies,* the *AME Church Review,* the *APA Newsletter on Feminism and Philosophy,* the *CLA Journal,* the *Black Arts Quarterly, Social Science Quarterly, Popular Music and Society,* and more. Yancy's book publications include *African-American Philosophers: 17 Conversations* (1998), which was named an Outstanding Academic Book by *Choice* for 1999, *Cornel West: A Critical Reader* (2001), *The Philosophical i: Personal Reflections on Life in Philosophy* (2002), and *What White Looks Like: African-American Philosophers on the Whiteness Question* (2004). He is currently coediting a book entitled *Narrative Identities* (2005). Yancy recently received the prestigious McCracken Fellowship from New York University. He is book review editor of the *APA Newsletter on Philosophy and the Black Experience.*